POLITICAL SCIENCE RESEARCH

A HANDBOOK OF SCOPE AND METHODS

◆ ◆ ◆

Laurence F. Jones

&

Edward C. Olson

Angelo State University

HarperCollinsCollegePublishers

To Sandy who gave me support,
to Dad who showed me tolerance,
to Mom who taught me discipline,
to David, Mark and Chrissie who made me laugh.
and
To Shelly. Her encouragement never faltered.

ACQUISITIONS EDITOR: Leo A. W. Wiegman
PROJECT COORDINATION AND TEXT DESIGN: York Production Services
COVER DESIGN: Sarah Johnson
MANUFACTURING MANAGER: Hilda Koparanian
ELECTRONIC PAGE MAKEUP: R. R. Donnelley and Sons Company, Inc.
PRINTER AND BINDER: R. R. Donnelley and Sons Company, Inc.
COVER PRINTER: Color-Imetry Corp.

Political Science Research: A Handbook of Scope and Methods

Library of Congress Cataloging-in-Publication Data

Jones, Laurence F.
    Political science research: a handbook of scope and methods /
Laurence F. Jones, Edward C. Olson.
        p.   cm.
    Includes bibliographical references and index.
    ISBN 0-06-501637-8
    1. Political science—Research.   2. Political science—Methodology.
I. Olson, Edward C., 1948– .   II. Title
    JA71.J59   1995
320'.072—dc20   95–45431
                                                             CIP
                                                             r95

95 96 97 98 9 8 7 6 5 4 3 2 1

CONTENTS

Preface xi

❖ **PART ONE**
An Introduction to Political Science and
Political Research   **1**

◆ **CHAPTER 1**
Conducting Systematic Political Research: An Overview   **3**

Introduction 3
The Importance of Political Research 4
Characteristics of Scientific Knowledge 5
Acquiring Scientific Knowledge 7
Obstacles to the Scientific Study of Politics 9
The Use of Theory to Investigate the Scope of Politics 10
Traditional Methods Used to Investigate the Scope of Politics 12
Modern Methods Used to Investigate the Scope of Politics 13
Composite Political Research: Our Method of Choice 15
The Systematic Research Process 16
Summary 18
Key Terms 19
Exercises 20
Suggested Readings 20
Notes 21

◆ **CHAPTER 2**
   The Problem: Essence of the Research Project   22

   Introduction 22
   Deciding on a Potential Topic 23
   The Research Problem 25
   Topic Selection: Some Concluding Remarks 27
   Summary 28
   Key Terms 28
   Exercises 28
   Suggested Readings 29

◆ **CHAPTER 3**
   The Literature Review: Becoming Familiar with Your Topic   30

   Introduction 30
   Purpose of the Review 30
   How to Begin the Search for Related Literature 31
   How to Write the Literature Review 36
   Summary 39
   Key Terms 40
   Exercises 40
   Suggested Readings 40

❖ **PART TWO**
   The Scope of Political Science   41

◆ **CHAPTER 4**
   The Political World   44

   Introduction 44
   Politics and Human Relations 44
   Politics and Human Nature 46
   The Political System 46
   Some Key Political Concepts 48
   The Major Political Questions 53
   The Political Science Discipline 59
   Political Science Subfields 60
   Summary 63

Key Terms   64
Exercises   64
Suggested Readings   65
Notes   65

◆ **CHAPTER 5**
   The American Political Process   **67**

   Introduction   67
   Political Environment: Revolutionary Ideals and Constitutionalism   68
   Some Key Questions   70
   How the System Works   79
   The American Political System   83
   Summary   97
   Key Terms   98
   Exercises   98
   Suggested Readings   99
   Notes   99

◆ **CHAPTER 6**
   Public Administration and Public Policy   **101**

   Introduction   101
   Public Administration: Our Working Definition   102
   The Who of Public Administration   102
   The What of Public Administration   104
   The How of Public Administration   117
   Administrative Ethics: A Fertile Field for Research   122
   Summary   128
   Key Terms   129
   Exercises   129
   Suggested Readings   129

◆ **CHAPTER 7**
   Comparative Politics   **132**

   Introduction   132
   The Study of Comparative Politics   132
   Approaches to the Study of Comparative Politics   134

Summary   152
Key Terms   153
Exercises   153
Suggested Readings   154
Notes   154

◆ **CHAPTER 8**
   International Relations   **156**

Introduction   156
The Study of International Politics   156
Key Concepts   157
Some Key Questions   165
Approaches to the Study of International Relations   176
Summary   179
Key Terms   180
Exercises   180
Suggested Readings   181
Notes   181

❖ **PART THREE**
   The Methods of Political Science   **183**

◆ **CHAPTER 9**
   Elements of Research: Determining Causal Explanations   **185**

Introduction   185
Constructing Causal Explanations   185
Multiple Causation   195
Summary   195
Key Terms   196
Exercises   196
Suggested Readings   197

◆ **CHAPTER 10**
   Understanding Measurement   **198**

Introduction   198

The Theory of Measurement   198
Measurement Validity   202
Measurement Reliability   203
Summary   211
Key Terms   212
Exercises   212
Suggested Readings   213

◆ **CHAPTER 11**
 Research Design   **214**

Introduction   214
The Research Design: An Overview   214
Experimental Designs   215
Nonexperimental Designs   223
Other Types of Research Designs   225
Obstacles to a Successful Research Design   227
A Comparison of Research Designs   231
Summary   233
Key Terms   233
Exercises   234
Suggested Readings   234

◆ **CHAPTER 12**
 Data Collection and Input   **236**

Introduction   236
Data Collection Techniques   237
Sampling   241
Sample Designs   244
Determining the Sample Size   250
Coding the Data   255
Data Input   255
Summary   256
Key Terms   257
Exercises   258
Suggested Readings   259
Notes   259

◆ **CHAPTER 13**
 Data Analysis: Univariate Statistics   **260**

Introduction   260

The Role of Statistics   261
Limitations of Statistics in Research   262
Univariate Statistics   263
Shape of the Distribution   284
Summary   288
Key Terms   289
Exercises   290
Suggested Readings   292

◆ **CHAPTER 14**
  Data Analysis: Bivariate Statistics   **293**

Introduction   293
The Rudiments of Association   294
Measures of Association   301
Statistical Significance and Hypothesis Testing   310
Bivariate Tests for Interval Data   320
Summary   330
Key Terms   331
Exercises   331
Suggested Readings   334

◆ **CHAPTER 15**
  Data Analysis: Multivariate Statistics   **336**

Introduction   336
On the Nature of Control   336
Methods of Control   338
Summary   348
Key Terms   349
Exercises   350
Suggested Readings   352

◆ **CHAPTER 16**
  Putting It All Together   **353**

Introduction   353
Theoretical Implications   353
Policy Implications   354

Writing the Report   354
A Sample Research Proposal and Research Paper   357
A Final Thought   357
Key Terms   358
Exercises   358
Suggested Readings   359

Appendix I: Sample Research Studies   360
Notes   377
Bibliography   378
Appendix II: Sample Data Sets and Selected Variables   380
Appendix III: Statistical Tables   385

Table A1: Random Digits   385
Table A2: The Standard Normal Distribution   390
Table A3: The Chi Square Distribution   391
Table A4: Levels of Significance for Student's T   393
Table A5: Critical Values of F   395

Glossary   399
Bibliography   418
Index   427

PREFACE

Political Science Research: A Handbook of Scope and Methods is an introductory text to be used by those schools requiring scope and methods course of second- or third-year political science majors.

We decided to write this text because of our general dissatisfaction with existing texts and our experience in teaching scope and methods courses. In our view, scope and methods is one of the most difficult courses in the curriculum for you and your professor alike. From your point of view, the course material is abstract and involves subject matter not typically encountered in a traditional liberal arts curriculum. Your instructor faces the difficult task of motivating you to engage material that, quite frankly, may not be very exciting to you. The material may also be more difficult than you have faced up to this point in your academic career. Additionally, the field poses many dilemmas as to what we can realistically expect to accomplish in a 16-week semester. Our experience has helped us learn "what works" and "what doesn't." It has also convinced us that existing texts contain too much of the "what doesn't."

We believe that much of the existing literature fails because it assumes a background that most sophomores and juniors do not have. Many texts are elaborate and abstract forays into the scope of politics while others inundate you with intricate statistical designs, models, and techniques. Few adequately introduce you to the discipline of political science and the research process in a meaningful and understandable way. We designed our text to help you develop a basic understanding of what political science is all about, to show you what to expect in other junior- and senior-level political science courses, to help you read and comprehend the literature of political science, and to teach you how to conduct basic political research without overwhelming you with statistical theorizing and calculation.

We wrote this book with three major objectives in mind. First, we want to teach you about the scope of political science. That is, we want to familiarize you with what political scientists do and study. Thus, we introduce you to some basic concepts and notions about public administrations and policy, international politics, and comparative politics and American government. We complete this introduction by exploring several of the major questions asked by political scientists in respect to these areas.

Second, we want to familiarize you with the methods of political science. In other words we want to teach you about the ways political scientists go about studying politics and pertinent questions. Thus, we introduce you to the statistical procedures and calculations that are a major part of political research. These procedures will help you to evaluate and assess the research efforts of others and to conduct your own independent empirical research projects.

There is no substitute for actually participating in a research effort. Therefore, our third objective is to provide you with a text that guides you through each stage of the research process: topic selection, literature review, hypothesis formulation, data collection, data input, data analysis, and the writing of the final report.

Our text is an introductory guide. As such, we assume no prior training in statistics and quantitative methods. Thus, it is not necessary for you to have an extensive background in empirical research. Rather than stressing statistical formulas and computation, we accent the conditions under which you should use such techniques. We also want you to have the ability to interpret the statistical results. The exercises concluding some of the chapters emphasize the discussions and help you understand and master the concepts and techniques we discuss. If you have mathematical limitations you should not be discouraged by the techniques we present. Instead, you should concentrate your efforts on understanding the utility of these techniques when examining political questions and concerns.

We believe our text surpasses existing scope and methods works for several reasons. First, its organization around the entire research process effectively integrates both scope and methods in a meaningful and understandable way under a single cover. Second, it provides a better introduction to the political science discipline by providing you with an overview of the subtopics in the field. Third, it stresses the application and interpretation of statistical results rather than statistical derivation and calculation. Fourth, it emphasizes the practical rather than the theoretical side of research. Fifth, the text contains several kinds of illustrations including figures, tables, and examples of research efforts. Sixth, chapters include exercises designed to help you understand the lesson and finish each phase of the research project. Finally, the appendices contain examples of student papers, critiques of the reports, and statistical tables necessary to assist you in interpreting statistical results.

In summary, some critics may assert that the coverage given each of our objectives may be too watered-down to be useful. We believe, however, that by attempting to introduce you to political questions and issues in an integrated and illustrated manner, you will gain an enhanced appreciation of the field and the entire research process. In addition, you will have a clearer understanding of the relationship each phase has with the other phases. Last, you will have attained a working knowledge of techniques that will benefit you throughout your collegiate years.

1

◆ ◆ ◆

AN INTRODUCTION TO POLITICAL SCIENCE AND POLITICAL RESEARCH

What is political science? As a student of politics, this is one of the first questions you should ask and answer (Isaak 1981, 3). Part One, an introduction and overview to political science and political research, provides the basis for answering this question.

Chapter 1 introduces you to the art of conducting systematic political research. At the start of the chapter you will read about the importance of political research and the characteristics of scientific knowledge. For example, scientific knowledge is nonnormative and can be analyzed and verified through empirical methods.

In the chapter we also spend some time discussing epistemology and ways to acquire scientific knowledge. Part of our discussion covers the debate that exists between the traditionalists and the behavioralists over the ways politics should be studied. In addition, we address factors that impede the scientific study of politics. For example, the extent of cooperation given by the subjects of a study and measurement difficulties can negatively influence the results of a research effort.

The theoretical approaches and methods political scientists use to investigate the political world precede our discussion of the characteristic features of research. In our discussion we identify and examine several steps you must follow when conducting scientific research. We conclude the chapter by telling you about some ethical concerns you must address when doing research—concerns that will contribute to the worthiness of the study and the dignity of research participants.

At the outset of Chapter 2, we emphasize the importance of deciding on a potential topic and defining a research problem. After all, your topic establishes the framework for the other major stages of the research process.

We also try to show you that, of all the stages of the research process, selecting a topic is the most difficult for us to provide guidelines. Nevertheless, we provide you with some general suggestions to use when developing a research topic. As such, we present possible sources you can review to identify topics and problems worthy of research. We also provide some guidelines to follow when evaluating possible topics.

You will also read about some suggestions to follow when writing your problem statement. For example, you must state your problem clearly and avoid half-statements, opinions, and those problems that you can answer with a simple yes or no. The chapter also stresses the importance of limiting the scope of your problem.

In Chapter 3 we present a comprehensive discussion about reviewing the literature. Consequently, we cover quite a bit of ground while emphasizing that the major purpose of the review is to become thoroughly familiar with your topic.

While the review is a separate part of the research report, it is, however, an ongoing task that impacts each stage of the research process. As a result we spend some time trying to help you see the purpose of the literature review. We also provide some direction so that you can master the steps involved in conducting a systematic review. Last, we give you some suggestions so that you can properly write your literature review.

As with every chapter in this text, we include several exercises designed to enhance your understanding of chapter material. We also include a list of terms you need to understand. Last, a list of suggested readings is included at the end of each chapter. A review of these readings should also contribute to your understanding of the material.

CONDUCTING SYSTEMATIC POLITICAL RESEARCH: AN OVERVIEW

❖ INTRODUCTION

Political science scholars see political research as exhilarating, informative, and, for the most part, fun. Political science students fulfilling the requirements of a semester research paper, however, may not have the same outlook. All too often they develop feelings of anxiety because they see the paper as another tedious task assigned by an all too demanding professor. True, the research paper is often the most crucial requirement in the syllabus. True, it is a major effort that requires an extensive literature review, hypothesis design and testing, empirical analysis, and discussion about theory and policy implications. In addition, standard manuscript style is often a requirement. But it is also true that most students discover, after the initial shock has diminished, that conducting political research can be a most invigorating academic experience. At last students can pursue their own intellectual interests. As one scholar noted, "The product of the research represents one's own work, reflective of one's own talents, imagination, and creativity" (Cole 1980, 1).

To maximize one's own talents and for utmost satisfaction, however, the research process should be systematic. Otherwise the effort may be frustrating, the results misleading, and the paper ineffective. In this chapter we introduce you to the systematic research process. An understanding of this chapter will enable you to:

1. See the importance of political research.
2. Identify the characteristics of scientific knowledge.
3. Distinguish between the inductive and deductive ways to acquire scientific knowledge.
4. Identify obstacles impeding the scientific study of politics.

5. Differentiate between the numerous approaches and methods used to investigate political questions and concerns.
6. Identify the characteristics of research.

❖ THE IMPORTANCE OF POLITICAL RESEARCH

Political research is an exacting and discriminating investigation undertaken by political scientists to discover and interpret new political knowledge. It often involves scientific activity to produce knowledge about political life. While there are several ways to conduct political research, we wrote this book as an introduction to scientific political research. Thus, we concentrate on a research method that objectively observes the political world.

Political science scholars tell us there are two types of research: applied research and basic research (Shively 1990, 4). Political scientists conduct applied research to help solve a particular problem. The collection and analysis of data to help solve the AIDS problem or the need for additional public housing are examples of applied research.

Applied research is important for several reasons. First, it alerts the public to problems that impact society. Second, it suggests remedies to fix identified problems. Last, government decision makers often use its results to address constituents' demands and to develop policy.

Basic research satisfies one's intellectual curiosity about some political question or phenomenon. For example, you may want to know why political and social unrest is so common in Latin America or why some Americans tend to be conservative or liberal. The researcher's goal is to enhance their understanding of a political phenomenon rather than use the findings to remedy a specific political problem. Basic research is important because it provides us with an understanding of political life. In addition, the findings lead to the development of theory—theory used to explain political events.

Political research also sustains the democratic process. A citizenry informed about their government and its activities is a premise of democratic theory. The public often receives political information from public opinion polls and data collected by the media. Consequently, the citizenry and the democratic process benefit. Thus, political research is also important because published findings inform us about our government and its activities.

As a result of this discussion you now understand the importance in having at least a working knowledge about political research. This knowledge will foster your understanding about political events and phenomena, help you collect information to satisfy your political curiosity, facilitate your comprehension of public policy and governmental activity, and prepare you to complete research assignments for political science courses.

❖ CHARACTERISTICS OF SCIENTIFIC KNOWLEDGE

Previously we said we would concentrate on a scientific approach to study politics—an approach based on an objective observation of political phenomena that produces scientific enlightenment and knowledge. When political scientists talk about the accumulation of scientific knowledge, they talk about a way of learning that is different from the other ways you learn about your environment. For instance, they say that **scientific knowledge** is verifiable and can be refuted, is nonnormative, is transmissible, is general, is explanatory, and is provisional. This means that you can observe scientific knowledge, it is value free, it can be observed by different persons, it applies to much of society, it can explain what is going on around you, and it can change.

Other ways we learn do not have these characteristics. There are people who, for example, reject that there is such a thing as a human soul. After all, the notion that we have immortal souls is not something that we can verify, or explain, in a strict, scientific sense. The majority of people who do support the existence of an eternal soul, however, maintain that assertion is a matter of religious belief. Therefore, with these ways of learning, you have to have faith. You have to believe. While proof is not essential to scientific learning, hypotheses developed to test theories must be refutable (see Chapter 9).

The scientific approach to knowledge is premised on some basic assumptions that are unproven and unprovable (Frankfort-Nachmias and Nachmias 1992, 6). These assumptions are necessary for the conduct of scientific discussion and represent issues in the area of the philosophy of science known as epistemology. **Epistemology** is the study of the foundations of knowledge. How do we know what we think is true? Frankfort-Nachmias and Nachmias assert that by studying the following assumptions we can enhance our understanding of the scientific approach and the claim that it is superior over other approaches to acquiring knowledge. First, nature is orderly and regular. Events do not occur randomly. Second, we can know nature and humans, and, as a part of nature, humans can be understood and explained by the same methods by which we study nature. Third, knowledge is superior to ignorance. That is, knowledge should be pursued for its own sake and for the improving of human conditions. Fourth, all natural phenomena have natural causes. This assumption implies that natural events have natural causes and rejects the notion that forces other than those found in nature work to cause natural events. Fifth, nothing is self-evident. As a result claims for truth must be objectively shown. Therefore, common sense or superstition cannot be relied on to verify scientific knowledge. The possibility of error is always present and even the simplest claims of knowledge require objective verification. Last, knowledge is derived from experience. In other words, if science is to help us understand the real world, it must be observable and rely on perceptions and experience. Now let's turn our attention to the characteristics of scientific knowledge.

◆ SCIENTIFIC KNOWLEDGE CAN BE VERIFIED AND IS SUBJECT TO DISPROOF

Scientific knowledge is empirical, which means that it is subject to experimental verification because it is grounded in observation and experience. We can observe political phenomenon such as the number of votes cast in an election or the number of Republicans in the United States Congress. We can record, measure, and quantitatively analyze scientific knowledge. We can verify, for example, the requirement that motor vehicle operators use seat belts by looking at a copy of the legislative act that established the law. In addition, theory based on scientific knowledge must be refutable and must be subject to disproof.

◆ SCIENTIFIC KNOWLEDGE IS NONNORMATIVE

The empirical research used to acquire scientific knowledge addresses what is and what might be in the future. Thus, it can predict. Scientific knowledge tries to determine what is needed to solve political problems. Scientific knowledge is value free because it does not judge observations as bad or good. It does not address "how." Students and researchers' choice and definition of concepts temper and shape what we regard as fact. Accordingly, it does not dictate ways to improve a situation. Examples include measuring the effect of welfare programs, analyzing the outcome of government subsidies, and evaluating the consequence of economic deregulation.

On the other hand, researchers use normative knowledge to evaluate a situation and, based on their ideology, prescribe ways to remedy the occurrence. Theorists such as Plato, Marx, and Adam Smith used normative research and knowledge to investigate inequities in their political, social, and economic surroundings. Their goal was to make political decisions based on theory (Shively 1990, 5). We will expand our discussion about normative and empirical theory in Chapter 4.

◆ SCIENTIFIC KNOWLEDGE IS TRANSMISSIBLE

Scientific knowledge is also transmissible. It is transmissible "because science is a social activity in that it takes several scientists, analyzing and criticizing each other, to produce more reliable knowledge" (Johnson and Joslyn 1986, 16). As a result, scientific knowledge helps identify and control biases that may enter research activities. In short, the research methods are made explicit to the reader to encourage analysis and duplication. It allows others to test the worth of the research.

◆ SCIENTIFIC KNOWLEDGE IS GENERAL

When you make a general statement you make a statement that includes a wide range of people, events, or objects. Your general statement helps account for a wider range of phenomena than specific knowledge. The same applies when we say that scientific knowledge is general. For example, it is more useful for you to know that African Americans, as a group, tend to vote Democratic than it is to know that Jesse Jackson supports Democratic political figures and policy. You cannot predict that African Americans will vote Democratic because Mr. Jackson supports the Democratic ticket. In sum, empirical generalizations are statements that communicate general knowledge and summarize relationships between individual facts.

◆ SCIENTIFIC KNOWLEDGE IS EXPLANATORY

Scientific knowledge is also explanatory because it provides reasons for behaviors, attitudes, or events; it answers "why" questions. For example, "Why are Catholics abandoning their loyalty to the Democratic party?" A possible answer may be the Democratic party's stance in the abortion debate. Hence, not only is it important to observe political activity, it is also important to explain political acts. Scientific knowledge provides us with such explanation.

The explanatory capability of scientific knowledge is also important because it is the basis for prediction. If we know why Catholics are abandoning the Democratic party, we can predict the voting results in a Catholic voting precinct. Additionally, explanation is the primary purpose of theory. While a purpose of theory is to organize and coordinate existing knowledge in a field of study, a theory's major function may be to explain singular facts and occurrences.

◆ SCIENTIFIC KNOWLEDGE IS PROVISIONAL

Scientific knowledge is provisional. It is provisional because it alerts us to the possibility that future observations may contradict currently accepted knowledge. Improvements in the methods of observation, measurement, and research design, may alter and improve our understanding of existing behavior. Although repeated analyses and tests may have confirmed explanations for political phenomena, "the provisional nature of scientific knowledge alerts us to the possibility that future observations may contradict currently accepted laws" (Johnson and Joslyn 1986, 19).

Now that we have discussed the characteristics of scientific knowledge, we turn to the acquisition of scientific knowledge.

❖ ACQUIRING SCIENTIFIC KNOWLEDGE

◆ DEVELOPING THEORY THROUGH INDUCTION

One way to acquire scientific knowledge is through induction. **Induction** occurs when a theory evolves based on the observation of phenomena. Thus, observation precedes theory. The researcher objectively observes the object of

TABLE 1.1

PARTY IDENTIFICATION OF FIRST-TIME VOTERS AND PARENTS

	Parent's Party	
	Democratic	**Republican**
First-Time Voter's Party		
Democratic	45 (90%)	5 (10%)
Republican	5 (10%)	45 (90%)
Totals	50 (100%)	50 (100%)

interest and records those observations. The researcher looks for patterns in the data and develops a theory that explains why the pattern occurred.

Let's look at an example dealing with political socialization, or how people learn political attitudes. For the purpose of illustration, assume no previous theory exists for this example.

A political science student collected data about the political party affiliation of first-time voters and their parents. The results are depicted in Table 1.1.

The table shows that, of 100 families, 50 sets of parents identified with the Democratic party and 50 identified with the Republican party. Additionally, the table shows that 90 percent of the first-time voters identified with the parties of their parents. After some analysis and deliberation, our hard-working student develops the theory that most first-time voters tend to identify with the political parties of their parents.

While this example may seem elementary to some, it does show how scientific knowledge can be inductively acquired. Our student collected data, observed patterns in the data, and then developed a theory about first-time voters.

◆ DEVELOPING THEORY THROUGH DEDUCTION

We also acquire scientific knowledge through deduction. **Deduction** occurs when we make observations based on some prior expectations or established premises. From these, we determine what type of pattern to expect in our data and then look for it among the observations. The problem lies in the "well-established premises" from which you are supposed to deduce theories. There simply are not many well-established premises in the social sciences that you can use to deduce anything (Shively 1990, 165). In addition, it may be difficult for you to deduce theory based on "prior expectations" at this point in your academic career. Thus, pure deduction will be difficult for you.

While pure deduction is rarely possible, many of you will predict certain occurrences based on some theory you have read about or studied in some other discipline. For example, you may decide to use Emile Durkheim's theory of Anomie to predict and explain the suicide rate in America. Then you observe and measure events to see if they occur as predicted. Thus, an awareness of important theories in other disciplines can be an important source for you when forming hypotheses.

As you can see from these elementary examples, the political scientist can acquire scientific knowledge based on observation (induction), or based on expectations or an existing theory (deduction). Whatever the method of learning, the alert student can also see there are similarities between both methods. For example, the researcher must collect and analyze data. Then, the researcher draws conclusions based on the data analysis. Finally, the conclusion is translated into theory or used to support an existing theory.

To this point we have based our entire discussion on the assumption that we can study politics scientifically. But is this a valid assumption? Can we study politics in a scientific manner? We think the answer is yes but some would say no. Even those who share our belief that we can study politics scientifically know there are problems in doing so. Thus there are some obstacles that impact the scientific study of politics.

❖ OBSTACLES TO THE SCIENTIFIC STUDY OF POLITICS

Why do some nations have a unitary government while others have a federalist structure? Why do some Supreme Court members consistently favor strong, central government, while others consistently decide for the states? Why do some nations go to war? These are questions that political scientists try to answer. As you can see by these examples, political science involves the study of people in order to explain their political behavior. However, to discover explanations and patterns of political behavior so that political theory evolves, people must act consistently. In other words, they must be predictable. For if people do not act in a predictable manner, how can political scientists explain their political behavior?

Although, some political scientists reject the idea of studying human behavior scientifically, many accept the notion that people do act in a consistent manner. They accept this idea based on their experience and the experience of others who preceded them. If you doubt the validity of this assumption, you should take ten minutes to analyze your activities and those of your family and friends. We are sure that you will see consistent patterns of activity. For example, you may find that you eat at the same restaurant every Friday night or listen to the same radio station on most days. We are also sure that, upon reflection, you will discover that this consistency is applicable to your political activity and the political activity of your family and friends. In sum, consistent activity within the population is paramount to the scientific study of politics.

At the same time, human beings do think for themselves and are capable of purposeful behavior. We are not lifeless objects. Our ability to think and reason, or to act out of emotion, creates obstacles to the scientific study of politics. Workers who know they are the subjects of a study designed to determine the impact of environmental changes on work productivity, for instance, may strive to enhance productivity despite the environmental changes caused by the researcher. When people know that they are the subject of a study, they often act in an atypical way because they think they are contributing to the success of the study. They do not realize that they distorted the results of a scientific study.

Individuals may also respond to survey questions to hide their true feelings because they think their attitudes are socially unacceptable. Consider the following question. Do you support the legalization of marijuana? Most may say no because they believe drugs are harmful and a threat to our social order. Likewise, individuals are often reluctant to tell a researcher the truth about some past behavior. What would be the probability of getting someone to tell a researcher that they committed armed robbery, had an abortion, or were frequent users of illegal drugs? Thus, respondents may answer the question differently than they actually believe.

It is also difficult to collect some data needed to test theories. How does one, for instance, collect data about racist attitudes?

Last, the wording of the survey question can be an obstacle to the scientific study of politics because it could bias the response. As an example, consider the following questions: Do you favor an organization that works to protect the rights of workers while ensuring maximum benefits for all members? Or, do you favor an organization whose activities result in increased costs to the consumer and periodic work stoppages? Each question, of course, is describing union activity. The wording, however, could influence the way someone responds to the question. In legal jargon, "the question is leading the witness." Why not simply ask survey participants to rate their feeling about unions and their activities? In sum, a poorly worded question could result in the collection of false information—information that can impede scientific political research.

❖ THE USE OF THEORY TO INVESTIGATE THE SCOPE OF POLITICS

When we talk about what political scientists study and do, we are talking about the scope of political science. On the other hand, when we talk about how political scientists accomplish their ends, we refer to the methodology of the discipline. In short, scope and methods in political science are considerations of how political scientists go about their work.

In the following pages we will briefly examine systems, power, and goal theories, as theoretical approaches used to study politics. Then we will discuss the philosophical, historical, comparative, and juridical methods, used by traditional political theorists, to investigate political life. We will conclude with a discussion about behavioralism and postbehavioralism. These methods, adopted by modern political scientists, differ from the traditional methods because they emphasize the use of scientific tools to analyze politics.

◆ SYSTEMS THEORY

There are several broad ways that political scientists investigate the scope of the political world. One way they accomplish this task is by analyzing the entire political environment. David Easton enhanced this approach through the use of a model that viewed the political world as a system (Easton 1952). He saw the "political system" as an ongoing process that involved citizen demands and support, linkage of institutions to articulate the demands to government decision makers, government action on the demands, output in the form of legislation or judicial decisions, feedback, and support of the output or, if necessary, new demands from the citizenry.

Political scientists use the systems model in several ways. First, they identify important public problems. Second, they identify the players who provide system input. Third, they examine the decision-making process. Fourth, they analyze important policy and output to determine whether the output is substantive and adequate to meet citizen demands. Last, they determine how other social sciences can contribute to problem resolution. As such, the systems model is an important and useful approach when studying politics. (A more elaborate discussion about this approach will appear in Chapter 3.)

◆ POWER THEORY

Power theory, another way to study politics, views politics as a world of political bosses, power brokers, corporate power, and a power elite. This approach suggests that some individual or group dominates the system through their power activities. Thus, it is an undemocratic model of government. It assumes that important government decisions are made by a small, but powerful, group of people who have great wealth and business connections. Consequently, important public policies reflect the class interests of this strata.

There are several ways political scientists examine power and use this approach. Those using the elite approach view society as a pyramid. There is a small group of power elites at the top who use the subordinate political elite to enact and implement policy that serves their ends. At the bottom of the hierarchy is the nonelite citizenry. This group is the recipient of policy resulting from elite goals and political manipulations. Therefore, government policies reflect elite values, not those of the general public.

That view differs from the liberal notion of pluralism. Pluralism sees policy resulting from a series of compromises between a wide range of interest groups vying for power and policy development (Williamson and Rustad 1985, 12). Pluralism also differs from elitism because no single group dominates across policy arenas.

On the other hand, Neo-Marxists assert there is a corporate, or capitalist, elite that dominates the working class while influencing political decisions (Williamson and Rustad 1985, 17). These power sources are so concentrated that a meaningful exercise of power by the working class, or nonelite, is impossible (Jones 1983, 186). As a result, the capitalist economic system has created a capitalist-controlled society. Thus, the elites have evolved to the point that they exercise social, cultural, and political power in addition to economic power (Parenti 1978, 215).

◆ GOALS THEORY

Moral, or goals, theory, is another way that some political scientists study the political world. It analyzes the direction and goals of politics. Simple power or process is not its concern. Its concern is the purpose of power and the goal of the process. It examines the political process to determine whether it is ethical and in concert with democratic goals. We discuss the morals approach more thoroughly in Chapter 4.

❖ TRADITIONAL METHODS USED TO INVESTIGATE THE SCOPE OF POLITICS

There are several theories used by political scientists to approach the study of politics. There are also several methods to accomplish this task. Methodology is the particular way political scientists operate within a theoretical approach to investigate political activity. It is important that you remember that political scientists use these methods with any one of the theoretical approaches discussed above (Schrems 1986, 70–82).

◆ THE PHILOSOPHICAL METHOD

When political researchers use the philosophical method, they ask "why" questions. For example, why do some men rule while others follow? Why do nations and states differ?

The philosophical method is deductive in nature in that it proceeds from certain generalities about man. Man is political. Man is social. Man is self-serving. Man was ". . . endowed by their Creator with certain unalienable Rights." From these generalities, proponents of the philosophical method arrive at particular conclusions and applications. Thomas Jefferson, for example, used much of John Locke's philosophy when writing the Declaration of Independence. Locke's political writings about the natural rights of man, the purpose of government, equality, consent, limited government, and the right to revolt were paraphrased by Jefferson.

Today, many political scientists use the philosophical method when studying the scope, purpose, and value pursuits of government. For example, how intrusive should government be in society? Should government allocate scarce resources to promote order, provide public goods and services, or promote equality? How should government resolve dilemmas between freedom and order, or between freedom and equality? In sum, as Schrems asserts, "The philosophical 'why' is not something which was settled in ancient writings or in nineteenth-century revisions. Contemporary political scientists . . . are known for their Aristotelian or philosophical generalizations" (Schrems 1986, 73).

◆ THE HISTORICAL METHOD

Political scientists use the historical method to determine the structuring principles and conditions that give rise to a particular state or governmental practice. For example, what factors contributed to the ratification of the United States Constitution? Or, what factors influenced the creation of the Commonwealth of Nations? The political scientist also wants to know if the influences still have relevance despite changes in the political system.

◆ THE COMPARATIVE METHOD

The comparative method is a continuation of the historical method. It expands the historical investigation by analyzing and contrasting the experiences of nations and states. Scholars use it, for example, to determine the value of, and the pros and cons of, various political systems practiced by different cultures and nations.

Several scholars use this method to conduct comparative voting turnout studies. Mackie, for example, conducted a study to determine why voter turnout in the United States was so low compared to 25 other nations (Mackie 1990). You might use this method in a similar way by examining voter turnout in several states in the United States.

◆ THE JURIDICAL METHOD

The juridical method emphasizes laws, institutions, structures, and roles founded upon law. This method gives the researcher and student a broad overview of politics. It focuses on questions such as the basis for the United States Constitution, the branches of government, and political parites.

❖ MODERN METHODS USED TO INVESTIGATE THE SCOPE OF POLITICS

American political scholars used the traditional methods of political research to produce pensive and pertinent political theories. While the "founding" role of the scientific method of research may be attributed to Merriam at the University of Chicago in the early 1920s, American political scientists did not extensively begin to use scientific research methods to test their theories until the 1940s. During this period European social scientists expanded the scientific research process to America. As a result, many began to use research surveys to collect data so they could study the behavior of individuals and groups (Isaak 1981, 38–39).

◆ THE BEHAVIORAL METHOD

Scholars who use the behavioral method study the actual behavior of political actors whether they be presidents of countries, voters in elections, or peasants revolting against their government. Instead of analyzing the intent of constitutions, or how institutions are supposed to work, "behavioralists" study what actually happens. **Behavioralism** is a scientific method. When using this method, statistical, mathematical, and other quantitative analyses of data are important. Value judgments are not as important as data collection and analysis.

There is a gap between behavioralism and the other more normative methods we discussed. As such, several criticisms evolved about using the behavioral method. First, many scholars worry that it does not consider values and "what should be." Adherents of the behavioral method, however, believe that it is their task to explain political phenomena, not change it. Change should be left to those having the means to apply the implications of the study. Second, some political scientists disapprove of the inclusion of economic, psychological, and social factors to explain political behavior. They believe this interdisciplinary approach coupled with "the imputed objectivity, value-freeness, and scientific pretension predetermine and limit the content of political studies and leave out the very political dimension of the political world" (Shrems 1986, 79). Third, some criticize the behavioral method because it involves the quantification of political theory. Last, behavioralism was criticized as being too limited in scope and having a need to be more comprehensive (Schrems 1986, 78).

◆ THE POSTBEHAVIORAL METHODS

Because of criticisms about behavioralism, many behavioralists turned to public policy and policy analysis to show the utility of scientific methods when studying political questions. As such, **postbehavioralism** emerged as a way to study politics. This method expands behavioralism by including additional dimensions to political studies. It addresses the criticisms discussed above. Hence, there are several postbehavioralist groups.

Some postbehavioralists perform all the steps of the scientific research process and then, based on their value preferences, propose recommendations for public policy. For example, the results of a research study may lead the researcher to recommend the curtailment of affirmative action programs. A postbehavioralist who believes that government should pursue equality in the work force, however, may recommend continuance of the program. In short, they believe there is a place for normative considerations and applications in their efforts.

Other postbehavioralists emphasize formal mathematics in lieu of statistics in their research efforts. They believe that advanced mathematics such as calculus, exponentials, and logarithmic applications enhance their research.[1]

While the postbehavioralists criticize behavioralism to some extent, they are not antibehavioralists (Schrems 1986, 81). As such, they try to expand the contributions of the behavioralists. Even though postbehavioralists use formal mathematics, such as calculus in their political analyses, they make value judgments about the politics they study (Schrems 1986, 78). They believe there is an explicit place for normative applications in their studies.

❖ COMPOSITE POLITICAL RESEARCH: OUR METHOD OF CHOICE

We have spent some time discussing ways political scientists go about their work. We discussed traditional methods such as the philosophical method, the historical method, the comparative method, and the juridical method. We also discussed the behavioral method and methods used by postbehavioralists which typify a modern approach to political study. We will, however, concentrate on a **composite approach** to political research that combines elements of behavioralism and postbehavioralism.

Our approach is a composite one because it embraces the need to observe actual behavior, the need to consider political activity observable through the traditional methods of political research, the attributes of systematic research, and statistical applications, and the need to prescribe action by government decision makers. Our method will not only provide explanations for political action, it will also provide recommendations for making necessary policy changes. While the procedure is value free, the recommendations may be value laden.

In sum, our approach is similar to postbehavioralism because it allows researchers to proclaim their value preferences when they make recommendations. It differs from postbehavioralism, however, because it does not call for value judgments to be made about the political activity under study. Additionally, unlike the formalistic postbehavioralists, we believe statistics is an important tool for the political scientist.

There are several reasons for proposing this method of political inquiry. First, we believe values, as much as possible, should be kept from influencing the investigation of political problems. This sounds like a difficult challenge. In fact some would assert that it is "impossible to conduct social research that is uncontaminated by personal and political sympathies" (Becker 1967, 239–247). Therefore, many political scientists would probably agree that values can influence problem definition, analysis, and solutions. Thus, an important question arises: If the researcher begins the inquiry with an ideological bias, how can objective research result? If the response is, "it cannot," then how can results and implications be unbiased? Sadly, the answer is, "they cannot."

We believe our composite approach to political research, however, lessens the problem of bias. Our method bases value judgments, expressed as theoretical or policy preferences, on the scientific study of politics. This is quite different than making value judgments based on inquiries "contaminated by personal and political sympathies." We recognize, of course, that it may be difficult to keep social research value free. It is not so difficult, however, to sensitize researchers to the way values bias their research. We see our composite approach as a way to provide this sensitivity.

Second, the composite method embraces the idea that studies using quantitative data are more likely to produce functional theories—theories that have value in policy making. Therefore, the composite method fulfills an important requisite of applied research.

Third, like the behavioral method, the composite method uses scientific knowledge. Remember we said that scientific knowledge has certain characteristics that distinguish it from other ways individuals shape their beliefs—characteristics that also make it provable through deductive and inductive reasoning.

Fourth, the composite method involves systematic procedures. It translates the strengths discussed above into research activities through an orderly research process. That is, there are guidelines that optimize the probability that the research effort will have important consequences.

In conclusion, the composite approach complements the more traditional approaches to political research. Our approach considers the impact of political institutions, decisions, and juridical processes and output, on the research problem.

Each approach we discussed has its own benefits and limitations. Whatever the approach and method of analysis used by political scientists, however, an orderly and systematic process of research will enhance the results. Therefore, let's turn our attention to the features of the systematic research process.

❖ THE SYSTEMATIC RESEARCH PROCESS

As we discussed, scientific knowledge is empirical, nonnormative, transmissible, general, explanatory, and provisional. These criteria are the basis of the systematic research process—a process consisting of several stages that are supported by an extensive literature review and theory. We will cover each stage and the literature review in subsequent chapters. At this time, however, we introduce you to the importance of a comprehensive literature review and theory, and the various stages of the systematic research process.

◆ THE LITERATURE REVIEW

A comprehensive literature review is an important part of the systematic research process. Although, the review is a separate part of the research report, it is an ongoing task that impacts each stage of the research process.

We cannot stress enough the importance of the literature review. First, the review helps you gain expertise in the chosen field of inquiry. Second, problems and research questions can evolve from the reading of other studies. Third, the review provides support for hypothesis construction and the clarification of research elements. Fourth, suggestions for possible ways to perform the research, to collect and input your data, to select appropriate statistical procedures, and to analyze your data, can result from an effective literature review. Last, the review provides theoretical support for your study.

Recall that deduction is one way you can acquire scientific knowledge. In addition, it is the most common method used by novice political researchers and students. Thus, most of you will acquire scientific knowledge based on the testing of a political theory. As you will see in the following chapters, theoretical support is essential to each stage of the systematic research process.

We will cover the literature review and the importance of theory in more detail in Chapter 3.

◆ IDENTIFYING THE TOPIC OF RESEARCH

The first stage of the systematic research process requires clear identification and definition of a research topic. While we will cover this stage in more detail in Chapter 2, we offer some brief comments at this time.

During this stage you should ensure that the topic interests you and is of interest to other scholars in the field. You must also make sure that you can complete your project within the time allotted and with the resources available. Last, it is important that you understand and consider the ethical considerations associated with research.

◆ CLARIFYING THE RESEARCH ELEMENTS

Another step in the research process is to succinctly clarify the research elements. This will require you to define the problem in a way that will allow you to gather information about the problem. This step often requires you to "conceptualize" and "operationalize." That is, the problem must be broken down into concepts that allow measurement. In political research, concepts are perceptions used to represent political characteristics. Examples of concepts used in political research are power, influence, political efficacy, political socialization, and political culture.

Next, you must translate the concepts into observable events. As an example, recall our discussion about the party identification of first-time voters. In that example, the concept of political socialization was measured, or operationalized, by comparing the party identification of first-time voters and the party choice of their parents.

We will discuss other elements of research, such as variables and hypotheses, in Chapter 9.

◆ **THE RESEARCH DESIGN**

The next step in the research process is to design the research procedure. This requires you to determine the sources of your data, consider ways to collect your data, and decide how to analyze your data. This subject will receive extensive coverage in Chapter 11.

◆ **THE REMAINING STEPS**

Many of the remaining steps in the research process will require you to put the research design into action. For example you will collect and input your data (Chapter 12), analyze your data through the application of appropriate statistical techniques (Chapters 13–15) and prepare a report relating the findings to some political theory or important policy issue (Chapter 16).

You may see that research is a cyclical process. It usually starts with a problem and ends in a tentative empirical generalization. The generalization ending one cycle starts the next cycle. This cyclic process continues indefinitely, reflecting the progress of a scientific discipline. The research process is also self-correcting because the sequential process allows one to reevaluate each stage to identify possible errors.

◆ **SUMMARY OF THE SYSTEMATIC RESEARCH PROCESS**

There are eight stages of the systematic research process: problem identification, hypothesis formulation, research design, measurement, data collection, data input, data analysis, and generalization of the results through theory and policy implications. In addition, the literature review and theoretical support are important to the process.

Figure 1.1 depicts the systematic research process as a wheel that is constantly turning. The eight stages of the research process are the spokes of the wheel. These spokes are held in place by a hub consisting of theoretical support. The wheel is inflated to keep it balanced and turning. The research wheel, however, is not inflated with air, but with the benefits of an effective literature review.

Throughout this text we will advocate the systematic approach to political research. If you follow the steps we briefly outlined, your research will be more complete and personally satisfying. More importantly, your research effort may make a small contribution to the existing body of literature for a particular political issue. Thus, the results will expand political knowledge.

❖ **SUMMARY**

In this chapter we introduced you to the systematic research process. We explained the importance of political research. We also examined the various characteristics of scientific knowledge. For example, scientific knowledge is not normative and you can observe and measure it through empirical meth-

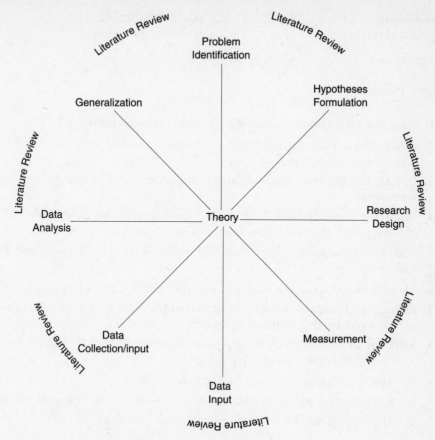

FIGURE 1.1   Systematic Research Process

ods. We also presented an in-depth discussion about the ways we can acquire scientific knowledge. In addition, we reviewed factors, such as subject cooperation and measurement difficulties, that impede the scientific study of politics. We also discussed some of the theoretical approaches and methods political scientists use to investigate the political world. We concluded Chapter 1 with a discussion about the characteristic features of research—a discussion that told you there are several steps and ethical concerns you must address when doing research to ensure the worthiness of the study and the dignity of the research participant.

❖ KEY TERMS

behavioralism   deduction
composite political research   epistemology

induction   postbehavioralism
political science   scientific knowledge

❖ EXERCISES

1. Why is it important for students to study research methods?
2. Differentiate between scientific knowledge and the other types of knowledge discussed in this chapter.
3. Distinguish between the inductive and deductive ways to acquire scientific knowledge.
4. What are some obstacles impacting the scientific study of politics? How can the political scientist overcome these obstacles?
5. Distinguish between approaches and methods used to investigate the political world.
6. Identify and discuss the stages of the systematic research process.
7. Identify and discuss ethical concerns that political scientists should consider when conducting political research.
8. Select an empirical study from a political science journal (*Publius* or *American Political Science Review*) and identify:
   a. The theoretical approach used by the author.
   b. Key points made by the author in each stage of the research process.
   c. Theoretical and/or policy implications of the study.

❖ SUGGESTED READINGS

Champney, Leonard. *Introduction to Quantitative Political Science.* New York: HarperCollins, 1995.

Durkheim, Emile. *Le Suicide.* New York: The Free Press, 1951.

Eulau, Heinz. *The Behavioral Persuasion in Politics.* New York: Random House, 1963.

Goldenberg, Sheldon. *Thinking Methodologically.* New York: HarperCollins, 1992.

Isaak, Alan C. *Scope and Methods of Political Science: An Introduction to the Methodology of Political Inquiry,* 3rd ed. Hometown, IL: Dorsey Press, 1981.

Johnson, Janet Buttolph, and Richard A. Joslyn. *Political Science Research Methods.* Washington, D.C.: Congressional Quarterly Press, 1986.

McCoy, Charles A., and John Playford. *Apolitical Politics: A Critique of Behavioralism.* New York: Thomas Y. Crowell, 1967.

Schmidt, Diane E. *Expository Writing in Political Science: A Practical Guide.* New York: HarperCollins, 1993.

Schmidt, Steffen W., Mack C. Shelley II, and Barbara A. Bardes. *An Introduction to Critical Thinking and Writing in American Politics.* Minneapolis/St. Paul: West Publishing, 1993.

Schrems, John J. *Principles of Politics: An Introduction.* Englewood Cliffs, NJ: Prentice-Hall, 1986.

Shively, W. Phillips. *The Craft of Political Research,* 3rd ed. Englewood Cliffs, NJ: Prentice-Hall, 1990.

❖ **NOTES**

1. See, for example, Manus I. Midlarsky, "Rulers and the Ruled: Patterned Inequality and the Onset of Mass Political Violence," *American Political Science Review* 82 (June 1988): 491–509.

THE PROBLEM: ESSENCE OF THE RESEARCH PROJECT

❖ INTRODUCTION

In the preceding chapter we introduced you to the systematic research process—a process involving several stages. In this chapter we will discuss items you need to consider when choosing a research topic or problem. While we discuss research topics, problem statements, and sources of potential research topics, we will not discuss the steps you should take to conduct a literature review. The scope and importance of the literature review requires a separate chapter (Chapter 3).

The initial stages of research are very crucial. We believe, however, that the choice of a research topic is perhaps the most critical. Your topic sets the stage for your entire research effort. It also establishes the framework for the other major stages of the research process.

Of the early phases of the research process, the selection of a topic is perhaps the most difficult for us to provide you with guidelines. Topic selection is personal and involves a great deal of originality, experience, and talent—talent that is sharpened over a period of time. Still, our purpose in this chapter is to provide you with some general suggestions that you can use to develop a worthy research topic.

An understanding of this chapter will enable you to:

1. Define a research topic.
2. Evaluate the worth of possible research topics.
3. Distinguish between personal and researchable problems.
4. Identify faults resulting from a lack of understanding about the nature of research.
5. Write a problem statement that fulfills the requirements of the composite research process.

❖ DECIDING ON A POTENTIAL TOPIC

The initial idea for possible research topics can come from numerous sources. Sometimes the professor will assign a topic for the class to research or will provide a list to select from. Many professors, however, will leave the decision up to you. After all, a major purpose of political research is to identify pertinent questions that require investigation. Therefore, you should have some capability in identifying and selecting potential research topics. We preface our discussion by emphasizing that it is ultimately your responsibility to select a research topic.

◆ SOURCES OF TOPICS

A cursory review of several journals and publications may provide you with some ideas about potential research topics. For example you may want to consult the *International Encyclopedia of the Social Sciences.* This publication consists of articles published by social scientists. Each article describes some of the major issues and questions in a particular subject area. It also provides you with additional references to major publications. Thus the *International Encyclopedia of the Social Sciences* is an invaluable source of possible research topics.

In addition, you should examine the leading journals and periodicals in the field of political science. Examples include the *American Political Science Review, The Public Administration Review,* and *Urban Affairs Quarterly.* When perusing these publications, you should take the following steps to simplify your efforts. First, read the titles of the articles. A simple review of the titles of articles in these journals will alert you to topics of potential interest to you. Second, read the abstracts that precede each article to get a better idea about the purpose of the article and its applicability to your field of interest. Third, examine the bibliography that follows each article. The bibliography can give you some ideas about what other scholars have written in your area of interest. If you follow these simple steps you should end up with several ideas for researchable topics.

Another source of topics that is often slighted by students is the basic textbooks you purchased for your political science classes. In particular, if your interest is American politics, your introductory text is an invaluable source of ideas. In addition, each chapter follows the general guidelines of a research paper. The chapters in Lineberry, Edwards, and Wattenberg's text *Government in America: People, Politics, and Policy,* for example, discuss the history, development, advantages and disadvantages, impact on politics, and reform initiatives for each subject matter. In addition, they use current data to support their arguments. The bibliographic references and suggested readings that follow each chapter are also invaluable sources of possible topics for your research.

◆ EVALUATING A POTENTIAL TOPIC

Richard Cole offers several criteria that you should consider when choosing a topic to research (Cole 1980, 9–10). First, ensure the topic interests you. You will devote several weeks, or even months, to your research paper. Nothing could be more tiresome than working on a project without the enthusiasm that accompanies a topic of interest. Additionally, nothing detracts from the ultimate quality of the final product than a lack of enthusiasm. Thus, you should select a topic that will be appealing throughout the length of your research effort.

Second, while the topic must interest you, it should also be of interest to other scholars in the field. A major purpose of research is to add to the existing body of knowledge. Your brief semester research project should relate to the context of existing theory or relate to current policy.

A major question often posed in our classes is, "How does one know whether a particular topic will interest other political scientists?" One way to answer this question is to review the social science indexes, journals, and abstracts to discover other work that is being conducted in your chosen area. A word of caution. If you find a large amount of material, your topic may be "over studied." Thus, it would be difficult to add much to what already exists. On the other hand, if you find little, or no, reference in the literature relating to your possible topic, your topic may be of no interest to the broader discipline, or it is too difficult to pursue. In either case, you should look for another topic.

Third, you should ensure that your topic is manageable. It is usually not too difficult to conceive of interesting and significant ideas. The problem often is selecting a topic that you can complete within the time allotted and with the resources available. Research is often time consuming and expensive. Thus, while you might find it interesting to survey all members of the U.S. Congress about their interests outside the Congress, you may also find it expensive, time consuming, and impractical for a one-semester course. On the other hand, interviewing city council members may be practical. In sum, you must take time to apply a good deal of foresight and common sense when selecting your topic. Know your own time and resource limitations and select a topic that is realistic and manageable.

Last, you need to understand the ethical considerations associated with research. Some scholars may see the importance of a study to the field of political science. Yet, others may consider the same study outside the ethical boundaries of research. Researchers exceed ethical limits when they do not consider the external implications of their findings.

W. Phillips Shively reminds his readers that conducting research is an extension of one's personal actions. As such, researchers must consider the ethics of their research (Shively 1990, 10). He identifies two comprehensive classes of ethical questions researchers must consider.

First, they must understand the consequences of their research on society. They should realize that their research could be a detriment to society. For example, think of the ethical questions confronting the Los Alamos scientists who designed the atomic bomb. Or, think of the ethical questions confronting social scientists who see the results of their research used by the government to support the elimination of welfare programs. While each of these efforts can benefit some segments of society, each can also disrupt some segments of society. Shively implies that researchers should consider all of society and the ethical questions inherent in their research prior to releasing their findings (Shively 1990, 10).

Shively also identified a second class of questions involving ethics. Shively asserted that ethics are also disregarded when researchers mislead subjects asked to participate in a study. In addition, a lack of ethics appears when researchers infringe on the rights of study participants. Thus, they must treat research subjects in a fair and humane manner (Shively 1990, 11). Failure to do so could put undue psychological stress on the subjects, place unreasonable demands on the participants, abridge the confidentiality of the subjects, and mislead the subjects (Shively 1990, 11–12). Hence, you must also take steps to treat your study participants with dignity while protecting their privacy. One way to accomplish this goal is to make the research results available to the participants. This action may also help you gain their confidence.

The problems identified by Shively pose difficult ethical questions for the researcher. Did the efforts of the scientists at Los Alamos benefit more people than they harmed? In 1946, many may have answered with a resounding yes. Today, after analyzing the long-range impact, however, many more may respond with an equally resounding no.

So what rule should we follow? We agree with Shively's firm rule "that people should never be coerced or tricked into participation and should always be fully informed before they agree to participate" (Shively 1990, 12).

Our final comment about ethics and political research concerns plagiarism. Studies can be replicated, but not plagiarized. Remember, a goal of research is to generalize the findings of one study to other geographical regions, segments of society, and population centers. Therefore there is nothing wrong in taking the same steps as other scholars when doing your research. To copy their findings, however, is plagiarism.

In summary, when conducting a political inquiry, you must understand the ethics of political research—ethics that consider the study's impact on society, the participants, and other scholars in your field of interest.

❖ THE RESEARCH PROBLEM

◆ PROBLEM STATEMENT AND CLARITY

After you decide on a research topic you must clearly state the problem you want to investigate. All research begins with a problem statement. A **problem statement** is a question you want to answer. For example, your topic may be voting in western democratic nations. The problem you may want to answer is "Why is the voting turnout higher in some western democracies than in other western democracies?"

There are, for the most part, two types of problems: personal problems and researchable problems. It is the latter type that fulfills the requirements of the composite method of research discussed in Chapter 1. A preliminary step in your research effort is to clearly state the problem so that you can take the appropriate steps to answer the question it poses. You should state the problem in a complete grammatical sentence. State the problem so well that anyone, anywhere, could read it, understand it, and react to it without benefit of your presence. In addition, you must state your research problem so that the purpose of your research is clear.

◆ WHAT TO AVOID WHEN WRITING YOUR PROBLEM STATEMENT

Do not write your problem statement as a meaningless half-statement. Consider the following statements for example: "Welfare and mass transit systems." "A voting turnout study." As stated, these are topics, not research problem statements.

These statements give the reader very little to go on. They also provoke questions of their own. What is the purpose of each study? Where will the studies be conducted? Who are the participants? Following are some possible ways to translate these statements, or topics, into meaningful problem statements:

1. The purpose of this study is to determine the effect that welfare recipients in Houston's Third Ward have on Houston's mass transit system and to identify ways to alleviate observed problems.

2. The purpose of this research is to analyze and compare the electoral systems of western democracies in order to identify reasons for differences in voting turnout and to identify ways to enhance overall turnout.

Generally questions you can answer with a simple yes or no are not appropriate research problems. Research problems must delve deeply into the subject. You must concern yourself with the qualitative differences that distinguish one situation from another. As a result, simple studies about a particular individual, company, or event, are not research because data analysis and interpretation to identify situational differences are not a part of the process. Thus, comparison is an important characteristic of research problems.

Some students also make the mistake of expressing their opinion when writing a problem statement. As a result, instead of having a research problem per se, they express an opinion that they want to defend or prove. For example, "The Republican party is better than the Democratic party." A possible way to restate this statement so that it meets the requirements of a problem statement is: "The purpose of this study is to identify differences between the Republican and Democratic parties to identify reasons why Republicans have dominated the executive branch since 1968."

A final comment about problem statements. Make sure your problem is limited. Do not attempt to research too much. Limit your study to a manageable geographical area with a limited population. Remember to consider your time and resource allocations.

❖ TOPIC SELECTION: SOME CONCLUDING REMARKS

Our discussion so far has given you some suggestions to follow when selecting and evaluating a topic to research. We also gave you some pointers about writing problem statements. Before we conclude our discussion, however, we want to offer some final hints for selecting your research topic.

◆ SELECT YOUR TOPIC EARLY

Many students have a glaring fault: they excel at procrastination. They wait until the last minute to select a topic, formulate a problem statement, collect as much information as possible about their topic, and attempt to write the report. The result is often an inferior report that violates the principles we have discussed. Early topic selection ensures greater access to materials, more time to carefully formulate hypotheses, more flexibility when collecting your data, and more time to analyze your data and write your report. Early topic selection will also, undoubtedly, result in a superior research project.

◆ LIMIT THE RANGE OF YOUR TOPIC

As a beginning researcher you may fall into a common trap. That is, like many novice researchers you may select a very broad topic and immediately find yourself inundated with information. You may, for example, want to investigate "political participation." Your investigation, however, reveals there are hundreds of articles and references on different areas of this general topic. Obviously, your topic is too broad and cannot be adequately researched and reported on within a single semester. Your task then is to limit the topic. Perhaps you can initially limit the range of political participation to "political participation in America." You can further limit the topic to "types of political participation in America." Further constricting could result in a paper about "unconventional political participation in America." This topic, however, is still too expansive. Perhaps the topic of your paper should be something like "the 1960s Civil Rights Movement in America and the impact of unconventional political participation on public policy." Anyway, we are sure you get the point of our discussion. Narrowing and defining a general topic makes your research tasks more manageable. It will also result in more interesting and definitive results.

◆ CONSIDER DUPLICATING ANOTHER STUDY

Duplicating another study is a legitimate way to conduct scientific research. The goal in such a project is not "to reinvent the wheel." It is appropriate, however, to see if the wheel works as well in a different environment or location. As long as you replicate, but do not copy, another study, you are within the ethical bounds of scholarly research. Consider these examples. It is acceptable to determine whether the social patterns contributing to political unrest in Third World nations found by previous research also have an impact in the large urban centers of America. It is also acceptable to see if the political attitudes found at Harvard match the political attitudes found at Brigham Young University. Remember, an important goal of research is to provide additional confirmation to whatever theory you tested. If you find differences, your goal is to determine reasons for the differences and suggest ways to modify the theory.

◆ ABANDON TOPICS THAT ARE IMPOSSIBLE TO COMPLETE

Another common mistake to avoid is to pursue a topic you cannot complete within the time parameters. When it is obvious that your references are limited, or your data cannot be collected, you need to consider another topic. Early topic selection makes it possible to reveal problems while there is time to change to another subject. It is better to select another topic than to turn in an inferior paper accompanied by excuses for your drab performance.

❖ SUMMARY

At the outset of this chapter we said that, although the initial stages of research are very crucial, the choice of a research topic is perhaps the most critical. Your topic establishes the framework for the other major stages of the research process.

We also said that of all the stages of the research process, topic selection is the most difficult for us to provide guidelines. Nevertheless, we provided you with some general suggestions to use when developing a research topic.

As such, we discussed possible sources you can review to identify topics and problems worthy of research. We also provided some guidelines to follow when evaluating possible topics. In addition, we gave you some suggestions to follow when writing your problem statement. You must state your problem clearly. You must avoid half-statements, opinions, and those problems that you can answer with a simple yes or no. We also stressed the importance of limiting the scope of your problem. We concluded the chapter by advising you to select your topic early, to consider replication of previous studies, and to abandon your topic if it becomes unwieldy.

❖ KEY TERMS

problem statement   topic evaluation

❖ EXERCISES

1. A student turned in the following list as possible topics for research. What is wrong with the list? Reword the proposed topics into suitable research topics and problem statements.

    a. Political socialization

    b. Political participation

    c. Ideology

    d. Political change

2. Referring to textbooks, political science journals, and your own areas of interest, develop three possible research topics.

3. Write problem statements for the topics you developed for question 2. Make sure they fulfill the criteria provided in the chapter.

4. Discuss the criteria for evaluating the worth of possible research topics.

5. Distinguish between personal and researchable problems.

6. Identify faults resulting from a lack of understanding about the nature of research.

7. Why is it important to select a possible research topic as soon as possible?

❖ SUGGESTED READINGS

Goldenberg, Sheldon. *Thinking Methodologically*. New York: Harper-Collins, 1992.

Johnson, Janet Buttolph, and Richard A. Joslyn. *Political Science Research Methods*. Washington, D.C.: Congressional Quarterly Press, 1986.

Leedy, Paul D. *Practical Research: Planning and Design,* 3rd ed. New York: Macmillan, 1985.

Mann, Thomas. *A Guide to Library Research Methods*. New York: Oxford University Press, 1987.

Schmidt, Diane E. *Expository Writing in Political Science: A Practical Guide*. New York: HarperCollins, 1993.

Schmidt, Steffen W., Mack C. Shelley II, and Barbara A. Bardes. *An Introduction to Critical Thinking and Writing in American Politics*. Minneapolis/St. Paul: West Publishing, 1993.

Shively, W. Phillips. *The Craft of Political Research,* 3rd ed. Englewood Cliffs, NJ: Prentice-Hall, 1990.

THE LITERATURE REVIEW: BECOMING FAMILIAR WITH YOUR TOPIC

❖ INTRODUCTION

The major purpose of the literature review is to become thoroughly familiar with your topic. A comprehensive literature review is an important part of the composite research process. Although the review is a separate part of the research report, it is an ongoing task that effects each stage of the research process.

An understanding of this chapter will enable you to:

1. See the purpose of the literature review.
2. Master the steps involved in conducting a systematic literature review.
3. Relate the literature to your research project.
4. Properly write the literature review.

❖ PURPOSE OF THE REVIEW

To properly conduct research, it is necessary to review what other scholars have to say about your topic. You want to thoroughly familiarize yourself with the available literature in your area of study. A precise **literature review** will also help you to narrow your topic and place the research in the proper theoretical or policy context. While topic familiarization is the major reason for conducting a literature review, there are other important reasons for reviewing the literature.

◆ REVEAL SIMILAR STUDIES

A review may reveal investigations similar to your own. It can show you how other researchers have handled their research. By studying the major research questions asked by others, the review will help you define your problem. The literature may also suggest other important questions and hypotheses that need research.

◆ THEORY IDENTIFICATION

Most of the research you will perform will start with a theory. Then you will design a research project that tests the applicability of the theory to your project. A thorough literature review may help you identify theories that explain your research question. It may also help you identify concepts and measurements that others used to explain political phenomena. The review can give you some insight by suggesting a research design for dealing with your research problem.

◆ DATA SOURCES

A major benefit of a thorough literature review is the possibility that someone else collected much of the data you need for your study. At the very least, your review may reveal sources of data you did not know existed.

◆ PERSPECTIVE

The literature review can help you put your study in perspective. It can help you see your own study in a historical perspective. It may also help you to evaluate your research efforts by comparing them with related efforts of other scholars.

The literature review familiarizes you with the approaches and techniques used by others, with the available data sources, and with the important questions that still need an answer. Thus, it gives you a framework to use when conducting your research.

❖ HOW TO BEGIN A SEARCH FOR RELATED LITERATURE

A thorough literature review requires you to search books, journals, abstracts, indices, and texts that deal with your topic. There are, however, several ways to conduct a literature review. If you are starting with only a general interest in a subject, you may want to locate a textbook covering the subject, read the appropriate sections, and then check out the sources cited in the footnotes and lists of references. The purpose of this type of review is to become familiar with the overall topic. After this initial review, however, your purpose changes. Now you want to review the literature so that you can narrow your topic and develop your problem statement. As a result, you can expect frequent trips to the library to complete the review.

You have probably learned how to do general research during Freshman orientation. Hence we will not present a detailed discussion about computer searches and software. Thomas Mann's excellent book, *A Guide to Library*

Research Methods, however, will tell you all that you need to know about these valuable research tools.

◆ INDICES AND ABSTRACTS

Generally, indices provide you with the author and topic information within a broad subject matter area. They are compilations listing articles, studies, and research reports in specified areas. For example, the *Social Science Index* is an important reference source that lists recent articles appearing in the various social science journals. Published quarterly, the index lists authors by subject matter for almost 300 periodicals in fields such as anthropology, economics, environmental sciences, public administration, sociology, and political science.

Another useful index is the *Bibliographic Index,* which is a cumulative bibliography of bibliographies. With luck you may find an entire bibliography appropriate for your topic. If you want to conduct research about public administration, for example, you will find in the *Bibliographic Index,* under the subject heading "Political Science," several entries dealing with bibliographies of public administration.

Other useful indices include the *Comprehensive Dissertation* indices. These indices are published by author and by subject matter. Each of these indices will alert you to the whereabouts of doctoral dissertations that may apply to your study.

The *Author Index* lists dissertations by authors' surnames. You can obtain complete bibliographic information for each entry. Where an author wrote more than one paper for a degree or received more than one doctorate, multiple entries may occur. If you want to write a paper about local government, for example, you would find in the *Comprehensive Dissertation Index,* 1991 Supplement, Author Index, Volume 5, p. 349, the following entry:

Jones, Laurence Frederick
   Representational change in Texas county government.
   (Ph.D. The Univ. of Texas at Arlington, 1990.) 215 pp.
   51-07A p.2515   DEY9033483

The first entry is the name of the author. The second entry gives the title of the dissertation. The third entry lists the name of the school granting the degree and the year the author earned the degree. The fourth entry gives you information about the number of pages in the dissertation. The paging reflects the number of exposures filmed and available from University Microfilms International. The fifth entry is the DAI citation. In our example, "51-07A p.2515" indicates Volume 51, Number 7, Section A, page 2515 of *Dissertation Abstracts International.* The sixth entry is the order number (DEY9033483). If the dissertation is available from University Microfilms International, the order number appears as the last item of information in the entry. You can get a copy of most other dissertations from the institutions that granted the degrees. Interlibrary loan and copy service information is also available from the individual schools.

The entries in the *Subject Index* are similar to those cited in the *Author Index*. The major difference is that the first entry will be a key word denoting the subject of the dissertation. All subject keywords are listed in alphabetical order. Each new keyword is displayed in boldface type at the extreme left of the column. The index lists individual dissertation entries under each keyword alphabetically by title. Referring to our example above, the entry in the *Subject Index* for this dissertation is:

Representational Change
    Jones, Laurence Frederick
    Representational change in Texas county government.
    (Ph.D. The Univ. of Texas at Arlington, 1990.) 215 pp.
    51-07A p.2515   DEY9033483

This entry is found in the *Comprehensive Dissertation Index*, Social Sciences and Humanities, Volume 4, p. 552.

A major limitation of the indices we discussed above is the fact that it takes time to publish an index. Therefore, there is often a lapse of time between the publication of a journal article and its subsequent reference in the appropriate index.

Newspaper indices, however, are very useful as a reference source to very current topics. Newspapers that are indexed and available on microfilm in most libraries are *The New York Times, The Wall Street Journal, The Christian Science Monitor,* and *The Washington Post.*

Abstracts are another useful source that will help you learn about your topic. An **abstract** is a summary of an article or a study. Abstracts differ from indices because they summarize the important points of the cited material. The typical abstract is often less than 500 words and is a favorite reference source for the researcher. Abstracts are more difficult to compile than indices because they provide more information. Thus, they are often less current than indices. Despite this characteristic, however, they are an extremely useful tool and thus merit your attention.

Some of the more popular abstracts that you might use include *Public Administration Abstracts, SAGE Public Administration Abstracts, SAGE Urban Studies Abstracts, Sociological Abstracts, Dissertation Abstracts International,* and *Urban Affairs Abstracts.*

◆ PROFESSIONAL JOURNALS

All thorough literature reviews include research reports and findings published in professional **journals** in Political Science and Related Fields. Today, there are numerous journals that you can use to enhance your review. While the following list is not exhaustive, it does give you a variety of sources to select from.

American Political Science Review

Published since 1906, this journal publishes the latest studies about political science questions, policy, and institutions. In addition, the American Political Science Association endorsed the journal as its official journal.

American Journal of Political Science

Published since 1957, this journal primarily publishes reports and articles about American government and politics.

American Politics Quarterly

Published since 1973, the articles in this journal deal primarily with American political behavior and culture.

Comparative Politics

Published since 1969, this journal publishes articles that address the political systems, institutions, and ideologies of the different types of government throughout the world.

International Studies Quarterly

Published since 1957, this journal publishes articles quite similar to those published in the *Comparative Politics* journal.

Policy Studies Review

Published since 1981, this journal publishes articles related to current public policy issues and programs.

Political Science Quarterly

One of the oldest journals in terms of publication, this journal, first published in 1886, publishes a plethora of articles about American politics, comparative politics, and international relations.

Polity

Published since 1968, this journal is the equivalent of the *Political Science Quarterly.*

Public Administration Review

Published since 1939, this publication publishes articles that advance the "science, processes, and art" of public administration.

Public Opinion Quarterly

Published since 1937, this journal is especially useful for students who use political opinion polls in their research efforts.

Public Policy

Published since 1953, this journal is an excellent reference for those who are interested in the formulation of public policy.

Publius: The Journal of Federalism

Published since 1971, this journal publishes articles that deal with intergovernmental relations in federal government systems.

Urban Affairs Quarterly

Published since 1965, this is the official journal for scholars interested in urban affairs and politics.

Western Political Quarterly

Published since 1948, this journal publishes articles dealing with political science and public administration.

◆ BOOK REVIEWS

While many of the journals listed above provide reviews and **critiques** of current political science books, there are also several review digests and indices that you may want to use during your literature review. These reviews are particularly useful because they also offer interpretations and explanations about political phenomena that may differ from those espoused by the author of the book being reviewed. Some of the better review digests include *Book Review Digest, Book Review Index, Perspective,* and the *Political Science Reviewer.*

◆ MAKE BIBLIOGRAPHIC CARDS

After two or three days of reference search in the library, you may find that you generated a lengthy list of sources that address your topic. In fact, you may have a long list of references without meaning. That is, unless you took steps similar to those we will discuss in the following passages, your list will only be a long slate of books and references, instead of a list that gives you an idea of how each entry will complement your research. Thus, when you begin to accumulate your material, you should follow this procedure:

1. Use 3 by 5 cards to log references applicable to your study.
2. The cards should be in bibliographic form. In addition, include a brief synopsis of the article on the card. For example:

   This article consists of a description of voting patterns of black citizens who reside in all-black communities contrasted with those blacks living in cities having a heterogeneous population. The article uses empirical methods to measure concepts of political alienation amongst black voters.

3. When completed, your cards should include all material that you intend to use in your paper. You can also use the cards to construct your bibliography.

◆ STAY FOCUSED

You should always relate your bibliography to your problem. That is, always keep your research effort problem-oriented. Continually ask yourself, How does this item of literature relate to my problem? Do not build a haphazard bibliographic collection. Some consider that a long list of sources is akin to a thorough literature search. However, irrelevant literature soon becomes apparent and will detract from the overall thesis.

❖ HOW TO WRITE THE LITERATURE REVIEW

◆ HAVE A PLAN AND AN OUTLINE

The review is a discussion of those other studies, research reports, or writings that bear directly on your own effort. Before you begin writing the review, you should have a plan. That is, make sure you know precisely what it is that you are trying to do. To help you with this goal, you should have an outline to guide you through the process. Your outline should begin with a discussion about the classic studies and theories that have prepared the way for your research effort as well as those of others. You should begin your discussion from a broad and comprehensive perspective, or as Leedy says, "like an inverted pyramid: broad end first" (Leedy 1985, 73). Then you want to deal with specific, or more localized, studies that focus closer on your specific problem.

The following is an example of the headings of a literature review for a research paper about the impact of interest groups on public policy in America. We follow Leedy's approach by arranging the topics in the form of an inverted pyramid to depict how the author of the paper did what we discussed in terms of an overall plan and outline.

Outline of the review of the related literature

The impact of interest groups on public policy

Historical overview of interest groups in America

Types and structure of interest groups

Political Action Committees

Interest group resources

Interest group problems

Interest group tactics

Iron triangles

Good or bad?

Summary

◆ RELATE THE LITERATURE TO THE RESEARCH PROJECT

Throughout the writing of the review, you want to constantly ensure that the literature you are discussing relates to your problem. Too many discussions of the literature are nothing but a chain of pointless and isolated summaries of the writings of others. For example, Dahl says, Lineberry says, Welch says. With this style there is no discussion or attempt to demonstrate how the literature relates to your research problem. Leedy offers the following suggestions to help you with this task.

First, prior to penning your review, write your research statement, or problem, at the top of the page to remind you of the central theme of your topic. Remember, everything, including the literature review, revolves around your problem statement. A possible research statement for the above example is: *The impact of interest groups on public policy in America.*

Second, dissect the problem into its subparts. Then, match each subpart with its related literature. Study these groups in relation to each other, with the view of planning and organizing the discussion of the related literature. Each entry in the above outline is a subpart of the research problem.

Last, write the review. Begin each section with headings whose wording is similar to components and theoretical bases highlighted in your outline. Each entry in the above outline, for example, would head each section of your literature review.

◆ REVIEW AND CRITIQUE THE LITERATURE; DO NOT REPRODUCE IT

It is more important what you say, or study, about the literature than what the author of the study has to say. Therefore, you should present your own discussion and critically analyze the study and the findings of the author. Effective **critiques** are not simply a summary of an article. Nor are they a list of the pros and cons of an article. Instead, effective critiques are an overall assessment and evaluation of articles and literature. You need to include the following items in your review.

Subject: Briefly discuss the subject of the reading.

> **Example:** This article explains the reciprocal relationship between interest groups, legislative committee members, and administrative agencies. These "iron triangles" are seen by the author as having a negative impact on the American political system.

Purpose Statement: Briefly discuss the author's purpose for writing the article.

> **Example:** The main purpose of this article is to analyze the ways iron triangles influence public policy in America.

Major Points: Discuss the major points made by the author throughout the article.

> **Example:** Special interest groups in America lobby, build coalitions, litigate, apply grass-roots pressure, and participate in the election process to influence public policy. They also form a "productive" liaison with the administrative agencies responsible for implementing the policy that addresses their demands.

Thus, the author asserts that interest groups contribute to fragmented public policy and an ever increasing budget deficit.

Analysis: Address, as a minimum, the following factors in your analysis of the article.

1. The significance of the article.

Example: This article is significant because it identifies ways that special interest groups influence American public policy.

2. Its current relevance.

Example: Today, interest groups play an important role in public policy. This article depicts the impact that interest groups have on current legislative bodies and administrative agencies. In addition, it was not unusual to hear presidential political candidates in the 1992 race for the presidency speak out against the influence of special interest groups as a major reason for the nation's budget deficit.

3. The effectiveness of the article in making the major points.

Example: This article used data that showed a relationship between interest group campaign contributions and support for interest group demands by the recipients of PAC political donations.

4. Theoretical implications of the article.

Example: The findings presented in this article support the subgovernment political theory that the reciprocal nature of iron triangles contributes to policy fragmentation and budget costs. The notion of hyperpluralism is also substantiated by the findings of the author.

5. Policy implications of the article.

Example: Congress should enact and enforce legislation to curb the influence of PAC donations to political players.

Personal viewpoint: Briefly discuss your personal agreement or disagreement with the article. Try to draw on your personal knowledge or experience when possible.

Example: Analysis of the data collected by the author suggests that hyperpluralism and iron triangles can contribute to fragmented policy and a budget deficit. The author, however, neglects to mention that, as linkage institutions for their constituencies, interest groups are the collective voice of their members. Thus, they represent the demands of their members. They also provide policy feedback and keep their members appraised of political activity that addresses their demands. Therefore, interest groups enhance the democratic process.

◆ PARAPHRASE

Throughout your review you should try to paraphrase the major points of the author. If necessary, try to use short direct quotations. Only use long quotations as a last resort.

◆ SUMMARIZE

Each literature discussion and associated research relating to the problem should end with a brief summary. In the summary you want to recap what you said and show its relationship and significance to the research problem. Thus, you want to tell the reader what it all means. Your summary should epitomize the discussion and show its direct relationship to the problem under study.

> **Example:** *The impact of interest groups on public policy in America.* This article relates to the research problem because it presents a negative view about the contributions of special interest groups towards public policy. While others assert that competing interest groups enhance the democratic process by providing a communications linkage to policymakers, the author of this article has a different viewpoint. Interest groups, as a part of the iron triangle reciprocal arrangement, contribute to fragmented policy and budget deficits. Therefore, they impede the notion of effective and efficient government.

❖ SUMMARY

In this chapter we covered quite a bit of ground in relatively few pages. However, this is not to slight the importance of the literature review. As we said in the beginning of the chapter, the major purpose of the literature review is to become thoroughly familiar with your topic. We also said that the review is a separate part of the research report. It is, however, an ongoing task that impacts each stage of the research process.

As a result, we spent some time trying to help you see the purpose of the literature review. We also gave you direction so that you could master the steps involved in conducting a systematic literature review. We also wanted you to be able to relate the literature to your research project. Last, we gave you some suggestions so that you could properly write the literature review.

The first steps of the composite research process are finished. You have a topic, know how to write a problem statement, and are thoroughly familiar with the literature and the relationship of your topic to that literature. In Part Two, we will discuss the scope of political science. As such, we will introduce you to the political world, present some key questions dealing with the American political process, and spend some time discussing public administration, comparative politics, and international relations.

❖ KEY TERMS

abstract   journals
critiques   literature review

❖ EXERCISES

1. Discuss the purpose of the literature review.
2. Identify and discuss the steps you should take when conducting a systematic literature review.
3. Discuss why it is important to ensure you show the relatedness of the literature to your research project.
4. Identify and discuss the sections of a literature review.
5. Review three empirical studies published in recent political science journals. For each study, report:
   a. The purpose of the study.
   b. The sources of information and data.
   c. The major findings.
   d. The major conclusions.
6. Select one of the research topics developed in exercise 2 in Chapter 2 and, relying on the various indices and abstracts discussed in this chapter, thoroughly review the literature in this area. List the 10 books or articles that appear most relevant to your particular area of interest and prepare a paragraph summary of each. Make sure you follow the steps discussed in this chapter.

❖ SUGGESTED READINGS

Johnson, Janet Buttolph, and Richard A. Joslyn. *Political Science Research Methods.* Washington, DC: Congressional Quarterly Press, 1986.

Leedy, Paul D. *Practical Research: Planning and Design,* 3rd ed. New York: Macmillan, 1985.

Mann, Thomas. *A Guide to Library Research Methods.* New York: Oxford University Press, 1987.

Schmidt, Diane E. *Expository Writing in Political Science: A Practical Guide.* New York: HarperCollins, 1993.

Schmidt, Steffen W., Mack C. Shelley II, and Barbara A. Bardes. *An Introduction to Critical Thinking and Writing in American Politics.* Minneapolis/St. Paul: West Publishing, 1993.

2

◆ ◆ ◆

THE SCOPE OF POLITICAL SCIENCE

In Part One we introduced you to political science and political research. In Chapters 2 and 3 we took you through the first two stages of a research project: topic selection and the literature review. In this section we present a more thorough introduction to the discipline of political science. Our purpose is twofold. First, we want to give you an overview of some major political science subfields. If you are a major or minor in political science, your college or university will probably require courses in several of these subfields. At the same time you will have room to specialize in a particular subfield. Our discussion will help you decide on areas to explore further in your college career. Second, we want to help you select a topic for your research project in your scope and methods course. In each chapter we provide a sampling of the major research issues posed by scholars in the field or subfield. Discussion of these issue will help you discover your own particular research interest.

Chapter 4 presents an introduction to the world of politics. We show how politics and political relationships are embedded in human existence. We discuss some of the central questions posed by the political world and why they are important. Much of the discussion involves questions raised in the political science subfield of political theory, which we do not attempt to cover here. You will not be slighted by this omission however. In a scope and methods course, it is likely your instructor will require a research project that incorporates the quantitative methods covered in Part Three of this text. These methods are foreign to traditional political theory. We conclude with a sketch of the remainder of the political science discipline and its subfields.

Chapter 5 presents the subfield of American politics. The American politics subfield is perhaps the most advanced in the discipline. We provide an overview of the American political system by examining the political environment, constitutionalism, and some key questions about how the system works.

We also discuss the major elements of the political system such as political parties, interest groups, Congress, and the presidency.

Chapter 6 explores public administration and public policy. Public administration refers to the government's role in delivering common goods and services to the community. Public policy is the goal-directed course of action by government to deal with a public problem. Here we provide an overview of the "who," "what," and "how" of public administration. We also explore the purpose and evaluation of various types of public policy and provide a general overview of the policy-making process.

Chapter 7 introduces the subfield of comparative politics. This subfield is the broadest and most difficult to summarize. It confronts the question of how to compare politics among nations and involves analysis of all the world's political systems. We do not pretend to cover the breadth of this subfield, but instead discuss how the subfield developed, why it is important, and how to compare political systems. The discussion will hopefully provide you with a flavor for this important, yet difficult, area.

Chapter 8 completes our discussion of the scope of political science with a description of the subfield of international relations. This subfield is also difficult to summarize because it is broad, and even international relations specialists do not always agree as to its boundaries. We first introduce you to some basic concepts in the study of international relations. These include the international system, nation-states, international organizations, multinational corporations, and other nongovernmental organizations. Second, we illustrate the conduct of international relations by discussing how nation-states play the game. We then discuss some important questions in the subfield giving particular attention to the causes of war. Finally, we summarize some of the different approaches to the study of international relations.

As you read and study Part Two it is important that you keep certain cautions in mind. You must not assume that our descriptions provide complete coverage of the political science discipline. Your scope and methods professor will probably point out that some subfields such as political theory (as we already mentioned) and political economy are omitted altogether. In an introductory text however, limitations of time and space preclude discussing all subfields in their entirety. We had to pick and choose. Therefore, we chose those subfields that dominate the undergraduate curriculum in political science at most colleges and universities. American and comparative politics, public administration and public policy, and international relations are taught virtually everywhere. Indeed, some would argue that areas such as political economy are part of other subfields. For example, the political science curriculum might include courses in comparative political and international political economy.

We also make no pretense that we cover completely the subfields we do discuss. That too would be an impossible task to complete in one text. There have been thousands of books and articles written in each of the major subfields we visit. Your professor might point out, for example, that Chapter 5 on American politics omits important issues such as the roles played by the media and the bureaucracy in the American political system. Likewise, the vast dimensions of *comparative politics and international relations make omissions unavoidable. A good example is our decision not to discuss the role of morality, and the moralistic approach, in the study of international politics.*

We have limited our effort to providing you with a beginning look at what the study of politics is all about. We provide an overview of the types of questions political scientists ask, and the major areas in which they ask them. In this regard, Part Two provides a solid introduction to the discipline, and it will help you begin to ask important political questions for yourself.

THE POLITICAL WORLD

❖ INTRODUCTION

We have introduced you to the nature of political research and how to begin a research project by selecting and learning about a topic. But we have not helped you decide what your topic will be. Before choosing a topic, you need information about the political world and the major questions it poses. You need to know what political scientists do. In this chapter we will explore the meaning of politics and its relationship to human existence.

We will discuss some of the central issues in the study of politics, and sketch the outline of the political science discipline.

An understanding of this chapter will enable you to:

1. Understand the meaning and importance of the political world.
2. Explain the core concepts of politics, influence, power, authority, and government.
3. Understand what questions concern students of politics.
4. Begin to narrow your research topic to one or two of the political science subfields.

❖ POLITICS AND HUMAN RELATIONS

Politics is one of those words often used to describe a whole host of situations, events, and outcomes without really understanding what we are describing. Politics is like love. It's hard to define. Unlike love however, we don't necessarily know when we're in it. In addition, in common usage, politics conjures up negative perceptions. For example, what do you think when you hear the word *politics?* Many citizens conjure up the following:

Politics is corrupt. Politicians are crooks in suits.

He got his promotion because of politics, not competence.

All politics is wasteful.

The legislature rejected our proposal to save the schools. It was all politics.

Would it not be strange to hear someone say, "The legislature adopted our proposal to improve the schools. It was all politics?"

Because of the negative view of politics, politicians, and government, it's not surprising many people hope to avoid politics altogether. "If politics will just leave me alone, I won't bother it?" Unfortunately, this is not a choice even for those with such an attitude. Politics is intertwined with all human relationships. We all play politics whether we realize it or not. Let's consider an example that should be close to home to most students.

You are probably reading this text in a college class on the scope and methods of political science. Your instructor hopes that most are in the class to learn and discover. She wants to help you become educated in the skills necessary to ask interesting political questions, and then try to answer them. She also knows, however, that for some students her hopes are only a dream. Many of you are in class because it is required. Others are present because the class filled a vacant slot in their class schedule. Still others enrolled because they heard the instructor was excellent. Whatever the motive though, all enrolled want to succeed, to pass the course at least, and hopefully make an A.

In such a situation, will you engage in political activity to increase your potential for success? Some of you won't (just as some never vote). Others of you will, whether you call it politics or not. To illustrate, answer these questions:

Do you think that students sitting near the front of the class get better grades?

Does it help your grade if the instructor knows your name and something positive about you?

Does it help your grade if you are attentive and interested in the subject matter and express that interest to the instructor?

Does it help you when the instructor gives hints about test questions?

If you get a test grade lower than expected, can you sometimes get the grade raised by discussing your test with the instructor?

If you answered yes to any, some, or all of these questions, you recognize that a political relationship exists between students and teachers and that political activity may affect your success. College teachers are human, too (contrary to the belief of some students). You can influence them. What can you do? You can sit up front, ask questions, see your instructor outside class, and express interest in the subject. You can ask for hints and encourage her to discuss the test. None of these actions will succeed in changing a C grade to an A. In borderline cases however, between A and B, B and C, politics can make the difference.

Your instructor also acts politically when she tries to influence those who dislike the subject nevertheless to learn about the subject. She may work hard to persuade you of the subject's importance and convince you of its significance to your future. If nothing else, she may use the threat of a bad grade to encourage your efforts.

We could offer other examples involving virtually all aspects of human life. Our relationships with friends, family, employers, and peers can be political. The reason? The source of politics is embedded in human nature. As a result, whether politics is good or evil, or a combination of both, it is an inevitable part of human life.

❖ POLITICS AND HUMAN NATURE

To say that human nature is complex is to understate the obvious. Philosophers have debated the essential ingredients for centuries. The range of debate spans the beliefs that human nature is entirely selfish (Thomas Hobbes 1651) to the acceptance that our nature is purely cooperative (Karl Marx).

Fortunately, we need not enter this debate to illustrate how human nature spawns political relationships. A famous political scientist, Robert Dahl (you will read much of his work if you continue to study political science), maintains there is common agreement over several aspects of human nature. Like all forms of life in this world, human beings face the task of dealing with their conflicts (Dahl 1976, 1991). Conflict among people stems from two central characteristics. First, we are social creatures. With few exceptions, we are unwilling or unable to live alone. Second, though we are not totally selfish, we are not completely unselfish either. Even when we act unselfishly, we may violate the interests of others. Conflict is the inevitable result. Unlike other forms of life however, we are endowed with the capacity to think, to reason, and to take conscious actions to deal with conflict and gain the advantages of community and cooperation (Dahl 1976, 9).

Politics is tied to the human condition because our nature inevitably leads to conflict. The way we participate in the conflict and the ways we try to resolve conflict and achieve cooperation is central to what we mean by the political world. Politics then is a process. In the words of Harold Lasswell, it is the process that determines "who gets what, when, and how" (Lasswell 1938).

❖ THE POLITICAL SYSTEM

Harold Lasswell's definition is admittedly broad. It could describe any kind of human conflict. It includes the political relationships between students and teachers described above. It includes "office politics," the conflict emerging within families or among friends, and any situation where someone tries to influence the behavior of another. Political scientists are not interested in studying all political relationships however. We are concerned only with those interactions about how and why government decisions are made, how governments relate to their citizens, and how governments relate to one another.

Let's look at Lasswell's definition from this political science perspective on politics. The "who" in his definition refers to those who participate in the political process. At the least, we can identify political leaders, political parties, interest groups, and voters as part of the "who." The "how" refers to activities in the political game. People play politics by voting, bargaining, campaigning, and lobbying. In some societies political activities are more sinister. Terrorism, assassination, bribery, and torture are all part of the contest. The "what" in the definition is what government does as a result of the game, or public policy. Governments build roads, provide benefits such old age assistance, tax, and go to war. They regulate individuals and business to protect environmental quality. They spend money on scientific research. The "what" can also be a change in the nature of the government itself. Such change occurs in military coups and political revolutions.

To try and better understand the political process as Lasswell defines it, political scientists devised the concept of the **political system** (Easton 1952, 1965). This concept attempts to link together the who, how, and what in politics. The political system is a model of how politics determines public policy. Robert Dahl defines a political system more broadly. He says that a political system is "any persistent pattern of human relationships that involves, to a significant extent, control, influence, power, or authority" (Dahl 1991, 4). Most political systems are models about how the politics of individual countries are conducted. Others are used to compare the politics of nations. One, the international political system, is used to explore the nature of politics among nations and other actors such as multinational corporations and international organizations like the United Nations. To illustrate the model of the political system, we will consider a model typically applied to politics in the United States.

Figure 4.1 presents a diagram of the model political system in the United States. Politics starts with people, living together with different interests, wants, desires, and beliefs. When these interests, wants, desires, and beliefs are in conflict, a political issue arises. Virtually anything can be the subject of political conflict (with your instructor, try to think of questions that could never become political), but government will not act on the conflict until it is brought to the policy agenda.

The policy agenda refers to those problems or issues that government officials and other political leaders pay attention to at any given time (Kingdon 1984). In the United States, the policy agenda is made up of items brought to the leaders' attention by linkage institutions. Political parties and interest groups struggle to get issues on the agenda. The media and election campaigns are forums where various subjects are given public attention.

The decision makers (government) respond to the policy agenda when they make public policy. Congress may enact legislation banning certain handguns. The president may restrict the sale of weapons to another country. An agency in the bureaucracy may issue a rule requiring "air bags" in new automobiles, and the Supreme Court could rule that abortion is no longer a constitutional right.

Each of these actions in turn impact people. Banning weapons affects manufacturers, target shooters, hunters, and those in fear of crime. They make life more difficult for criminals and safer for potential victims of crime. Mandatory air bags may increase the price of automobiles, lessen the number of highway deaths and increase profits for insurance companies. Banning

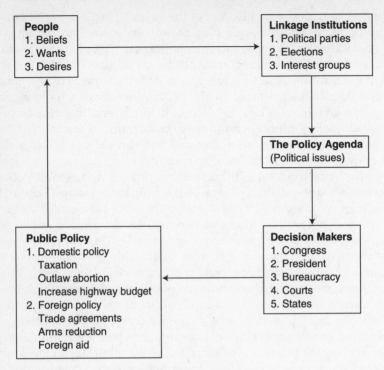

FIGURE 4.1   **U.S. Political System**

abortions may increase the number of unwanted children, increase the number of illegal abortions, and increase loyalty of citizens who believe that abortion is morally wrong. In short, public policies impact the people's wants, desires, and beliefs. These create new political issues on the policy agenda for decision makers to consider. They in turn make new, or modify old, public policies.

Political scientists study how political systems work. In the example given, we want to know what people think and why. We want to know how linkage institutions operate and which ones are the most significant. We want to know how political leaders interact and how they formulate and implement public policy. And we want to know the effects of government policy. Did government action achieve stated goals? Who are the winners and losers? Will today's losers be tomorrow's winners? Or, do some people always win while others always lose?

❖ SOME KEY POLITICAL CONCEPTS

We have argued that politics is universal and that political systems exist everywhere. To begin the study of politics and political systems, we need to understand some core concepts essential to the political world. Concepts are basic building blocks necessary to asking and answering political questions. We call them core concepts because it is impossible to study politics without them. In Chapter 9 you will find a more detailed discussion of concepts and how they relate to the research process.

We have already discussed two important political concepts—politics and the political system. But when you read Dahl's definition of the political system above, did you understand it? Let's review. A political system is "any persistent pattern of human relationships that involves, to a significant extent, *control, influence, power, or authority.*" The *italic* words are critical to the study and understanding of politics and political systems. What do these terms mean? Is their meaning clear or elusive? How do they relate to the study of politics?

Since politics is about the conflict among human beings, control, influence, power, and authority among people are the essential elements in the study of politics. As Bertrand Russell concluded many years ago, "Power is to politics as energy is to physics." Without energy, there is no physics. Without power, there is no politics. However, the "power terms" in Dahl's definition of the political system have no common definitions. This is true in ordinary usage and among social scientists. One person's power is another's influence, is still another's control. Fortunately, for an introductory course, we need not get into the intricacies and complexity of these concepts.[1] Instead, we will provide some working definitions of influence, power, and authority (we won't bother with control since it is a function of the other power terms). These definitions will not satisfy all students of politics. Nevertheless, they will give us the tools to study some fundamental political problems, and they will lead us into a discussion about why we should study them.

Before defining what these "power terms" mean, we must limit their scope to the political arena. In common usage, we often hear about man's power over nature, man being subjected to the forces of nature, and man's control over the animal world. From a political perspective, we must limit the power terms to relationships among human beings. Since politics is about conflict among people, the power terms help explain the outcomes of these conflicts.

Political influence is a process. It involves the use of political resources to achieve one's goals. Our working definition of **influence** is the following: *The use of political resources by one or more individuals so their wants, desires and preferences affect the actions, or predispositions to act, of others* (don't panic, read the following to help you understand the definition).

Remember your scope and methods teacher? She wants you to learn and understand the meaning of the power terms. One way to achieve her goal is to tell your class that no student will pass the course unless he or she can write an essay that explains political influence and accurately compare it with political power and authority. She is using a resource (a failing grade, making you repeat the course, possibly losing a scholarship, etc.) to influence your actions. If you study, think, and learn, as a result of her threat, she has influenced your action. Even if you don't act, but were predisposed to do so, she has exercised some influence. In the political arena, you may try to influence a school board member to fire the football coach by threatening to withdraw your vote in the next election if the coach remains.

In our discussion of influence above, your teacher used her ability to give a grade as a resource to influence your behavior. You used your right to vote to influence the school board member. These are just examples of many political resources one can use as means of influence. Most human beings, though not all, have at least some resources that they can use to influence the actions or predispositions of others. However, in any political system, some have more resources than others. The wealthy have more than the poor, the knowledgeable more than the ignorant. This applies to individuals within a nation or relations among nations. The United States has more political resources than Ghana, for example. Political power involves the quantity and importance of the political resources possessed by an individual, group or nation.

Our working definition of **political power** is: *The capacity to use political resources to influence successfully the actions, or predispositions to act, of others*. Another way of looking at power is to ask the question, "Who is the most powerful person in the United States?" Answer: "The one with the largest number of significant political resources."[2] Remember, influence is a process. From our definition, power is the capacity to successfully engage in the influence process. We could also then think of influence as exercising power. Those having power do not have to use it. Two equally wealthy individuals may use their wealth differently. One will attempt to influence the outcome of elections (exercising power), the other will aid charities of all types (no influence).

If power refers to the capacity to influence, what makes up this capacity? We have defined it as the quantity and importance of political resources possessed by a political actor. But, what do we mean by political resources? How do we determine their significance? The first question is relatively simple to answer. The second is much more difficult, yet much more significant to understanding the political process.

Broadly defined, a **political resource** is any attribute that an individual, group, or nation can use to influence others. Information, money, votes, the threat of force, friendship, knowledge, and even food can be political resources (can you think of other political resources?). For example, a candidate for public office that can raise substantial campaign funds through friendship, political connections, and knowledge of fundraising techniques will have more power than a candidate without these resources. The candidate with these resources will have more money that, as a resource in itself, can be exchanged for those necessary to influence voters—professional campaign consultants, public opinion polls, TV, and radio advertising.

Comparing the significance of political resources is much more difficult. Oftentimes the significance of a given resource varies with the context in which it is used. This makes it difficult for social scientists to compare the power of individuals, groups, or nations. Consider the following hypothetical situation. Suppose we have two individuals, Hank and Mary, who possess the political resources listed in Table 4.1. Each has five political resources, and

TABLE **4.1**

COMPARING POLITICAL RESOURCES

Hank	Mary
Ph.D in Political Science	Lawyer
Professional Political Consultant	Support of Organized Labor
Former member of Congress	Former member of City Council
Well liked by wealthy individuals	Voted to lower property taxes
Close ties with well-known media	A Medal of Honor in Operation Desert
Personalities	Storm

both are running for a seat in the United States Senate. They seek to use their "power" to influence the voters of their state. Who is the most powerful?

With what we know about voters and elections, political scientists would compare the two candidates' resources and probably conclude that Hank has the "most power." As a political scientist and political consultant he has more knowledge about the process. He has access to two critical electoral resources (money and the media), and has more experience as a former member of Congress. Mary can count on her union support for volunteer participation in her campaign (Hank will have to pay for help). She has some political experience. She can use her proven record against taxes and her status as a "war hero" to influence voters, but only if she can raise the money necessary to inform the voters of these traits. If there were such things as "electoral bookies," they would probably say Hank has the distinct edge in the race.

Suppose however that during the course of the campaign two major industries in the state lay off thousands of union workers, and several of the "laid off" are veterans of Desert Storm. Congress is disgraced by money scandals involving wealthy contributors, and the press reveals that Hank voted against the extension of veteran's benefits while a member of Congress. Suddenly, Hank's political resources become political liabilities while Mary's resources become more significant. Her union support and veteran status, coupled with her "outsider" status having never been a member of Congress, propel her to victory in the new electoral context. She was more powerful.

The significance of political resources varies with the context of their use. As a result, there is little agreement among political scientists about who has the most political power in any political system. For the United States political system, there is a perennial debate about who has power, who is powerless, and who is in between. The debate continues over who benefits and who suffers as a result of the distribution of political resources.[3]

However, most analysts agree that one political resource is of particular importance in the power equation. It is our third power term—authority. Authority is a very special political resource. Acting with authority is the most efficient and effective form of influence. It allows leaders to rule (get their way) without expending other political resources. If you have authority, you can sway the actions or predispositions of others by giving an order, through argument, or by simply asking for what you want. Unfortunately, as with the other power terms, authority is difficult to define.

Authority is related to our perceptions of right and wrong, knowledge (expertise), and legitimacy. Someone who "has authority" is perceived by others to be the most capable to make decisions. The person with authority has a right to decide because of expertise, or because the person in the position to decide has the legal, or moral right, to be there. We comply with the wishes of those in authority because we think it is right to do so, or that we have an obligation to do so. We comply with our doctor's wishes because of his medical expertise. Subjects in the Middle Ages followed the queen's commands because they believed she acted in God's name. To disobey her was to disobey God. Most Americans today obey the laws of our land because they believe it is right to do so, not because of fear of punishment. Why is it right? Because those who made the laws were elected under constitutional procedures that we accept as legitimate (correct).

Unlike other political resources, authority is bestowed by the perceptions of others. It is not inherent in anyone. It lies in the eyes of the beholder. Our working definition of **authority** is: *The ability to affect the actions or predispositions of others because people feel obliged to comply because compliance is right or correct.* There are two types of authority. The first we call *de jure* authority. This means authority in law (if you continue to study political science or law you will confront many more Latin phrases). This type of authority develops when a set of rules and procedures, accepted as legitimate by most everyone, are used to determine who will be in authority (Benn and Peters 1959, 20; Weber 1947, 300–1). Peasants followed the queen because of the principle and procedure of "divine right." The U.S. president has authority because he is duly elected under widely accepted constitutional and legal procedures.

The second type of authority is *de facto* authority. This means authority in fact. Such authority derives from the personal history, credentials, or achievements of an individual (Benn and Peters 1959, 21). The medical doctor deserves deference because of her expertise, developed through rigorous study for many years. Teachers have authority for the same reason.

Most political authorities have different mixes of both types of authority. Your scope and methods teacher has *de jure* authority because she is your teacher. She will have even more influence over you however if she shows great knowledge, is a good educator, and earns your respect—*de facto* authority. Likewise, the mayor may have legal authority to administer a city budget. His priorities are more likely to be followed if he has the respect of the city council and city employees.

We now have working definitions of the important political concepts of influence, power, and authority. These concepts are central to the study of all things political. On page 48 we argued that political scientists study how political systems work. In doing so, students of politics try to understand the process that determines who gets what, how, and why. Understanding the power terms is essential to this task.

❖ THE MAJOR POLITICAL QUESTIONS

An understanding of the power terms, and their importance to the study of politics, also shows us why it is important to study the political process. Power is unequally distributed in any political system. Some are more powerful than others. They are more influential. They get their way more often. Political analysts have observed unequal political influence for thousands of years. The ancient Greek philosopher Plato advocated rule by philosopher kings (*The Republic*). His student, Aristotle, tried to justify the differences in authority between master and slave, husband and wife, parent and child (*The Politics*, Book 1). Some 2000 years later, Rousseau and the "father of the U.S. Constitution," James Madison, argued that the source of inequality and conflict was the unequal distribution of property (*A Discourse on the Origins of Inequality*, 1775; Federalist #10). Arguing along similar lines, Karl Marx and Friedrich Engels created a revolutionary doctrine that "shook the world" of the twentieth century (*Communist Manifesto*, 1848; *Das Kapital*, 1894).

If you recall our discussion of human nature and political conflict (p. 46), it should be obvious why the distribution of power and influence is important. Human nature is sometimes selfish. Those with greater power may use their influence to achieve noble ends, or they may act to further their own gain regardless of the cost to others. Let's imagine a political system where one person has all the political resources available in the system. He or she would have absolute political power (there has never existed such a system though the German system under Hitler and the Soviet system under Stalin were close approximations). The person with power could use it to help all subjects to achieve their goals. He could also enslave everyone. How do you think our fictitious leader would behave?

The possibility that a leader with complete power would act to enslave us, or that those with the most power in a political system will use it to their benefit at our expense, leads to the fundamental questions of political science. How should people be governed? Who should govern? What is the purpose of government?

These questions introduce another important concept in the study of politics—**government.** We have mentioned the concept before, but avoided a specific definition. We have noted that politics is an inevitable part of human existence because humans are social and self-interested creatures (at least some of the time). As a result, conflict (and politics) is inevitable. We also argued (p. 46.) that humans are rational, that they can use reason to help them resolve conflicts. As far back in human history as we can see, men and women have searched for ways to resolve conflict with a minimum of violence and bloodshed (Dahl 1976, 10). Their solution has always been some form of government.

In every political system, the government is the set of individuals and political institutions that has, or makes the claim to have, the *de jure* authority to make the rules that resolve conflict. It helps if those who make the rules have the political resources to enforce them.[4] Those with governmental authority usually make decisions according to the standards of justice held by those who make the rules. Viewed in this way, because politics is an inevitable part of human existence, so is government.

To argue that government is inevitable does not mean all governments are good, however. It only means they exist. Governments, like people, can be good, bad, or somewhere in between. When they are bad, they can approach pure evil. Adolph Hitler's government exterminated 6 million people!

In whatever manner governments act, the governed will be the beneficiaries or the victims of their actions. Thus, the central questions of political science are also central to the quality of human life. Let's examine them more carefully.

◆ HOW SHOULD PEOPLE BE GOVERNED?

As rational creatures, human beings are capable of asking if life could be better than it is. Since governments by definition influence people, some have always asked the question, "Which government is best?" This is not surprising given the potential of government to do such great harm.

Answering this question is one of the most interesting, difficult, and important tasks facing political scientists because people have defined the "best government" differently throughout history. Since our perceptions of human nature vary, philosophers, scholars, and political leaders have differed on how much government should control the people's behavior. For example, if we believe that humans are inherently and completely selfish (Hobbes), then government should tightly restrict their behavior. If we believe human nature is purely cooperative, then government can perfect people so that no government is ultimately necessary (Marx and Engels).

These represent the extreme views of human nature, however. Many others view human nature as more complex. All views, moreover, fall on a continuum based on assumptions about human potential for cooperation. Table 4.2 provides a description of this continuum and the corresponding amount of government control associated with each.

William Meulemans provides handy labels for these different perceptions of human nature and the corresponding need for social control (1989, 81–85). From the left to the right of the political spectrum:

TABLE 4.2

HUMAN NATURE AND CONTROL

Views of Human Nature	Type of Government Control
Purely cooperative people can be perfected to live in harmony.	Once perfected, no control
People are nearly cooperative and can be improved.	Little control
People can learn to be sensitive to other's needs and help one another.	Some control
People are selfish and must be guided to protect social stability.	More control
People are selfish and cannot master their own weaknesses.	Absolute control
People are selfish, passionate, aggressive, and violent.	Oppressed

Revolutionary radicals believe human beings are perfectible.

Radicals believe humans can be improved.

Liberals assume that people can reform to become more sensitive to others.

Conservatives assert that individuals need guidance.

Reactionaries faithfully believe that humans need absolute control.

Revolutionary reactionaries know that people must be oppressed.

Each perspective yields a different answer to the question, "Which government is best?" In general, those on the left end of the spectrum would favor governments and other political institutions that emphasize humanistic goals. They emphasize that people are unlikely to abuse the benefits, rights, and freedoms the political system provides. On the other side, government must control the pathological aspects of human behavior. It also preserves the privileged position of those in authority.

More specifically, the *revolutionary radical* sees no government as the best government. Political institutions are based on a classless society where everyone is completely free and equal. Ironically, these revolutionaries see violent revolution and at least a short-term dictatorship as necessary steps to achieve the classless society.

Radicals imagine a government and political system based on guaranteed rights where all are assured of the basics of life. These rights not only include basic political rights, but economic rights to adequate food, clothing, housing, and health care as well.

Liberals say the "best government" is one that provides equal access through a broader redistribution of both wealth and power. Political institutions should foster equality of political power.

Conservatives believe that government should promote individual opportunity to succeed economically in a society that rewards competition. Government cannot perfect, improve, or reform human behavior. At best, it can guide or control behavior to preserve competition.

Reactionaries believe in human weakness, so government must establish strict rules and enforce them. Government control is necessary to force people to perform their obligations.

Revolutionary reactionaries hope to create a society where the people's passions and aggressiveness supports complete allegiance to the leader. The leader will lead the society to glory.[*]

Which of these alternative definitions of the "best government" would you choose? Most American students usually respond with either a liberal or a conservative view. This shouldn't be surprising since these views are most compatible with the historical experience of the United States. Thomas Jefferson is a good example of the liberal we described above. Alexander Hamilton exemplifies the conservative. Most Americans shy from the radical, but it is compatible with the American experience as well. The Reverend Martin Luther King Jr. comes to mind.

All three of these views, radical, liberal, and conservative are compatible with *democratic government*. The revolutionary radical on the left and the reactionaries and revolutionary reactionaries on the right are compatible with *authoritarian* or even *totalitarian government*. The distinction among these concepts leads us to our next question.

◆ WHO SHOULD GOVERN?

The answer to this question depends on two related dimensions of analysis. The first involves the number of individuals involved in the governing process. Dictatorship is rule by one. Pure democracy is rule by all. The second involves the human or social qualities most desirable in those who govern. Is there a natural ruling class? Should governors earn their *de jure* authority through merit? Should governing be everybody's business regardless of personal or social qualifications?

Dictatorship and Democracy   The concepts dictatorship and democracy are far more complex than their common usage implies. We will discuss this complexity in more detail in Chapters 5 and 7. In comparing democracy and dictatorship, one thing is clear in their definitions. In political systems where only a few individuals have political power, the closer we are to dictatorship. In systems where the many have power, the closer we are to democracy.

*The above adapted with permission by Prentice Hall, Upper Saddle River, New Jersey. William Meulmans, *Making Political Choices: An Introduction to Politics*, 1989, pp. 81–85.

In known history there has never been a pure dictatorship where one person has unlimited political resources and everyone else has none. Likewise, there has never been a pure democracy, where political resources are equally distributed to all. Nevertheless, classifying political systems according to the number of rulers is as old as the ancient Greek philosophers. Aristotle classified constitutions according to the number of individuals entitled to rule. Rule by one is kingship. Rule by the few is aristocracy. Rule by the many is polity (Aristotle, *The Politics*, 116).[5] The debate over democracy and dictatorship remains today.

The justifications for rule by the few or by the many rest on the second dimension to the question, "Who should govern?" Kings and queens rule because of some form of divine right. They act with God's authority. Some dictators rule because of the people's devotion to them because of their heroism or exemplary character. Max Weber called this "charismatic authority" (Weber 1947). In a democracy, the many should govern because of the human and social qualities of freedom and equality (Locke, Rousseau, Jefferson).

Justifying authoritarian political systems requires the assumption that some people are more fit to govern than others. Monarchy not only postulates the divine right of kings, but also that there is a natural governing class, the aristocracy, that governs through birthright. Vladimir Lenin, the engineer of the now defunct Soviet communist autocracy argued that the Communist Party must lead the proletariat (industrial working class) in their historic march toward communism. The working class was incapable, of seeing its mission (Lenin in Tucker 1975, 24)

In considering democratic political systems, there is substantial debate about who should actually govern. Some democracies, such as Great Britain, institutionalize rule by the majority. Constitutionally, the minority has no *de jure* authority. Others, such as the United States, provide for majority rule tempered by specific constitutional limits on its authority (found principally in the Bill of Rights). Thomas Jefferson believed that democratic institutions would create a meritocracy. Rulers would rise through merit from all social classes. Modern students of democracy have even created a new theory called "democratic elitism." It is based in part on the assumption that only the elite possess democratic values and therefore, we cannot trust the mass of people to protect these values (Bachrach 1967).

Democratic elitism is also based in part on the common observation that substantial numbers of people in democracies have no political life in the system whatsoever. They are apolitical. They don't vote. They know little about the political system. They don't belong to political organizations. They pay little attention to political news. Should these unconcerned be part of the governing process? Should they have as much say as those who do participate? Political scientists disagree over the answers to these questions.

Ultimately, the debate over the question "Who governs?" turns on our assumptions about what governments should do. How we are governed and who actually governs is important because governments have influence over us. How governments use this influence shapes the quality of human existence.

◆ WHAT IS THE PURPOSE OF GOVERNMENT?

At a basic level we have already answered the question on the ultimate purpose of government. The answer depends on our assumptions about human nature discussed above. Politics is an inevitable part of human life because our nature leads to conflict. The purpose of government is to deal with conflict.

To Hobbes, since man is purely selfish, life without government would be a life of total conflict. In his famous phrase, living without government (Hobbes called this the "state of nature") would mean "continual fear, and danger of violent death and the life of man, solitary, poor, nasty, brutish and short" (Hobbes 1651, 82). The purpose of government is to protect human beings from themselves.

Others contend human beings are not such dismal creatures. As we argued earlier, the perceptions of human nature range from the purely selfish to the purely cooperative. Except for these two views, human beings will seek to use some form of government to facilitate the advantages of cooperation and to provide the mechanisms to resolve conflict that is inevitable in community life. Philosophers such as Plato believed that the ideal government should resolve conflict to achieve *justice* (Plato, *The Republic*, Book IV, 162–65).

Aristotle, as we already mentioned, classified political systems according to the number of rulers. We cheated you a bit in that discussion because he really classified political systems according to two criteria. Systems were divided not only on the basis of who governed, but also on the basis of whose interest rulers served. Was the purpose of government to serve the interest of the community as a whole, or did rulers serve their own selfish interest? Table 4.3 presents Aristotle's sixfold system. Ideally, government's purpose was to rule in the interest of the whole community. Recognizing the self-interest of human beings meant rulers might govern only to further their own interests to the detriment of others.

Can governments achieve justice? Will they rule in the interests of all? Political theorists have debated these questions about the purpose of government for most of recorded history. At another level, political scientists have debated the proper role of government intervention in regulating the lives of

TABLE 4.3

ARISTOTLE'S POLITICAL SYSTEMS

Number of Rulers	Rule in Interest of All	Rule in Interest of Rulers
One	Kingship	Tyranny
Few	Aristocracy	Oligarchy
Many	Polity	Democracy

The Politics, Book III. Baltimore: Penguin Classics, 1962, p. 116.

its citizens. As political systems evolve, new generations face new problems and issues that nobody even thought about even a few years earlier. Suddenly, the public becomes divided. Some want government to initiate immediate change. Others seek to block that change. Consider the following sources of modern controversy in the United States:

Should government require mandatory drug tests for employees in sensitive or important positions?

Should government establish national health insurance to cope with runaway health-care costs?

Should government require mandatory AIDS tests for high-risk groups?

Should government prohibit surrogate mothers?

If we answer yes to any of these questions, we are asking for more government intervention in our lives. Importantly, there was no controversy over drug and AIDS testing 15 years ago. The debate over national health insurance has been around for some time, but it leaped to the forefront of the public mind with the rapid rise of health-care costs in the 1980s and 1990s.

As new issues emerge over time, one thing is clear. Government regulation of our behavior increases. Only a few years ago using asbestos for insulation, smoking in public, dumping toxic waste, abortion, being searched before boarding airplanes, and hiring and firing employees were all questions outside the public domain. Individuals could act freely in these "private arenas." Today, each of these areas are considered of great public importance and government regulates individual behavior in each.

Political scientists, politicians, and average citizens alike debate whether such government intervention is desirable, necessary, or inevitable. Some contend that regulation gives us better choices by protecting the public from certain harmful activities. Others argue that so much needless and counterproductive regulation reduces our freedom, standard of living, and the quality of life. Underlying these positions are two contrary views of the central purpose of government, protection, and freedom. The debate continues because of the conflict between these two goals. Government protection means regulation (limiting freedom). Individual freedom risks injury and exploitation of others. Should we allow the property owner next door the *freedom* to bury toxic waste that will pollute our water supply?

❖ THE POLITICAL SCIENCE DISCIPLINE

The political science discipline is the study of political systems for the purpose of answering the major political questions. Hopefully, you are now aware that there is little agreement over the answer to these questions. The reasons for this are many. The most significant perhaps is that human beings are very complex creatures. Therefore, studying human behavior is more difficult than studying other life forms or inanimate objects. Legend has it that Albert Einstein was once asked why he did not turn his great genius to solve the political problems of the world. His reply was, "Because politics is more difficult than physics."

What makes human beings so complex is our ability to think and reason, our emotional complexity, and our consequent system of values including our perceptions of right and wrong. Einstein's response reflected his belief that there was much more to know and learn about human beings than about stars, quarks, and energy.

The central questions of political science represent this human complexity. Each of the three are *normative* in nature. Questions posed by the physical world are *empirical*. This fundamental distinction between the normative and empirical worlds is necessary to the introduction of the political science discipline.

When our concerns are normative, we want to know or describe how life ought to be. Normative questions are tied to the human capacity to make judgments about right and wrong. They are tied to our morality, our values, and our perceptions of how to achieve the best life. For example, when we ask, "Who should govern?" we are asking people to make value-laden judgments about the "best governors." Normative questions are at the center of all social science. They are the reason we study human behavior.

Empirical questions aim at describing how things are. Asking whether the earth is flat or round is an empirical question. No matter how much members of the flat earth society want the world to be flat, they are empirically wrong.

Political science involves empirical as well as normative questions. For example, let's suppose we conclude normatively that democracy is the "best" form of government. This conclusion would also lead us to the empirical question, "What are the conditions necessary to produce democratic political systems?" The answer will help us better understand how to achieve our normative goal of democracy, or whether we can hope to achieve it at all. We also might want to examine existing political systems that claim to be democratic and ask whether their actual operation meets democratic criteria. We may find our normative criteria are completely unrealistic. Such an empirical finding would help us rethink our definition of democracy. We will see later that empirical studies of the United States led to a revision of democratic theory.

❖ POLITICAL SCIENCE SUBFIELDS

The political science discipline is divided into several subfields of study. This reflects both disagreement about how to study politics and the varying types of political systems in the world. We discuss four major subfields in Chapters 5–8. As we noted in the introduction to Part Two, we do not cover all of the subfields, including traditional political theory. However, we have given you a taste of what political theory is about in this chapter.

The subfields of American politics, public administration and public policy, comparative politics, and international relations are the principal subjects for the scientific study of politics. Your teacher will probably encourage you to study in one of these areas for your research project. This is where the most interesting and answerable scientific questions are found.

◆ AMERICAN POLITICS AND GOVERNMENT

The subfield of American politics involves the analysis of the American political system. Some scholars argue that we shouldn't consider it a subfield of the political science discipline at all. Instead, it more properly belongs as just another area of study in comparative politics (Easton 1957). After all, the United States is just another of the many political systems in the world.

Nevertheless, we consider the study of American politics a unique subfield for several reasons. The first is the most obvious. Most likely you are a student in a college in the United States. You are a U.S. citizen. If not, you chose to study in the United States. American politics is a subfield of political science because most American political scientists believe it essential for American citizens to understand the operation of their own political system. A similar argument might be made by French and Japanese political scientists about their own political systems.

Second, the United States lays claim to the title of the first new nation of the modern world (Lipset 1963). It was the first major colony to win independence through revolution. It was the first modern country to experiment with democratic institutions (though British values were their impetus). It was the first nation founded on the revolutionary principles of equality, individual freedom, and consent. People should be equal under the law. People should be free to pursue life with as little government interference as possible. Since government is the creation of the people, it should exist and operate only with the consent of the governed.

Third, today the United States is the major economic and military power in the world. Our political system contributed to our emergence as a world power. Political scientists are interested in explaining if and how this is so. People around the world are curious about how such a giant works.

Unlike other subfields, the study of American politics is centered on democratic theory. As the "first new nation," political scientists study the development and operation of our system to ascertain whether or not the United States lives up to democratic ideals. As we will see, we study our institutions, the Congress, presidency, bureaucracy, courts, and the states, to determine their responsiveness to the people. We study the political behavior of the people (in elections, in interest groups, or in protest) with an eye toward the peoples' responsibility in a democracy. We study public policies such as those concerning taxation, the environment, and civil rights. We make judgments about who benefits and who suffers. We are always interested in evaluating whether or not public policy is responsive to the people and the public interest.

◆ PUBLIC ADMINISTRATION AND PUBLIC POLICY

Public administration refers to the the government's role in the delivery of common goods and services to the community. It refers to the implementation of public policy. Public policy is a goal-directed course of action by government to deal with a public problem.

Students of public administration are concerned principally with the execution of public policy. As such, they study the "who," the "what," and the "how" of policy execution. The central concern is with the unelected bureaucracy in the executive branches of government at the national, state, and local levels. They are also increasingly concerned with what we call the "administrative state."

Students of public policy focus on two separate, but related, dimensions of policy. First, they concern themselves with the purpose and evaluation of various types of public policy such as economic policy (such as taxation) and social policy (such as abortion or civil rights). Second, they analyze the process of policy making as a series of activities that leads to a policy decision and its implementation. The central concern of the second dimension is to use the policy-making process to develop a better understanding as to how the entire political system works.

◆ COMPARATIVE POLITICS

Comparative politics is without doubt the broadest and most challenging of the political science subfields. Its scope is immense and there is little agreement about how to study politics in a comparative way. Basically, there are two broad approaches to study in the field. The first, also called the traditional approach, is based on the assumption that all political systems are unique (Macridis 1955; Scarrow 1969). Each nation's history, culture, and society are so distinct that we cannot compare political systems at all. For example, we may observe that two (or more) nations have legislatures, but the history and culture of each nation determines how they will behave. Traditional comparative politics focuses on case studies of the politics in individual nations. The traditionalist approach is evident in book titles focusing on a single country, such as *The Politics of France, British Politics in Historical Perspective*, or *Ghana: The Politics of Economic Failure*.

The second approach assumes that the political world is more similar than different. We can compare political systems in a meaningful way to help find and understand fundamental elements of politics and the political process. It is important to study the politics of individual nations, but we should focus on what the politics of one nation tells us about the political process in general. This can only be done by truly comparing political systems. Books with titles such as *Comparative Political Parties, Comparative Legislatures* or *The Politics of Development* reflect this comparative perspective. The comparative approach dominates the subfield today.

Comparative political scientists use the model of the political system (see p. 48) in their study. They note that all nations have a relevant public, linkage institutions, and government decision makers that make public policy. They use this model to make comparisons between different nations. To illustrate, they try to explain why one nation may have many political parties while others have only a few. They try to understand the conditions that produce democracy in some countries and authoritarianism or even totalitarianism in others. They try to explain why violent change is the norm in some countries while others remain peaceful and stable over long periods of time. They want to know why some nations are as rich as Midas while others remain wretchedly poor.

There are more than 180 different political systems in the world. Given this single empirical fact, you can see the enormity of the challenge posed by comparative politics.

◆ INTERNATIONAL RELATIONS

We distinguish the international political system from others by one important fact. It is a system where there is no effective government. International organizations such as the United Nations exist, but in no sense can we consider them governments in the same way we describe the government of France. Recall our definition. A government makes rules for the society and *has the power to enforce them.* The UN has little enforcement power unless the national governments all agree to, and are willing to pay for, enforcement actions.

The international political system is made up of independent, sovereign nation-states. A sovereign state has supreme authority over its citizens or subjects. In a system made up of sovereign states, where there is no higher authority, politics resembles life in the Hobbesian state of nature. Nation-states, if they choose, can act to further their own self interest unfettered by government control. Their actions are limited only by the power of other actors in the system. Those with the most political resources win. Those with less, lose.

Increasingly, actors other than the nation-state have joined the international system. These include supranational organizations such as the new European community and multinational corporations. There is little consensus yet as to the impact of these organizations on the international system.

Scholars of international politics study how nation-states and supranational organizations interact. They want to learn what motivates nations to act as they do. They study the sources of power in the international political system. Most significantly, in the Hobbesian world of international politics, they study the causes and consequences of war.

War and conquest have been the central issues of the study of international politics since the ancient Greeks. This is not surprising given the horrors and consequences of such international conflicts. The development of nuclear weapons, with their potential to destroy all human life, has given new urgency to understanding the causes of war.

❖ SUMMARY

This chapter introduced you to the nature and importance of the political world. We argued that politics is a process human beings cannot escape because the source of politics lies in human nature itself. Since humans are social, self-interested creatures, conflict is inevitable. The way we participate and try to resolve this conflict is the essence of political life. As long as we are human, we cannot avoid politics.

Virtually any relationship among humans can be political. Politics exists within families, between teachers and students, and between employers and employees. However, political scientists are only interested in those relationships involved in the model of the political system. Political scientists study political systems to learn how and why government decisions are made, how governments relate to their citizens, and how governments relate to one another.

In studying political systems, political scientists must study patterns of influence, power, and authority. Each of these concepts is complex, and there is little agreement over how to define them. Nevertheless, they are essential in studying the political process. We provided you with working definitions of influence, power, and authority. These definitions will help you understand the nature of the political process.

The definitions also help us all understand why it's so important to study politics. In the known history of human society, some have always possessed more power than others. Those with more power can, and often do, abuse that power. This fact leads to the central questions of political science: How should people be governed? Who should govern? What is the purpose of government?

Political scientists study political systems with the hope of answering these fundamental, normative questions in at least five separate subfields. These include political theory (discussed in this chapter), American politics, public administration and public policy, comparative politics, and international relations. The following four chapters explore the last four subfields in more depth.

❖ KEY TERMS

authority   political power
comparative politics   political resources
government   political system
influence   politics
international relations

❖ EXERCISES

1. Describe the relationship between the political world and human nature.
2. What are political resources? How are they relevant to power and influence?
3. What are the advantages and disadvantages of the following?
   a. Rule by one.

b. Rule by the few.

c. Rule by the many.

4. What human activities should government regulate and which should be beyond the power of government regulation? Be prepared to discuss your reasoning in each instance.

5. On your first mission to Mars, your spacecraft lands, but is unable to leave. Help from Earth will not arrive for ten years. Your crew and passengers number more than 500 people. Food and water are scarce. You have no knowledge of the life-support resources available on the planet. Violence among the population erupts in the struggle for food and water. You control the initial violence because you and your crew possess the only weapons. The passengers cease hostilities because they fear your laser guns. You realize their fear will soon wane if only because you have no power source to recharge your weapons. Rule by fear is only a temporary solution to controlling violent conflict. You meet with the crew and some concerned passengers to discuss what to do. What would you suggest and why? List and be prepared to discuss the steps necessary to control conflict and encourage cooperation among the new community until help arrives from earth.

❖ SUGGESTED READINGS

Dahl, Robert. *Modern Political Analysis,* 5th ed. Engelwood-Cliffs. Prentice-Hall, 1991.

Funderburk, Charles, and Robert Thobaben. *Political Ideologies,* 2nd ed. New York: HarperCollins, 1994.

Lasswell, Harold, and Abraham Kaplan. *Power and Society.* New Haven: Yale University Press, 1950.

Lipset, Seymour Martin. *Political Man.* Garden City, NY: Anchor, 1959.

Meulemans, William. *Making Political Choices.* Engelwood-Cliffs, NJ: Prentice-Hall, 1989.

❖ NOTES

1. If you continue to study political science you will see that political scientists continue to debate the definition of these concepts.

2. It is difficult to measure the significance of different political resources, and hence, power. Some argue that power is only one form of influence. Power is associated with influencing people by threatening severe deprivation or punishment (see Lasswell and Kaplan 1950).

3. This debate has three sides. Some contend that political resources are concentrated in the hands of the few (Mills 1957; Domhoff 1990). Others such

as Robert Dahl hold that power is more widely, and fairly, distributed (Dahl 1956, 1961). Still others argue that power is too widely distributed, making government inefficient (McConnell 1966; Lowi 1978).

4. For example, many describe the nation of Lebanon as a country without government. There is an official president and a legislature. These governmental institutions make rules, but there are many groups that have the resources to resist their enforcement.

5. He actually added another dimension to these different political systems. It involved whether or not rulers rule in the interest of all or in their own interest. This dimension is taken up below.

THE AMERICAN POLITICAL PROCESS

❖ INTRODUCTION

The subfield of American politics involves the analysis of the American political system. In many ways it is the most advanced subfield in the political science discipline. This is true for three basic reasons. More scholars (at least in the United States) have spent more time studying American politics than the other subfields. Because of the democratic character of the United States, scholars have access to information unavailable in the other areas. The financial commitment to research in many U.S. universities has led to impressive data collections relevant to virtually every aspect of politics and government in the United States. As a result, the American politics subfield provides you with more than just exciting topics for your research project. It offers you a unique opportunity to use current and reliable data to explore your topic.

An understanding of this chapter will enable you to:

1. Understand the environment of the American political system and the importance of democracy in studying our politics.
2. Identify the key questions confronting the political system as a whole.
3. Explain the basic controversies over how our system works.
4. Identify some key issues involving each aspect of the American political system.

In Chapter 4 we argued that you can use the model of the political system to analyze the politics of any country. We said that all political systems are in the same business of translating the wants of the relevant public into public policy. We did not say that political systems have the same character, however. Some involve ruthless dictators who care nothing for their people. Others have advanced systems of social welfare that provide cradle-to-grave services to minimize poverty and suffering. What often distinguishes a political system's character is its environment. Many argue that America's political environment is unique in the world.

The political environment refers to the forces that influence how the political system operates. It involves a country's history, economy, society, and culture. It helps determine what issues confront the political system. It also limits the system's acceptable response to a problem. For example, it is unlikely that health-care crisis in the United States will lead to socialized medicine. The people's broad commitment to a free enterprise economy excludes this option from the choices decision makers have to provide universal access to health care.

❖ POLITICAL ENVIRONMENT: REVOLUTIONARY IDEALS AND CONSTITUTIONALISM[1]

The cultural environment of the U.S. political system has had an important, and some would say, revolutionary impact on the political system. We have argued that the United States is the "first new nation" of the modern world. It was the first major colony to win independence through revolution. The new government spawned by this revolution found its basis in the revolutionary ideas of liberty, equality, consent, democracy, and constitutionalism. They were revolutionary because most countries throughout the world were monarchies of some sort. Monarchy rejected each of these principles. Let's consider each in turn.

Liberty refers to individual freedom and limited government. It means that each individual should enjoy as much freedom as is possible. Government should restrict individual freedom only as necessary to preserve order and protect the freedom of others. The power of government is therefore limited.

The idea of individual liberty has both personal and political dimensions. In the United States, most individuals believe they have the right to free expression and to pursue whatever road they want to take. As people, we are free to believe and act as we choose in the social, economic, and political arenas. Liberty also has an important impact on the political system. Freedom of speech and press and the right to vote and organize into political groups impact how the political system functions.

The Declaration of Independence committed the United States to the principle of **equality.** Thomas Jefferson's famous statement that "all men are created equal" has been expanded by our history and culture to include groups other than white males. In effect, Jefferson's statement today reads "all people are created equal."

While the United States is committed to the principle of equality, we have never really agreed on what it means. Does it mean simply political equality where all have the right to vote, the right to run for office, and the right to be treated equally under the law? Or, does it also imply a right of the individual to have equal opportunity to develop his or her talent and skills? If the answer to the second question is yes, does government have the duty to develop policies to ensure that all, regardless of sex, race, or economic background, have that opportunity?

Though there is little agreement on what equality means, historically there has been a broad consensus on what it doesn't. Equality does not mean equality of result (we will see that some groups advocate policies to achieve equal outcomes). People should have similar life chances, but there will always be winners and losers.

The idea of **consent** means that governments should exist and operate only with the approval of the governed. The people create government to help them and their communities, and to preserve certain rights. If government fails to serve the community needs or violates the people's rights, the people have the obligation to install new government. The notion of consent is in direct opposition to the underlying basis of monarchy, the divine right of kings. This principle basically held that government is the creation of God, not people.

The belief in democratic government follows from the ideas of liberty, equality, and consent. Democracy is the best way to protect these other values. Through time, **democracy** has taken on many meanings. However, all contain the same core. In the words of Abraham Lincoln, government is "of the people, by the people and for the people."

The problem is how to create such a government. The United States is known as a representative democracy. The people keep ultimate control of government by electing representatives who then make policy in the people's name. In a representative democracy, we must amend Lincoln's famous phrase. Government is of the people and for the people, but not directly by the people.

The idea of **limited government** establishes the principle of constitutionalism. We should control government not only through elections, but by limiting the powers of government in a written document and/or in widely shared, deep-seated beliefs. Constitutional governments, unlike monarchies, are governments of law and not individuals. No one is theoretically above the law. The U.S. Constitution sets down the fundamental governmental structures and procedures. It also sets limits on the activities of government. These limits are intended to prevent government leaders from making decisions based solely on political ambition or whim instead of on constitutional principles.

The attempt to institutionalize these cultural ideals in the American political system is what makes the United States the "first new nation." The cultural aspects of our political environment went against most of the common wisdom of the times.[2]

The idea that we could create a government based on these ideals was considered by many as absurd. So the U.S. political system began as a unique, some would say radical, experiment. The unique cultural environment means that today the system remains a bold experiment. Let's examine why.

❖ SOME KEY QUESTIONS

In analyzing the American political system as a whole, the cultural environment poses the key questions. These questions involve both the type of issues confronting the system and how the system operates.

◆ LIBERTY

How much freedom should a person have? In a political system based on the ideal of liberty, this is a crucial and difficult question. We gave the simplistic answer to the question when we said people should have as much freedom as possible without infringing on the freedom of others. In the words of a former Justice of the United States Supreme Court, "The right to swing my fist ends where the other [person's] nose begins." The dilemma for the political system is to determine where the other person's nose begins.

Prior to the establishment of the "first new nation," most governments provided only the oldest duty of government—**order.** If government has no other duty, it must protect its citizens (remember Thomas Hobbes?). Throughout history, order was the first, and in many instances the last, purpose of government. There was little concern with the freedom of the people. The political environment in the United States challenges the political system to provide both freedom and order.

The challenge presents a dilemma because at some point the values of freedom and order contradict one another. We all agree with freedom of speech, but what if my speech could incite a riot? Should government limit that speech because of its duty to maintain order?

The political system must somehow decide where to draw the line between freedom and order. The difficulty is that there is no easy and obvious place for the line. Consider the following example involving freedom of expression.

The U.S. Supreme Court declared in 1957 that obscene material is entirely excluded from constitutional protection in *Roth v. United States* (354 U.S. 477). State and local governments have since attempted to ban allegedly obscene material on the grounds that it is a threat to the social order. It corrupts community moral standards, it may lead to criminal conduct, and it is a danger to children. Yet in many American communities today, pornography flourishes in adult movie theaters, bookstores, and nightclubs. How can this be? The problem comes in trying to define what is obscene. For example, is the Academy Award–winning movie, *Carnal Knowledge,* obscene because it had a scene showing actress Ann Margaret's bare midriff? Can the directors of an art museum be punished for displaying the 175 piece display of a famous photographer because five of the pictures depicted homoerotic and sadomasochistic acts while two used nude and partially nude children? The courts answered that neither of these instances involved obscenity in *Jenkins v. Georgia* (418 U.S. 87 [1974]) and *Osborne v. Ohio* (Sup. Ct. 1691 [1990]). Instead, each was a form of expression protected by the U.S. Constitution.

The Supreme Court has long struggled to define obscenity, but with little success in developing an objective test. The reason for this difficulty is that obscenity rests in the eyes of the beholder. D. H. Lawrence, author of the classic work *Lady Chatterly's Lover* (banned in the United States for some time), summarized the problem by concluding, "What is pornography to one man is the laughter of genius to another." Former Supreme Court Justice Potter Stewart evidenced his frustration over the issue when he declared that he could not define obscenity but, "I know it when I see it" *Jacobellis v. Ohio* (378 U.S. 184 [1964]).

The important point you should remember from this discussion is that in most countries, questions involving free expression pose no dilemma for the political system because order is their prime concern. In Iran for example, certain sexual acts are punishable by death.

◆ EQUALITY

The American commitment to equality also confronts the political system with difficult questions. What is the meaning of equality? What should government do to promote equality? Different answers to the first question yield different answers to the second. Because we use equality in different senses, different groups use it to support different causes in the political system.

As we argued, we define political equality in America as the right to vote, the right to run for office, and the assurance that everybody's vote counts the same in elections. This concept is central to a representative democracy. The United States has pretty much achieved this definition of political equality. However, when some people advocate political equality they mean much more than the right to run for office and "one person, one vote." They argue that the chairman of the board of Exxon Corporation and the local plumber are not politically equal even though they both have one vote. For true political equality, we must first achieve social equality. Social equality requires equality in wealth and education.

Various interests have advocated two paths to achieve social equality, equality of opportunity, and equality of result. Each represents different conceptions of equality. We have already identified equality of opportunity as deeply ingrained in the American political culture. Equality of result is not.

Equality of opportunity means that every individual has the same chance to develop his or her talent, and the same chance to succeed in life. Some argue that when the political system achieves equality of opportunity, social equality follows. We see this principle in the U.S. Constitution. It bans titles of nobility, and there is no property requirement for holding public office. The system of free public education represents a major commitment by the political system to equal opportunity. Many laws today prevent discrimination in hiring, housing, and voting.

Yet the commitment to equality of opportunity still creates controversy. For example, the system of public education provides access to all children, rich and poor. We all know however, that the schools themselves are not equal. States and local governments control public education. The schools vary according to the wealth of the state, teacher qualifications, and the type of taxation used to fund schools. The last difference is a current source of controversy.

The states rely heavily on local property taxes to fund public education. The amount of revenue produced varies by the tax rate and the property values in the local school district. Where property values are high, a low tax rate still produces enormous revenues for schools. Where property values are low, even high tax rates fail to produce revenue equal to that of rich school districts. As a result, there is inequality in funding. The presumption is that children in property-poor districts do not have the same opportunity for quality education as those in property-rich districts.

Attempts to reduce the funding inequality have been controversial. Some states have increased income taxes to directly fund poor districts (income taxes are never popular). Others have forced a transfer of revenue from the rich districts to the poor, Robin Hood style. Others have simply failed to resolve the issue because of its controversial nature.

To other groups in the political system, we can achieve social equality only through equality of result. These groups believe that government must see to it that people are equal in fact. It is not enough to ensure equality of opportunity. Government must redistribute wealth and status to achieve social equality.

While not deeply embedded in the political culture, the political system has produced laws designed to produce equality of result. Laws today mandate equal pay to men and women for the same jobs. They mandate affirmative action programs to recruit members of minority groups into jobs. They prohibit discrimination in employment, public services, and public accommodations on the basis of physical disability. Some states have even passed legislation mandating much more than equal pay for equal work. They require equal pay for comparable work. Under comparable worth legislation, women must receive the same pay as men even if they are in a different job as long as the work is of comparable value.

Equality of result creates far more controversy in the political system than equality of opportunity. By definition, the government, by redistributing wealth and status, creates winners and losers. At the same time, equality of result is controversial because it conflicts with the first idea in the U.S. cultural environment—liberty.

Most Americans believe that equality and freedom go hand-in-hand. However, they actually clash when government attempts to achieve equal outcomes. Policies mandating equal or comparable pay limit employer choice. The policy forces them to pay more than the free market would allow. Forced school busing to achieve equal proportions of African Americans and whites in public schools limited freedom to choose where children go to school.

These examples illustrate the controversies created when government tries to promote equality, particularly social equality. Once again, we remind you that these challenges exist only because of our commitment to the principle of equality.

◆ CONSENT

How do we know when the people withhold their consent? In some cases in the world it is obvious. The United States was born in revolution. The Declaration of Independence clearly stipulated that King George III's government no longer had the consent of the colonies. The people of the Soviet Union withheld consent and the Communist government fell. The Confederacy of the old South seceded from the United States and was returned only after a bloody civil war.

In other cases it may not be so easy to determine. The U.S. government appears to operate with the consent of the people. There are some disturbing facts however. Many citizens lack the most basic information about our political system. Only one in three can identify their representative in the U.S. House of Representatives. Only 60 percent know there are two U.S. Senators from every state. Depending on the survey, between 50 and 70 percent of the adult population cannot identify a single aspect of the U.S. Constitution's Bill of Rights.

Additionally, fewer and fewer people bother to vote in national elections. Turnout is lower in the United States than in all other modern democracies except Switzerland. Only 53 percent voted in the 1992 presidential election, and this represented an increase from the 50 percent that voted in 1988. Survey after survey reports rising frustration and cynicism among the people toward their government.

Do these facts mean the people are withholding their consent? While we do not have the answer to this question, we can say that democratic political systems depend more on the active consent of the citizens than do other forms of government. If the answer to the question is yes, then the system is confronted with the challenge of how consent can be restored.

◆ DEMOCRACY

Is the United States a political democracy? Democracy, as we have argued, is a system of government where the ultimate political authority rests with the people. However, there are different beliefs as to how we can establish the people's ultimate authority in practice. There are also questions about whether the people do in fact have the ultimate authority in the U.S. government.

The original idea of democracy came from the ancient Greek city-state of Athens. The Athenian government is the historical model of direct democracy. Direct democracy is a system where the people directly govern themselves. In Athens, all issues were placed before an assembly of all citizens for a vote. In other words, all citizens were members of the law-making body (women and slaves were excluded since they were not citizens).

In some ways we can consider direct democracy as an ideal form of democracy. This is because it demanded a high degree of participation from each citizen. As a result, debate over public issues was a continual part of community life.

The United States is a representative democracy as we described earlier. The framers of our constitution believed that direct democracy wasn't a very good idea for two reasons. First, ancient Athens had relatively few citizens. The United States was simply too populous (about 3–4 million in 1787) for direct democracy to work efficiently. Second, they believed the mass of citizens to be too uneducated to govern themselves. The masses were prone to demagoguery, and were likely to violate the rights of the minority.[3]

Representative democracy, where the people were only indirectly involved in policy making, seemed to solve both of these concerns. Elected representatives would act in the people's name.

Today, representative democracy in the United States demands four conditions. The first is universal suffrage. This means that all adult citizens have the right to vote in the election of government officials. The second is majority rule. Since each vote counts the same, the only fair decisions are those decided by some majority. The third is minority rights. We must protect the rights of the minority from any majority that wants to become oppressive. Fourth is something called responsiveness. Elected representatives must respond to the wishes of the people.

The debate over whether the United States is a political democracy centers on the fourth requirement of representative democracy. To most analysts, the United States has complied, to one degree or another, with the first three rules. However, there is little agreement as to whether the political system is responsive to the people. Even for those who agree that it is responsive, there is disagreement as to how.

We will discuss the different answers to our question "Is the United States a political democracy?" in more detail in the next unit. We want you to know now however, that there are at least three answers to the question. The first is a definitive no. In spite of the fact that the United States has universal suffrage, majority rule (as defined above), and basic support for minority rights, the system responds to the wishes of a narrow economic and social elite. The other two answers are yes, but they provide different interpretations as to how the system is responsive. The first holds that the system of representative democracy works as described above. The system of elections ensures that representatives respond to the wishes of the majority. The second, called pluralist democracy, holds that government responds to the people through their participation in, and representation by, competing interest groups.

We hope it is obvious to you that the issue of democracy is the most important one governing the study of the American political system. When we study each aspect of the political system, whether it be the electoral process, political parties, or the U.S. presidency, the underlying normative concern is how each contributes to the quality of democracy in the United States.

◆ CONSTITUTIONALISM

The principle of constitutionalism poses many important questions in the analysis of the American political system. As we stated, a constitutional government limits governmental powers through a written, or in some cases unwritten, contract. Constitutionalism in the United States attempts to put into practice the values in the political environment cited above.

What kind of government did the framers of our written Constitution intend? How has constitutional government evolved over time? Has the U.S. Constitution been an effective limit on the powers of government? Is our eighteenth-century constitutional government sufficient to cope effectively with twenty-first century problems? These are just a few of the important questions in the analysis of constitutionalism in the United States.

We cannot begin to attempt to answer these questions completely in this text. There have been volumes written about each one. We will, however, try to give you a taste of how each question came about and why it is important.

The first question above involves the intent of the framers. The most significant aspect of the U.S. Constitution was that it created a strong central government where none had existed. It is easy to forget that the Constitution is really the second constitution governing the United States. The Articles of Confederation was our first constitution. It governed the new nation from 1781 through 1789. The Articles created a loose confederation of the 13 states. The central government was extremely weak. It was difficult to maintain economic and social order under such a system. For this, and other reasons, dissatisfaction with the Articles grew, leading to sympathy for creating a stronger national government.

The government created at the Constitutional Convention in 1787 hoped to strike a delicate balance to achieve order without threatening the people's liberty (see p. 68). In doing so, the framers created an intricate web of governmental institutions and processes designed to make it difficult for any individual or group to tyrannize the people. Ultimately, the Constitution created a government based on five central principles. It is sometimes said that the framers followed the "Madisonian model of government" in designing the new constitution because four of these principles were forcefully argued by James Madison (Lineberry, Edwards, and Wattenberg 1990, Ch. 2).

The Madisonian Model consisted of the following.

1. *Republicanism:* This is a form of government where the people rule through their elected representatives. The framers of the Constitution were somewhat fearful about the people having a direct say in the government. As a result, much of government was placed beyond the reach of the average citizen. The president was elected indirectly through the electoral college. U.S. Senators were elected in the legislatures of the various states. Supreme Court Justices were appointed by a president not directly elected by the people and confirmed in the Senate also not directly elected. Only

members of the U.S. House of Representatives stood before the voters for election. Even then, the "voters" consisted of white males with property in most states.

2. *Separation of Powers:* This meant assigning the basic powers of all governments—lawmaking, law enforcement, and law interpretation—to independent legislative, executive, and judicial branches of government. The separation of powers protects liberty because all government power cannot fall into the hands of a single group of people. In theory, the separation of powers means that one branch cannot exercise the powers of another.[4]

3. *Checks and Balances:* This concept provides each separate branch of government with the ability to have some control over the others. The framers reasoned that checks and balances such as the president's veto would prevent one branch from ignoring or overpowering another.

4. *Federalism:* As a principle of government, this is the one distinctly American idea of government. It provides that the powers of government are shared by a central body and territorial units. We are citizens of both the national government and the government of the state in which we reside.

In essence, the Madisonian model attempted to establish order and protect liberty by dividing power both horizontally and vertically. The Constitution divides power within the national government. It also divides power between the national government and the states.

The fifth principle of our constitutional government is the very essence of constitutionalism. *Limited government* means that government does not have absolute power. As we argued, all constitutional governments have limited power. The U.S. Constitution, however, mainly through the Bill of Rights (the first ten amendments to it), attempts to specifically protect the rights of the individual and place certain actions beyond the scope of government's power. We are all familiar with the basics of the Bill of Rights such as freedom of expression, freedom of religion, and due process of law.

The Bill of Rights represented a compromise with those who opposed ratification of the Constitution (The Anti-Federalists). The Bill of Rights was not part of the Madisonian Model. Madison actually opposed those amendments even though he wrote them. He believed them unnecessary to protect freedom and believed that at some later date leaders may restrict other rights not specifically stated in the Constitution.

Each of the five central features of the U.S. Constitution provide a fertile area of research on the political environment of our political system. They also provide the kickoff point for answering our second question, "How has the Constitution evolved over time?"

Again, in answering this question we must be suggestive and illustrative rather than comprehensive. Suffice it to say that the literature on the subject is immense. Because of the immensity, however, there are literally hundreds of potential research topics in the area.

The Constitution changes through two mechanisms. The first is the formal amendment process established by the framers. Through a cumbersome and difficult process, amendments can be added.[5]

The second method is informal. It involves changes in the meaning of the Constitution through interpretation or political practice. The informal process has resulted in more substantial change in the Constitution's meaning. It has also provided the most interesting and challenging questions about the political environment. Let's consider some examples coinciding with some of the central features of the U.S. Constitution.

As we argued, the Constitution created a republican form of government. It did not create a democracy, however. Recall that the people played at most an indirect role in governing themselves. The meaning of the Constitution has changed over time to produce a more democratic political system. Through political practices, states created universal, white male suffrage by the 1850s. Constitutional amendments created direct election of U.S. Senators, gave women the vote in 1920, and eliminated some of the barriers preventing African Americans from voting.

The political practices leading to the development of political parties made the selection of the president more democratic. The electoral college has become little more than a rubber stamp of the choice of average voters in each state and the District of Columbia.

Under the electoral college system each state was to select electors as they saw fit. These electors would then meet in their respective state capitols to cast their votes. The candidate receiving a majority (50% + 1) of the votes became president. The intention of the constitutional framers was for the states' elite to select electors. The competition among political parties in the states soon led all to select electors in general elections. Today, we vote directly for these electors in each state.

It is a common myth that the framers of the Constitution intended by the separation of powers to create three separate and equal branches of government. Though there was some ambivalence on their part, the Constitution intended that Congress would be the most influential. It was given the power to make law, raise and spend money, and declare war. The Supreme Court was to be the least powerful branch. Article III creating the Court was purposely ambiguous. While the Constitution established the Supreme Court as the highest court in the land, the framers could not agree on the size, composition, or procedures of the national judiciary. So they left these issues to Congress.

By interpreting the meaning of the Constitution, the Supreme Court gave itself the power of judicial review, the power to declare acts of Congress unconstitutional in *Marbury v. Madison* (1803). Today, through both practice and constitutional interpretation, the president attempts to influence the legislative process by setting the legislative agenda for Congress. The president can bypass the Senate in foreign policy by negotiating executive agreements instead of treaties. Likewise, presidents, not Congress, make the decision to go to war.

In short, the separation of powers looks very different today than its intent in 1787. Many go so far as to say we now have presidential instead of congressional government (Lowi 1987). With the power of judicial review, the Supreme Court is no weak sister. There are many interesting research topics analyzing the rise of the president and the Supreme Court. It is also fascinating to examine why Congress declined in power. The Republican 104th Congress (1995–97) attempted to reverse this trend. Was it successful? Why or why not?

The political history of the United States is in many ways the history of federal relations between the national government and the states. The U.S. Constitution is somewhat ambiguous and contradictory about the powers of the national government and the states. The clash over the limits of national power over the states ultimately led to the Civil War.

The meaning of federalism has dramatically changed as well. For example, the Constitution contains two contradictory provisions concerning the power of the national government. The Tenth Amendment seems to limit the national government to only those powers specifically stated in the Constitution. It says that the powers not delegated to the United States, nor prohibited to the states, are reserved to the states (the reserve clause). However, Article I of the Constitution gives the Congress all powers "necessary and proper" (the elastic clause) to carry out its duties. For most of the nineteenth century, the U.S. Supreme Court used the Tenth Amendment to limit the scope of the national government's power. For most of the twentieth century, the Court has justified an expansive national government based on the elastic clause in *McCulloch v. Maryland* (1819). The national government is now involved in nearly all aspects of government. It is involved in education, hamburger making, and even influencing the drinking age and the speed limits in the various states.

The principle of limited government has also gone through significant change. As our population grew and our economic and social lives became more complex, the Bill of Rights has confronted situations the constitutional framers could not have imagined. The Supreme Court today must deal with issues such as test-tube babies and surrogate motherhood. It must apply the Bill of Rights to questions of abortion and the right to die. It has decided that the separation of the church and state means no prayer in public school classrooms, but the Navajo Indians have no protected right to use peyote in their religious services.

We hope you get the picture. Constitutionalism in the United States constantly confronts changing circumstances and historical development. The study of these confrontations is one of the most fascinating aspects in the study of the political environment. So far, the confrontation has led to adaptation of constitutional principles to changing times. However, in recent years, some have questioned whether our eighteenth-century document, based on eighteenth-century principles, can provide solutions to the complex problems of governing in the twenty-first century.

The argument goes something like this. The world of the twentieth and twenty-first centuries is fundamentally different than any previous era. It is a world of over 6 billion people interacting at different levels of development. With jet travel and modern communications capabilities such as satellites, fax machines, and television, the world has become more interdependent. This is particularly obvious when we look at the interdependence of the economy. What happens economically nearly anywhere in the world can impact the United States as well as other nations. The United States is no longer the only major economic force in the world. We must compete effectively with nations who play by different rules than we do. Changing the way we play the game may not be possible given our constitutional division and fragmentation of power. Our governmental structure with separated power, checks and balances, and federalism makes decisive action by government difficult, if not impossible.

At home, the growth of population, diversity, and government has created an unprecedented number of highly organized interests that are single-minded and unwilling to compromise. The fragmentation of power described above makes it easy for groups to literally paralyze government and prevent actions necessary to deal with the enormous problems we face (Lowi 1979). The kind of decisions required to remedy problems associated with a $5 plus trillion national debt, economic restructuring, environmental destruction, and a multicultural society, can't be made under our constitutional environment. The only hope in this scenario is a changed constitution to increase government's ability to act decisively.[6]

Not everyone agrees with this view. Many contend that our constitutional structure is adapting to changing times. The critics have missed the changes toward less fragmentation (Berry 1989), or understated America's success in coping with modern problems (Schwarz 1988). We might also remember that the Constitution fragmented power in our government for a purpose—to prevent tyranny. Would constitutional reform lead to a less democratic form government?

❖ HOW THE SYSTEM WORKS

We have introduced you to the environment of the American political system. You should recall that the environment is important in helping explain the differences among political systems. As we have argued, the environment also helps us pose the fundamental questions confronting the political system. In analyzing the U.S. political system, our interests always get back to democracy. Is the United States a political democracy? It is now time to get back to this question and examine how the system operates.

We previewed the debate over our question in the discussion of democracy as an aspect of the political environment. What we want to do now is sketch out the possible answers. These answers will then help us ask more specific questions about how the political system works.

There are at least two models of democracy in the modern world (recall, we have dismissed direct democracy as impossible). The first resembles the ideal representative democracy described. We will call it the "majoritarian model of democracy."

The **majoritarian model** tries to approximate the people's role in a direct democracy within the confines of representative government. Procedurally, it reflects the classic requirements of representative democracy, universal suffrage, political equality, and majority rule. All adults must have the right to vote in free elections, their votes must count the same, and the majority makes the decisions in elections and within government.

Each of these procedures are prerequisites for the majoritarian model of democracy, but they are not sufficient to guarantee democracy. From this perspective, we achieve democratic government only if the elected representatives in government respond to the wants and desires of the majority of the public. The model presumes that the citizenry actively participates in the political process, that citizens are knowledgeable about government and politics, and they make rational decisions in voting for their elected representatives. Elections are not the only means to select representatives, but they are the means through which the majority influences what government does or does not do. The people decide for whom to vote based on the candidates' stand on political issues. Once elected, representatives should make policy based on what the majority elected them to do. If they fail, the majority may vote them out of office at the next election.

As you will see in your own research on the American political system, the majoritarian model is in trouble. Much research on the American public shows a lack of interest and knowledge about the political process. Statistics show that it is only a minority of people who vote regularly in all elections. Even in the last few presidential elections, voting participation has barely exceeded 50 percent!

Does this mean that the United States is undemocratic? For years, students of the political process lamented their inability to reconcile the lack of interest and knowledge of the people with the majoritarian model. If they have no interest, "Why talk about democracy?" During the 1950s however, other researchers developed a different model. This model assumed the limited knowledge and participation of the "real electorate." Instead, government responded to the people through their participation in, or representation by, groups. This conception formed the "pluralist model of democracy."

The **pluralist model** of democracy argues that Lincoln's "government by the people" really means government by people operating through competing interest groups. This model of democracy exists when there are many private (nongovernmental) groups that make demands on government and even challenge government (Dahl 1982). As noted, the model changes the criterion for democracy from responsiveness to the majority of the public to responsiveness to organized groups of citizens.

The character of American society and the nature of our constitutional structure make an ideal setting for the pluralist model. Our society is diverse, creating a multitude of different interests. We have also noted that the nature of constitutionalism in the United States divides and fragments government decision-making power. As a result, the multitude of interest groups have relatively easy access to public officials with the power to make decisions. Where the political system centralizes power, such as in the United Kingdom, most decisions are made by a relatively small number of decision makers. These few leaders are far too busy to hear and consider the competing claims of numerous groups. Under our decentralized system, groups have alternative points of access.[7]

Let's consider an example. We all recall that it was government policy in many states to segregate African American and white citizens in the public schools. Many organizations, but particularly the National Association for the Advancement of Colored People (NAACP), failed to get these states to change their laws. White supremists dominated these state governments. But losing in the states was not the end. The NAACP turned to the U.S. Congress for relief. The Congress, too, failed them. But, because of the separation of powers, the war was not over. The NAACP turned to the federal judicial system, which did what even Congress would not. It outlawed school segregation. Had segregation been a major issue in the United Kingdom's centralized political system, the NAACP would have had only one chance "to win" its point of view.

The pluralist model requires all of the procedural requirements of the majoritarian model, but it does not presume that all citizens will be active or knowledgeable. It requires activity and knowledge only of those who are concerned about certain issues and willing to act through organized groups. Importantly, it presumes that the basic political liberties in the American political environment and the fragmentation in our governmental structure ensure that all citizens can have access to government if they choose. The key words in the pluralist model of democracy then are, *divided power, fragmentation,* and *open access.*

The major differences between the majoritarian and pluralist models of democracy summarizes the approach to our previous discussion about whether our constitutional structure is obsolete for the problems of the twenty-first century. Those who argue that we need constitutional reform believe in the necessity of the majoritarian model. Those opposed are pluralists. What are these major differences?

In majoritarian democracy, the mass of citizens control government, not interest groups. Citizens must be knowledgeable and active. The electoral process must be sufficient to harness the power of the majority to influence government decision makers. Centralized governmental structures and decisive elections are the means to aid majority rule.

Pluralist democracy demands less knowledge and participation from the citizenry at large. It requires only group action. It relies on strong groups and a fragmentation of governmental power so that many groups can be heard. Such conditions interfere with majority rule thereby protecting group (minority) interests. Pluralism allows minorities to rule, through groups, as long as the majority remains unorganized.

The third and final model of the American political system is not democratic at all. It answers our question "Is the United States a political democracy?" with a definitive no. We call this model "elite theory."

There are various versions of **elite theory.** However, all maintain the following. Despite the procedural characteristics of majoritarian democracy and the presence of a multitude of different groups, a very small minority makes all the important government decisions. Additionally, government is responsive to the interests of a small group of people with similar characteristics. The two major characteristics shared by this minority are business connections and great wealth (Mills 1956; Dye 1990).

The elite theory argues that only the few govern America because they control the key economic and political institutions of American society. They dominate the largest business corporations where the wealth of these corporations provide them with power. They dominate the key government institutions such as the legislative and executive branches, because an inner circle of corporate leaders supplies the people for top government jobs. These business and government leaders are advocates for their companies and the broader capitalist economic system.

In elite theory, the United States may look like a representative democracy, but it is really an oligarchy (rule by the few). The powerful few determine which issues come to the attention of government. They define those issues on their terms. They then constrain government decisions to suit their own interests.

The appeal of elite theory is to those who believe that wealth dominates politics. Critics of elite theory have noted that many government decisions don't appear to serve the interests of the wealthy elite. For example, in two recent controversies pitting environmental groups against wealthy corporate interests, government decisions sided more with the environmental side than the so-called elite interest. In 1990, Congress passed, and President Bush signed, the Clean Air Act. This act, among other things, will force large industry to spend billions of dollars on environmental protection. Likewise, large logging interests lost to environmental interests when the government set aside 11.6 million acres of forest to preserve the habitat of the endangered spotted owl (Abramson 1991).

Elite theorists reject these kind of criticisms based on individual decisions. They contend that such research doesn't really test the influence of the power elite because much of the elite's power is to keep issues off the political agenda. In other words, the issues of most concern to the elite are never even considered by government leaders (Bachrach and Baratz 1962).

Which of these models best explains the American political process? You may have already concluded from our discussion of the three models that the majority of scholars believe that pluralist democracy best explains how the

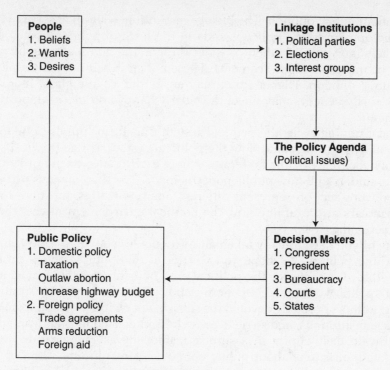

FIGURE 5.1   **U.S. Political System**

political system operates. At the same time however, elite theory has a substantial following, while some reformers find pluralism inadequate and advocate majority rule.

In the next section we explore some more specific questions confronting each aspect of the American political system. We will expose you to the questions, analysis, and some possible answers that led to these different conceptions of politics in the United States. You will also most likely find a multitude of research projects that may help us understand which view is most correct.

❖ THE AMERICAN POLITICAL SYSTEM

We have now discussed three important issues in the American politics subfield. We examined important aspects of the political environment and the key questions it poses for the political system as a whole. We also presented the three basic views about how the political system operates. We want to now return to the political system model we discussed in Chapter 4. For your convenience we have reprinted it above in Figure 5.1.

Let's briefly review the model as we apply it to the American political system. When we speak of the beliefs, wants, and desires of the people, we are talking about public opinion. The linkage institutions identified serve to channel public opinion to the policy agenda in the form of political issues. Decision makers (government) then consider these issues and make public policy (actions or inactions of government). These policies then impact people and affect public opinion. Higher taxes may anger the middle class. Increasing Social Security benefits may make the elderly happy and more supportive of government.

In a continuing cycle, the political system transforms public opinion into public policy. To understand how the political system works, political scientists study each part of the system and how each relates to the others. The hope is to understand how public policy is made. The three models presented in the previous section represent different answers to this question. Importantly, scholars also examine how the political environment affects the system's functioning (see p. 68).

Many of you have already taken an introductory course in American government and politics. We hope you will recall that your textbook probably began with a discussion of the political environment (the first few chapters dealt with political culture, the economy, and various aspects of constitutionalism). The authors probably devoted the subsequent chapters to public opinion, the linkage institutions, and so on. Researchers interested in American politics usually divide their efforts in a similar fashion by asking separate, though often related, questions about public opinion, interest groups, the Congress, the presidency, and the courts. Some study the major areas of public policy, such as economic, environmental, and defense policy. We treat each in turn.

◆ PUBLIC OPINION

Public opinion is important in a democracy because democratic government should respond to the wishes of the people. In analyzing the actual role of public opinion in the United States political system, we face several practical questions. What is public opinion? How do we measure public opinion? How do we learn our political beliefs and attitudes? How powerful is public opinion, and whose opinion counts?

The first problem in studying public opinion is the confusion over how it's defined. Defining public opinion is an iffy proposition because there is no single public. For example, we often say public opinion favors a particular issue such as a constitutional amendment to balance the budget or increases in Social Security benefits. However, a more accurate description of these types of statements would be 68 percent of the public support each, 22 percent oppose each, and 12 percent have no opinion or simply don't know. There are really many publics out there. We might define public opinion then as a collection of individual attitudes, or beliefs, shared by some portion of adult citizens.

The problem with this definition is that it includes private opinions, those that are unrelated to the political system. We might have private opinions about the president or the upkeep of a neighbor's house. To be public, the opinions have to be publicly expressed and related to some aspect of the political system. Borrowing on V. O. Key's definition (Key 1961), we will revise our definition as follows. **Public opinion** is the collection of individual attitudes, or beliefs, shared by some portion of adults that government finds prudent to heed.

Once we have decided on a workable definition, we need to know how to measure public opinion. The chief, and best, means is the public opinion poll. We will not discuss the polls here, because much of this text is about survey research. However, measuring public opinion involves several dimensions as well. These include intensity, stability, knowledge, consensus, and conflict.

Intensity refers to how strongly people feel about an issue. For example, most people have an opinion on the issue of gun control, but they don't have strong opinions. Only a relatively small minority have intense feelings about the issue. Intense opinion is the most likely to generate government response.

Stability refers to the tendency of some opinions to remain constant over time, while others tend to be highly volatile. Our attitudes toward the two major political parties remains similar for long periods of time, but our views toward the Soviet Union changed rapidly, and dramatically, following World War II.

Knowledge refers to the level of information people have about politics and their political attitudes. Usually, the more intensely someone feels about an issue, the more knowledge he or she will possess. In general, the American population has little knowledge about politics and government. For example, polls show consistently that much less than 50 percent can identify who represents them in the U.S. House of Representatives. The level of knowledge is an important element in the study of public opinion.

Consensus and conflict refer to the level of agreement or disagreement on a particular question. The American public is in overwhelming agreement on issues such as requiring school children to repeat the pledge of allegiance in school, but the public is divided over abortion.

The next question involves how we learn public opinion. The basic answer is the process of political socialization. Political socialization is the way individuals acquire a set of political attitudes. It involves the study of what, when, and how we learn. Of particular concern is the how. There are many research questions concerning the role of the family, schools, peers, religion, political events, and race in socialization. Since the advent of television, the power of the media as an agent of political socialization is one of the most debated topics in political science. This is because of the concern that public opinion can be manipulated.

The final research problem in the analysis of public opinion involves the power of public opinion and whose opinion counts. In many ways this is the most important problem because it focuses on the key question in a democratic political system, "Is government responsive to the people?" It is here that the debate between the majoritarian, pluralist, and elitist models of the system begins. In trying to answer the question, we are led to the next part of the political system as well, the linkage institutions.

◆ LINKAGE INSTITUTIONS

Recall that **linkage institutions** are the channels which transfer public opinion to the policy agenda. They include at least political parties, elections, and interest groups. Some now believe that the media not only is an agent of political socialization, it also can help place issues directly on the policy agenda.

Political parties are organizations that sponsor candidates in elections for political office under the organization's name. They run candidates to attempt to capture control of the machinery of government by winning majority support from the public. They contribute to democratic government by attempting to perform four functions.

First, political parties nominate candidates in elections. They try to recruit talented candidates to run under their banner. They also serve as a form of peer review to increase the quality of candidates running for office. The party wants to win, so they need good, electable candidates.

Second, political parties help voters by structuring, or simplifying the vote choice. Parties reduce the number of candidates on the ballot who have a serious chance in elections. The established political parties in the United States, Democrat and Republican, have acquired a loyal following among voters over the years. This discourages nonparty candidates and new parties because the chance of victory is remote. The fewer the candidates, the less amount of information is necessary for voters to make intelligent choices.

Third, political parties propose alternative government programs. The two major parties in the United States have different, though not drastically, philosophies or ideologies about what government should or should not do. Even if voters know nothing of the candidates, they can vote rationally by selecting the party closest to their own fundamental beliefs.

Fourth, parties coordinate the actions of government officials. The parties, once elected, try to implement the programs that they advocate. They work to propose legislation and then get it passed in the name of the majority that elected them.

The last two functions are particularly crucial to the success of the political party as a linkage institution. The party must propose a governmental program, voters must respond to that program, and the party must implement that program once in office. Strong parties are good linkage institutions. Weak parties are less effective. Strong political parties are also necessary to implement the majoritarian model of democracy.

Research in the area of political parties focuses on how well the major parties perform their functions. The general conclusion has been that they perform them less well than in some other countries. This is one reason many conclude majoritarian democracy does not exist in the United States. Many of the reforms proposed by advocates of constitutional reform are designed to strengthen the political parties and make them more effective linkage institutions.

Major questions you might want to explore include the following: What makes for strong or weak political parties? How effective are political parties in performing the major system functions? How have political parties evolved in the United States? What explains the two-party system in the United States? Do political parties offer the electorate a real choice?

The most visible activities of political parties involves elections, the second linkage institution. Ideally, the political parties nominate candidates who compete with one another in order to capture government control. As we argued, voters must choose between the competing policy proposals of the parties for the parties, and elections, to be effective linkage institutions. Students of the electoral process study whether this is or is not the case.

We can approach studying the electoral process from at least two different perspectives. First, we can adopt the perspective of a candidate seeking public office. What hurdles do the political system place before a candidate in the quest for public office? Second, we can adopt the perspective of the voter in the electoral process. Why do citizens choose to participate or not participate? How do voters decide for whom to vote?

The serious candidate faces two separate contests in most American elections. To have a serious chance of election, he or she must first win the nomination of one of the two major parties. As a two-party system, it is extremely rare for an independent or a representative of a minor party to win a general election. Once nominated, the candidate must defeat the other major party nominee in the general (constitutional) election. Thus, we can divide the electoral process into the nomination game and the election game.

In addition, the electoral environment facing the candidate varies with the office sought. The race for the presidency presents a very different ballpark than a race for the U.S. House of Representatives. To conserve space, we will treat the campaigns generically, but keep in mind that you may want to compare the different environments posed by races for different offices.

The nomination game in the two major parties for the most part involves primary elections. Depending on the office sought, these involve the direct, or indirect, nomination of the candidates by rank-and-file party members. Candidates for the party nomination run in elections pursuing the votes of fellow partisans.

The existence of party primary elections is one of the reasons our political parties are not good linkage institutions. All a candidate has to do to receive the party's nomination is to win the primary. Since it is average voters making the decision, the party leadership has little say in who the party's candidates will be. As a result, once elected, the party leadership has less influence over how the new official will behave in office.

The research questions posed by the nomination game reflect the hurdles a candidate faces. What are the rules of the nomination game? Do the rules effect campaign strategy? Who are the primary voters? How do candidates influence them? What kinds of candidates do the parties usually nominate? How has the nomination process changed over time?

The general election game involves the contest between the two major party nominees. It is the constitutional election. The rules facing the two candidates vary by state and level of office. For example, the electoral college method of selecting the president makes this race unique in the United States (and the world). In races for most other offices, the candidate with the most votes from the electorate wins.

The questions most often posed by the general election apply to the nomination game as well. How is strategy developed? How are campaigns financed? What is the impact of money on the electoral process? How can candidates influence voters?

The last question brings us to the second perspective in studying the electoral process—the voter. Many political scientists have devoted their entire careers studying voting behavior. Over the years, we have also developed a voting behavior database that is the most extensive in political science.

Our interest in voting behavior goes back once again to our concern with democracy. Traditional democratic theory (whether it be direct or representative democracy) places the responsibility of government on voters. As a result, we want to know if citizens live up to democratic ideals. We have already mentioned that much research suggests most American voters fall short. Hence, the development of the pluralist model of democracy.

There remains much debate over the issue however, and there are many unanswered questions about the American voter. As noted, the two basic questions involve voter participation and how the voter decides.

By most accounts, voter participation in the United States is appallingly low. In one study, voting in the United States was the lowest in a comparison of 27 countries with competitive elections (Congressional Research Service 1987). The problem is how to explain low voter participation in the United States.

You may want to explore this question in your own project. You might examine the factors associated with voting and nonvoting. Scholars have examined such factors as age, education, race, income, and the level of competition in elections to help us understand why some vote and others don't. You might also find it interesting to explore the claims that more and more people refuse to vote because they are cynical (withhold consent?) about the system and believe their vote makes little difference.

How voters decide in elections is one of the most researched issues in political science. Yet, there remains little agreement as to the principle factors associated with the individual's vote choice. As argued, the democratic ideal has the citizen deciding on the basis of knowledge about the candidates and the policies they propose. Some have argued in this vein that voters are not fools (Key 1966). Most, however, contend that though voters may not be fools, they fall short of the democratic ideal.[8]

In exploring the vote decision, you might want to consider one of two types of factors. The first is socioeconomic. Such factors include, education, income, class, religion, geographic region, and gender. The second is psychological. These include party identification (does the voter have a long-term identity with a political party?), candidate image (the voter's perception of the candidates), and issue preference (the voter perceives candidate's position on the issues as similar to his or her own). These factors are psychological because they are rooted in the attitudes and beliefs held by individual voters (public opinion).

Our view of how voters behave is critical in our analysis of the majoritarian and pluralist models of democracy. The majoritarian model requires a high level of participation in elections. Voters must participate on an informed basis. Their decisions must include the candidate's position on issues and policy positions. The pluralist model requires less participation and information. It presumes that the citizenry best expresses public opinion through the third linkage institution—interest groups.

Interest groups are organized bodies "of individuals who share some political goals and try to influence public policy decisions" (Berry 1989, 4). Parties also want to influence policy. However, political parties seek to actually make policy by winning control of government. Interest groups participate in the electoral process by helping candidates sympathetic to their cause, but they do not actually run candidates for office.

A perennial debate in American politics involves the role of interest groups in a democratic society. On the one side, James Madison warned of the "danger of faction" (Federalist #10). He believed that groups threatened the interests and liberty of others as well as the interest of the community as a whole. Echoing Madison's early concern are those today who believe that organized interests thwart the will of the majority (majoritarians) and those who believe that only the few wealthy groups control public policy (elitists).

On the other side, Alexis de Toqueville, a French visitor to the United States during the eighteenth century, wondered at the number of Americans belonging to groups. He suggested that so many associations were possible because of the strong democratic culture (in Heffner 1956, 198). In more modern times, those advocating the pluralist model of democracy (see p. 80) see interest group activity as essential in holding government accountable to the people.

The "bad side" of interest groups is easy to see. They do press their own selfish interests at the expense of others. They sometimes are involved in scandalous activities as well. The image of well-paid lobbyists in Gucci shoes passing out money to elected officials is well-entrenched in American political folklore.

The good side of the group process is not so clear. In the pluralist model of democracy, interest groups perform five essential functions.

1. *Representation:* Interest groups represent people before government. Just as elected officials have constituents, so do interest groups. The group's representative is a lobbyist.

2. *Participation:* Interest groups also provide a means for people to participate in the political process. People who have similar concerns and interests can pool their money and resources to act collectively. It is easier to get government to listen to a group than to an individual.

3. *Education:* Groups educate the public on political issues in order to increase membership and lobby government.

Box 5.1

Foreign Policy Issues and Voting: A Research Example

Researchers in American politics have long debated how American voters decide for whom to vote in presidential (and other) elections. Much of the research since the 1950s has focused on the relative importance of three short-term psychological factors. These include individual attitudes toward the two major political parties, the image of the two major candidates, and the voter's perception of relevant political issues. The bulk of traditional research has found political issues the least important of the three influences. To the extent that issues are relevant to the vote decision, domestic issues seem more important in the vote choice than those concerning foreign policy. However, in recent campaigns, Hess and Nelson (1985) note that the presidential candidates base their campaign principally on foreign affairs (not so for 1992). Given the findings of traditional research, such strategy raises a contradiction. The strategy of presidential candidates is either misguided, or the prevailing wisdom on vote choice is somehow flawed. John Aldrich, John Sullivan, and Eugene Borgida sought to explore this contradiction by reexamining the role of foreign policy issues in the voters' choice. Aldrich and his colleagues used survey data generated from the University of Michigan's National Election Study and the Gallup Poll to study the role of foreign policy issues in the 1980 and 1984 presidential elections. In order to determine whether voters respond to issues in a campaign, the authors first identified the conditions necessary for issue voting. First, the voter must have the issue stored in memory (issue availability). Second, the issue must be readily accessible to the voter. That is, the attitude must be readily recalled from memory when stimulated by the media, the campaign, or other sources. Third, the voter must perceive a difference between the two major candidates and parties on the relevant issue. Using certain scaling techniques and probit analysis (a form of regression; see Chapter 14), they analyzed these conditions required for determining issue voting on domestic and foreign policy issues in 1980 and 1984. In contrast to much scholarship, they found that the public has more available and accessible foreign policy opinion and information than previously thought. These attitudes were accessed through candidate discussion in the campaign. Likewise, voters perceived a difference between the candidates on foreign policy questions and responded to these differences with their votes. More specifically, the authors concluded that:

Continued

BOX 5.1 (CONT'D)

FOREIGN POLICY ISSUES AND VOTING: A RESEARCH EXAMPLE

1. Peace stands with prosperity as an enduring goal of the public.
2. With the exception of 1973–80, foreign policy issues have been cited as the "most important problem" facing the nation.
3. Candidates campaigning on foreign policy issues is a source of attitude accessibility for much of the public.
4. Foreign policy differences between the candidates were important determinants of the vote.
5. Therefore, the contradiction disappears. Candidates do not waltz before a blind audience. It appears that the only blind audience is a significant part of the academic community.

Source: John Aldrich, John Sullivan, and Eugene Borgida, "Foreign Affairs and Issue Voting: Do Presidential Candidates 'Waltz Before a Blind Audience'?" *American Political Science Review* 83 (1989):123–141.

4. *Agenda building:* Interest groups serve as linkage institutions by bringing issues to the policy agenda. They do so in their roles as channels for participation, education, and representation. There are many problems in American society. Not all of them get attention. Interest groups bring new issues into the limelight.

5. *Responsiveness:* Interest groups monitor government programs, keeping their members, and others, abreast of what government is doing, or not doing.

We have hinted that, empirically, interest groups are the strongest linkage institutions in the American political system. We do not take a position on the "goodness" or "badness" of them. Instead, we will leave that to you. We will, however, suggest some questions that, when answered, may help you decide whether or not the group process is healthy for the political system.

How do groups form? This question is critical because the pluralist model of democracy presumes that people can easily organize and that no group of people is more capable of organizing than others. An important part of pluralist theory is that new interest groups form when some people's interests are threatened (Truman 1951).

Are some interests represented while others are not? Elite theory argues that only the wealthy and powerful belong to groups to which government listens. Many, even nonelitists, have observed that not all interests have group representation.

How do interest groups operate? Pluralist democracy presumes that groups work in similar fashion to represent their members. They recruit membership, hire lobbyists, and communicate with government officials. They raise money for campaigns and communicate with government officials and constituents. Do all groups have similar resources? Elite theorists say no, pluralists say yes.

◆ Decision-Making Institutions

Whatever we conclude about the relative strength of the three major linkage institutions, political issues do end up on the policy agenda. Government **decision makers** confront these issues and make public policy. In the U.S. political system, the decision makers are uniquely influenced by their political environment, particularly the constitutional principles of the separation of powers, the system of checks and balances, and federalism. For the sake of brevity, we will limit our discussion to the three major decision-making agencies of the United States government—the legislative, executive, and judicial branches.

The United States Congress is the chief law-making institution in government. You know it is a bicameral legislature consisting of a House of Representatives (435 members) and the Senate (100 members). You also need to recall that the framers of the Constitution intended the Congress to be the most powerful decision maker. Students of the Congress want to explain how it operates (a considerable task). They also want to know whom it represents. This requires an understanding of to whom and to what the Congress is most responsive. Is it political parties, constituents, or groups? In other words, does the operation of Congress support the majoritarian, pluralist, or elitist models of decision making in the United States?

Though Congress plays many roles in the U.S. government, its chief duty is lawmaking. As students of Congress, we are interested in how the lawmaking process works. While we lack the space for a detailed discussion here, we need to know that the legislative process is dominated by the system of committees and subcommittees. Members of Congress introduce bills that are then referred to the relevant committee, which then refers it to a subcommittee. These committees and subcommittees study the bill, hold hearings, and make amendments to the bills. Afterward, the committees either make a recommendation to pass the bill in the whole House or Senate, or kill the bill. Usually, the Congress will take the recommendation of the committees. Congressional committees are thus the real workhorses in Congress. Since Congress usually takes their recommendations, they are also the real power in the legislative process.

The committee and subcommittee system has the effect of fragmenting power in the Congress. This in turn encourages the pluralist model of democracy. For example, representatives from agricultural regions of the country strive to land seats on the agriculture committees. They then tend to support agricultural interests. Since Congress responds to its committees, agricultural groups influence lawmaking by gaining the support of only a handful of representatives on the agriculture committees.

We are also interested in what the most important influences on legislators might be. There are several factors that we might research. Among these are political parties, interest groups, constituents, and the president.

We have previously argued that political parties have only limited influence in government. This is because they do not really control the nomination and finance of candidates for Congress. Party leaders in each house do try to influence the rank and file, however. Depending on the issues involved, leaders sometimes succeed and sometimes fail. The Republican leadership in the 104th Congress enjoyed extraordinary success in organizing the rank and file behind their budget priorities.

Interest groups have substantial influence in Congress because they provide members with resources necessary for their campaigns (money and workers). They also provide valuable information, and other help to aid members in the legislative process. Finally, as argued above, interest groups usually need to influence only a small number of members on the relevant committees.

A legislator's constituents are the people who live in his or her state or district. Their opinions should have enormous influence on the member because it is the member who represents them. However, many constituents are uninformed about issues and make few demands on their representatives.

In the twentieth century, the president has come to play an important role in the law-making process. In spite of the separation of powers, the president has become the "chief legislator." While the president cannot vote in Congress, he recommends the bulk of legislation for Congress to consider. Most of what Congress does is to react to the president's proposals. The president's success depends on his ability to persuade the Congress to go along.

There is little agreement as to which of the above have the most or the least influence on the behavior of Congress. Depending on the political context and the issue involved, one, some, or all can be significant. In general, however, much evidence points to interest groups as the most active elements attempting to influence Congress, supporting once again the pluralist model of democracy.

If you select the Congress for your research area, the potential topics are numerous. You may want to look at the impact of the factors listed above on the legislative process. You may want to examine the committee and subcommittee system. It is possible to compare the operation of the House and the Senate. Or, you may want to study how different types of policy issues are treated in the legislative process.

The executive branch of government is really two politically separate entities. The president is the center of the executive branch. However, the sprawling executive bureaucracy, consisting of the cabinet departments, the executive agencies, and the independent regulatory commissions often operates independent of presidential control. Political scientists even study the two separately. There are scholars who focus almost entirely on the presidency. Others concentrate on the bureaucracy (see Chapter 6). Once again for the sake of brevity, we will limit our discussion here to the American presidency.

In studying the presidency, scholars have focused most intensely on the question of presidential power. The framers of the Constitution were somewhat ambivalent about how powerful the president should be. They feared executive power because of the experience with the king of England. They also wanted the president to have the ability to check the power of Congress, which they believed would have the most influence in the new government.

Despite this last concern, today most scholars see the president as the center of American government. During most of the twentieth century, the responsibility and power of the presidency has grown. When we examine presidential power, we see at least three categories. These include constitutional powers, extraconstitutional power, and power deriving from political skill.

The constitutional powers are those specifically given by the Constitution. On the surface they are quite limited. Article II gives the president the executive power and makes him the chief diplomat and the commander in chief. He can convene Congress, grant pardons and reprieves, and veto legislation passed by Congress. Compared to the number and specificity of the powers granted Congress, the president's stated powers pale in comparison.

However, the president's constitutional powers, though stated, are not well defined. For example, while the constitution gives the president the positions of chief executive and commander in chief, it does not define the specific powers these include. Some presidents have challenged Congress and defined these powers broadly. Recent presidents have argued that the position of commander in chief implies that the president can commit U.S. military forces without the consent of Congress. They claim this power even though the power to declare war is given to Congress in the Constitution.

Though the president has often gained additional power by challenging Congress, Congress sometimes willingly delegates power to the president. Congress gave Franklin Roosevelt latitude to do what he thought necessary to solve the economic problems of the Great Depression. Likewise, it gave Richard Nixon the power to implement wage and price controls to deal with inflation. Even the 104th Congress, seemingly bent on the reestablishement of congressional leadership, will probably give the president a form of the item veto, yielding more budgetary power to the president.

Occasionally, presidents assert what we can best describe as "extraconstitutional" or "inherent powers." These are powers that go beyond the Constitution. Inherent powers derive from the president's duty to protect the national security. During the Civil War, Lincoln increased the size of the army beyond what Congress authorized, instituted a blockade of southern ports, and suspended the right of habeas corpus. He argued that he must circumvent the Constitution in order to save the nation. One president, Richard Nixon, unsuccessfully argued that whenever the president acts, by definition it is constitutional.

The final source of presidential power is political skill. The influence of an individual president depends on his ability to use the powers and resources at his disposal to get what he wants done. According to one scholar, the power of the president is little more than the power to persuade (Neustadt 1960). For example, we have argued that today the president is the chief legislator. We measure the president's success by how well he persuades Congress to legislate what he wants. The difference between strong and weak presidents often lies in their abilities to skillfully choose priorities, bargain, compromise, and use the resources of the office. In short, powerful presidents are skillful presidents.

The topics available on the executive branch are also numerous. We have just touched the surface in our discussion of the presidency. What explains the growth of presidential power in the twentieth century? What is the ultimate source of presidential power? How do presidents persuade Congress? The bureaucracy? The people? What explains presidential success and failure?

Scholars have treated the judicial branch of government as a subfield of American politics. There are two broad concerns. The first is constitutional law. Scholars in this area focus their attention on how the U.S. Supreme Court applies and interprets the Constitution. This area is what we earlier referred to as constitutionalism. The Court is confronted with a variety of circumstances to which the Constitution does not clearly speak. We gave you some examples near the beginning of this chapter. Over time the major areas of constitutional law have included the powers of government, civil liberties, and civil rights.

We have already mentioned that the Constitution is often vague in defining the powers of government. The Supreme Court ultimately decides what the powers of the president, the Congress, and even the Court really are.

Likewise, the Supreme Court must apply the Bill of Rights to specific situations such as pornography and certain religious practices. In modern times, the Court has gotten more involved in protecting the civil rights of disadvantaged groups.

We do not recommend that you choose constitutional law as your research topic, though we do suggest you take a course in constitutional law before you graduate. It is a very important and interesting subject. However, the complexity of the field means it is difficult for beginning students.

The second concern is judicial behavior. Here we are interested in the policy impact of the judicial system and how it operates. If our interest is the U.S. Supreme Court, we want to study its impact on policy relative to the Congress and the president. We might want to know how the Court works and how the justices make up their minds. We might want to know if certain justices consistently vote with others on certain issues and are consistently opposed on others. For example, we might find that over time three justices may vote the same on issues involving the rights of the accused but disagree consistently on issues involving freedom of religion (see Appendix II for a way to research this topic).

In studying the larger judiciary, the other federal and state courts, scholars are interested in the whole process. They want to know how judges, prosecutors, and defense attorneys interact. How do juries behave? Are defendants in criminal trials really presumed innocent until proven guilty?

These questions are important because the Bill of Rights in the U.S. and state constitutions presumes the judicial process will work in certain ways. Criminal defendants have the right to a fair trial. Juries are supposed to be fair and impartial in determining guilt or in deciding who should get custody of the children following a divorce.

What we find in most cases is that the system does not quite work as presumed. One example will suffice. All criminal defendants have the right to a fair trial. However, most criminal cases never go to trial. Approximately 90 percent of criminal cases end with a plea bargain. This is a deal where the prosecution, defense, and judge agree to allow the defendant to plead guilty to a lesser crime and receive a specified sentence. Such is hardly what the framers of the Constitution intended.

You might have already guessed that you cannot really study the decision-making institutions in isolation from one another. As we noted at the beginning, the separation of powers really means separate institutions sharing powers. We cannot really understand how Congress behaves without understanding the president's veto or the Supreme Court's power of judicial review. Likewise, to govern, the president must have the cooperation of Congress and, like Congress, the acquiescence of the Court. To understand the decision-making institutions, we must study how they interact with each other (and the linkage institutions) to make public policy.

◆ PUBLIC POLICY

In our discussion of the political system we have nearly come full circle. All political systems make **public policy** which affects the public and hence public opinion. Thus, the process begins again. Public policy scholars have shown two major interests (see Chapter 6). Many develop an expertise in the different areas of public policy. As argued, almost any issue can become a question of public policy. Traditionally however, political scientists have focused on those issues most often on the policy agenda.

As a result we have experts on economic, environmental, civil liberties, civil rights (equality), energy, and foreign policy. The questions on the decision maker's plate most often fall into one or the other of these broad areas. From time to time, others, such as health care, become center stage on the policy agenda. However, they usually are at least related to one of the major areas. For example, the health-care issue is ultimately an economic question.

The second interest in public policy is much broader. Many who call themselves public policy specialists are really less concerned with specific policies than with how the policy is made. These researchers study certain environmental policies to learn more as to how the system works. They want to know if the system operates differently when we consider different types of policies. The most obvious distinction is between domestic and foreign policy. Foreign policy is basically the prerogative of the president. The public, Congress, and the courts play only a secondary role. This is not true for domestic policy where the president must deal with interest groups, parties, and Congress all at once.

In short, students of public policy examine the political system to try and see which of our three models—majoritarian, pluralist, or elitist—best explains how a particular type of policy is made. One reason each model continues to have adherents is because each captures a portion of the truth, at least for some policy issues. The elitist model best explains many foreign and defense policies. The pluralist model best explains agricultural subsidies. When a political issue is particularly controversial, and large numbers of people are concerned, the majoritarian model is closest to the mark.

We have now completed our tour of the American political system. We hope you are armed with many questions that may serve as a "kickoff" point in your search for a research topic. We say "kickoff" point because most of what we have discussed is much too broad for a term project. Instead, we designed the discussion to introduce you to a number of issues and areas where you can look for an interesting and manageable topic. The next three chapters will introduce you to other potential topics in public administration and public policy, comparative politics, and international politics.

❖ SUMMARY

In this chapter we introduced you to the subfield of American politics. It is the longest chapter in this book. This is no accident. Though you will see in Chapter 7 that comparative politics is more challenging, more work has been done on the American political system than on any other.

The American political system is unique because of its cultural environment. This environment made the United States the first new nation of the modern world. The United States was the first nation to expect its system to operate in the context of liberty, equality, consent, democracy, and limited government.

The commitment to these ideals also poses the key questions facing the political system as a whole. How much freedom should the system allow? What should government do to promote equality? How do we know when people withdraw their consent? Is the United States a political democracy? Does the U.S. Constitution effectively limit government?

Each of these questions is complex, with no simple answer. As a result, we have very different responses to the same questions. For example, there is little agreement as to the meanings of freedom, equality, and democracy. Where there is little agreement on the question's definition, there will be little agreement on the answers.

We then turned to the question of how the system works. We identified three different models that attempt to explain the American political process. Each purported to explain how the system translates public opinion into public policy. Two of the models, majoritarian and pluralist, were found compatible with at least some democratic values. The third, elitism, was not.

With three competing views of the political system, we began to explore each aspect of the political system. We examined the major issues associated with the study of public opinion. We then turned to the linkage institutions followed by the decision makers and public policy. Each area posed many specific questions and problems in studying the political system. Many issues can be starting points for developing research topics.

Throughout our discussion, we noted that the pluralist model of democracy won the support of the majority of political scientists. However, the other two models are alive because they may explain some public policies that the pluralist model cannot.

❖ KEY TERMS

consent	linkage institutions
decision makers	majoritarian model
democracy	order
elite theory (elitism)	pluralist model
equality	public opinion
liberty	public policy
limited government	

❖ EXERCISES

1. Describe why the United States is described as the first new nation.

2. Identify three political issues (other than those listed in the chapter) that illustrate the tension between the governmental goals of freedom and order.

3. Describe and discuss the impact of constitutionalism on the American political system.

4. Compare the majoritarian, pluralist, and elitist models of the political system.

5. Write a research proposal on a topic associated with public opinion, the linkage or decision-making institutions.

❖ SUGGESTED READINGS

Cronin, Thomas. *Direct Democracy*. Cambridge: Harvard University Press, 1989.

Dahl, Robert. *Dilemmas of Pluralist Democracy*. New Haven: Yale University Press, 1982.

Dye, Thomas. *Who's Running America: The Bush Era*. Engelwood Cliffs, NJ: Prentice-Hall, 1990.

Fiorina, Morris. *Congress: Keystone of the Washington Establishment*, 2nd ed. New Haven: Yale University Press, 1989.

Lipset, Seymour Martin. *The First New Nation*. New York: Basic Books, 1963.

Lowi, Theodore. *The Personal President*. Ithaca, NY: Cornell University Press, 1987.

Martin, Janet. *Lessons from the Hill*. New York: St. Martin's Press, 1994.

Mundo, Phillip. *Interest Groups*. Chicago: Nelson-Hall Publishers, 1992.

Obrian, David. *Storm Center: The Supreme Court in American Politics*, 2nd ed. New York: Norton, 1990.

Phillips, Kevin. *Boiling Point*. New York: Random House, 1993.

Toqueville, Alexis de. *Democracy in America*. ed. Richard Heffner. New York: John Wiley, 1956.

Wills, Gary. *Explaining America: The Federalist*. Garden City: Doubleday, 1981.

❖ NOTES

1. We will discuss only these cultural aspects of the political environment in the United States. We leave out the economic and social elements of the environment for the sake of brevity and simplicity. We also believe these cultural elements have been the most important for the development of the American political system. Moreover, the same elements of the economic and social environment interact with the cultural environment to pose the fundamental questions facing the American political system.

2. The astute student will find there are marked similarities with our discussion of John Locke in Chapter 5. This is not an accident. The people most active in founding the United States were much influenced by Locke's writing.

3. There remain vestiges of direct democracy in the United States. Many states have either, or both, the initiative or referendum. In the former, citizens can place proposed legislation on an election ballot. In the second, legislatures propose laws or constitutional amendments that must then go before the voters at large for approval. Additionally, in New England there remain small towns that are governed by "town meetings" where all citizens gather once or twice a year to make decisions affecting their town.

4. In practice, the separation of powers is far from complete. At least one scholar contends that instead of a separation of powers, we have separate institutions sharing powers (see Cronin 1989, 47).

5. There are two mechanisms to formally amend the Constitution. The first requires Congress to propose the amendment by a two-thirds vote, then ratification by three-fourths of the states. The second has Congress calling a National, Constitutional Convention at the request of two-thirds of the states. The convention would then propose amendments for consideration by the states. The second method has never been used.

6. Charles Hardin and Grant McConnell argue that we need to reform the system so it resembles parliamentary systems such as that in the United Kingdom (see Hardin 1974; McConnell 1966). Theodore Lowi argues that there is nothing wrong with the Constitution that can't be cured by a re-evaluation of the purpose of government. Our new ideology, interest group liberalism, has led to a system where government cannot govern (see Lowi 1979).

7. You may be scratching your head here remembering our discussion about how some scholars contend that organized interest groups now paralyze government, rendering it helpless in coping with modern problems. These critics are the ones who would like to reform the system to coincide more with the majoritarian model of democracy. They believe, for reasons you may want to explore, that the pluralist model is neither real democracy, nor an effective form of government.

8. The list of works supporting this view is too long to cite. However, the classic study is Campbell et al. (1960).

PUBLIC ADMINISTRATION AND PUBLIC POLICY

❖ INTRODUCTION

In the early years of our republic, George Washington, Thomas Jefferson, Andrew Jackson, and other American leaders spent much time deciding how to administer the affairs of a new government. It was not until 1887, however, that political scientists began to look at public administration as a professional field of study and application (see Wilson 1987). Since that time, political scientists have spent much time debating the role of politics in public service and the "politics-administration" dichotomy. They have also examined the structure, the decision-making processes, and the interaction between public managers and their subordinates.

While we spend some time looking at these areas, we will spend more time tracing the evolution of public administration in America. Specifically, we will talk about the "who," "what," and "how" of public administration. We conclude the chapter with an examination of the ethics of public administrators.

An understanding of this chapter will enable you to:

1. Define public administration.
2. Trace the development of the field.
3. Identify the major functions of public administrators.
4. Identify the stages of public policy making.
5. Understand the role of public administrators in public policy.
6. Identify ways public administrators make decisions.
7. Understand the ethical problems facing public administrators.

❖ PUBLIC ADMINISTRATION: OUR WORKING DEFINITION

Public administration is an important area of study in most political science and government curriculums. Many government majors also find themselves working as public administrators upon graduation. Before we consider the nature and scope of public administration, it is important to have a working definition. Public administration is two terms: *public* and *administration.* Thus, we need to define each term before we can gain an understanding of the field.

Public has to do with people, a community, or a society. It involves the community's shared resources. For example, public schools, public parks, and public services, implies that these resources belong to each member of the community.

Administration is the coordination and provision of personnel and monetary assets to accomplish a group's goals. A group may be your fraternity or sorority, a school board, a local police department, or the Department of Defense. The groups we study in public administration are governmental groups found at all levels of government.

For our purposes, **public administration** refers to the government's role in the delivery of common goods and services to members of a community be it at the national, state, or local level of government. As such, public administration involves the study of the "who," "what," and "how" of public administration. It also involves the challenges confronting the administrative state.

Public administration is an activity common to most countries and levels of government. But public administrative processes and structures differ from country to country. As such, many scholars have expended considerable time in the subfield of comparative public administration. This chapter, however, is concerned with public administration in the United States.

❖ THE WHO OF PUBLIC ADMINISTRATION

◆ THE EARLY YEARS

The U.S. Constitution provided for a federal political system having departmental administrative functions. It also provided the nation's leaders with a difficult question: Who should administer the nation's affairs?

George Washington and John Adams, Federalist presidents, believed that public administrators should be appointed based on talent, education, and moral character. At this stage of our history, only the socially elite had most of these characteristics. Thus, they were chosen to fill government posts.

Washington and Adams also rewarded individuals who were loyal to the Federalist cause by appointing them to administrative positions. Thus, patronage or the "spoils system" emerged as a factor in appointing public officials.

◆ PARTICIPATORY DEMOCRACY IN THE PUBLIC SECTOR

Thomas Jefferson also believed that talent should be a requisite for appointment. Jefferson, however, opposed the idea of rule by the social elite. He believed in **participatory democracy** where people from all walks of society have the opportunity to participate in the processes of government. This notion also applied to the administrative sector. Thus, under Jefferson, the "personnel pool" was expanded.

During his time in office, President Andrew Jackson attempted to actualize as much of the Jeffersonian belief about public administration as possible. His ideas of popular government and participatory democracy were extensions of Jefferson's. He believed in rotation in administrative office, national nominating conventions, and the idea that the president was a direct representative of the people.

Jackson's efforts, however, resulted in accusations that he introduced the spoils system and did not display respect for administrative skill or merit. But some argue that Jackson would not have supported the theory of the spoils system. His position on rotation in office was merely a way to reform a government badly in need of reform and new participants.

Jacksonian democracy contributed to the growth of the pool of potential public administrators and the size of the governmental administrative body. Many were still concerned, however, that appointments were made because of "who you knew versus what you knew." This concern was magnified when a disappointed office seeker assassinated President Garfield in 1881. As a result, Congress established a civil service merit system when it passed the Pendleton Act in 1883. The objective of the legislation was to fit the best qualified with the administrative position and restore integrity and efficiency in the public service.

◆ INFLUENCE OF THE PROGRESSIVE MOVEMENT

The **Progressive movement** had an important influence on the development of American public administration. The Progressives, concerned about increased urbanization, immigration, the growth of governmental corruption, and the loss of traditional values, offered several solutions to the problems they envisioned. They wanted, for example, to make government more efficient and businesslike. Thus, they called for the professionalization of public agencies and functions. They also wanted to expand the system by returning power to the common people. To accomplish this goal, they introduced such devices as the initiative, the referendum, the recall election, party reform, and other direct democracy suggestions.

Their goals implied that the administration of politics would be accomplished by the elite, but the political process would be influenced more by the people. To some, this also implied that administration and politics were separate functions not to be fused.

President Woodrow Wilson, for one, agreed with this notion. He believed in a clear line of demarcation between politics and administration. The broad plans of governmental action were political activities. The detailed execution of those plans were administrative functions. Wilson argued that public administrators should not involve themselves with general legislation, and legislators should not interfere with administrative details. For Wilson, there was a major distinction between politics and administration. He believed that politics had no place in public service. His concern was that public appointments should be based on merit, rather than partisanship. Thus, Wilson helped to craft the politics-administration dichotomy—a dichotomy, that while refuted by many scholars today, is still a matter of debate amongst some practitioners.

Wilson also looked to Max Weber's concept of **bureaucracy** as a way to professionalize the administrative function. While today we associate the bureaucracy with the public sector, a bureaucracy is any large complex organization. And, while the bureaucracy did not become a prominent organizational system in American government until the nineteenth century and the spread of industrialization, bureaucracies existed in the early Catholic church, ancient China, and the Roman Empire.

Weber identified several characteristics and roles of the bureaucracy. The essential characteristic in Weber's model was hierarchy. The principle of **hierarchy** means there is a tightly structured system of supervision and subordination in which supervision of the lower offices is done by the higher ones. Weber also believed in authority resting in the position, not in the person. Subordinates complied with their superior's orders because of the authoritative position they held, not because of who they were.

◆ PUBLIC ADMINISTRATION TODAY

In 1789 less than 2,000 civilians worked as federal government employees. For the next 100 years several departments and commissions such as the Department of the Interior, the Department of Justice, and the Interstate Commerce Commission were created. As a result, over 140,000 civilians worked in federal government. Today, over 3 million civilians work for the federal government as employees of the departments, administrative agencies, White House staff, Supreme Court, and Congress.

The size and scope of the administrative state provide a fertile field of study for political scholars. In the following passages we will examine the political nature of public administration, the activities of public administrators, and challenges faced by the public administrator.

❖ THE WHAT OF PUBLIC ADMINISTRATION:
THE FUNCTIONS OF PUBLIC ADMINISTRATION

◆ PERSONNEL ADMINISTRATION

Personnel administration is an integral part of every public management activity. In this section we will describe personnel administration functions, the impact personnel offices have on public managers, and how reform initiatives have changed personnel administration at the federal level.

Personnel Administrative Functions   The personnel function consists of those procedures and behaviors that combine the needs of organizations and people to achieve common goals. It involves every aspect of an employee's work-related activity. It is that part of public administration charged with shaping the quality and quantity of public employment. This charge is realized when personnel managers work with other departmental employees to achieve organizational goals.

The personnel function involves personnel administration and human resource management. Personnel administration is the management of those activities, or functions, associated with recruiting and placing a satisfactory work force in the organization. On the other hand, the responsibility for enhancing job satisfaction and productivity is an important part of the manager's job and part of human resource management.

We will not spend time examining the tasks associated with human resource management. Instead, we will concentrate on personnel administrative functions such as recruitment, selection, position classification, compensation, training, evaluation, and adverse action or employee disciplinary processes.

The goal of the recruitment process is to identify a large pool of available people who are interested in public employment. The most common recruitment technique is to fill vacancies from an available pool of qualified candidates. A longer-range strategy is manpower forecasting and planning. Forecasting is used to predict the capability of the employment market to fill an agency's future personnel needs. Planning is used to develop manpower strategies.

A major purpose of the selection process is to choose the best applicants identified during the recruitment process. As such, personnel administrators use application forms, examinations, and interviews. The first step in screening job applicants is the completion of an application form. Then, civil service examinations are used to qualify and rank applicants. Those individuals with the highest scores are then referred to the official with authority to interview and hire the applicant. Thus, the last two steps in the process are usually the interview and selection process which includes notifying the individual of his or her selection. These steps are important to the personnel system in that they contribute to the maintenance of a selection process based on merit versus patronage.

A **position classification** system is used by personnel administrators to provide for an equitable and effective personnel management system. This function involves the classification of positions, not people, with the person hired automatically assuming the title and benefits associated with the position. The advantages of position classification are its ability to structure the work being done in the organization, describe jobs to employees, and protect against violations of the merit system. A good position classification system that delineates the duties and responsibilities of each job is also central to the creation of compensation plans.

Compensation plans are a major concern of public personnel administrators. By combining duties and responsibilities, the personnel system attempts to ensure equal pay for work of equal value. Compensation plans in most public agencies are established by surveying agency positions, gathering comparative data from other organizations, formulating a pay schedule, and integrating it with the position classification plan. Compensation can also include employee benefit packages, health and accident compensation, and retirement plans.

Compensation is a reward for existing ability. Thus, employee training is used in equitable personnel systems to improve employee abilities. Typical training programs include orientation sessions, probation periods, supervisory training, remedial or refresher classes, and courses in specific subjects. Seminars, programmed instruction, case studies, and conferences are methods of instruction used by personnel managers. On-the-job training and job rotation, while perhaps mandated by the personnel administrator, are usually part of the human resource management end of the personnel system continuum.

Another important function of the personnel administrator is the maintenance of an evaluation system. The goal of a rating system is to improve individual performance by ensuring discussion between the employer and employee about work quality. Appraisal procedures can be an important factor in personal motivation, organizational communication, supervisory understanding, and personnel actions, such as promotions and pay raises. They can also provide a check on the effectiveness of other personnel processes like recruitment.

Evaluations can also lead to **adverse personnel actions** against employees such as reprimands and dismissals. The purpose of adverse actions is to correct a situation in which an employee is incompetent or has violated established agency policies and practices.

The Impact of Personnel Activities on Public Managers   The functions we have discussed, although seemingly independent, have an interactive impact on each other and on the management of public organizations. For instance, the recruitment objective raises several questions. What type of person should be encouraged to work for the government? Should an agency seek liberal arts majors or experts with graduate degrees for management positions? In other words, is the public interest best served by generalists or specialists?

The personnel administrator also helps determine why individuals are recruited. Should people be recruited who are trained to fill the vacancy? Or should the agency assume responsibility to reduce unemployment by providing compensatory training opportunities?

The recruiting efforts of the personnel administrator can impact other personnel administrative functions and the agency's management activities. They present managers with a work force that may require different training programs, compensatory packages, and possibly adverse actions. As such, the philosophy of the personnel administrator may require managers to be more flexible and knowledgeable about different management theories.

There is also a multiplicity of public personnel structures with each branch having its own personnel system. As a result, recruitment practices differ. Within the executive branch there are four distinguishable personnel groupings, each having distinct values and allegiances. First, there is a patronage system where selection is based on a combination of competence and political loyalty. Examples include the cabinet positions. There is also a unionized system, where most personnel actions are determined through labor and management negotiations. Recruitment within the third system, the professional service system, is based largely on previous education and experience. Examples include the Senior Executive Service. The final grouping is the classified merit system, where entry and advancement are determined through competitive examination. The complexity of this personnel system creates problems for the personnel administrator, worker, and manager. Numerous rules and requirements must be understood and followed when performing the various personnel functions. Consequently, much criticism has arisen.

Critics believe the merit system, for example, promotes employee protectionism. Subsequently, the work force becomes stagnant and effectiveness deteriorates. The system was also charged with using racially discriminate testing and screening activities.

Critics of the professional service have charged that academic institutions responsible for producing the professional are too far removed from the operations of government to be the judges of what public employment requires. Thus an ongoing question is, can institutions offering graduate degrees in public administration produce effective and professional public administrators?

Due to these criticisms and concerns, some factions have called for personnel administration to be made an integral part of the executive function so that personnel systems could be measured in terms of their contribution to better government rather than by the number of personnel transactions they complete. The implication is that personnel systems under the control of top administrators would be less protective of poor performers.

Reform Initiatives   During the 1970s, concerns about productivity, public sector unionism, the impact of affirmative action, a lack of administrative ethics, and criticisms of the merit system contributed to the reform movement in the federal civil service. As a result, Congress passed the **Civil Service Reform Act (CSRA) of 1978**.

The act replaced the Civil Service Commission by establishing the Office of Personnel Management to act as the president's civil service staff administrator. The Merit System Protection Board was also created to hear cases involving personnel controversies. In addition, the Senior Executive Service was created to professionalize upper management positions.

The CSRA also resulted in staffing and training changes, the elimination of nepotism, a system of performance appraisals to serve as the basis for salary increases, and safeguards and appeal rights for those judged to have unacceptable performance. A minority recruitment program to overcome perceived staffing discrimination also had to be implemented. To further complicate the manager's job, the CSRA recognized employees' rights to organize for collective bargining. Thus, the CSRA significantly changed the way public personnel and agency managers were to perform their duties.

◆ THE BUDGET PROCESS

Public budgeting is a technical and political process. As such, the approaches to public budgeting can influence the extent and exercise of political power by appointed professionals and elected officials. In this section we will describe different approaches to public budgeting. We will also spend some time describing how the approaches to public budgeting can influence the exercise of political power.

The Budget Process as a Source of Administrative Power   Many critics of public budgeting have asserted that the process contributes to political power and bureaucratic growth. For example, if an administrative agency is to accomplish its mandated tasks, it needs an adequate supply of money. Money is one way that public agencies demonstrate their political clout and their importance to the rest of the political system.

On the other hand, the budgetary process can also be the arena in which elected political officials demonstrate and enhance their power. They can do this in two ways. First, they can show their concern for the taxpayer by limiting the amount of money allocated to the public sector, especially to the less popular government programs. Second, they can lend their political support to agencies that are supported by major interest groups and the representative's constituency. As a result, they can attain political backing by each group.

The increased complexity of public issues has led many public executives to delegate executive functions to the administrative agency. This includes becoming deeply involved in the various stages of the budgetary process. This involvement, in turn, leads to the promotion and justification of agency needs and an enhanced power base without stressful executive oversight.

Public budgets are political instruments that can contribute to agency growth and power. Agencies, for example, allocate resources to provide politically feasible and desirable public goods and services. Any curtailment in service delivery could result in community repercussions. Many budgeteers use this rationale as budget support.

Agencies also tend to be politically sensitive in that their budgets cater to the prevailing political agenda. As a result, political support for budgeted items is often available. In fact, many legislative representatives demand that agencies seek the necessary budgetary requirements to ensure agency survival and service provision for the representative's constituency.

The traditional form of public budgeting also contributes to bureaucratic growth. The annual, fragmented, and incremental budget builds on previous budgeted line items. This approach permits policy to continue indefinitely without excessive scrutiny. Incremental budgeting tells us how much government spends and what it buys, but not why. Therefore, the budget continues to grow and agencies continue to receive additional funding each year—funding that contributes to agency survival.

Some scholars of public budgeting contend that the traditional form of public budgeting is mindless because its line items do not match programs, irrational because it deals with inputs instead of outputs, shortsighted because it covers one year instead of many, fragmented because as a rule only changes are reviewed, and conservative because changes tend to be small and ineffective. As a result, scholars and practitioners have offered several **analytical budgeting** alternatives to remedy the process.

Analytical Budgeting Alternatives   **Management By Objectives (MBO)** is a management tool used to promote a sense of participatory management in the workplace. Although objectives are specified by management, both the manager and worker decide on the performance standards to use in the attainment of objectives. Because a basic budgeting step is to develop objectives, MBO objectives are translated into the budgetary process while also serving as a tool to evaluate employee performance during the appraisal process (see Drucker, 1954).

Another alternative to the traditional budget process is **Planning, Programming, and Budgeting System (PPBS).** This method was used by Robert MacNamara, President Kennedy's Secretary of Defense. It is influenced by cost-benefit analysis and concepts of system analysis. That is, all procedures involved in a task or program are identified, analyzed, and quantified. In sum, PPBS involves the establishment of goals, objectives, program statements, work packages and units, and individual tasks (see Schick 1987).

Zero-Based Budgeting (ZBB), another alternative, originated in the private sector at Texas Instruments. ZBB is supposed to highlight program efficiency while requiring each program to be completely reevaluated each year. The process also involves the use of middle-management decision packages that are ranked according to their need with subsequent funding a result of the prioritization (see Phyrr 1987).

Advantages of Analytical Alternatives   These alternative budget models were developed, in part, to control the exercise of power in public organizations. All management levels are involved in the development of programs and goals. This makes it essential for the executive to review and be involved in agency budgetary activity. The models emphasize and highlight program effectiveness. Thus, ineffective programs can be identified and terminated. They also involve a systematic analysis of alternative courses of action. This makes it possible to identify and implement more efficient and effective operations.

These models place less emphasis on line item incrementalism with all program aspects being consolidated in the budget. In addition, they require a periodic evaluation and possible restructuring of agency goals, establishing communication between administrators and subordinates because of their participatory characteristics, and force managers to determine all financial aspects when developing programs. As a result, bureaucratic growth through budgetary enhancements can be controlled.

Disadvantages of Analytical Alternatives   There are several disadvantages to using these reform approaches. First, time and paperwork increases dramatically in that programs are constantly evaluated and restructured. Second, many departments may devote more time to defending an established program versus looking for better alternatives. Third, the efficient application of the various reforms require training and effort which may be lacking. Fourth, many executives want to see expenditures centralized in the budget instead of piecing together budget items from the various programs. Fifth, because of the complexity involved in the application of the reform models, many executives and legislators do not understand their concepts and support requirements. As a result, the reform models can be mystifying to those outside the agency. Last, their technical nature tended to strengthen the position of the agency in relationship to political executives. For example, program budgeting requires considerably more information about the activities of the agencies than is required for traditional line item budgeting. Since the executive may not have the staff or expertise to fully understand the information, the advantage is still on the side of the agency.

In summary, the budget process is an important base of administrative power. Because budgeting is a crucial process for both government and citizens, it determines to a great extent who will receive what from government, who will pay for it, and what agencies will exist to provide it. Success in the budgetary process can be a means for tabulating the winners and losers in political struggles, with budgetary outcomes indicating trends in the interests and priorities of government.

While agencies gain power from budget activities by attaining the funds to ensure agency continuation, elected political officials also use the budget to demonstrate their power. They do this by showing the public that they can control governmental spending or ensuring the continuation of popular government programs through approval of agency budget requests. While there are some problems associated with budget reform efforts such as ZBB, they can be used to control political power and growth by requiring agencies to establish goals, objectives, and program statements, while providing support for the continuation of programs and policy.

◆ Public Administrators and Public Policy

Introduction   A **public policy** is a general plan of action adopted by a government to solve a social problem (housing, welfare), to counter a threat

Box 6.1

BUDGET REFORM AND POLITICAL REFORM: A RESEARCH EXAMPLE

Researchers have posited the notion that the incremental, line item budgeting approach used at the federal level has inherent problems. It is time-consuming, inefficient, and narrow in scope and vision. That is, agencies devote more time to defending an established program than looking for alternatives. Despite this, budget reform has received little support at the federal level of government.

At the other levels of government, and particularly at the municipal level however, budget reform initiatives are often used. Irene S. Rubin used the case study method (see Chapter 11) to evaluate the interaction of budget reform initiatives and political reform in six American cities. The purpose of her study was to investigate the differences and the similarities between cities in their adoption of budget reform initiatives. Her analysis suggested that the more politically reformed cities (city manager-council, merit appointments), were more likely to adopt budget reform innovations than lesser politically reformed cities (weak mayor, strong departments, patronage appointments).

Rubin concluded from her analysis that the more politically reformed cities adopt budget reforms much more quickly than the intermediate or least reformed cities. The cities also tend to differ in their motivations and use of budget reforms. The more reformed cities adopt budget reforms because they help the city to adapt to environmental threats and demographic shifts in the population. The intermediate cities wait to see what works, what can be easily implemented, and what appears to address the environmental and technical problems they confront without changing the political structure. The least politically reformed cities use budget reforms to address immediate environmental problems but also to help change the political structure towards more central control and policy accountability of the departments. In short, the less politically reformed the city, the more political the budgeting process.

In any case, Rubin's findings are good news for budget makers and budget reformers. Budget reforms are widely used at the municipal level. They are used by officious managers and politicians to solve problems. They also render a larger set of alternatives for elected officials who do not have control over independent departments, and who do not know how to regain the support of a disatisfied public. This raises an interesting research question: What steps would be necessary to initiate budget reform at the federal level of government?

Source: Irene S. Rubin, "Budget Reform & Political Reform: Conclusions from Six Cities." In Frederick S. Lane, *Current Issues in Public Administration,* 5th Edition. New York: St. Martin's Press, 1994, pp. 306–326.

(crime, illegal drugs), or to pursue an objective (tax policy). Public policy is a goal-directed course of action, taken by government, to deal with a public problem. Thus, public policies are choices made by official government bodies and agencies that affect the public interest. Public policy making involves a series of activities that leads ultimately to a policy decision and the implementation of that decision.

Types of Public Policy

Regulatory Policy   A major goal of **regulatory policy** is to maintain order and prohibit behaviors that endanger society. Government accomplishes this goal by restricting citizens, groups, or corporations from engaging in those actions that negatively impact the political, social, or economic order. Examples include attempts to control criminal activities such as robbery, providing traffic ordinances, and prohibiting people from using certain drugs. Another goal of regulatory policy is to protect economic activities and business markets. This is accomplished by prohibiting industry from practicing activities detrimental to the free market (the creation of monopolies, for example). Regulatory policy is also evident in the implementation of laws designed to protect the work place and the environment.

Distributive Policy   **Distributive policy** refers to the provision of benefits to citizens, groups, or corporations. It is also used by the government to encourage certain activities. Tax abatements and farm subsidies to promote economic development, and tax write-offs for homeowners to promote the housing industry are good examples. Distributive policy is also evident when the government promotes the purchase of U.S. savings bonds.

Redistributive Policy   The major purpose of **redistributive policy** is to promote equality. The government redistributes the wealth from one group in our society to another group. This occurs when the government provides benefits directly to citizens through social programs such as welfare. Progressive taxation, where tax rates increase as your income increases, is also a redistributive policy.

The Process   Scholars have identified seven stages in the policy-making process (Wayne et al. 1995). The first, and often the most critical, is **problem recognition.** Before an issue can be considered, it must be recognized as a problem requiring public attention.

The second stage, **agenda setting,** means that the issue is considered by a government body empowered to make decisions to resolve the problem. Interest group strength, political support, and the severity of the issue determine whether the issue reaches the agenda setting stage. There are many problems that our government could address. Not all of these problems are visible political issues. For years and years, toxic wastes were getting into our ecological system, but not many people were paying attention. Now this is a significant political issue. Something happened to put the issue of toxic wastes on the policy agenda.

By **policy agenda,** we mean the range of issues the political system is working on. There is no one official agenda for all of government, so we are not referring to a formal document. Once an issue is on the agenda, the institutions of government will consider different policy solutions. Quick action is not necessarily taken. Being on the agenda can still mean there is a long road for the issue to travel. Congress struggled with immigration reform for years, but only in 1986 did it finally get a bill through. Once one institution takes action, it is likely that the others will be drawn into policy making, too. For example, if Congress passes a bill creating a new program or amending an old one, an administrative agency will probably have to write regulations for it. Somewhere along the line, it is very likely that there will be a court challenge to the way the agency is implementing the program.

Policy formulation, the third stage, involves the shaping of specific proposals addressing the problem. It is important to formulate policy in such a way as to maximize official and public support for the measure, thereby helping to ensure its adoption and implementation.

The fourth stage is **policy adoption.** This is the most political stage of the policy process. It involves bargaining, compromising, and negotiation. Seldom does a proposal emerge from the process as originally formulated. Thus this stage involves compromising and the use of policy negotiating tactics such as pork barrel politics and logrolling.

Policy implementation, the fifth stage, involves putting the policy into action. This is normally the responsibility of an administrative board or agency. Policy implementation is often left to the discretion of the administrative agency with the Congress playing an oversight role.

The sixth stage is **policy evaluation**. After an agency puts a program into operation, it must evaluate the policy's success or failure. Evaluation can take place when an agency assigns staff members to examine how well a program is working. Using social science methodology, the staff will try to design a valid means of collecting data to find out how well the program is working. Outside consultants may be hired to do evaluations if in-house personnel are not available. In a less formal way, evaluation takes place through communication from the field. Those who work in the field offices implementing the program and dealing with the agency's clients on a day-to-day basis will quickly develop strong impressions of what works and what doesn't. They will encourage the headquarters in Washington to change those policies that aren't working well. Change can come from new agency regulations or by asking the Congress to change the statute.

The final stage is **policy termination.** Policies must be terminated when they become dysfunctional or unnecessary. This stage is often neglected by government. As a result, the size, scope, and influence of government grows.

◆ SOURCES OF POLICY INITIATION

Policy making does not always begin as part of the predictable cycle described above. What is it that gets an issue attention in the first place? Roger Cobb and Charles Elder use the concept of triggering devices to explain how some issues get onto the political agenda (Cobb and Elder 1972).

Natural catastrophes can induce policy activity. Floods, earthquakes, and hurricane damage often results in demands for government action to address private and public property damage. Agitation by sectors of the society in response to natural catastrophes also provoke government action. For example, a mine cave-in at Consolidated Coal Company's No. 9 mine resulted in the death of 78 miners who were trapped inside. Agitation by miners led to government action.

Unanticipated human events such as terrorism in the past few years have caused our government and others to take action. For example, the bombing of the World Trade Center in New York and the Oklahoma City bombing led to an evaluation of our antiterrorist policy and citizen demands to review our immigration policy to countries associated with terrorist activity.

Technological advances have produced environmental harm. Our industrial society produces acid rain, creating an environmental problem. As a result, government has taken steps to address it.

Policy is also initiated when groups perceive there is an imbalance in resources between groups. Strikes by unions reflect their members' feelings that they are not sharing fairly in the distribution of resources. This perception often results in the group's call to government to take action to rectify the perceived disparity. The government was asked, for example, to take steps to resolve differences between major league baseball owners and players.

Social change, such as changing patterns of marriage, divorce, and childbearing have led to new policy problems. Government's role in addressing the problems associated with single mothers, individuals seeking abortions, and the call by some groups to recognize the sanctity of same sex marriages, are also examples.

International conflict and the threat of conflict, are also **policy triggering devices.** The events in Bosnia, Somalia, and Haiti, for example, have resulted in demands from Americans and citizens of other nations for our government to take action.

◆ PUBLIC ADMINISTRATORS AS POLICY MAKERS

There are numerous players in the policy-making process including chief executives, the legislature, the courts, interest groups, political parties, and

Box 6.2

CLASSIFICATION OF PUBLIC POLICY ANALYSTS: A RESEARCH EXAMPLE

Public administrators spend a great deal of time analyzing policy in an effort to find ways to improve the operation of their departments and agencies. **Policy analysis** is a disciplined and logical approach to determine what might be done in any given circumstance.

Laurence E. Lynn Jr. believes this approach has four components: identifying the purposes of government actions, identifying and evaluating alternative ways of achieving given purposes, choosing specific designs for governmental actions, and evaluating the capacity of the government to perform certain actions. Lynn found that, because of the growing importance of policy analysis, and because of the time required to perform an effective analysis, many public departments have a staff of qualified policy analysts who perform the work.

But how do you determine the effectiveness of a policy analyst? Arnold Meltsner tried to answer this question by devising a model (see Chapter 11) for classifying analysts. Meltsner ranked analysts as high or low in two separate dimensions: analytical skill—the ability to do competent technical work, and political skill—the ability to function effectively in a government agency and to communicate with public administrators. His model is illustrated in Table 6.1.

Lynn makes an interesting observation about Meltsner's model. He observes that at first glance, one might believe that a public executive would want to hire as many entrepreneurs as possible. Conversely, the executive would not look to hire

TABLE 6.1

POLITICAL SKILL

	High	Low
Analytical Skill		
High	Entrepreneur	Technician
Low	Politician	Pretender

Continued

BOX 6.2 (CONT'D)

**CLASSIFICATION OF PUBLIC POLICY ANALYSTS:
A RESEARCH EXAMPLE**

pretenders. The one-dimensional technicians would be a last resort. In actuality, however, Lynn asserts that many public executives are reluctant to hire entrepreneurs because they may distrust analysts having high political skill despite their technical competency. As a result, the technician who is apt to be comfortable in a role that requires no political aptitude would be a perfect match for executives who are fearful of politically adept analysts.

The Meltsner construct is an excellent example of how scholars create models to help them understand political phenomenon. Students who are interested in studying the political and analytical skills of public policy analysts could use this model as a starting point in their research.

Source: Laurence E. Lynn, Jr., Policy Analysis." In Frederick S. Lane *Current Issues in Public Administration,* 5th Edition. New York: St. Martin's Press, 1994, pp. 336–344.

private citizens. Public administrators are also influential because they often play a role in each stage of the policy-making process.

Administrators are responsible for delivering services to the public. As such, they often identify problems not envisioned by those who enact public policy. Thus, administrators may call for the legislature to place the problem on the political agenda. Since they are the experts in implementation and are closest to the constituency, their demands are often addressed.

Administrators impact policy during the formulation stage because they have the information concerning the substantive impact of the policy. They also have the expertise to determine how the policy can be changed to meet the needs of the majority of the possible policy beneficiaries. Their knowledge and advice is also called on during the adoption stage of policy making.

Administrators most impact policy development during the implementation stage. Because legislation or executive orders establishing policy are normally vague, administrators often specify policy as they implement it. Legislative bodies are often understaffed and without the necessary expertise to comprehend all facets of program needs. Therefore, they often delegate policy-making tasks to the administrative agencies with the required expertise. Thus, administrators not only implement policy as an official part of their daily operation, they also put the finishing touches on the policy itself.

The burden of securing compliance with public policies also rests primarily with administrators. They strive to shape, alter, or use the values people find important when making choices. They seek to limit the acceptable choices by attaching penalties to undesired alternatives and rewards or benefits to desired alternatives. They also try to interpret and administer policies in ways designed to facilitate compliance with their requirements.

Administrators are also active during the policy evaluation stage. They take steps, for example, to determine the substantive impact of policy. They also maintain the records that are reviewed by congressional oversight committees and other groups evaluating policy. As such, they possess and control the evidence of the policy's impact.

By gaining the support of their clientele, administrators can eventually impact the termination phase of the policy-making process. Agencies often build a power base of constituents who are convinced that they need the service offered by the agency. By calling forth that support, the agency may convince legislators that the program is valuable and should be continued.

Administrators can also influence policy through the processes of rule making, adjudication, and law enforcement. In their quasi-legislative rule-making capacity, an agency issues rules with the force of law that apply to all persons under their jurisdiction. Adjudication is a quasi-judicial process where agencies charge individual's suspected of violating a rule and try them. If violations are found, the agency imposes sanctions on the guilty party.

❖ THE HOW OF PUBLIC ADMINISTRATION

◆ INTRODUCTION

Whether the purpose of government is to maintain order through regulatory policy, distribute public goods and services through distributive policy, or provide benefits and entitlements through redistributive policy, it is often accomplished because of the decisions made by public administrators. Thus, public administration students need to be familiar with the complexities and workings of public organizations so they can understand how administrative decisions are made.

In this section we will examine the public decision-making process. Specifically, we will spend time describing the bureaucratic and systems approaches. Then we will look at some other approaches public administrators use when rendering administrative decisions.

◆ THE BUREAUCRATIC APPROACH

The bureaucratic model evolved from theories espoused by Max Weber. It is used by political scholars to analyze the activities of government agencies and to identify phenomena associated with large-scale complex organizations.

Characteristics of the Bureaucratic Model According to the bureaucratic model, government agencies are characterized by several pivotal structural attributes. First, there is a well-defined and integral chain of command that has each subordinate reporting to one superior. The number of subordinates is kept to a small number to enhance the unity of command.

Second, departments below the chief executive are separated by function and by processes or tasks. This divides the work flow so that no employee or work unit handles a complete operation. The positions in these departments are called **line positions**. Employees in line positions provide the agency's services.

Third, there is a system of procedures and rules for dealing with all contingencies. This reinforces the detachment of each work unit or person and thus supports the unity of command.

Fourth, relations between organization members and between them and their clients are formal and impersonal. Services are delivered without bias.

Last, in addition to the line positions, **staff positions** exist to help the chief executive control the total system. Examples include internal auditors, budget experts, and functions not directly involved in the provision of agency services. As such, staff positions are considered as advisory only and outside the chain of command.

Advantages of the Bureaucratic Model There are several advantages to using a bureaucratic form of organization in the public sector. The decisive reason for the advance of bureaucratic organizations is its structural superiority over any other form of organization. The bureaucratic organization provides enhanced precision, speed, effectiveness, and efficiency. These advantages occur because administrative functions are specialized according to objective considerations, and workers operate in accordance with clear rules.

These advantages supposedly enhance the decision-making process because decisions are made rationally and by administrators trained in the specifics of the organization who are found at the upper point of the hierarchy. In addition, implementation and adherence to the rules are enhanced because of a limited span of control and reduced hierarchical layering of functions.

Disadvantages of the Bureaucratic Model There are also some disadvantages associated with the bureaucratic model. As discussed, the model focuses on the internal aspects of the bureaucracy such as hierarchy, specialization, and span of control. As such, the model is inadequate because it ignores the impact of social factors and does not attempt to understand the bureaucracy's political role.

Proponents of the bureaucratic model argue that organizations could improve productivity if they maintained a reduced span of control by minimalizing the number of subordinates who reported to a superior. They have asserted that this would improve supervision and the communication of decisions. At the same time they stress that performance and communication would be further improved if the number of layers in the hierarchy were minimized. For any given number of people in a bureaucracy, reducing the span of control will actually increase the number of layers in the hierarchy, and vice versa. Thus, these principles of the bureaucratic organization are contradictory.

◆ THE SYSTEMS APPROACH

During the 1940s and 1950s, social scientists, scholars, and practitioners in the field of human resource management began to use systems analysis to analyze human behavior. They wanted to formulate a generalized scientific language and methodology they could use to define a set of principles that were valid for all organization systems regardless of the nature of their component elements and the relations between them. Identifying principles of scientific explanation common to all types of systems would make it possible to use the knowledge from highly understood systems to explore less understood systems.

Systems theory views an organization as a complex set of dynamically intertwined and interconnected elements. The system includes inputs, processes, outputs, feedback loops, negative entropy, equilibrium amongst the systemic components, and the environment in which the system operates. A change in any element of the system inevitably causes changes in its other elements. The interconnections tend to be complex, dynamic, and sometimes unknown. Thus when management makes decisions involving one organizational element, unanticipated impacts can occur throughout the organization. Systems organization theorists study interconnections, frequently using organizational decision processes and information and control systems as their focal points for analysis. Whereas bureaucratic organization theory tends to be one dimensional and somewhat simplistic, systems theory tends to be multidimensional and complex in its assumptions about organizational causal relationships. The bureaucratic model viewed organizations as static structures while the systems school sees organizations as dynamic processes of interactions among organizational elements. Thus, organizations are adaptive systems that must adjust to changes in their environment if they are to survive.

Effective application of systems theory by administrators is valuable in that it can allow them to obtain information that will help them reach decisions when implementing policy. By knowing the players, the inputs, the throughput processes, and interactions, the administrator can structure the decision-making process and obtain direction in the implementation of policy. This can be useful should the administrator have to apply some measure of discretion when implementing the policy. As such, systems theory and its application in administration can encourage a concern with normative issues that involve individual rights, representation, and administrative discretion. Systems theory can be used to enhance change, democratic control, and enhance the administrator's capability to make ethical decisions during policy implementation.

While the systems approach does alert the administrator to the significant interrelationships of the various participants in the policy process, its usefulness is somewhat limited by its highly generalized nature. It fails to contribute enough insight into and explanation of how decisions are arrived at and policies made within the decision-making structures themselves. Therefore, it is important that one be aware of other constructs such as the rational, incremental, and mixed-scanning models.

◆ THE RATIONAL APPROACH

The **rational** model of decision making is a widely accepted theory. It usually includes several elements. First, decision makers and administrators are confronted with a given problem that can be separated from other problems or at least considered meaningfully in comparison with them. Second, the goals, values, or objectives that guide decision makers are clarified and ranked according to their importance. Third, the various alternatives for dealing with the problem are examined. Fourth, the cost and benefits resulting from the selection of each alternative are investigated. Fifth, each alternative, and its consequences, are compared with the other alternatives. Last, decision makers choose the alternative that maximizes the attainment of their goals, values, or objectives.

The rational construct can be useful to administrators because it helps them to make correct cost-benefit comparisons of alternatives and make more accurate predictions of the consequences of each alternative. The rational model is used extensively by public agencies because it's considered the optimal method for implementing the policies of legislatures and chief executives. In short, the rational model stresses the need to maximize utility, clearly define problems, weigh costs and benefits of decision options, select the best approach, and evaluate the decision.

As with any model, however, there are several criticisms of rational decision making. Decision makers are not always faced with concrete, clearly defined problems. Thus, decision makers must identify and specifically define the problems they face prior to making the decision. Because there are many factors that impact a problem, this process can be difficult. A second criticism holds that the rational model is unrealistic in the demands it makes on the decision maker. As discussed above, the model assumes that there is enough information about the alternatives for dealing with a problem and, as a result, the decision maker will be able to accurately predict the costs and benefits of each alternative while comparing the alternatives. This process requires sufficient time, knowledge of, access to all the information, and the capability to evaluate all relevant factors. There is also the problem of sunk costs. Previous decisions and commitments and investments in existing programs may eliminate many alternatives from consideration in the decision process. Thus, the rational model may be an incomplete and unbalanced guide for public administrators.

◆ THE INCREMENTAL APPROACH

The **incremental** theory of decision making avoids many of the problems associated with rationalism. Incrementalism is more descriptive of the way in which leaders actually make decisions. It can be summarized in the following manner. The selection of goals or objectives and the empirical analysis of the action needed to attain them are closely intertwined with one another. The decision maker only considers some of the alternatives for dealing with a problem, and these will differ only incrementally from existing policies. For each alternative, only a limited number of important consequences are evaluated. The problem confronting the decision maker is continually redefined; that is, incrementalism allows for countless ends-means and means-ends adjustments that have the effect of making the problem more manageable. There is no single decision or right solution for a problem. Thus, incremental decision making is essentially remedial in that it is geared more to the correction of present problems versus the promotion of future social goals (Lindbloom 1978).

Incrementalism can be especially useful to public administrators who are burdened with exhaustive schedules and agendas. That is, incrementalism is realistic because it recognizes that decision makers lack the time, knowledge, and other resources needed to engage in comprehensive analysis of all alternative solutions to existing problems. Additionally, people are essentially pragmatic, seeking not always the single best way to deal with a problem but something that will work, or something that will be **satisficing,** that is, meeting the decision maker's minimum standard of satisfaction. A practical application of incrementalism in the public sector is evident in the budget-making process.

◆ THE MIXED-SCANNING APPROACH

Etzioni agrees with the criticism of the rational theory but suggests there are also some shortcomings in the incremental theory (Etzioni 1978). For instance, decisions made by incrementalists often reflect the interests of the most powerful and organized interests in the organization, while the interests of others may be neglected. Moreover, by focusing on the short run and seeking only limited variations in current policies, incrementalism may neglect the organization's social needs. Thus, Etzioni introduced the mixed-scanning theory of decision making.

Mixed-scanning combines both rational and incremental decision processes. It provides for rational decision- and policy-making processes which establish the basic policy goals and direction. Incrementalism is then applied so that decisions can be reached and effectively implemented. Mixed scanning also allows the decision maker to use the rational or incremental approach, depending on the situation. In some instances, incrementalism will be adequate, while in others, a more thorough approach along rational lines will be needed.

Public administrators can use the mixed-scanning approach in the decision-making process by regularly scanning the entire organization environment. So long as no major issue appears, decisions can be made on a routine, incremental basis. However, when an important problem does occur, a second level of analysis should take place focusing on overall goals. Mixed-scanning can also be used to address problems and as a basis for program development. As a practical example, suppose we want to create a program to reduce traffic congestion in the community. The rationalistic approach would seek an exhaustive survey of traffic conditions through detailed observations and by scheduling reviews of the entire community as often as possible. This would yield much data, would be costly to analyze, and would perhaps overwhelm the capabilities of the agency. However, an incremental approach may only focus on those areas in which there were past traffic control problems. As a result, it may miss those areas that deserved attention if traffic control problems arise.

A mixed-scanning strategy would include elements of both approaches by first using an information-gathering device that covered the entire community, but not in great detail, and a second device that would zero in on those areas revealed by the first device as requiring in-depth examination. While mixed-scanning might miss areas in which only a detailed device could reveal trouble, it is less likely than incrementalism to miss obvious trouble spots in unfamiliar areas.

❖ ADMINISTRATIVE ETHICS: A FERTILE FIELD FOR RESEARCH

Administrative agencies continue to grow and expand their power. Reasons posited for this phenomenon include the increased use of discretion, expanded involvement in the functions of the three branches of government, and intensification of agency solidarity through alliance formation and unionization.

While some believe this growth is necessary to balance the increased fragmentation of our political system (Meier 1993, 1–7), others believe it could lead to the abuse of several aims of our Constitution, such as the separation of powers (Butler et al. 1984, 426). This latter belief suggests an interesting question: Is there a conflict between the basic aims of constitutional government and the goals and methods of modern public administrators?

◆ WHAT ARE THE STANDARDS OF AMERICAN BUREAUCRATIC LEADERS?

Before we answer this question we want to spend some time analyzing the professional standards and ideals of our public administrative leaders. The values of civil servants are an important aspect of administrative responsibility and are a basis for much concern and interest in the professionalism of the public sector. It was asserted, for example, that public administrators need to periodically perform an "inner check" to help them recognize and observe the standards and ideals of their profession (Gaus 1936).

But what are the professional standards and ideals of American civil servants? Opinions vary on a continuum from those who view civil servants as "power-mad, undemocratic minions of satanic, un-American forces," to those who view them as "all-benevolent, responsive servants of the public, possessing the wisdom of Plato's philosopher-kings." The answer, of course, lies somewhere between the two extremes (Hill and Hebert 1979, 423).

One scholar of public administration surveyed a sample of high-level federal bureaucrats to determine their attitude about the democratic ideals of limited government, the right to counsel, and no self-incrimination (McClosky 1964). The results created considerable controversy because many of the respondents (a little over 25 percent) did not embrace the ideals (Hill and Herbert 1979, 423).

Some critics, however, were not convinced that the results meant that public administrators held undemocratic attitudes and thus should be restrained so that they did not abuse the public's civil liberties (Hill and Hebert 1979, 424). As support, they argued that the results were similar to those of a comparable survey completed earlier by the public. They also believed the survey statements described abstract theoretical possibilities versus actual situations that were related to the work accomplished by most civil servants. Last, they asserted that public administrators are constrained by a number of structural and legal rules when making and implementing decisions that concern the public.

Many scholars agree that there is an excess of structural and legal rules that can work to constrain public administrators. The rules may be core rules which represent the core technology of the agency and are the standard and essential rules used to process clients according to agency procedures. Examples include arrest and booking procedures in police departments and welfare eligibility criteria. There are also lesser rules that are often ignored by the administrator as a way to conserve time so that the overall agency mission can be accomplished. The willingness not to pursue speeders who are within 5 miles-per-hour of the speed limit is an example (Prottas 1979, 92–93). However, instead of constraining the public administrator and negating the impact of the questionnaire results discussed above, this excess of rules can contribute to the use of discretion which can result in the withholding of benefits (Prottas 1979, 99).

Public administrators can also become obsessed with departmental decisions and precedents despite the injustice or hardship they may cause in individual cases. As a result, they often develop an indifference towards the feelings of clients. This enthusiasm for regulations and formal procedure coupled with an employee's fixation on his or her department leads first to an inability to consider the government as a whole. Second, it inhibits the employee's ability to recognize the relations between the governors and the governed which is an essential part of the democratic process (Robson 1964). Thus, while some believe that bureaucratic decision making is limited by the regulatory demands of the agency, others see a quite different picture.

So far we have presented a negative outlook towards the values of the bureaucracy. This is not to be construed as an effort to delineate the bureaucracy as an unnecessary part of the public sector. After all, as far back as Woodrow Wilson, the administrative sector was recognized as an important factor to support the functions of the executive branch, alleviate the onus of a crowded docket on the judicial branch, and implement the laws initiated by the legislative branch. Additionally, there are scholars and analysts who believe that many agencies are client centered, believe in client participation, and are representative of the citizenry (Waldo 1955, 196). Still others argue that the bureaucracy protects constitutionalism because of its representativeness (Long 1954). Last, while confirming the importance and need of the bureaucracy, some believe that administrative agencies can be controlled through various bureaucratic monitoring mechanisms, thus somewhat sterilizing the negative consequences of their activity. So, the problem is not the reduction of administrative power but its control.

◆ WHAT SHOULD BE THE PROFESSIONAL STANDARDS AND IDEALS OF PUBLIC ADMINISTRATORS?

Unfortunately, no response to this question will be accepted without significant retort. Some will ask, whose values are we talking about? Or, others will label identified values as being out of date. After all, the framework in which someone's values are judged differs from one culture to the next and from one era to the next (Gardner 1990, 3).

However, many treatments of the question suggest that democratic norms are important. That is, a slate of standards based on the democratic principles espoused in our Constitution. But what are these democratic norms, and how can they be applied to the administrative sector? A noted scholar of public administration wrote that a workable democracy can be achieved through the interaction of leaders in strategic positions of influence who are forced by the complexity of interests involved in a decision-making situation to pay attention to all the interests in the society (Redford 1969, 199–200). Within this workable democracy, administrators should adhere to three values that collectively yield a democratic morality. First, individual realization involves the protection of men from restraints imposed by others, the establishment of favorable conditions for individual development, and the creation of social mechanisms that continuously operate for humane purposes. Second, the equality of man asserts that all men have worth deserving social recognition. Third, participation is the notion that liberty only exists through involvement either in decision making or in control of leaders who make the decisions (Redford 1969, 9–22). Thus, a democratic morality posits an open society where there is access to information, access to forums of decision, an ability to open any issue to public discussion, an ability to assert one's claims without fear of retaliation, and consideration of all asserted claims as a precondition for the attainment of a society dedicated to the people (Redford 1969, 8). In short, a democratic administration is a method of carrying on the administrative process in such a way as to encourage participation in the decision-making process by those affected by the decision (Lorch 1980, 100).

Democratic morality also rejects the right of any elite within the public sector to impose its will on the people. Therefore, it is acceptable for medical experts to inform the public on the hazards of smoking, for example, but not acceptable for the experts to initiate a rule that bans smoking (Redford 1969, 32). Thus, an essential role and value of public administrators is to be responsive to the populace without imposing on their basic constitutional rights.

Others believe that because of the many immoral actions that have characterized our past behavior and because we set demanding moral standards of political behavior while morally judging people who make moral judgements, we must search for morality in the Constitution (Goldwin 1979, 2). Therefore, if there is to be political or democratic morality, then its premise must be established so that there is a precedence for judging the morality of the public sector, that premise being our Constitution.

But we often indulge ourselves in excesses of morality. Such self-indulgence and excess have the same impact as do all other forms of extremism. Therefore, the framers of the Constitution believing that political liberty unavoidably involves some immorality at the expense of the public and that the American people are unrelenting moral judges, penned the Constitution so that the abuses of immorality could be controlled. The objective was to make governmental representatives consistent with the American character and consistent with the principles of liberty and equality of rights (Goldwin 1979, 6). Thus, the framers did not attempt to recast the moral fiber of Americans but to accept them for what they were. They wanted to lead the populace to habits of right action in order not only to control the tendency towards self-interest and self-advancement but to turn them to the benefit of the populace (Goldwin 1979, 10).

In sum, there are several criteria we can use to judge the bureaucracy in a democratic setting and as a basis for establishing professional standards and ideals of American civil servants. First, public administrators must be responsive to the needs of the citizenry without imposing on basic constitutional rights. Second, administrative directors must be alert to the need for individual development while creating social mechanisms that exist for humane purposes. Third, the administrative sector must recognize the equality of man through equal representation. Fourth, administrators should be open to public input to ensure all citizens have an opportunity to participate in decisions that impact them. Fifth, public administrators must adhere to the principles set forth in the Constitution, which was written to delineate the proper functions of the government.

◆ IS THERE A CONFLICT BETWEEN THE CONSTITUTION AND THE BUREAUCRACY?

The basic aims of constitutionalism were to establish a constitutional government, to establish constitutional law, and to restrict any one branch of government from the arbitrary exercise of governmental power. The purpose of constitutional law is to say what governmental branches may or may not do (Lorch 1980, 61). Constitutional government implies a government that is regulated by laws which control and limit the exercise of political power (Woll 1977, 1).

Under constitutionalism there were several additional principles that were established. First, due process of law as provided in the Fifth and Fourteenth Amendments. This process can be, and is, used to evaluate administrative action. The constitutional requirement of due process demands that the parties under jurisdiction of administrative agencies be fairly notified no matter what statutes may say concerning time limits or any other facet of law. Fairness is measured by reason and it is a requirement that stands above statute (Lorch 1980, 128). Second, the concept of separation of powers stresses the need for the branches of the government to be separate and distinct entities so that no one branch can become all powerful (Federalist Papers 47, 48, and 51 in Woll 1977, 15–19). Third, power must not be delegated. Congress was established to represent the people, who in theory have delegated power to Congress to represent them. The Congress, in turn, is supposedly not permitted to redelegate that delegation without the approval of the people (Lorch 1980, 79–80).

Therefore, through the establishment of courts, Congress, and an executive branch, the Constitution attempted to create a system of checks and balances where separate and distinct governmental branches oversee the activities of the other branches to ensure that the basic rights of the people are protected. The Congress, however, is often slow in administering to clients, is unable to compete with administrative agencies as an innovator because of a lack of specialization and technique, is apt to be inefficient in providing quick and consistent action, and is not adept at follow-up to ensure laws and edicts are implemented. Consequently, public administrators have assumed much of its powers. Additionally, Congress has delegated much legislative and judicial power to administrative agencies. The branches of government do not have the time, knowledge, or ability to devise detailed rules for the many areas in which the law operates (Lorch 1980, 79). Last, the executive branch is also delegating more and more responsibility to the bureaucracy for reasons similar to those discussed above. As a result, the administrative arm of our government is assuming more power at the expense of the three branches of government. We can no longer dismiss the bureaucracy as simply a part of the executive branch of the government (Woll 1977, 6). In fact, it can be argued that they have emerged as a fourth branch of government (Meier 1993, 1–7).

These actions have resulted in expansive government and bureaucracies that are quasi-independent of legislative restriction. The delegation of quasi-legislative and judicial power to administrative agencies has blurred the distinction between the three constitutional branches of government. There is no longer as distinct a separation of power as embodied in the Constitution. Our traditional image of constitutional government is now outdated.

It is important to note, however, that the separation of powers has never been interpreted to mean complete or total separation. Instead, what we have is separated institutions sharing power. For example, administrators were always asked by legislatures to perform various discretionary duties, were given the job of making rules, were asked to apply or enforce certain laws, and were given the approval to fill in the details of statutes. This is not a new phenomenon nor is it avoidable. What is new is the magnitude of the overlap and the extent of delegation of power to this new "fourth branch" of government.

There exists today some tension between the aims of constitutional government and the aims and methods of modern public administrators. Because of the factors enumerated above, some arbitrary action occurs within administrative agencies and their activities have become difficult to control. Additionally, courts will seldom try to impose consistent standards on the rule-making function of agencies except those few required by statutes (Lorch 1980, 158). One important reason for this reluctance is that the courts recognize that without administrative law their agendas would be heavily burdened.

◆ CONCLUSIONS

Although there appears to be a conflict between the aims of the Constitution and those of administrative agencies, without an in-depth study it is impossible to say that public administrators do not hold values nor act in an ethical way. The existence of administrative agencies, law, and courts tend to enhance the due process of law concept in that they relieve much pressure from overburdened courts and as a result enhance one's chances of obtaining judicial relief. Agencies do have mechanisms in place to provide for human needs and services. They have written and implemented rules to enhance equal representation within the sector. They have also provided ways that citizens, through interest groups and public forums, can participate in the administrative decision-making process. Last, while some departure from basic constitutional aims, such as the separation of powers and delegation of powers concepts, may have occurred, many agree that it is a necessary departure if our government is to be truly representative of the people.

In sum, there are probably some public administrators who symbolize the "power-mad, undemocratic minions of satanic, un-American forces." There are, however, probably many more who are responsive public servants with values that are consistent with the American character and with the principles of liberty and equality of rights.

❖ SUMMARY

This chapter traced the historical development of the American public administrative state. We spent time discussing the early years and the impact Washington and Adams had on the staffing of the American bureaucracy. We also looked at the influence that Jefferson and Jackson and their notion of participatory democracy had on public administration. The influence of the Progressive movement in American government and Weber's bureaucratic structure concluded our discussion about the "who" of public administration.

Much time was also devoted to the functions, or the "what," of public administration. Specifically we talked about the personnel function and its impact on public managers. We also discussed the budget process as a source of administrative power. Our discussion evolved into an analysis of some analytical budgeting alternatives that could address the budget function as a power base. This section ended with a succinct presentation of public administration and public policy. We talked about the types of public policy, the process of making policy, sources of policy initiation, and public administrators as policy makers.

The "how" of public administration included a discussion about several approaches that are used to fulfill the functions of the administrative state. We examined, for example, the bureaucratic approach, systems analysis, rational decision making, an incremental approach to making decisions, and the mixed-scanning approach used by some administrators to render decisions.

The chapter concluded with a discussion of administrative ethics and serving the public interest. As such we talked about the standards and ideals of public administrators. We also analyzed the question, is there a conflict between the basic aims of constitutional government and the goals and methods of modern public administrators?

We said that while there appears to be a conflict between the aims of the Constitution and those of administrative agencies, it is difficult to conclude that public administrators do not act in an ethical way. After all, the existence of administrative agencies, law, and courts tend to enhance the due process of law concept. In addition, agencies have written and implemented rules to enhance service provision and to enhance equal representation within the sector. They have also provided ways that citizens, through interest groups and public forums, can participate in the administrative decision-making process.

❖ KEY TERMS

administrative ethics
adverse personnel actions
agenda setting
analytical budgeting
bureaucracy
Civil Service Reform Act (CRSA)
  of 1978
compensation plans
distributive policy
hierarchy
incremental decision making
line positions
Management By Objectives (MBO)
mixed-scanning
participatory democracy
Planning, Programming, and
  Budgeting System(PPBS)
policy analysis

policy adoption
policy agenda
policy evaluation
policy formulation
policy implementation
policy termination
policy triggering devices
position classification
problem recognition
Progressive movement
public administration
public policy
rational decision making
redistributive policy
regulatory policy
satisficing
staff positions
Zero-Based Budgeting (ZBB)

❖ EXERCISES

1. Discuss the evolution of American public administration.

2. Discuss the impact the Civil Service Reform Act of 1978 had on the activities of public administrators.

3. Discuss the budget process as a source of administrative power.

4. Discuss the various analytical budgeting alternatives to include advantages and disadvantages.

5. Discuss the stages of policy and how public administrators are key actors at each stage.

6. Compare and contrast the various approaches public administrators use to analyze policy and make decisions.

7. Some scholars believe there is a conflict between constitutionalism and the aims of public administrators. Debate this belief.

❖ SUGGESTED READINGS

Butler, Sanera, and Weinrod. *Mandate For Leadership II*. Washington, D.C.: The Heritage Foundation, 1984.

Cobb, Roger W., and Charles D. Elder. *Participation in American Politics: The Dynamics of Agenda Building.* Boston: Allyn and Bacon, 1972.

Drucker, Peter F. "Management by Objectives and Self Control." In *Classics of Organizational Behavior*, ed. Walter E. Natemeyer. Oak Park IL: Moore Publishing, 1978.

Etzioni, Amatai. "Two Approaches to Organization Analysis: A Critique and a Suggestion." In Jay M. Shafritz and Philip W. Whitbeck, *Classics of Public Administration*, 2nd ed. Oak Park, IL: Moore Publishing, 1978.

Gardner, John. *On Leadership.* New York: Free Press, 1990.

Gardner, John W. *Attributes and Contexts.* Washington, D.C.: Independent Sector, 1987.

Gaus, John M. "The Responsibility of Public Administration." In *The Frontiers of Public Administration.* Chicago: University of Chicago Press, 1936, pp. 39–40. Quoted in Larry B. Hill and F. Ted Hebert, *Essentials of Public Administration.* North Scituate, MA: Duxbury Press, 1979.

Gerth, Hans H. *From Max Weber: Essays in Sociology.* London: Oxford University Press, 1973.

Goldwin, Robert A. "Of Men and Angels: A Search for Morality in the Constitution." In *The Moral Foundations of the American Republic*, 2nd ed., ed. Robert H. Horwitz. Charlottesville, VA: University Press of Virginia, 1979.

Goodnow, Frank J. "Politics and Administration." In Jay M. Shafritz and Albert C. Hyde, *Classics of Public Administration*, 2nd ed. Chicago: Dorsey Press, 1987, pp. 26–29.

Hill, Larry B., and F. Ted Hebert. *Essentials of Public Administration.* North Scituate, MA: Duxbury Press, 1979.

Horowitz, Donald L. *The Courts and Social Policy.* Washington, D.C.: The Brookings Institute, 1977.

Lane, Frederick S. *Current Issues in Public Administration*, 5th ed. New York: St. Martin's Press, 1994.

Lindbloom, Charles E. "The Science of Muddling Through." In Jay M. Shafritz and Albert C. Hyde, *Classics of Public Administration*, 2nd ed. Chicago: Dorsey Press, 1987, pp. 299–318.

Lorch, Robert S. *Democratic Process and Administrative Law.* Detroit: Wayne State University Press, 1980.

Long, Norton E. "Public Policy and Administration: The Goals of Rationality and Responsibility." *Public Administration Review* 14 (winter, 1954): 22. Quoted in Delbert Taebel, *The Bureaucracy and Democratic Theory*, unpublished.

Lynn, Laurence E., Jr. "Policy Analysis." In Frederick S. Lane *Current Issues in Public Administration*, 5th ed. New York: St. Martin's Press, 1994, pp. 336–44.

McClosky, Herbert. "Consensus and Ideology in American Politics." *American Political Science Review* 58 (June 1964): 361–82. In Larry B. Hill and F. Ted Hebert, *Essentials of Public Administration.* North Scituate, MA: Duxbury Press, 1979.

Meier, Kenneth J. *Politics and the Bureaucracy: Policymaking in the Fourth Branch of Government,* 3rd ed. Belmont, CA: Wadsworth, 1993.

Meltsner, Arnold. *Policy Analysts in the Bureaucracy.* Berkeley: University of California Press, 1976.

Prottas, Jeffrey Manditch. *People-Processing.* Lexington, MA: Lexington Books, 1979.

Phyrr, Peter A. "The Zero-Base Approach to Government Budgeting." In Jay M. Shafritz and Albert C. Hyde, *Classics of Public Administration,* 2nd ed. Chicago: Dorsey Press, 1987, pp. 495–505.

Redford, Emmette S. *Democracy in the Administrative State.* New York: Oxford University Press, 1969.

Robson, William A. *The Governors and the Governed.* Baton Rouge, LA: Louisiana State University Press, 1964, p. 18. In Larry B. Hill and F. Ted Hebert, *Essentials of Public Administration.* North Scituate, MA: Duxbury Press, 1979.

Rourke, Francis E. *Bureaucracy, Politics, and Public Policy.* Boston: Little, Brown, 1969.

Rubin, Irene S. "Budget Reform and Political Reform: Conclusions from Six Cities." In Frederick S. Lane *Current Issues in Public Administration,* 5th ed. New York: St. Martin's Press, 1994, pp. 306–26.

Schick, Allen. "The Road to PPB: The Stages of Budget Reform." In Jay M. Shafritz and Albert C. Hyde, *Classics of Public Administration,* 2nd ed. Chicago: Dorsey Press, 1987, pp. 299–318.

Sylva, Ronald D. *Public Personnel Administration.* Belmont, CA: Wadsworth, 1994.

Waldo, Dwight. *The Study of Public Administration.* New York: Random House, 1955.

Wayne, Stephen J., G. Calvin Mackenzie, David M. O'Brien, and Richard L. Cole. *The Politics of American Government.* New York: St. Martin's Press, 1995.

Wildavski, Aaron. *The Politics of the Budgetary Process,* 4th ed. Boston: Little, Brown, 1984.

Wilson, Woodrow. "The Study of Administration." In Jay M. Shafritz and Albert C. Hyde. *Classics of Public Administration,* 2nd ed. Chicago: Dorsey Press, 1987, pp. 10–25.

Woll, Peter. *American Bureaucracy,* 2nd ed. New York: W.W. Norton, 1977.

COMPARATIVE POLITICS

❖ INTRODUCTION

The comparative politics subfield is the broadest and most challenging in political science. It includes analysis of all the world's political systems in a comparative way. The field is more than immense however. There is little agreement about how to study politics comparatively. This results from both the size of the task and the complex issues associated with comparing political systems.

Nevertheless, the field is of great interest and importance to political scientists. The comparative perspective allows us to develop more general theories about politics and government (remember that one goal of scientific knowledge is generalization). It also helps us understand the multitude of differences in the world community. Finally, the questions posed in comparative politics are fundamental to the study of politics. Why are some political systems free and democratic while others tyrannize and torture their own people? In short, the field provides an opportunity to scientifically examine the fundamental political question, "which government is best (or at least better)?"

An understanding of this chapter will enable you to:

1. Describe the subfield of comparative politics.
2. Discuss some different approaches to the study of comparative politics.
3. Explain some key concepts and questions involved in studying politics comparatively.

❖ THE STUDY OF COMPARATIVE POLITICS

Comparative politics traces its origins to Aristotle's comparison of the Greek city-states. As a subfield of political science however, it emerged more recently during the two decades between World War I and World War II. American political scientists began studying the political systems of Europe basically to understand how different countries, with different kinds of governments and ideologies, operated. Students of European politics were principally concerned with questions involving the advantages and disadvantages of presidential and parliamentary types of governments, whether government should adopt a unitary or federal structure (remember our discussion of federalism in Chapter 5.), and the origins, character, and significance of democratic, socialist, and other authoritarian governments.

Following World War II the world changed again. One by one, colonies in Africa and Asia moved toward independence from the colonial powers. The Cuban revolution and the rise of Castro threatened American domination in the western hemisphere. Scholars began to expand the horizons of the comparative subfield to include the emerging political systems of what we now call the Third World. This new focus, beyond the traditional emphasis on the European-American confines, created new questions, concepts, and methodologies in the field.

The new focus led students of comparative politics to broaden their horizons. As a result, they had to search for new concepts and theories to help explain the great diversity of political systems in the world. They also began to look more carefully at the possibility that political systems may not be unique in themselves.

This new perspective led to a more systematic approach to the study of comparative politics. Scholars such as Seymour Martin Lipset (1959), Gabriel Almond and James Coleman (1960), and Samuel Huntington (1968) advanced controversial approaches to study how political systems develop. Lipset saw democracy as the culmination of the modernization process. Almond proposed a set of functions that we could use to compare nations at different levels of development. Huntington devised a theory that attempted to explain not only how political systems develop, but how they decay as well. The "action" in the subfield shifted away from Europe. Scholars began to apply these new frameworks to the study of politics in the Third World.

By the end of the 1960s, the discipline changed yet again. With the world stuck in the ideological Cold War between the East and West, Marxist theorists challenged the earlier theories about economic and political development. The social and economic ills of the Third World came from its dependence on the major industrialized nations of the First World. Capitalist and Marxist ideology clashed even in the halls of the world's major universities. The result was disunity in the subfield. Instead of seaching for ways to systematically compare developed and undeveloped political systems, researchers retreated to their respective area specialities. Latin American enthusiasts studied Latin America. Those interested in communism studied communist countries. There was little attempt to compare European nations with those in Africa.

Today, the subfield remains in a state of intellectual disarray. Many scholars continue to seek a new consensus on how to study politics comparatively. Others have begun to question whether meaningful theoretical comparisons can be made (Wiarda 1985). Still others remain locked in ideological competition.

The challenges of the subfield will intensify as we approach the end of the twentieth century. We are experiencing a global transformation at least as significant as the one following the end of World War II. The collapse of the Soviet Union and the Soviet bloc, the move toward a market economy in China, and the democratic experiments in nations as different as Russia, the Phillipines, and Brazil create both challenges and opportunities to the systematic study of comparative politics.

The subfield of comparative politics is a difficult one to describe. The transformations described above indicate the lack of agreement over both what and how we should study politics comparatively. We won't even attempt to settle the conflict. What we will do is lay out a few major issues in comparative politics. Hopefully, this will clarify why the subfield is so complex.

❖ APPROACHES TO THE STUDY OF COMPARATIVE POLITICS

We have already introduced you to the three basic approaches to the study of politics—traditional, behavioral, and postbehavioral. Scholars of different persuasions have also used each to study comparative politics. However, in the comparative politics subfield, each approach has some unique implications. These implications involve more than just how we study politics, but include what we study as well.

Historically, as in the study of all politics, the traditional approach to comparative politics liberally combined fact and value to develop theories of the political process. In the twentieth century, the traditional orientation shifted its focus to study the history, institutions, and processes of individual countries—the "cases." These **case studies** analyzed the structure of the state, elections, political parties, and even interest groups. They attempted to explain how the political systems of individual countries worked. Importantly, they described institutions without comparing them except by pointing out the contrast between democracy and authoritarian regimes and contrasting parliamentary and presidential forms of government.

The underlying assumption of the traditional method was that each nation's politics is unique. The differing national experiences, cultures, and traditions made theoretical comparisons among countries a fruitless task. Unfortunately, this belief made the traditional approach "noncomparative, descriptive, parochial and static" (Macridis 1955). Traditional students of comparative politics learned a great deal about individual countries but were unable to help us understand politics more generally in other than anecdotal ways.

The traditional approach had other weaknesses as well. In studying individual countries, scholars focused on the historical evolution of political institutions. For example, some studies traced the evolution of the British Parliament and the consequent decline of the monarchy. While important, such analyses were not generalizable. Likewise, these studies centered on legal forms such as constitutions. They were concerned with how government under particular constitutions were supposed to work instead of how they in fact operated. Finally, most of the traditional studies limited their research to Western European institutions. They ignored the array of political activity and institutions throughout most of the world.

For the reasons stated above, the traditional approach to comparative politics came under attack by scholars such as Macridis. The parochial and static character of comparative politics could not satisfy the new movement toward a more scientific and theoretical approach to social science.

The behavioral approach in comparative politics was a reaction to many of the weaknesses identified in the traditional method. As noted in Chapter 1, the behavioral approach argues that we can best understand politics and political systems by studying how political systems behave instead of how constitutions intend them to operate. The chief goal of behavioral research is to explain how people act and why. As an early advocate of the behavioral approach concluded, behavioral research seeks to explain "why people behave politically as they do, and why, as a result, political processes and systems function as they do" (Eulau 1963).

As applied to the study of comparative politics, the behavioral approach had a revolutionary impact. Its underlying assumption differed radically from that of the traditional school. The behavioral approach presumed that human activity was the subject of study. Human beings are creatures with far more similarities than differences whether they be American, French, or Laotian. Therefore, by studying human behavior, we could make comparisons among different political systems. Moreover, by studying politics in a comparative way, we could develop more general and scientific theories about human political behavior. In short, we could study the various aspects of politics scientifically.

For example, political scientists are interested in why people vote the way they do (see Chapter 5). The comparative behavioralist would study voting behavior in democratic nations to discover similarities and differences in levels of participation in elections, and the role of political parties, election structures, and education in the vote decision. The goal would be to learn more about what motivates democratic citizens to vote in the first place and to understand why they vote the way they do. By studying voting behavior under different political environments, we develop a better understanding of human voting behavior.

In sum, the behavioral approach to comparative politics attempts to apply the following tenets to the study of politics:

1. Identify regularities or uniformities in political behavior which we can express as general theory.

2. Verify by testing the validity of the theory.

3. Use quantitative, statistical techniques to measure, examine, and evaluate gathered empirical data.

4. Scientifically understand political behavior without making value judgments about the implications of the new knowledge for social or political problems.

5. Integrate political research with the other social sciences.[1]

6. Abandon ethnocentrism and expand the boundaries of study to all the world's political systems.

During the 1960s and 1970s, the behavioral approach itself became the subject of attack. Many reacted to the "pure science" approach that seemed to reject humanism and the important normative (value) questions in politics (Chilcote 1981, 58). Critics attacked behavioralists for a lack of substance and an overemphasis on study methods. Critics also charged that behavioralists studied trivia. Because reliable quantitative data was unavailable, behavioralists could not study the most interesting and pressing questions.

This dissatisfaction ultimately led to a third approach to comparative politics—postbehavioralism. Postbehavioralism attempted to combine some elements of the traditional and the behavioral approaches.[2]

The postbehavioral approach emphasized the following:

1. Substance must supercede technique so that the world's most important social problems become more important subjects of study than the tools of investigation.

2. Science cannot be separated from values in the study of human behavior. We can use a scientific approach to study behavior, but values at the very least inform us of what behavior we should study and why.

3. We should not automatically assume that there are universal laws that govern human behavior. There may be, but they remain undiscovered. We must therefore focus on the differences between political systems, as well as their similarities, because some may not lend themselves to generalization.

4. Intellectuals must not become mere technicians, isolated from the substance of their work. They should defend human values and bear the responsibility for their society.

5. The intellectual should put knowledge to work and enter the debate over social progress for the betterment of humankind.

The postbehavioral researcher is one who makes value judgments that guide his or her research, uses the scientific (or other) technique to increase knowledge on the subject, and then becomes an advocate of social change based on the new knowledge.

Much of the disarray in comparative politics stems from the confusion over which approach to the subfield is best. The theme of this book, however, recommends that we employ the composite approach to political research (see Chapter 1). In so doing, we avoid confronting the current debate over approach and still provide you with a variety of research topics and techniques to help you understand the research process in political science.

There are other difficulties in the study of comparative politics, however, that we cannot dismiss so cavalierly and still do justice to the subfield. Once we have agreed that political systems can be compared, we still face the question of how we can compare them. The astute student will observe that we still haven't gotten to the substantive questions of democracy and dictatorship, and political change and development. This is because the key concepts and questions in comparative politics are both methodological as well as substantive. We will treat each in turn.

◆ KEY QUESTIONS AND CONCEPTS: METHODS

The behavioral and postbehavioral approaches to comparative politics both assume, more or less, that we can compare the politics of different nations. However, they do not directly tell us what we should compare.

The first "what question" shows us the immensity of the task before the comparative political scientist. What countries should we compare? Should we compare only similar political systems such as the United States and the United Kingdom? Or should we try to compare nations across different historical and ideological experiences? Does it make sense to compare the United States and Ghana, for example?

Focusing on similar countries forces us to center on comparisons rather than contrasts. In this strategy we try to neutralize certain differences to better analyze other contrasts. For example, if we are interested in studying the difference between presidential and parliamentary democracies, we will want to select countries that have linked cultures and historical experiences. Thus, it makes more sense to compare the United States and the United Kingdom instead of the United States and Japan. Though both the United Kingdom and Japan are parliamentary democracies, Japan lacks the common Anglo-Saxon cultural ties of the United States and the United Kingdom. Thus, if we observe differences in how laws are made in the United States and the United Kingdom, we can be more confident that the difference results because of the dissimilarity between political institutions and not differences in culture. Comparing the United States and Japan would not allow the same level of confidence in our conclusions.

When the focus is on countries with dissimilar experiences, institutions, and cultures, our concern begins with contrasts. We fix our attention on situations that present maximum differences in how the political systems operate. The similarities we observe are secondary to identifying and explaining the differences among systems. In comparing the United States and the former Soviet Union for example, we would begin with the assumption that the two represented opposite political worlds. We would also expect our analysis to reveal the underlying forces that explain these fundamental differences.

A related problem is to decide how many countries we want to compare. There are over 180 independent states in the world today. If we compare just two countries, we learn a good deal about their similarities and differences, but do we learn anything that we can generalize to other states? On the other hand, if we focus on 30 countries, we may lose our ability to see the nuances in particular political systems.

Generally speaking, when researchers begin with a comparision of two countries, they later expand their studies to others. When the approach is to compare similar countries, the task is to expand the analysis to other similar countries. When the two countries contrast, we might consider each as a prototype of two different types of countries. We would try to find other political systems that fit with each new type. The most obvious examples include democracies and dictatorships or developed and developing countries.

As we have argued, one of the major concerns of comparative politics is to develop a more general understanding of politics. We can try to achieve this goal by studying individual countries or by comparing two or more countries. Then we can gradually expand the number of cases to develop typologies. To develop general political theory, however, we must ultimately study all political systems. We must develop and test hypotheses of general application to politics in all human society. This dilemma leads us to the second "what question" in comparative politics. What should we compare among countries?

The answer to this question is relatively simple when we are comparing only a small number of countries. In comparing similar countries, we compare their histories, cultures, and their political, social, and economic institutions. If we are studying two or three democracies, our concern will be to analyze the development of the democratic culture and how their institutions operate. We can make a similar argument about comparing contrasting countries. For example, there are political parties in both the United States and Communist China. However, the Chinese Communist Party is a very different animal than the Democratic and Republican parties in the United States.

Nevertheless, if our goal is to develop broader political theory, we must develop concepts that are even more abstract, that can encompass the great political diversity of our world. One attempt at this is our old friend the political system. You recall that the concept of the political system presumes that the political processes of all countries are essentially the same. All political systems are in the same business. They perform the same functions. These functions are performed by political structures that may be very different depending on the cultural and ideological environment. Structure may also vary with the political system's level of development.

The key to developing more general political theory is to identify the key system functions and then find the political structures which perform them. With the assumption that all systems perform the same functions, the goal of the comparative political scientist is to identify these functions and the corresponding structures in all political systems.

This approach to comparing political systems was developed by political scientist Gabriel Almond (Almond and Powell, 1966). Almond's approach represented a major attempt to develop a general and dynamic theory of politics in its various manifestations. We call it **structural-functionalism.** We will see that structural-functionalism has many critics, but it is still used in one form or another to organize comparative research.

Let's once again review our discussion of the political system. In Chapter 4 we argued that all political systems are in the business of translating the wants and desires of the *relevant public* into public policy. Public policies run the gamut from building monuments and performing rituals, to engaging in nuclear war. Each political system performs essentially the same functions so that the opinions of the relevant public are translated into public policy. To Almond, these functions include the following:

a. Input functions
   1. Political socialization and recruitment
   2. Interest articulation
   3. Interest aggregation
   4. Political communication

b. Output functions
   1. Rule making
   2. Rule application
   3. Rule adjudication

The input functions involve the process where the wants and desires of the relevant public get placed on the policy agenda for government decision makers to consider. Political socialization refers to the process whereby people learn the system's political values and their role in the system. For example, children in a democracy learn the importance of voting and speaking their minds. Children in a primitive tribe learn to obey the chieftain. Recruitment refers to how people become part of the political classes. Again, in a democracy, rule makers are mostly elected. In an absolute monarchy, leaders are chosen through birthright.

Interest articulation and aggregation involve how demands get on the policy agenda. Interest articulation refers to the demands made by the relevant public. Interest aggregation involves bringing together different interests and demands behind a common front. It's the process whereby individuals and groups with differing, yet compatible wants unite to push a common program.

Political communication serves all the above input functions. Political recruitment, socialization, articulation, and aggregation all occur through some form of communication.

The outputs refer to the different types of government actions (public policy making). Rule making is law making of one form or another. Rule application is rule administration, and rule adjudication involves judicial interpretation of both rule making and application.

Once we have identified these key system functions, we compare political systems by looking for the **political structures** performing these functions. Political socialization in modern societies occurs in the family, schools, interest groups, political parties, and even the media. In less developed countries it may occur only in the family and through rituals or cermonies. Interest articulation and aggregation occurs through political parties, interest groups, elections, or other political structures, the so called linkage institutions in our model of the political system.

The output functions are performed by the decision-making institutions of government. In the United States, rule making is performed by legislatures (both national and state), by bureaucratic agencies, and in some cases by the president. The executive branch of government performs rule application, and the judiciary performs rule adjudication. In an absolute monarchy, the monarch performs all decision-making functions.

Public policy decisions, as we have argued, impact the relevant public who then articulate new demands or support for those actions. Government structures make new public policy and the system hopefully adapts to new environmental conditions.

Structural-functionalism also allowed classification of political systems into several categories. They could be modern or premodern, industrial, postindustrial, or agrarian, and developed or underdeveloped. Almond essentially saw political systems at different levels of development. At the higher stages of development, structures are more numerous and differentiated than in primitive political systems. So in modern democracies, there are many socialization agents (structures performing political socialization). In underdeveloped systems there are relatively few.[3]

After an initial surge of enthusiam, structural-functionalism came under attack. The critics addressed three problems. Structural-functionalism had an inherent conservative bias, it offered ambiguous concepts, and it failed in its promise to be universally applicable.

The conservative bias in structural-functionalism comes from its reliance on systems theory and its underlying belief that political development would lead to political democracy. The ultimate goal of system functions is system preservation, not change. Many critics held that Almond and his colleagues injected their personal ideologies into the description of political development. The "natural modernizing forces" were driven by the quest for freedom and the market economy. Structural-functionalism seemed to evade or ignore the alienation and pain caused by modernization. For example, the industrial revolution caused enormous suffering and dislocation. By avoiding the downside of development, structural-functionalism missed the conclusion that political development does not necessarily lead to human fulfillment.

Critics also found structural-functional concepts ambiguous. It was difficult to adequately define what the system is and to delineate the system's boundaries (Groth 1970). The definitions of structures and functions were only restatements, in a more confusing way, of existing concepts such as the state, constitutionalism, and law. "What Almond had to say could have been said without using this systems approach and it would have been said more clearly" (Finer 1969/70).

Finally, some found that structural-functionalism did not help us generalize about politics. Some scholars discovered it difficult to apply to historical and contemporary cases (Holt and Turner 1966). For example, its definition of modern political systems as democracies meant we could not really use it to analyze nations such as the former Soviet Union.

The debate over approaches such as structural-functionalism ultimately led to the disarray in the field of comparative politics today. Nevertheless, structural-functionalism did help shift comparative politics toward a more comparative and scientific focus. Today, scholars do much more in the field than compare constitutions and government types. They are more attuned to comparing how political systems actually work.

◆ KEY QUESTIONS AND CONCEPTS: SUBSTANTIVE

We have already discussed the immensity and diversity of the subfield of comparative politics. You should also have gathered from the previous discussion that there is little agreement as to how, or whether we can, study politics comparatively. The substantive questions in the subfield are equally diverse, and we cannot pretend to cover even a majority of them. However, we have selected some of the major questions and concepts using the standards established by our composite approach to political research.

The first question has been of particular interest to students and scholars residing in the United States. Why are some political systems democracies, others authoritarian, and still others ruthless dictatorships? In some ways this question is as old as political philosophy itself. For specialists in comparative politics, the question became intensely relevant following the experiences of the former Soviet Union, particularly under Stalin, and Hitler's Third Reich.

The underlying reason for this question is clearly postbehavioral in scope. Analysts make the value judgment that democracy is superior to other forms of government. Once we make this judgment, it becomes the job of the researcher to discover empirically the conditions of democracy.

To show you how scholars have tried to answer this question we must first discuss several important concepts. These include political culture, political socialization, which we briefly discussed earlier, and political development.

For the modern student of comparative politics, political culture refers to the "collective perceptions of individuals as they attempt to understand the institutions, processes, and formal beliefs of the political system in which they are located" (Cantori and Ziegler 1988, 159). It is the set of broadly based beliefs people have about politics, government, public policy, and their role in the political system.

In fact, for research purposes we can break the definition of political culture into three levels. First, there is the system culture. This refers to the people's attitudes toward the nation, the regime (the government as a whole), and the leaders of the country at any given time. Second, the process dimension of political culture refers to the attitudes toward the role the individual plays in the system and the attitudes about the role of others. Third, the policy culture focuses upon the results of the political process, or what government should or should not do (Almond and Verba 1980).

Political socialization is the process by which the people develop the norms and attitudes of their political culture. Students of political socialization want to know what political attitudes various peoples develop and how they develop them. They study the agents of political socialization such as the family, schools, religion, media, and the workplace. They want to know the extent to which values are transmitted across generations and what stimulates change in the indivdual's values and the political culture of entire political systems.

If we are interested in explaining the similarities and differences among political systems, it is important that we add a time dimension to our analysis of various countries. Without concern with where we have been, we probably cannot know where we are, or where we are going. To ignore the past is to fall victim to the assumption that the political world remains the same. Just as times change as to fashion, political eras change. What is acceptable behavior in one era may seem outrageous 100 years later. During the European Middle Ages, a person had to confess his or her crimes to God in public before they could be punished. Without the confession, there could be no punishment. People did confess, however. Various instruments of torture, from thumb screws to the rack, were effective in extracting the confession. Modern Europe would find the practice of torture completely unacceptable.

If we want to know why some nations are democracies and others dictatorships, we have to study how political systems develop. The concept of **political development** refers to how political systems evolve over time. It involves studying the conditions of democracy and authoritarianism, wealth and poverty, stability and political change. You should recall that one of the criticisms of structural-functionalism was that it is static, it cannot account for, or explain, political change (see p. 140).

The concept of political development led to an entire developmental approach to the study of comparative politics during the 1960s. Like structural-functionalism, it came under intense criticism.

There are many variations of the developmental approach. However, a series of studies instituted by the Committee on Comparative Politics of the Social Science Research Center[4] concluded that political development centered on a number of crises that all nations experience. These crises include the crisis of identity, the crisis of legitimacy, the crisis of penetration, the crisis of participation, and the crisis of distribution.

The Crisis of Identity   The crisis of identity centers on the following question: How do individuals and groups describe themselves politically? The first major hurdle in the process of development is the need for citizens to develop a national identity. Individuals must begin to think of themselves as one people. Failure to do so leads to national trama and maybe even civil war. This crisis is particularly acute in African nations where tribal identity still takes precedent over national consciousness. For example, in the late 1960s Ibo tribesmen tried to break away from Nigeria that the Hausa tribe dominated. A bloody civil war ensued resulting in countless hardships and slaughter for the Ibo.

The crisis of identity is not limited to the so-called Third World, however. The United States experienced its identity crisis in two different eras. In the late eighteenth and nineteenth centuries, we had to learn to think of ourselves as Americans rather than New Yorkers or Georgians. Then, in the buildup to the Civil War, large numbers of Americans began thinking of themselves as something other than American, for example, southerners. It was only following the Civil War that a true national identity emerged. Today we can see similar crises of identity in Lebanon and even Canada.

The Crisis of Legitimacy   Legitimacy is another important concept in the study of comparative politics. It suggests that the people believe that the government in power has a right to exist and is acting acceptably. Large segments of the population may at times disagree with the specific actions of the government (public policies), but they don't question the government's legitimate power to make those decisions.

When a government loses its legitimacy, it can stay in power only through coercion and force. Usually social disruption will be substantial, and in some instances the government will fall. Many French Canadians in the Quebec province do not accept the government in Ottawa. Much violence has occurred in India where the Sikh minority rejects the Indian government. The world watched between 1989 and 1991 as communist governments in Eastern Europe and the former Soviet Union fell as their peoples withdrew support.

It is an impossible task to define precisely the point when a regime develops or loses its legitimacy. In every political system there will always be some who support and reject the government. Established, legitimate political systems can withstand more internal criticism than newer ones because they have more "past legitimacy" in the bank. Depending on the political system involved, at some point a loss of legitimacy reaches a critical mass and the system collapses in revolution, civil war, or both.

The Crisis of Penetration   The crisis of penetration generally refers to a government's ability to enforce its decisions in all geographical regions and at all levels of society. Governments that are not able to enforce their decisions are less stable than others. For example, are there geographic areas in the country (or the country at large) where laws are ignored? During the "era of prohibition" in the United States, alcohol consumption flourished in spite of the law. Many Latin American and African nations have failed in their attempts to limit population growth.

The Crisis of Participation   The crisis of participation involves two dimensions of participation. The first is the amount of participation. If a new country has its first democratic election and only 10 percent of the eligible voters participate, it may indicate a lack of legitimacy. The presumption is that the trend toward democracy is part of the developmental process. The goal is to increase citizen participation in the democratic process to increase the legitimacy of the government. On the other hand, too many demands from the people may overburden the government's ability to cope and also threaten system legitimacy. We noted in Chapter 5 that some argue the United States political system faces demands from too many interest groups with conflicting demands that are unwilling to compromise. The result may be overload which ends in a loss of legitimacy.

The second dimension involves the type of participation. It is possible that a small number of demands could put considerable stress on the system. For example, the racial majority in South Africa demanded political opportunity in a regime that has a long history of racial discrimination. The mass demonstrations following the attempted coup against Michail Gorbachev in Moscow that led to the downfall of the Soviet Union is another recent example.

The Crisis of Distribution   One of the most visible problems in most countries today is an economic one. The availability of food, medicine, water, housing, and power are either completely insufficient or are not equitably distributed throughout society. The problem is particulary acute in the poorest countries of the world, but, even in the wealthiest of nations, there are often pockets of abject poverty and suffering. Countries that contain large groups that believe they are denied adequate material benefits is a political system ripe for revolution.

Political development is the process of coping with these crises. We label successful political systems developed. Those that fail are either undeveloped or developing. Students of political development attempt to understand how this process works.

How then can we use the concepts of political culture, political socialization, and political development to help us analyze why some nations are democracies and some are not? One approach is to examine the political cultures of different types of countries to see if there is a cultural dimension to democracy and authoritarianism. In other words, do democracies have common cultural traits that distinguish them from more authoritarian systems? Some classic studies dealing with this question include Almond and Verba, *The Civic Culture* (1963) and *The Civic Culture Revisited* (1980).

Another area of research is to focus on how democratic or authoritarian attitudes come about. We can study political socialization in various systems to understand how attitudes develop, how they are conveyed to new generations, and how these attitudes change.

Political development is the most significant concept in answering our question. As we argued, the developmental approach, if nothing else, focuses our attention on the process of change, on how a particular country got from point A to B over a period of time. The approach helps us to look for the prerequisites for democracy and other forms government. For example, early developmental theorists found an important link between economic development and democracy (Lipset 1959). Economic growth helped political systems cope with both the crisis of participation and distribution. Others looked to the social conditions of democracy (Moore 1966).

One classic study of political development by Walt Rostow focused on the "psycho-cultural" prerequisites of development. Even so, its conclusions centered on the relationship between economic development and democracy. In his book *The Stages of Economic Growth: A Non-Communist Manifesto* (1960), Rostow suggested there were five stages of growth in the development process:

1. *Traditional society*—prescientific with little economic development.
2. *Preconditions for takeoff*—limited scientific development and expanded agricultural and industrial output. Stage similar to that achieved in Western Europe by the eighteenth century.
3. *Takeoff*—characterized by a rapid rise in the gross domestic product and expansion of business and economic institutions.
4. *The drive to technological maturity*—Expansion of the investment base for the economy (capital accumulation and investment), and increased export markets.
5. *High mass consumption*—economy based on consumer goods and services. Examples are modern, politically developed countries such as the United States, Western Europe, and Japan.

Rostow, and others (see p. 144), clearly argued that capitalist economic development led to mature, politically developed democracies. As countries developed economically, political roles and institutions multiply and become more specialized. More and more people would participate in the political process. Just as consumers decide which companies offer the best products, the educated citizen would demand participatory rights and choose political leaders in elections. Voters would base their choices on which candidates offer the best in political goods and services.

This type of reasoning led many developmental theorists to conclude that political democracy was the end point of the continuum between traditional and modern political systems. The term *development* implies progress, and progress meant steps toward democratic politics.

While there was much criticism of this approach, the answer it offered to our question is clear. Democracy was the inevitable result of the developmental process. Undeveloped societies could rapidly modernize because of the diffusion of economic and technological innovations, education, and ideas from the modern, Western countries of Europe and the United States.

Our second substantive question in the comparative politics subfield also stems from the concept of political development. Why are some political systems developed or developing, while others seem stuck in an undeveloped state? Because of the identified relationship between political and economic development, a corollary question might be, "Why are some countries as rich as Midus, while others remain wretchedly poor?"

To scholars such as Lipset, development was more or less inevitable so interest in our question was somewhat misplaced. The new nations formed during the decline of colonialism would develop and become more wealthy and democratic (Lipset 1959). However, empirical observation seemed to prove this view wrong.

The political development approach came under attack by those who noticed that in many undeveloped countries, the so-called development that development theorists tried to explain simply wasn't occurring. Instead of a new crop of fledgling democracies throughout the world, many countries remained trapped in poverty, corruption, and tyranny.

Technical innovations from the modern world planted by foreign investors failed to spread to the rest of the economy. Agricultural production failed to keep up with industrialization and the massive movement of people from rural areas to the cities created inflation and food shortages. Economic growth came, but it often failed to generate domestic investment. As a result, the developing country remained dependent on foreign sources of capital and technology. Introducing modern medical technology to these countries did reduce both the death rate and infant mortality. However, it also led to over-population. Agricultural production failed to keep up with population growth, leading to deepening poverty and starvation. The introduction of "democratic political institutions" in cultures based on personal or familial relationships led to political systems typified by nepotism and corruption.

By the late 1970s, democracy had collapsed in much of the developing world. In Latin America alone 17 of 20 countries were under military-authoritarian rule (Wiarda 1991, 44). What was wrong? Why didn't development begin? And where it had, why did it stop? Two theories emerged to explain the apparent failure of political development. These included a revised theory of modernization and development based on our concept of political culture and dependency theory.

The revised modernization theory argued that the barriers encountered by many developing countries came principally from the persistence of traditional values and norms. Many of these traditional values, such as the importance of ritual, personal relationships, and family ties, were hostile to the values required to modernize the economy, society, and government—individualism, the work ethic, and proceduralism. Attitudinal factors short-circuited the development process.

To get back on track, scholars had to focus on the problem of cultural change. This was no easy task. Cultural norms and values are by definition deeply engrained traits. They are the filters whereby individuals make sense out of their world. Some authors came to believe only political violence and revolution were viable means of destroying vested interests and changing traditional norms.

Dependency theory represented a radical challenge to theories of political development. Drawing on the Marxist point of view, dependency theorists contended that barriers to development stemmed from the results of integrating developing nations into the international capitalist economy. Ultimately, this integration led to economic and political exploitation of the Third World by the developed countries.

Two sets of forces worked to throttle economic and political development. The first involved impersonal economic forces stemming from the dependent country's reliance on only a few (sometimes only one) exports and reliance on only a few trading partners and suppliers of aid. The second involved the influence of multinational corporations (see Chapter 8) who pursued their own economic interests in opposition to the national interest of the developing nation.

The economies of many developing countries depended on the export of a single agricultural good such as cocoa in Ghana. With so little diversity, such countries are extremely vulnerable to swings in the world price for the economy. A sharp drop in the world price of the good, not only weakens, but does nearly irreparable harm to the economic base. This deepens the country's dependence on aid from the First World.

The interest of multinational corporations had little to do with developing the domestic economies of local economies. In many cases their goals were cheap labor, extraction of raw materials and profits (without reinvestment in the local economy), and the maintenance of a monopoly on technology.

The usual pattern was for the multinational to create an unholy alliance with the political elite in the nation, making them very rich in exchange for the economic exploitation of the country as a whole. The political elite and the military kept a lid, often by brutal methods, on social unrest, arresting the developmental process. As development founders, the local economy weakens even as the political class prospers. Social unrest heightens requiring even more brutal repression.

Today, two empirical observations have discredited dependency theory. Economic growth is occurring in even the poorest of countries. For example, between 1960 and 1979, growth in Latin American GNP averaged 3.3 percent per year (Crotty 1991, 51). By 1980, the developing countries of Asia defied dependency theory's predictions. For example, some of the most dependent countries of all, South Korea, Singapore, and Malaysia, enjoyed 20 years of stable economic growth with only moderate inflation unmarred by balance-of-payments crises. Additionally, agricultural production was up, and income distribution remained comparatively equitable.

Finally, many of the dependent countries have moved toward more open and democratic political systems. With the collapse of the Soviet bloc, democratic ideals have swept the world's political landscape. This fact leads us to the last of our substantive questions in the subfield of comparative politics.

Is political democracy the end of the developmental process? As with all of our questions, the answer to this one is unsettled. For a period of time, the answer was no. In this new world political culture, however, democracy seems resurrected as a model of development.

Our question begs a discussion and critique of the whole developmental approach to comparative politics. As noted, the developmental approach became dominant during the 1950s and 1960s. At the time it appeared to be the most intellectually stimulating approach. Soon, however, the critics multiplied. Their criticism was diverse, but central to most was the view that developmental theory was biased and ethnocentric. It automatically assumed that a developed state was a democratic one. The central criticisms include the following:

First, critics focused on the Western developmental experience (remember our criticism of structural-functionalism?) as a model for political development. The models of political development had some form of political democracy as their endpoint. Critics argued that such models were of doubtful use in analyzing non-Western countries and were of only limited use even with some Western ones (Wiarda 1991, 36). Societies lacking cultural heritage from Greece, Rome, and even the Bible, and those without the historical legacy of feudalism and capitalism, simply do not follow the Western pattern of development.

Second, in regard to timing, developing countries today face different problems than the West faced during its development. For example, in the West, feudalism preceded capitalism. In much of the developing world, the two are intermingled or exist side by side. Coping with different historical circumstances may lead to a different developmental result.

Third, the international context is different today than in earlier eras. The international system is much more interdependent than in the 1950s. The developing world is caught up to a much greater degree in dependency relationships, international conflict, alliances, and the world culture of taste, travel, and communications. This interdependence could have profound impact on the process of development. The impact could be toward greater democracy or toward authoritarianism. We have already implied, and will argue below, that the trend is toward democracy.

Fourth, the Western bias in the development literature had a Cold War basis. Political development had to proceed along the path to democracy to keep the developing countries out of the communist camp.

Fifth, the Western bias to development, when accepted by the leaders of many developing countries, actually harmed the development process in many countries. It led to the destruction of many traditional institutions. These institutions, such as the extended family, clan, and tribal groupings, could have provided the social and cultural glue necessary to bridge the transition to more modern institutions. Instead, many countries have few traditional forms, and the modern ones remain primitive and dysfunctional. Development remains arrested.

Finally, critics challenge the notion that there is a developmental endpoint at all, whether it be democracy or some other political form. For example, as we have already noted, Samuel Huntington (1968) argued that many theorists viewed development as inevitable progress toward a democratic end. In fact, political change is cyclical. Countries both develop and decay. Huntington saw political development as the institutionalization of political norms and practices, regardless of whether this institutionalization came within the democratic framework. Therefore, the Soviet Union was a politically developed system. Ironically, the demise of the Soviet Union may be a classic example of **political decay.**

The developmental approach with its so-called Western bias lost favor when democracy failed to materialize in many countries. We discussed attempts, such as dependency theory, to explain why the developmental approach lost support. However, looking at the empirical record since the late 1970s may lead to a revival.

Nations as diverse as the Phillipines, South Korea, and the Republic of China have moved strongly and quickly toward democracy. Where in the late 1970s most Latin American countries had military governments, today 18 of 21 are either democracies or are moving toward democracy (Wiarda 1991, 44). Of course, we have not yet mentioned the incredible, and unpredicted, political change in the former Soviet bloc. For the most part, the new and old nations of Eastern Europe are moving toward democracy. Even in Communist China, the move is toward more openness and competition in the economy. If the early developmental theorists are right, demands for political freedom will accelerate, and those demands will alter the political system as well.

Political democracy may yet prove to be an end of political development. Several factors lead to this conclusion.

With over 30 years of experience with development, we now have an empirical base to make judgments about what works in the developmental process. With abundant case studies and comparative analyses, we know that what works is representative institutions, open markets, personal and group security, stable governments, social modernization, and peaceful, moderate change. These are all elements identified by early theorists such as Lipset and Rostow.

Today, the world political culture, though difficult to precisely define, is clearly in favor of democracy. Over the last ten years the change has been revolutionary. No one seems to want authoritarian, military regimes or Marxist-Leninist ones either. Such regimes have been overthrown or discredited. Even if there are bumps in the road to democracy, most ask the question, "What are the alternatives?" At least so far, there are none that have captured the imagination of more than a handful of people and nations.

A third force in favor of democratic development is U.S. foreign policy. Most transitions to democracy stem from domestic conditions. However, U.S. policies in favor of democracy have been important. The United States has always defended democracy and human rights on moral grounds. It has also been in our national interest to do so. As a result, advocacy of human rights and democracy has gained bipartisan support. Therefore, it is unlikely any future administration would abandon them as tenets of American foreign policy. As the only world superpower, our policy to support democracy and human rights should be even more significant in the developmental process.

In reassessing the developmental theorists, we must take into account the changes noted above. It may be that these scholars were wrong in the short run but may prove to have the last laugh. The criticism that their portrayal of development was too simplistic remains true. They based their theories too much on the Western experience. However, their conclusions about political development and democracy have gained new respect. Though there is no necessary and automatic connection between development and democracy, the trend toward democracy in the last 20 years is unmistakable. Of course, if change is cyclical as Samuel Huntington argued, even mature democracies can decay.

◆ THE STATE OF COMPARATIVE POLITICS

After reading this far, you probably now understand why we began this chapter by saying the subfield of comparative politics is in disarray. The problems and questions faced in studying politics comparatively are massive. We assure you that there are many more we simply omitted. You might also conclude that given the problems, and the fact that all of these scholars with graduate degrees can't agree, you should avoid choosing a topic from this area. We understand your fear and concern. However, in spite of the disagreement there has been much progress. There has been massive amounts of research using the traditional, behavioral, and postbehavioral methods. We know far more about government and politics in other countries than ever before. Through cross-national studies, we have made progress towards understanding more generally how politics works. Even the debate over approaches such as structural-functionalism and development represent progress in our learning. So we hope you will give some thought to selecting a research topic in this area. Here are some suggestions that may help you decide.

We suggest that in selecting your research topic and your method of research that you bypass most of the theoretical debate we discussed. (You don't have to! For you curious and ambitious students, we bet your instructor will help you find a topic exploring the debate further.) We included these discussions because they represent very important issues within the subfield. We want you to know about them and your instructor does too. At the same time, we believe you can select a topic and help increase your knowledge in the area without getting into this complicated debate.

Instead, we suggest you focus on a particular aspect of structural-functionalism or political development. You could compare the structures and functions of different countries by focusing on the major aspects of most political systems—public policy, political behavior, and government institutions. For example, you will recall that public policy is what government does. You may want to try and explain why different nations have different approaches to economic, education, and health-care policy. Health care is a topical issue today in the United States. How have other nations approached this issue? We can ask similar questions about education, economic, or welfare policy.

If you choose political behavior, you can focus on voting behavior, leadership, party behavior, and even the question of political change (development?) and revolution. You can compare and explain why people vote the way they do in different countries. You can ask questions that might help explain why young people vote more in Canada than in the United States. You might explore political development by identifying the economic, social, and political factors that explain political violence. For example, why do people rebel?

Focusing on political institutions allows you to compare legislatures, bureaucracies, courts, and political parties. There has been much research

Box 7.1

COMPARATIVE VOTER PARTICIPATION: A RESEARCH EXAMPLE

One of the perennial issues in the study of political democracies is the number of people who vote in elections. According to the classical variants of democratic theory, the more people participate, the better and more stable the democracy. But when we compare voting levels in the United States with those of most other Western democracies, we find that U.S. voter turnout is consistently lower. The different levels of voter participation led many scholars to try and explain why this is so. This required them to identify the factors that influence and discourage people from voting.

Over the course of several decades of research on the American voter, various scholars have identified at least three types of factors. The first set include attitudinal factors such as the level of political awareness, political interest, and partisanship. The second set is demographic, such as the level of education, income, social status, and gender. The third group involves the legal and institutional context in which individuals act. For example, the existence of the secret ballot, registration and residency requirements, and the strength of political parties and interest groups could influence the overall level of voting.

Unfortunately, research findings on voting in the United States were mixed. There is little agreement about the most important factors. G. Gingham Powell tried to help increase our knowledge of voting and nonvoting by using a comparative perspective. He studied attitudes, demographic and institutional factors, and the level of voting in 20 modern democracies including the United States. His data included information from public opinion polls, the various governments' census information, and the various legal requirements and restrictions on voting.

Using the sophisticated statistical technique of regression (you will learn about it in Chapter 14), Powell determined that the American voter presents an interesting paradox. Americans seem to be more politically aware, interested, educated, and wealthy than citizens in most of the other nations studied. But, Americans vote less! In the last three decades, the vote for president averaged about 54 percent where the average in national elections in the other 19 countries averaged near 80 percent. Powell also found that the legal environment in many countries encouraged voting in some nations and discouraged it in others such as the United States. Some examples include these. In Australia, voting is mandatory. In most of Europe, voter registration is automatic—the government registers voters. In the United States, registration is on the shoulders of the individual, and most states require registration at least 30 days before an election.

By adopting the comparative perspective, Powell increased our understanding of why people vote or abstain. His analysis led to at least four following observations:

Continued

BOX 7.1 (CONT'D)

COMPARATIVE VOTER PARTICIPATION: A RESEARCH EXAMPLE

1. Voter particpation is much less in the United States than in other democracies.
2. American attitudes should be more favorable to voting than in other democracies.
3. The American legal and institutional environment inhibits voter participation.
4. The most important factors explaining voter turnout are institutional.

There are many implications of these findings, but one should be obvious. If we want to increase voter turnout in the United States, we need to remove the institutional barriers to voting such as individual registration and residency requirements.

Source: G. Bingham Powell, "American Voter Turnout in Comparative Perspective," *American Political Science Review* 80 (1986): 17–43.

along these lines. You might want to look for, and compare, the factors most important in determining how members of different democratic legislatures vote on particular types of issues. Another example might be to ask whether certain types of political parties lead a more representative democracy. Finally, you might explore the intriguing differences in how various countries approach law and the role of the judiciary.

❖ SUMMARY

In this chapter we introduced you to the subfield of comparative politics. It is by far the most complex and diverse in political science. At the same time, the comparative study of politics is extremely important in our effort to understand political relationships. This is so because the comparative subfield offers the opportunity to study politics more generally, understand the multitude of differences in our world, and look more systematically at the question, "Which government is best?"

Unfortunately, the subfield is currently in a state of disarray. This stems from a lack of agreement as to if and how we can study politics comparatively. As a result, we can see three stages of change in the area. The first involved using the traditional case study to explore the politics of each country (mainly Europe). The presumption was that the politics of individual countries is unique. The second involved the application of behavioral and postbehavioral approaches to study comparative politics. Though different, each started with the presumption that we could study politics more generally. This led to theories such as structural-functionalism and political development to help us understand how we can compare politics across countries.

Third, the criticism of both structural-functionalism and political development ultimately led to the confusion we see now in the subfield. There remains little agreement as to the best approach to the study of comparative politics. Today we see an eclectic subfield where research involves some doing stage one research and others stage two.

Because of the disagreement over method, it is difficult to answer the substantive questions: Why are some countries democratic and others not? Why are some countries modern and rich and others undeveloped and poor? Is democracy the end point of political development?

You can avoid much of the debate over how to answer these questions in selecting a research topic, however. There are many, less grandiose questions that will increase our knowledge of the political process. We suggested that you use either a policy, behavioral, or institutional approach to ask important political questions. It is important to know how different nations confront the issues that face us all as humans. It is important to know how different people, with different cultures, behave politically, and it is important to discover how different cultures, and peoples organize their governments.

❖ KEY TERMS

case studies	political development
input functions	political structure
output functions	structural-functionalism
political decay	

❖ EXERCISES

1. Describe the evolution of the comparative politics subfield.

2. With the help of your instructor, try and list several reasons politics might be unique in each country. Then try to list several reasons why politics may not be unique to a specific country.

3. Identify and analyze the two "what questions" confronted in deciding how to compare politics among countries.

4. Discuss the problems with understanding why some countries are democracies and others are not?

5. Is political democracy the end point of political development? Why or why not?

❖ SUGGESTED READINGS

Almond, Gabriel, and Sidney Verba. *The Civic Culture Revisited.* Boston: Little-Brown, 1980.

Barbour William, and Carol Wekesser. *The Breakup of the Soviet Union.* San Diego: Greenhaven Press, 1994.

Biskup, Michael. *Europe.* San Diego: Greenhaven Press, 1994.

Cantori, Louis, and Andrew Ziegler. *Comparative Politics in the Post-Behavioral Era.* Boulder: Lynn Rienner Publishers, 1988.

Chilcote, Ronald. *Theories in Comparative Politics.* Boulder: Westview Press, 1981.

Crotty, William. *Political Science: Looking to the Future.* Vol. 2. Evanston, IL: Northwestern University Press, 1991.

Easton, David. *A Framework of Political Analysis.* Engelwood-Cliffs, NJ: Prentice-Hall, 1965.

Ethridge, Marcus, and Howard Handelman. *Politics in a Changing World.* New York: St. Martin's Press, 1994.

Huntington, Samuel. *Political Order in Changing Societies.* New Haven: Yale University Press, 1968.

Mahler, Gregory S. *Comparative Politics,* 2nd ed. Engelwood Cliffs, NJ: Prentice-Hall, 1995.

Moore, Barrington. *The Social Origins of Dictatorship and Democracy.* Boston: Beacon Press, 1966.

Rostow, Walt. *Stages of Economic Growth: A Non-Communist Manifesto.* New York: Cambridge University Press, 1962.

Rustow, Dankwart, and Kenneth Erickson, eds. *Concepts and Models in Comparative Politics: Political Development Reconsidered—and Its Alternatives.* New York: HarperCollins, 1991.

Wiarda, Howard. *New Directions in Comparative Politics.* Boulder: Westview Press, 1985.

Wiarda, Howard. *Latin America at the Crossroads: Debt, Development and the Future.* Boulder: Westview Press, 1987.

❖ NOTES

1. The behavioral tenets are adapted from Easton (1956).
2. The reader should review our discussion of composite political research, which goes beyond the postbehavioral approach in Chapter 1.

3. Almond revised his structural-functional approach in his 1966 book cited. He increased the number of system functions and structures. He added the notion that political systems exist in an environment that affect them. He also noted that there is a constant interaction between the system and its environment, allowing for change in both the system and its environment. These changes came in response to some of the criticisms structural-functionalism received. We will not elaborate on the complexity of Almond's revision because it is not a true reformulation, but only an extension of the earlier work.

4. This committee was located at the Center for Advanced Study in the Behavioral Studies at Palo Alto, California. Princeton University Press published the results throughout the 1960s in a series called *Studies in Political Development*. Examples include Lucian Pye, ed., *Communications and Political Development* (1963); Joseph La Palombara, ed., *Bureaucracy and Political Development* (1963); Lucian Pye and Sidney Verba, eds., *Political Culture and Political Development* (1965); and Leonard Binder et al., *Crises and Sequences in Political Development* (1971).

INTERNATIONAL RELATIONS

❖ INTRODUCTION

Our tour of the political science discipline is nearly complete. Hopefully, you now have a basic understanding of the relationship between human existence and the political world and how we as human beings have organized ourselves within various political systems. We have asked fundamental questions about the best type of governments, and we have discussed how these questions can be analyzed and theorized about. By now, you should have a whole list of potential research topics for your research paper.

But hold on. The subfield of international relations involves a unique political system, one in which there is no effective government, and where the characteristics of the Hobbesian state of nature are often illustrated. The collapse of the Soviet Union in 1990–91 and the end of the Cold War brought about sea changes in the nature of world politics and the international political system. The questions posed in this system are as interesting as they are important for understanding the political world.

An understanding of this chapter will enable you to:

1. Describe the nature of the subfield of international relations.
2. Describe the key concepts and actors in the international system.
3. Understand some key questions posed in the subfield.
4. Discuss the basic approaches to the study of international relations.

❖ THE STUDY OF INTERNATIONAL RELATIONS

Scientists believe that the planet we call earth is at least 4.5 billion years old. Human life began only about 340,000 years ago (Childe 1982). Only for the last 5,000 years is there a record of human history. We have noted that politics is imbedded in human nature (therefore, politics is as old as human existence), but the nature of politics has changed over the course of history. Modern international politics began with the Treaty of Westphalia in 1648. This treaty established the nation-state as the dominant actor in the political system. The nation-state system rejected subservience to the Pope and the Roman Catholic Church over the fiefdoms and principalities of Europe. A new system of self-ruling political entities that accepted no higher authority was born (Papp 1988, 17). The international relations we know today centers around the interactions among these nation-states and other transnational actors such as multinational corporations, and international organizations such as the United Nations. The subfield of international relations involves the study of these interactions in both the public and private spheres. It is a broad field that includes international politics, international economics, international law, and international security. In other words, nations and other actors interact politically, economically, and legally to improve their political and economic situations and to make themselves more secure.

Like most other subfields of political science, international relations seeks to understand political systems, particularly the international political system. We want to know what makes the system tick, how nations interact, why, and with what results. A central concern is to understand the ultimate form of political conflict, war.

❖ KEY CONCEPTS

As with all types of politics, international relations involves conflict, power, influence, and authority. In addition, the unique nature of the international political system requires some new concepts to help us ask important questions in the field. These concepts involve the types of players in international politics, the international system itself, and international law.

◆ THE PLAYERS

Those who play the game of international politics have differed over time. As we noted above, the modern system of international relations stems from the end of the Thirty Years War and the birth of the nation-state as the principal actor in the international system. In more recent times, other players, such as international organizations, multinational corporations and other nongovernmental organizations have joined the nation-state in the international arena. Let's consider each in turn.

The Nation–State The concept of the **nation-state** involves two separate notions—nation and state. A *nation* is a grouping of people who have a common identity. People perceive themselves as part of a unique whole, linked together by ethnicity, history, or culture. The *state* is a territorially bounded entity ruled by a central government that is capable of making and enforcing laws within its boundaries. Nations do not necessarily correspond with the state. The Jewish nation had no territorial control until the establishment of Israel. Many modern African states are home to more than one nation. The same was true of the former Soviet Union.

The nation-state is a state whose residents consider themselves a nation (Papp 1988, 19). In practice, we often use the terms *state*, *nation* and, *nation-state* interchangeably. This practice has become widespread within the sub-field of international relations. The reason is that even states that house many nations attempt to transfer old national loyalties to the new state. For simplicity's sake, we will continue the practice.[1]

The evolution of the nation-state system developed in two broad phases. The first phase began with the establishment of the Westphalian system in 1648 and ended with the consolidation of the state system during the nineteenth century. The second phase saw a major expansion in the number of nation-states.

The Westphalian state system was a system of empire. Even before the 1648 treaty, the English, Spanish, Dutch, and Portuguese had begun to use their military power to create overseas empires. The motivation was wealth and power. The economic philosophy of mercantilism, put forward by Jean Baptiste Colbert, justified building such empires. Mercantilism argued that a nation-state's power derived from wealth and, therefore, the state had to increase wealth in any way possible. Colonization was "the way" under mercantilist views. Colonies became the source of valuable resources and captive markets for the colonial power. Mercantilism was a way to build a powerful state and state system.

The teachings of Adam Smith in his *Wealth of Nations* led to a decline in the popularity of mercantilist philosophy and a new emphasis on free trade. Smith taught that colonial plunder was not the key to national power. Instead, capital and goods were. With this logic, colonies became less important, and concerns closer to home distracted attention from the colonies. During the late eighteenth century, the American Revolution, the French Revolution, and its nineteenth-century offspring, Napoleon, questioned the very existence of the Westphalian system of states.

The European state system, with few exceptions, was dominated by monarchy. The answer to the question "Who should rule the state?" was a given—the king or queen. The American Revolution of 1776 first challenged the system by rejecting King George III's right to rule the colonies. The French Revolution of 1789 completely rejected the concept of regal authority. In addition, this rejection threatened the legitimacy of the state itself.

You probably remember this story from your history courses. King Louis XVI was beheaded and a reign of terror swept France. The reign of terror is probably best symbolized by the guillotine as an instrument of execution. Many innocents lost their lives and chaos was the political norm. After many military victories, Napoleon Bonaparte restored order and became Emperor of France.

Napoleon wanted to replace the state system with something akin to the Holy Roman Empire. After many conquests, he nearly succeeded. However, as subsequent conquerors discovered, Napoleon overextended his power by attacking Russia. Defeated by the Russian winter, Napoleon's empire declined. Final defeat came at the hand of a coalition of states in 1815 at the Battle of Waterloo. Napoleon's loss revived acceptance of regal authority and the state system.

During the last third of the nineteenth century a new wave of imperialism began. By the early twentieth century, European states had once again built colonial empires in Africa and Asia. By 1900, Great Britain ruled 20 percent of the Earth's landmass and over one-fourth of its people. The United States and Japan joined the European states as colonial powers. The United States acquired the Phillipines, the Panama Canal Zone, and Hawaii, while Japan colonized Korea and Formosa. This second wave of imperialism ultimately led to the creation and collapse of new empires and the expansion of the numbers of nation-states.

Colonial expansion led to rivalry and competition among European states. New states formed through one of two methods. First, national groupings broke from traditional empires (Serbia and Albania). Second, smaller territorial units formed modern nation-states by joining together (Germany and Italy). The proliferation of states increased competition that fostered fear and concern for national security. Many nations forged rigid alliances that led to World War I (see p. 175).

World War I was savage, but out of the war came the the powerful principle of national self-determination. Self-determination of people, espoused by U.S. President Woodrow Wilson, meant that nationalities should determine who would rule them. Acceptance of this principle led to the expansion of the nation-state system.[2] Although World War I threatened the nation-state system, it also led to its expansion.

In addition to the proliferation of nation-states, two new types of states were born. The Russian Revolution of 1917 ultimately created the world's first communist nation—the Soviet Union. For the first time, a nation-state challenged the legitimacy of other states on the basis of an ideology hostile to capitalist economics. The Soviet Union challenged workers in other states to overthrow their rulers and offered help. Likewise, a new type of state emerged in Germany. Nazism, based on racial superiority and the consequent subservience of other peoples to Germany, preached expansionism. The German nation-state under Hitler became an assault on non-Germans and the nation-state system. The European theater of World War II was an attempt to reduce Europe to a German vassal.

We all know what happened to Hitler and his Third Reich. We need not belabor the history. The end of World War II saw another expansion in the number of states. Shattered Europe began to lose its colonial empire. New nations in Africa, Latin America, and Asia bloomed like spring meadows. Within 35 years following the war, European empires were history. By 1985, there were over 170 nation-states in the world. With the collapse of the Soviet Union in 1991, that number now surpasses 180.

The state system was well established by the close of World War II. Understanding international relations in such a system involves understanding how and why states interact. During the Cold War (1945–91) the competition between the United States and the Soviet Union dominated the international system. Today the system is more complex, and there is little agreement as to what the new structure of world politics will turn out to be (Spiegel and Pervin 1994, 5). The proliferation of states has made international relations much more complicated because there are now so many possibilities for interaction. The proliferation also complicates the conduct of foreign policy. Though some states are more significant than others, and some can be ignored all together, each nation's foreign policy must consider its impact on far more actors than before. The situation is further complicated for states in the "new international system" because other actors (discussed below) have taken on a new significance. At least one scholar believes that the nation-state is no longer central to the international system (Mansbach 1994).

International Organizations **International organizations** by definition are organizations made up of two or more sovereign states. They usually meet regularly and have a permanent staff. International organizations that Americans are most familiar with include the now defunct League of Nations, the United Nations, and NATO (North Atlantic Treaty Organization). International organizations vary in function and purpose, but all are voluntary and their actions usually have no binding force on participating states. What this means is that international organizations usually have no coercive power to enforce decisions on a reluctant party unless powerful member nations have the will to enforce them. We say *usually* here because there is some evidence that some organizations such as the European Union may soon resemble a truly international government.

International organizations are born by treaty or executive agreement between two or more nation-states. States are motivated to create international organizations to provide a forum for cooperation when it is advantageous for the member states. The purpose of international organizations spans the entire spectrum of human interest. It may be political, military, economic, cultural, social, or technical in nature. For example, NATO is an organization created to protect the security of the member states. The Organization of Petroleum Exporting Countries (OPEC), though pursuing political goals, attempts to protect the stability of oil prices and the oil profits of member nations.

International organizations, like the nation-state, have proliferated in recent years. Since the end of World War II, the world has become more complex, dangerous, and interdependent. For example, what happens politically in the Middle East, and its oil reserves, has a profound effect on the ecomony and standards of living of people throughout the world. Likewise, the existence of nuclear weapons that could destroy the world gives all an interest in their control. States have viewed international organizations as necessary to deal with this danger, complexity, and interdependence. Prior to World War I there were fewer than 50 such organizations. Today, there are over 375 (Papp 1988, 54).

With the increased complexity of the world, we should expect that the power and influence of international organizations will increase. Since the end of the Cold War, the United Nations has sponsored military actions and economic sanctions in Iraq, Bosnia, several African states, and in Haiti. You may be interested in examining the increase in influence for your research topic. However, we do not want to exaggerate the power of these organizations. All are the creatures of the nation-states and guarantee the sovereignty of member states.[3] The nation-state remains the more significant actor in the international arena.

Multinational Corporations   A **multinational corporation** is a business corporation with headquarters in one nation-state that owns and operates subsidiaries in other countries. Many multinational corporations are household words in the United States. We bet you've eaten a Nestle's chocolate bar, seen an advertisement for a Toyota, filled your car with Exxon gasoline, and taken a Bayer aspirin. Multinationals are in virtually every business imaginable. Some, such as Coca Cola and Sony, produce consumer goods. IBM and ITT deal in high technology. Still others such as Anaconda Copper deal in raw materials.

Multinational corporations are, for the most part, huge and experience strong economic growth. Many such as General Motors, Exxon, and Ford are larger economically than all but a few nations. Indeed, at least one estimate holds that by the turn of the twenty-first century, multinationals will account for about 50 percent of the world's economic product (Modelski, 1979).

No other actors in the international political system generate as much scholarly (and nonscholarly) controversy. They are either praised as providers of world prosperity or condemned as organizations that economically enslave states and people perpetuating poverty and misery in much of the world. Defenders argue that the multinationals provide economic opportunity in places where none exists and produce economic efficiency which helps maximize the production of goods and services at lower prices. Thus, the world's standard of living increases because of the multinationals. Critics hold them to be agents of economic imperialism that ruthlessly pursue profit and political control with little concern for the environment or human advancement.

The actual role of the multinational corporation is probably somewhere in between. Regardless of where we fall in this debate, however, the size and productive capacity of these giants ensure for them an important role in the international system.

Economically, multinationals can often make or break the national economies of the smaller nation-states. They can provide investment, education, and jobs. They can also take each away. Likewise, many large corporations have cornered a particular product market and can use this market power to increase profits in times of international crisis. During the gasoline shortages of the 1970s, many Americans believed that the "seven sisters of oil" had conspired to keep oil off the market to drive the price higher (ask your

Mom and Dad if they remember those days.) No one ever proved these charges. However, the point is this. The seven largest oil companies were large enough to do so if they had wanted to.

The economic power of multinationals also translates into political power. In the 1992 U.S. presidential election, for example, independent candidate Ross Perot tried to make an issue of foreign companies hiring lobbyists from the ranks of high-level government officials. Where the multinational corporation is important to the host country's economy, the government is often forced into making economic concessions to the company. These concessions, for example, involve taxation and property. In an extreme case, ITT was implicated in the overthrow and assassination of an elected leader in Chile (Spero 1985).

Multinational corporations have become important international actors. Some contend that they threaten the nation-state system itself (Heilbroner 1977). Governments have lost some of their abilities to control decisions in their countries as a result of the decisions of multinationals. If Ford moves plants from Detroit to Mexico City, it hurts the U.S. economy and helps the Mexican economy.

Nation-states have adopted several approaches to controlling the multinationals. Actions range from requiring nationals to own part of the company to banning the export of profits out of the country. As the world becomes ever more interdependent economically, the multinationals may further threaten the soverignty of nation-states. Another potential topic for your paper could involve how nation-states interact with multinational corporations.

Nongovernmental Organizations   The last actors participating in the game of international relations that we will discuss are **nongovernmental organizations.** These organizations by definition are not associated with governments, though some terrorist groups claim to be governments in waiting. Moreover, these organizations play only a subsidiary role in the international arena. Nation-states, international organizations, and multinational corporations are the dominant players.

Nongovernmental organizations differ as to size, purpose, and influence. They range from bodies such as the International Olympic Commission and the International Red Cross to political groups such as the Palestine Liberation Organization (PLO) and guerrilla organizations such as Peru's Shining Path.

For the most part, nongovernmental organizations have little impact on the nation-state international system. However, some are very visible in their activities, and some do have an impact on the behavior of the other actors in the international system. The International Red Cross is visible to all during disasters. Every four years the world's attention focuses on the Olympic games. You should be aware that the activities of the PLO and other political and terrorist organizations in the Middle East have a powerful effect on the foreign policy decisions of many nations with interests in that part of the world. Much research has begun in recent years on terrorism and its effect on the international system. You might find the subject of interest yourself.

◆ THE INTERNATIONAL SYSTEM

By now you are probably tired of us harping on about political systems. We do so because they are so important in studying and understanding the political world. In any event, the **international system** is unique among political systems and deserves further analysis. Recall Robert Dahl's definition of a political system from Chapter 4. He defined a political system as "any persistent pattern of human relationships that involves to a significant extent, control, influence, power, or authority. Most political systems involve individual nation-states where there is a centralized political authority (government) that processes demands of political actors. The centralized authority, at least for the most part, makes binding decisions accepted as legitimate by the political players.

To understand the international political system, we must be more specific about the type of human relationships we are talking about. One student of international relations defines the international system as any collection of *independent* political entities which interact with considerable frequency and according to regularized processes (Holsti 1965, 27). The key refinement of Dahl's definition is the word *independent*. The international system involves human relationships, control, power, and authority. However, it lacks the centralized political authority of most political systems. This is what makes the international system unique.

The international system is made up of sovereign nation-states that are accountable to no higher authority. Hence, the principal actors in this system live essentially in a state of anarchy. What are the implications for such a political system? Where there is anarchy, there is no automatic harmony. Each state is the final judge of its own cause. For example, a state will choose force to achieve its goals if its leaders value those goals more than they value peace (Waltz 1959, 160).

Unlike other political systems, the anarchic nature of the international system can influence the behavior of individual actors. Because any state at any time may resort to force to achieve its goals, all states must be ready to counter the use of force or pay for its weakness. The Hobbesian international system imposes the requirement on each state to provide for the strongest defense it can afford. Since each state is the guardian of its own safety, all other states are potential enemies and are treated with distrust. All states become concerned about their own strength and power relative to others. The old adage "If you want peace, prepare for war" reflects the impact of the international system on the behavior of nation-states. Therefore, in studying international relations, we must be aware that, while the international system is made up of its several actors, at the same time it has a life of its own.

The impact of the system on states varies with the structure of the system. In the nineteenth and early twentieth centuries, several states had relatively equal power. This generated a system of fluctuating alliances known as the balance of power system. During the Cold War, the standoff between the world's superpowers, the United States and the Soviet Union, profoundly impacted the behavior of all states. The international system had a bipolar structure. In the post–Cold War era, it is unclear whether the United States will remain a superpower in a unipolar world or whether a highly complex, multipolar structure will evolve (Spiegel and Pervin 1994, 5).

International Law   After our discussion of the anarchic nature of the international system, you might think that the idea of international law is a contradiction in terms. How can there be laws limiting the behavior of nation-states when there is no international government to make and enforce them? It's a good question that we can only answer by saying once again that the international system is unique. It's a system where anarchy and law are not necessarily contradictions.

The source of international law is obviously not a product of world government. Instead, we can best view international law as a set of agreements between or among the actors in the international system, usually nation-states, that defines how they will conduct relations. The sources of international law are international convention, customary law (Spanier 1990, 478), and subsidiary law (Papp 1988, 452).

International conventions are the specific treaties and other agreements among nations that bind the participants to particular actions. Some treaties involve relatively few actors. Others are more general. You have probably heard of the Geneva Convention which spells out the "rules of war."

Most international law is customary. It is not codified. Certain norms of conduct have evolved over time that at some point become accepted as binding even though they are not codified. Laws governing diplomatic immunity and much of the laws of the high seas developed by custom. Did you know that foreign diplomats committing crimes in another country (even murder) cannot be prosecuted? It's true, under the customary law of diplomatic immunity.

Subsidiary law, and its sources, is more vague. It basically comes from interpretations of international law by different courts, particulary the International Court of Justice. Such international courts are different in an important respect from national courts. Their decisions are not binding and they have no way to enforce them. So when the United States sued Iran for the takeover of the American Embassy in 1979, Iran simply denied the Court had jurisdiction. Later, the Sandinista government in Nicaragua sued the United States for its aid to the Contra rebels. The United States ignored the Court's ruling in favor of the Sandinistas.

In the anarchic international system, actors, particularly nation-states, obey international law when it is in their interest to do so. Sometimes powerful actors may find it in their interest to enforce the law against another state. As noted, the United Nations has taken a stronger role in policing the world community. The recent war following Iraq's invasion of Kuwait is a prime example. However, even strong actions such as the Gulf War were possible only because members of the UN Security Council (nation-states) found it in their interest to act aggressively.

❖ SOME KEY QUESTIONS

Americans live in a world of foreigners. However, so do the French, British, Japanese, and the Brazilians. Indeed, no nation-state contains even close to a majority of the world's population. Only about one in twenty are Americans. The most populous nation, China, represents only about one-fourth of the world's total.

No nation in the world has a monopoly of geographic size, population, wealth, or talent. Russia is the largest nation in the world. It spans eleven time zones. You could comfortably place the United States, China, and Western Europe within its borders. Yet it makes up only about one-eighth of the world's landmass. The United States has the world's largest economy, but this amounts to less than 25 percent of the gross world product. No nation enjoys a monopoly of scientific discovery and invention. Nobel prizes know no national boundaries. We can say the same about scientific, literary, and philosophical knowledge.

What the minority status of all nations means is that, like it or not, each must take into account what "foreigners" are doing. Because each nation has limited resources, it must gain cooperation from others to achieve its goals. The problem nations face probably seems obvious to you. However, gaining the cooperation of other nation-states is difficult because the "foreigners" we have described are very different. By the year 2000, some three-fourths of the Earth's population will be nonwhite. Over two-thirds of the people are nonChristian. But Buddists, Muslims, Jews, and Hindus are also in the minority. The world's people are irrevocably diverse in religion, language, culture, ideologies, and governments.

While people and nations are diverse, they are also becoming more interdependent. Today, what happens at home is more effected by what happens abroad than ever before. Television and jet travel have made the world smaller. CNN has made the world a more familiar place to most of us. Remember the Gulf War and Operation Desert Storm? We watched much of it live on TV. Some have said that Saddam Hussein's intelligence information even came from CNN! The internet makes international communication inexpensive and fast. Economically, the world depends on Middle East oil, Japanese and German electronics, and U.S. computer technology. Many nations are not self-sufficient in food production and must rely on others to feed their people.

In an interdependent yet diverse world, nations have no choice but to play the game of international relations. The game is more complicated today because of the multiplication of nation-states, the end of the Cold War, and the actors of the new international system—multinational corporations, more viable international organizations, and new nongovernmental entities. The new actors may dominate many areas of international relations and even threaten national sovereignty in a way that could transform the international system (Mansbach 1994). Nevertheless, though its role has diminished, the nation-state remains at the center of today's international system. As such, the nation-state system still poses the major questions (though not all) in the subfield of international relations. What do nation-states want? How do they play the game? What are the causes of war? A corrollary question to the last is, how can we preserve peace?[4]

◆ THE GOALS OF NATION-STATES

National Security   Since nations are diverse with different interests, conflict among nations is inevitable. In the anarchic international system, where no government is present to resolve these conflicts, each nation-state must provide its own **national security.** Because failure to provide sufficient security could lead to the state's extinction, it should not surprise you that protection against military threats is the number one priority of the nation-state. The number one goal is physical survival.

No state today can obtain total security. Where there are so many national actors, a state could only achieve such a goal by the conquest of all other independent states. Therefore, states can only feel relatively safe. The difficult question is how much security is enough? The answer to that question depends on the perceived level of threat by a nation's leaders, their ability to form alliances, and the nation's economic ability to build a strong military.

We can further break down national security into two other types—territorial security and political independence. Each state wants to protect its territorial integrity, or its frontier boundaries. Many international conflicts have erupted over the question of territorial integrity. Iraq claims Kuwait is its nineteenth province. Syria claims the Golan Heights, seized by Israel, as part of its territory. Territorial integrity is an integral part of a state's identity and self-esteem.

Political independence refers to the ability of a state to remain as free from foreign, or unwanted, influence as possible. In an interdependent world, no state can remain completely free in this sense. Nevertheless, each has a security interest in preserving its national values, lifestyle, and way of life. The United States and the Soviet Union during the Cold War intervened in many parts of the world because they feared the "other nation's values and actions" threatened their political independence. The United States intervened and overthrew Panamanian dictator Manuel Noriega in 1989 because allegedly Noriega was aiding in the drug trade to the United States, a perceived threat to our political independence and national values. In the new international system, concerns over drugs, the global environment, human rights, and economic performance complicate the quest for political independence. International organizations, multinational corporations, and other nongovernmental organizations even threaten state sovereignty over these new international issues. At the the same time subnational actors, tribes, and terrorist groups threaten political independence from within.

National Prestige   **National prestige** involves the way others perceive a nation-state. It is closely associated with military power and the willingness to use military resources to achieve the state's goals. Economic success is another key ingredient to national prestige.

We should not think a nation arrogant because it wants to improve its national prestige. If a nation has high prestige, other nations may not challenge it, and war is avoided. Or, a nation, when feared by others, may get its way with other states without threats. National prestige is an important resource in any nation's power base.

A state gains and maintains national prestige by developing a strong military and then using it to further its interests and make good its commitments. For example, the United States lost prestige with its defeat in Vietnam. The loss strengthened Soviet resolve to expand its influence in places such as Angola and Ethiopia. Even a weak nation, Iran, was bold enough to seize our embassy in Tehran. This was a blatant violation of international law that not even Hitler attempted. The United States strengthened its national prestige during the presidencies of Ronald Reagan and George Bush with successful military actions in Grenada, Libya, and the Middle East (Operation Desert Storm). President Clinton's perceived foreign policy waffling in Somalia, Bosnia, and Haiti could damage U.S. prestige.

Lesser nation-states are also concerned with prestige. France, Britain, and China developed the atomic bomb as a symbol of prestige. Even the poorest nations strive for recognition by creating their own airlines and establishing diplomatic missions in other countries.

Economic Security   For nation-states to be militarily secure they obviously need economic wealth to buy such protection. Armies, navies, and air power aren't cheap. Only nations with relatively strong economies can be strong militarily.

In addition, in an interdependent world a nation's security can be undermined by economic competition and decline. Nation-states compete economically as well as politically. The former Soviet Union maintained superpower status through its military might. The cost was to undermine its economic security and ultimately its ability to survive.

A decline of economic competitiveness today threatens the economic security of the United States. A decline in our economic base lowers our standard of living and we become vulnerable to "foreign penetration" of our economic infrastructure. Foreigners today own over 10 percent of the manufacturing base and 20 percent of the banks in the United States as well as 46 percent of the real estate in Los Angeles. In addition, foreign interests own such American giants as Pillsbury, RCA, CBS records, and United Artists/MGM (Tolchin 1989). Though U.S competitiveness has improved in the 1990s, the threat to economic security remains.

Several factors contribute to this threat. We have a national debt of $5 trillion that grows daily. In 1986 we became a debtor nation for the first time in history. We owe other nations more than they owe us. We see a decline in the quality of our labor force. Our school children are undereducated relative to many of those in Europe and Japan. Consider this comparison. American children on average attend school for 180 days a year for an average of 6 ½ hours per day. In Europe the average is 220 days for 8 hours and in Japan it is 240 days! Our children fall far behind their European and Asian counterparts in science and mathematics. This makes it difficult to compete in the world of high technology.

The message should be clear. A nation-state's internal problems can threaten its security as much as an external threat. Internal weakness leads to vulnerability in the international system. Economic security is therefore an important national goal.

Ideology   A final goal of nation-states is the advancement of an ideology. Recall that an ideology is a set of fundamental beliefs that explains the world and how the world should be. Communism is probably the most recognized of these ideologies. But democratic doctrine and religious beliefs have been ideological goals of nation-states as well.

Most states, however, do not have the promotion of a political ideology as their primary goal. To many, ideology isn't a goal at all. However, nations and governments born with a revolutionary ideology tend to believe that they have a unique role in spreading their faith. Thus, France after the French Revolution attempted to expand its influence. Its actions ended with defeat in the Napoleonic Wars. Likewise, the Soviet Union, from its birth in 1917 to its collapse in 1991, energetically sought to expand its power and advance the communist ideology. The Ayatollah Khomeini following the Iranian Revolution in 1979 sought to spread his brand of Islam to the rest of the Islamic world.

The United States has also articulated ideological goals for its foreign policy. President Woodrow Wilson justified our participation in World War I by "making the world safe for democracy." We justified the Cold War as a defense of democracy and freedom in the world. President Carter made "human rights" a cornerstone of his foreign policy.

While ideology remains a goal of some nations, the goals of national security, national prestige, and economic security remain paramount. For most of the history of the nation-state, the impact of ideology on the international system has been to intensify the conflict between nations rather than cause them (Spanier 1990, 85). For example, the United States and the former Soviet Union would have been rivals without the divergent ideologies. There would have been conflict. However, the different belief systems ensured that the conflict would be more intense and less open to compromise. Each nation saw itself as representing the "true path" and the other side as representing evil. In such situations, compromise is nearly impossible and the conflict of interest is overshadowed by mistrust, hostility, and fear.

◆ HOW STATES PLAY THE GAME

The anarchy of the international system automatically places nation-states in adversarial relations with one another. In such a political system, determination of who receives what, when, and how depends on the interactions of states under the rule of "every state for itself" (Spanier 1990, 96). There is no legitimate government to make the determination. In such an environment, each state must rely on itself to provide for its political independence, prosperity, and territorial integrity.

In an insecure world, nation-states try to reduce their insecurity by expanding their power. The interactions of nations most always involve power relationships and actions to increase their power vis à vis others. Recall the working definition of power we provided in Chapter 4. It refers to the "capacity to use political resources to influence successfully the actions, or predispositions to act, of others." Nation-states play the game of international politics by trying to increase their political resources and their capacity to use them. As a famous student of international politics once concluded,

> International politics, like all politics, is the struggle for power. Whatever the ultimate aim of international politics, power is the immediate aim. (Morganthau 1973, 27)

How do nation-states enhance their power? Some constituents of power are beyond the control of nation's leaders. For example, geography and natural resources are often a matter of chance. Some nation-states are endowed with an abundance of resources and a geography that provide a multitude of political capital. The size of Russia and its harsh winters contributed to the defeat of Napoleon, Kaiser Wilhelm during World War I, and Hitler during World War II. However, it also lacks an ice-free port in the winter. Some countries such as Bolivia and Zambia are land-locked, making them dependent on neighboring countries for access to the sea. Likewise, some countries are well endowed with natural resources. Imagine what influence Saudi Arabia would have without oil. Others have few, if any, of the things valued in the world (Chad and the Sudan).

Within certain limits, national leaders can act to enhance the political resources that increase the nation's power in the international system. We can group these resources into three broad categories—economic, military, and psychological (or sociopolitical).

Economic Dimension of Power   Economics contributes to the power equation in international politics in several ways. The most obvious is the relationship between wealth and military power. Satellite reconnaissance systems, armies, navies, and air forces are expensive. Cruise missiles, nuclear submarines, and missiles also are not cheap (the Tow missiles used so effectively in Operation Desert Storm cost nearly $1 million each). The richest countries play the largest roles in the international system because only they can realistically pay for a large, modern military arsenal. However, economics plays other, less obvious roles in the international power equation.

Today's world is economically interdependent. Trade is an important part of most domestic economies. If you don't believe this, ask yourself what would happen to our standard of living without Middle Eastern oil. Nations competing economically provides another example. From the 1970s to the mid-1980s the prices of American-made cars went up while quality went down. Foreign-made cars (particularly Japanese) rose in quality yet remained affordable. Sales of American-made cars plummeted while U.S. consumers went on a foreign car buying binge. Unemployment skyrocketed in Detroit. Similar events developed in other U.S. industries such as electronics, steel, and textiles. International competition directly effected our economic base.

Economic resources can also be used directly as weapons in the conduct of international affairs. In the 1970s OPEC blocked the sale of oil to the Western world. The embargo drove up prices, created shortages, and threatened the economic health of Europe, Japan, and the United States. The United Nations placed economic sanctions on Iraq following its invasion of Kuwait in 1991. Member nations refused to buy Iraqi oil to try and force compliance with their demands.

Rich nations may influence the behavior of poor nations by providing foreign aid or threatening to withhold it. Poor nations often depend on richer nations for their products. A boycott could destroy their fragile economies.

Even the relations between rich nations have a strong economic component. For example, Japan's influence in the United States has grown enormously over the last 25 years. Japan's monopoly in the production of certain products, such as computer chips, makes many U.S. industries dependent on Japanese suppliers. Whenever the American government begins to react to Japanese pressure, U.S. industry often becomes a Japanese ally fearing that supply of necessary products will be cut. Additionally, the Japanese have run an enormous trade surplus with the United States for many years. (We buy more products from them than they do from us.) Very simply, this means they have more American dollars than they can spend on our products. So, they begin to buy property and businesses in the United States. As a result, Japan becomes increasingly more influential in our economy and politics.[5]

Military Dimension of Power The high potential for violence is the best way to explain the nation-states' quest for power in the international system. In the anarchial system, the threat of violence, or its actual use, are the principal means states use to impose their will on others. As a result, military might is the chief political resource in a nation's power base. During the Cold War, the United States and the now defunct Soviet Union were "superpowers" because no other nation came close to their nuclear capability. Their economic strength was secondary.

As noted, military power is related to the economic capacity of the nation. Rich nations have the potential for more military might than poor ones. But just because a nation has a strong military does not necessarily mean that a nation will get its way. The influence that derives from military resources can only be tested in combat. The United States and its allies under the United Nation's mandate proved their power by driving Iraq out of Kuwait in 1992. Conversely, despite an overwhelming advantage in firepower, the United

States and the Soviet Union failed to impose their will in Vietnam and Afghanistan, respectively.

The relationship between military capability and power has both objective and subjective components. The amount and quality of military hardware and the skill of military personnel does not guarantee victory on the battlefield. At the same time, the quantity and quality of a nation's military is an important part of the national prestige nation-states seek. If others perceive a state strong and willing to use force to achieve its objectives, an implied threat of force may be sufficient to achieve the state's goals. This national prestige is built with a strong military and a proven record of its use to achieve its objectives.

In fact, the threat of force stands in the background of most negotiations between states. The desire to avoid war, particularly if the nation's leaders fear losing, is an incentive to compromise. Even the dominant power will normally prefer some compromise rather than war for two reasons. There is never any guarantee of victory (recall Vietnam and Afghanistan). War is costly both in money and human life, even for the victor.

The existence of nuclear weapons in a nation's military arsenal creates a special case in the international system's power equation. Most nations consider possession of nuclear capability part of national prestige and power. At least six nation-states have exploded nuclear devices. They include the United States, the former Soviet Union, China, France, the United Kingdom, and India. Many experts also believe that Israel has the capability to assemble a weapon in only a few days. Some believe that Pakistan, Argentina, Brazil, South Africa, and North and South Korea are very close to a nuclear capability. As a result of the Gulf War in 1992, we know that Iraq possessed the material and expertise to create a nuclear bomb. With the breakup of the Soviet Union, former Soviet Republics such as Ukraine and Russia have the bulk of the Soviet arsenal.

Ironically, the possession of these weapons of mass destruction do not necessarily increase a nation's ability to translate power into influence. The nuclear arms race during the Cold War illustrates this point.

Because of their destructive power, the Soviet Union and the United States engaged in a race to increase the capacity and sophistication of their nuclear arsenals. However, this buildup in capacity did not result in an increase in either's net power base. What fueled the arms race in the nuclear age was a strategy designed to deter the use of nuclear weapons. We built ever bigger and more sophisticated weapons to ensure they would never be used!

We justified the arms race on the theory of **deterrence.** The logic of deterrence relies on the belief that one side has the military capacity to convince the other that it is not worthwhile to attack. Nuclear deterrence depends on what we call mutually assured destruction (MAD). Each nuclear power must be convinced that if it launched a nuclear attack, the other side could absorb the first strike and respond with enough destructive power to destroy it as a functioning society. In such a situation, no rational leader would launch such a war unless suicide was the goal.

The deterrent depends on each side obtaining and maintaining a "second strike" capability. So when one side expands its weaponry, the other must respond to maintain its second strike capability. The result? More and more money spent on more and more weapons to achieve no increase in real influence in the power equation. At the height of the nuclear buildup, the United States and the Soviet Union had the capacity to destroy the world several times over with no net increase in their power.

The Psychological Dimension of Power   When we think of the political resources that make up a nation-state's power potential, we usually focus on the economic and military capabilities discussed above. It is also important to consider how and for what purposes leaders use these resources, and their skill and willingness to use them to achieve the nation's goals. What we are referring to here are the intangible aspects of the power equation involving the psychological predispostions a nation's people and its leaders. For example, things such as political will, morale, and character are all part of the power equation even though they are difficult to measure.

Though intangible, these psychological resources are important. We have already discussed the failures of the United States and the Soviet Union to impose their will on Vietnam and Afghanistan. Superior firepower could not save the Shah of Iran against the fundamentalist ideas of the Ayatollah Khomeini in Iran. Likewise, the British were driven from India by the power of nationalism fueled by the ideas and commitment of Gandhi.

The intangibles of will and morale are linked. Will refers to the determination of leaders in pursuing national goals. National morale is the "popular dedication [of the people] to the nation and support for its policies, even when that support requires sacrifice" (Spanier 1990, 155). Examples of will and morale are most evident during wartime. North Vietnam's leading general, Vo Nguyen Giap, predicted victory over the United States because he believed democracies quickly lose patience in a long, drawn-out struggle. They lose the will to win. Likewise, German bombing of London in the Battle of Britain in 1940 backfired by increasing the morale of the British people.

Character is an even more difficult concept than will and morale. The existence of a national character presumes that certain intellectual and emotional qualities are valued more highly in one actor than another (Waltz 1959; Arnand 1981). Russians have a long-standing mistrust of the outside world. Germans tend to be philosophic and have militaristic tendencies. The French are more emotional and artistic. Americans are industrious and pragmatic.

Character relates to the power equation because certain policies or strategies stem or are proscribed by character. For example, Americans are impatient. North Vietnam bet that we would not fight a protracted war. The British are determined. Hitler in 1940 and Argentina in 1982 misjudged this trait. Determination alone may account for the British refusing to yield during the battle of Britain. In 1982 this determination allowed Prime Minister Margaret Thatcher to wage a long-distance and expensive war to recapture the Faulkland Islands.

A final psychological resource is leadership. There are many aspects of leadership, but as a psychological resource we will consider just one. Leaders of nation-states that have the skill to formulate and implement strategy to achieve their goals will enhance a state's power. Those without a strategy will experience a decline. President Richard Nixon and his Secretary of State Henry Kissinger formed a comprehensive strategy toward China and the Soviet Union. It increased our freedom of action in the world and limited that of both the Soviet Union and China. Between 1969 and 1974 the United States sought to make cordial relations of paramount importance to both of these nuclear powers. The result was to limit Soviet and Chinese interference in Vietnam (Kissinger 1982).

Likewise, the leadership skills of Dag Hammarskjold as Secretary General of the United Nations built the prestige and influence of the UN. He convinced others that peacekeeping was a legitimate UN function and pushed the UN to accept international responsibilities. Without his leadership it is unlikely that the UN would have acted following the Iraqi invasion of Kuwait in 1990 or during the current crisis in the Balkans.

The Causes of War   "What causes war?" is perhaps the most intriguing question posed by the field of international relations. War and conflict are as old as human history. However, the existence of weapons of mass destruction made the question more important because they provide the means to literally destroy civilization.

Karl von Clausewitz, in a famous answer to the question, observed that "war is a continuation of politics by other means" (Clausewitz 1976). War was just another way that nation-states play politics in order to achieve their goals. Today, warfare is a tool of other international actors as well. Terrorist groups such as the Palestine Liberation Organization and the Irish Republican Army take their crusades to win national independence to civilians. Most research focuses on war among nations, but there are lots of potential research projects in analyzing these new types of warfare.

The seeming irrationality of international violence, the loss in life and property, coupled with its pervasiveness in the world, makes war and its cause the subject of intense interest. The study of war is as old as recorded history and the answer to its causes remains in dispute. Basically, there have been three approaches to the study of war between states elucidated in the classic work *Man, the State and War* by Kenneth Waltz (1959). Scholars have looked to the nature of man, the nature of states, and our friend the international system itself.

Human Nature   Recall once more that the source of politics is human nature (Chapter 4). Many philosophers argue that the ultimate form of politics, war, has its roots in human nature as well.

Traditional theorists as diverse as St. Augustine, Reinhold Niebuhr, and Confucius held firm to the belief that war springs from man. St. Augustine's chief culprit was original sin. Perfectly good men cannot war, but because of original sin, there are no perfectly good men. Niebuhr believed war was clearly in the nature of humankind. War stemmed from "dark unconscious sources in the human psyche" (Niebuhr 1938). Confucius put it quite simply, "There is deceit and cunning and from these wars arise" (Waltz 1959, 16).

From this perspective war results from selfishness, aggressive impulses, stupidity, or a combination of all three. Other causes of war are secondary. Eliminating war can come only by the enlightenment of all humanity.

The Nature of States   The second approach to the causes of war focuses on the character of particular nation-states. The type of government and economy as well as its culture are the primary determinants of war. From this perspective, some states are superior to others. They reach a state of being that eliminates the motivation and necessity of war. Unfortunately, there has been little agreement over the character of the superior state.

Emmanuel Kant (a famous philosopher that terrifies students by the complexity of his philosophy) believed that the purpose of the state was to make man act morally. The state should promote what is right. But no existing states were completely good or completely bad, so war was inevitable. As a result, states must actively seek to improve themselves internally. The ideal form was a republic. The political system should not be a monarchy. It had to be based on at least some popular representation of people other than the king's or queen's family. To Kant, a republic was a type of state which was unable to injure any other by violence" (Kant 1914).

V. I. Lenin, the founder of the Soviet Union, argued that private ownership in the economy caused class conflict within states and between states. Capitalist economies ultimately led to states colonizing others which led to conflict and war with other imperialist nations. Eliminating capitalism and creating a socialist society would eliminate injustice within a state, and as a bonus would eliminate the state's need for colonies that propelled them to war. Socialism brought peace (Lenin 1961).

President Woodrow Wilson, who led the United States into World War I, had a completely different view. The cause of war was neither private ownership of the economy nor the lack of a moral state. The chief foe to a peaceful world was the absence of political democracy. Democratic states, by definition, would not war. To Wilson, World War I itself would make the "world safe for democracy." The problem was to make states democratic. Wilson believed the first task was to defeat tyranny and provide for the "self-determination of peoples" which would lead to democracy. In the interim, a world confederation of democratic states (The League of Nations) would provide security and spread the democratic creed.[6]

All of these approaches can't be right. In spite of the great differences in belief however, there are two common, and important, threads in their arguments. The character of the nation-state is the most important cause of war. More importantly, each believed that we as humans could influence what our states would become. We have the power to end the bloody spectre of war.

The International System   The final approach to the study of war focuses on the character of the international system as the primary cause of war. As we have discussed, the international system is anarchic. In such a system, each state must fend for itself and provide for its own security. Since there is no higher authority or comprehensive standard of conduct, states pursue their interests by any means, including the use of military force. War is a simple result of competing states pursuing their own selfish interests. From this perspective, war is inevitable even if all states are led by angels and have achieved "superior internal structures" however defined.

The character of the international system creates other forces that lead to war. Since states compete with one another, and all fear for their security, there is little trust among nation-states. Leaders of one nation cannot be sure that leaders of others are speaking truthfully about their intentions. Uncertainty and the possibility of misperception plague all leaders in plotting and implementing their nation's foreign policy. Consider the following examples.

To increase national security in an uncertain world, nation-states have often formed alliances to improve their collective security. NATO is such an alliance as was the Warsaw Pact until the demise of the Soviet Union. The existence and necessity of alliances such as these in the international system led the world literally to fall into World War I.

The two principal European alliances involved were the Triple Entente of Great Britain, France, and Russia and the Triple Alliance of Germany, Austria-Hungary, and Italy. In addition, the several alliance states had secret agreements with others not in either major alliance. When Austria-Hungary's Archduke Ferdinand was assassinated in Sarajevo, Austria-Hungary prepared to march on Serbia. Russia mobilized because of a secret pact with Serbia. Germany mobilized against Russia. Austria-Hungary refused to respond to a series of communications from Berlin and marched into Serbia. World War I had begun. An Austrian diplomat was later asked how the war had begun. His frightening reply was "God, if we only knew." Distrust, uncertainty, and fear led leaders to enter a devastating war that nobody wanted.

Likewise, the modern theory of deterrence, as previously explained, stimulated an arms race based on the strategy of mutually assured destruction. Distrust and misperception contributed to this arms race and the various (fortunately hypothetical) theories of how World War III would begin. A popular novel of the 1960s, *Failsafe*, posited an accidental nuclear attack by the United States on the Soviet Union. Soviet leaders were told it was an accident, but that there was nothing we could do to call back the bombers. (If you were president, would you believe the leaders of the Soviet Union if the situation was reversed?) Moscow and its surroundings would be destroyed. The Soviets prepared to respond. Retaliation would mean World War III and the possible destruction of the planet. In the novel, the world avoided total war, but only because the United States government destroyed New York City with our own nuclear weapons to prove we were telling the truth.

❖ APPROACHES TO THE STUDY OF INTERNATIONAL RELATIONS

The three approaches to the study of war also help provide us with a framework to analyze all of international relations. As with the subfields of American politics and comparative politics, students of international relations have used traditional and scientific methods of analysis. Regardless of method however, we can study international relations from three different levels of analysis suggested by the various approaches to war. These are the state-system level, the nation-state level and the decision-making level.

The state-system level focuses attention on the international system's influence on the behavior of nation-states. As noted above, the anarchic nature of the international system may be the primary cause of war. At this level of analysis, the actions of states are for the most part determined by external forces generated by the international system. The character of individual states and their leaders really make little difference in how states will behave.

Proponents of this level of analysis focus their attention on the character of the international system and how it influences the behavior of actors in the international system. From this perspective we know that states are concerned about security, power, and their perceived national interest. They pursue their interests in a world of mistrust, uncertainty, and danger.

State-system analysis also concerns itself with problems of change in the international system and its impact on the behavior of states. For example, communications technology and economic necessity is making the world a much more global community. The world has become smaller and more interdependent as a result. Environmental problems such as acid rain, global warming, and ozone depletion know no national boundaries. How will states respond to these changes in the system?

Likewise, in this text we have de-emphasized international actors other than the nation-states for the sake of brevity. This does not mean they are unimportant, however. The rise of large multinational corporations, terrorist organizations, and other international and nongovernmental organizations are changing the international system. In the new international system these nonstate actors are proliferating. Their impact provides a fertile field for research.

The nation-state level focuses on how the internal structure of states influences their behavior. We categorize states as either democratic or authoritarian, capitalist or socialist, revolutionary or stable, rich or poor. Various students of war hypothesized that the character of a state determines its slant toward international violence.

We can also study whether it is more difficult for leaders in a democracy to make war than for those leading authoritarian states. Revolutionary states, such as France following the French Revolution and Iran following the overthrow of the Shah, reject the traditional order of things. Their revolutionary beliefs fuel their behavior. Thus, Napoleonic France believed it was in a "just

Box 8.1

GOVERNMENT STRUCTURE AND ALLIANCE: A RESEARCH EXAMPLE

The study of alliances among nation-states is a core element in theories of international relations and war. The neorealist view is that nation-states form, rearrange, or dissolve alliances to increase their security in the anarchic international system. From this perspective, alliance instability is unrelated to who governs a particular nation-state. This is another way of saying that partisan politics stops at the "water's edge."

Randolph Siverson and Harvey Starr explore the possibility that the above hypothesis is wrong. They postulate that governmental change within nation-states impacts their alliance behavior. Different groups, or group coalitions, serve different constituencies, have different ideologies or world views, and therefore, bring different priorities and values to government when they gain office. As such, Siverson and Starr expect states experiencing regime changes will show a greater propensity to change alliances than states experiencing no change.

The authors note that two basic types of regime change are possible. First, there are those changes where government leaders change while the rules of the game remain the same. Such changes take place when a Democrat replaces a Republican as president of the United States. Second, there are regime changes when not only rulers change, but the entire way politics and government are conducted. Such change occurs, for example, when a violent revolution occurs. Siverson and Starr are interested in only the latter type of change.

Within this second category of regime change, the authors identify three types: change that results from loss of a war to an external party, change that results from internal violence, and change that stems from internal political upheaval and crisis that stops short of overt violence. Siverson and Starr use data primarily from European international relations between 1816 and 1965 gathered from the POLITYII and Correlates of War data sets.

Using regression analysis (remember, you will learn about it in Chapter 14), the authors compare the impact of the various types of change and the alliance behavior of nation-states. They conclude in general that regime change has a definite impact on the alliance behavior of nation-states. More specifically, they find that change caused by loss of a war to an external party has the strongest effect in changing alliances.

Siverson and Starr carefully note that their findings do not mean that the neorealist search for security is irrelevant to the alliance behavior of nation-states. Instead, their findings suggest a nation's alliance portfolio is a product of forces other that pure security concerns.

Source: Randolph M. Siverson and Harvey Starr, "Regime Change and the Restructuring of Alliances," *American Journal of Political Science*, 38, no. 1 (February 1994): 145–61.

war" to establish international peace. The Iran of the Ayatollahs supports terrorism and takes other actions to spread its form of Islamic fundamentalism.

Finally, the decision-making level of analysis focuses on who makes the foreign policy decisions of a nation-state and how they make them. States don't actually make decisions, leaders of states do. Students of the decision-making perspective study the perceptions and values of the policy makers, the different kinds of decisions made, and the nature of the decision-making process itself. Usually, scholars adopt this perspective because it allows them to study specific decisions in some detail.

The foreign policy perceptions of a nation's leaders are important in explaining state action. President Jimmy Carter looked at the revolutionary Sandinista government of Nicaragua, though Communist, as a government born of years of repression by the ruthless Somoza government. His policy toward Nicaragua was one of live and let live. Carter's successor, Ronald Reagan, viewed the Sandinista government as another tumor of communist expansion that threatened the free world. U.S. policy under President Reagan blockaded and mined Nicaragua's harbors and supported the Contra rebels trying to overthrow the government.

Misperception is also a subject to study. British Prime Minister Chamberlain's failure to see Hitler's true intent probably made World War II unavoidable. How do leaders' perceptions develop? How do they affect foreign policy? How do perceptions affect other leaders? How do leaders perceive the post-Soviet international system? Each of these questions have been the subject of much research.

Students of the decision-making perspective also examine the kinds of decisions made. Basically, they study the differences between crisis and noncrisis decision making. Crisis decision making usually involves confrontations between great powers. You have probably read about the Cuban Missile Crisis of 1962. For 13 days in October the United States and the Soviet Union stood at the brink of nuclear war after President Kennedy discovered that the Soviets had introduced nuclear missiles to the island of Cuba. How decision makers react in such times of crisis are of obvious interest in the field of international relations.

Noncrisis decision making involves the more mundane, yet critical, decisions concerning issues of national security, power, and economic goals. How big should a nation's defense budget be? Should foreign aid be expanded or cut? What should the state's position be on trade, tariffs, and the environment? Studying these questions may not be as sexy as studying crisis, but they are critical in understanding the behavior of nation-states.

Finally, we want to know how leaders make foreign policy decisions. We might want to know if democratic countries have different processes than nondemocracies. We can even wonder if different types of decisions involve different processes in the same country. For example, in times of crisis, the bureaucracy is not part of the decision process in the United States. The president and his closest advisors decide without much input from anyone else.

Noncrisis decisions involve the president, the bureaucracy, the Congress, interest groups, and even the media.

After consideration of each of these three approaches to the study of international relations, you might wonder, which one is best? The answer is obviously a subject of debate, or there wouldn't be three different perspectives. Debate exists because we can use each to explain some, but not all, of the behavior of international actors.

They also reflect differing opinion as to the primary causes of international events. For example, consider the question "What caused World War II?" The answers vary with the approach. Allan Bullock in his book *Hitler: A Study in Tyranny* concludes without hesitation that Hitler and the perceptions of opposing leaders were the cause. He clearly believes the decision-making approach is best in explaining the war. British historian A. J. P. Taylor argued that Hitler was irrelevant. Conditions in the international system led to war. In other words, it mattered little who led Germany at the time—the world would go to war (Taylor, 1964).

❖ SUMMARY

The subfield of international relations is a broad one. It involves much more than "just politics." Culture, history, economics, and geography are all part of the international arena. Like other subfields of political science, however, international relations involves the study of political systems, particularly the international system. This system is unique because it is essentially in anarchy. Unlike most, the international system consists of actors many of which are sovereign nation-states. There is no international government to resolve disputes.

Analyzing international relations involves some concepts and questions not specifically seen in other political systems. The players consist of nation-states, international organizations such as the United Nations, large multinational corporations such as Exxon and ITT, and nongovernmental organizations such as the PLO. How these actors interact, and the result of this interaction, are the chief interest of students of international relations.

The international system creates a unique environment for the study of politics. Its nature determines how actors, particularly nation-states, interact and behave. Nation-states' first concern in the international system is their own security. Since there is no central authority to resolve disputes, each state is ultimately responsible for providing its security in a potentially violent and definitely uncertain world. Miscalculation can lead to national extinction.

Two other goals of nation-states are related to the issue of national security. These include national prestige and economic security. National prestige allows states freedom of movement in the international system. A state that is perceived as strong is less likely to be challenged by others. Economic strength provides prosperity for its people, stability and support of leaders at home, and the wherewithall to build a military arsenal to provide security.

A final goal of some nations is to spread a particular ideology such as communism or democracy. Usually, however, ideological goals are secondary to those related to national security.

The character of the international system also dictates how nations play the game of international politics. States will try to achieve their goals by expanding their power in the system. We described three dimensions of power (capacity to influence) in the system. These include the economic, military, and psychological dimensions of power. Because nation-states are insecure and pursue their goals in a system of anarchy, conflict can end in war. The study of war is a central concern in the subfield.

There have been three basic explanations of war. The first begins with the assumption that the cause of war is human nature itself. To end war we must perfect humanity. The second focuses on the character of the state. Is it democractic or socialist? The third looks at the anarchical international system as the primary cause.

Finally, students of international relations have studied the important questions in the field from three levels of analysis. These parallel the approaches to war. Some study the international system. Others examine how the character of the state affects its behavior. Still others focus on the leaders of states and how foreign policy is made in each. All three approaches are useful. Each captures a portion of the truth about the behavior of states, but none by itself captures the whole truth.

❖ KEY TERMS

deterrence	national prestige
economic security	national security
international organizations	nation-state
international system	nongovernmental organizations
multinational corporations	war

❖ EXERCISES

1. Discuss the evolution of the nation-state system in the international arena.
2. Using our definition of power in Chapter 4, describe how nation-states build power in the international arena.
3. With the help of your instructor, develop three (or more) hypotheses about how the international system is changing in the post–Cold War "new international system."
4. Do you believe that a nation-state's national security is better protected in a democracy or in an authoritarian state? Why or why not?
5. Which is the best approach to the study of war? Justify your choice.

6. With the help of your instructor, develop at least three topics for papers on the causes of war.

❖ SUGGESTED READINGS

Bullock, Alan. *Hitler: A Study in Tyranny*. New York: Bantam Books, 1961.

Clausewitz, Karl von. *On War*. Princeton: Princeton University Press, 1976.

Freedman, Lawrence, ed. *War*. New York: Oxford University Press, 1994.

Kissinger, Henry. *Years of Upheaval*. Boston: Little-Brown, 1982.

Mansbach, Richard. *The Global Puzzle*. Boston: Houghton Mifflin, 1994.

Spiegel, Steven, and David Pervin. *At Issue: Politics in the World Arena*, 7th ed. New York: St. Martin's Press, 1994.

Taylor, A. J. P. *The Origins of the Second World War*. Middlesex, UK: Penguin, 1964.

Waltz, Kenneth. *Man, the State, and War*. New York: Columbia University Press, 1959.

❖ NOTES

1. We should also note however, that the distinction between nation, state, and nation-state is sometimes important to understand activities in the international system. Terrorism in the Middle East and Northern Ireland are examples of national activities with international impact based on a rejection of the existing state.

2. The number of nation-states in Europe alone jumped to between 35 and 40 by the early 1930s.

3. Even the proposed European Union with its European Parliament, common currency, and supranational authority, receives its power from member states. At least in theory, the states may revoke that authority.

4. As with our earlier discussions of other political science subfields, we make no pretense that these are the only important questions in international relations. They are important ones, however, and will give you a flavor for the field. They also should provide you with suggestions for your research topic.

5. The rising influence of Japan is well documented. It has recently been popularized in novel form. For an exciting read, see Michael Crichton's *Rising Sun*.

6. You will recall that Wilson negotiated U.S. membership in such a "League of Nations," but the U.S. Senate failed to ratify the treaty (see Waltz 1959, 117–19).

3

◆ ◆ ◆

THE METHODS OF POLITICAL SCIENCE

Part One introduced you to political science and research. As such, you read how to conduct systematic political research, decide on a potential topic, and conduct a systematic search for related literature so that you could write a comprehensive literature review.

Part Two introduced you to the scope of political science. Several chapters were devoted to telling you about the political world, the American political process, public administration and public policy, comparative politics, and international relations.

Now the relatively smooth road we have traveled starts to get a bit bumpy. In Part Three, we discuss the basic elements of scientific research. We introduce you to terms such as concepts, variables, hypotheses, causation, and measurement. But do not worry. Our vehicle has brand new shocks, we drive slowly, and, as a result, we give you a smooth ride over the rough road we travel.

In Chapter 9 we cover the elements of research. You will learn all about nominal and conceptual definitions, variables, and hypotheses. An understanding of the chapter will enable you to identify the factors necessary to have a causal relationship and define multiple causation.

In Chapter 10 we introduce you to a notion that is very difficult for novice political researchers to grasp—measurement. We discuss the theory of measurement, the various threats to measurement, and how to enhance the reliability and validity of measurement instruments. We also explain how measurement is used to answer questions about topics such as voting turnout, the governmental structure of other nations, and why people revolt. Last, we discuss the different levels of measurement and their importance to the research process.

In Chapter 11 we introduce you to the different types of research designs you can use to complete a research study. Research designs provide you with a plan to use when collecting, analyzing, and interpreting data you believe provides answers to your research problem. As such, they are an important part of the research process.

We also highlight the advantages, disadvantages, and differences between the experimental and nonexperimental designs. Experimental designs, for exam-

ple, are stronger in internal validity, but weaker in external validity than the nonexperimental designs. An experimental design enables you to enhance the comparison, manipulation, and control, of your study's components. On the other hand, you cannot generalize the results as readily as you can with a nonexperimental design.

In Chapter 11 you will also read about several obstacles to the internal and external validity of your study and ways to overcome those obstacles. A clear definition of your population, probability sampling techniques, and a shorter period of study will help overcome the internal validity threats we discuss. The way you select and assign members to your test and control groups can influence the external validity of your study.

In Chapter 12 we deal with the various techniques political scientists use to collect and input data. We also examine the fundamentals of sampling theory and the aims of sampling. You will read about the central concepts of sampling such as the population, the sampling unit, the sampling frame, and the sample itself. We also look at probability and nonprobability sampling designs. The latter part of the chapter covers ways to determine the size of the sample, coding of the data you collected, and inputting the data to a statistical analysis software package.

In Chapters 13 through 15 we cover the various ways you can analyze your data. Chapter 13 deals with univariate statistics which are used to examine a single variable. In this chapter we look at some important tools to use in the preliminary stage of data analysis such as frequency distributions, measures of central tendency which describe the distribution's main characteristics, and measures of dispersion which depict the extent of variance from the typical value or average. We also tell you how to use frequency polygons to determine how extreme scores can affect the measures of central tendency we discuss.

The statistics discussed in Chapter 13 help the political scientist understand data distributions. These descriptive statistics, however, are only a first step in data analysis. Once summarized, researchers often want to discover relationships between variables. We turn to this issue in Chapter 14 by discussing bivariate statistics, or the analysis of two variables. We introduce you to the rudiments of association and the various measures of association you can use to determine whether there is a relationship between two variables. We also spend time discussing two important notions—statistical significance and hypothesis testing.

Chapter 15 is a complex chapter. In this chapter we talk about multivariate statistics, or the analysis of three or more variables. We cover control and ways to use statistics to determine causality and explain the political phenomena we observe. Cross-tabulation control procedures, partial correlation coefficients, and multiple regression techniques, for example, are very useful because they allow us to examine the correlation between variables.

In Chapter 16 we try to bring everything together by summarizing the steps in the research process and by examining and critiquing the efforts of other political science scope and methods students. We also talk about the possible theoretical and policy implications of your study. Last, we suggest ways to write an effective research report.

ELEMENTS OF RESEARCH: DETERMINING CAUSAL EXPLANATIONS

❖ INTRODUCTION

Having completed the literature review stage of the composite research process, you should be thoroughly familiar with existing writings, theory, and research in your area of interest. The next major stage is to identify and specify the various elements of your research project. As such, we will teach you about concepts, variables, hypotheses, and causation—terms that are new to most of you.

An understanding of this chapter will enable you to:

1. Define theoretical population, units of analysis, concepts, variables, and hypotheses.
2. Identify the factors necessary to have a causal relationship.
3. Define multiple causation.

❖ CONSTRUCTING CAUSAL EXPLANATIONS

Earlier we said that political scientists accept the notion that people act in a consistent manner. We also said that political science involves the study of people in order to explain their political behavior. These statements imply that the research process begins with an observation of behavior—a process that looks for differences in the way people act and behave. We study political leaders, members of political parties and interest groups, and the citizens of America and other nations.

As such, political scientists specify questions based on the observations they make. Typically they are interested in accounting for entire classes of events or relationships. Consider the following questions, for example. Why are social programs in some cities more successful than those in other cities? Why are some governments more authoritarian than others? Why do voters belong to different political parties?

As educated people, we assume that such variations are not just random. That is, cities with successful social programs are different than those with less successful programs. It is your task to identify the differences that determine the success of social programs implemented in the communities under study. Similarly, nations with authoritarian regimes differ from those without. Individual voters are different. Again, your task is to identify those differences among nations that cause them to differ with respect to government structure, or to explain differences among citizens that contribute to their affiliation with different political parties.

In short, your task is to do research. Through the composite research process, you need to take those steps that will provide scientific explanations to questions similar to those we discussed above. In order to take the proper steps, however, we need to explain the building blocks of the research process.

◆ THEORY

A **theory** is an integrated set of plans intended to explain or account for a given phenomenon. The goal of theoretical research is to expand your knowledge about political events and why they occur as they do. Theoretical research is empirical and strives to discover facts about politics. It tries to develop new political theories, change existing theories, or confirm existing theories. As such, the major goal of theoretical research is to advance theories that link observed facts about politics (Shively 1990, 7).

Anthony Downs, for example, developed what is called a "spatial theory" to explain how voters choose between political parties in American elections. The basic argument of his spatial theory is that you can reduce all political issues to a single ideological scale and place all politicians and voters on the scale (we discuss scales in more detail in the next chapter). The scale can range from 0, an extreme liberal position, to 100, which is an extreme conservative position. On this scale, you might place a liberal such as former Democratic presidential candidate George McGovern at 5. On the other hand, you might place a conservative such as former Republican presidential candidate Barry Goldwater at 85. To continue the example, you might place more moderate political figures such as former Presidents Jimmy Carter and Gerald Ford, towards the center of the scale, for example 30 and 70, respectively.

Downs asserts that the voters know where the parties and their candidates stand on the issue scale. As a result, they vote for the party that best represents their beliefs and values.

In America, those parties tending to have a centrist position have enjoyed the most electoral success. Thus, while individual politicians may find themselves somewhat "off center" on the scale, the two major political parties tend to seek a centrist position on the scale. The belief is that those parties that find themselves towards one pole or the other on the scale reduce their chances of electoral success. Therefore, if the parties' major concern is to win elections, they should nominate candidates as close to the center as possible (Downs 1957). This may explain why political candidates are so eager to label their opponents as liberal or conservative and scoff when their opponents profess to have moderate political beliefs. It may also help explain why Goldwater and McGovern were soundly defeated at the polls.

◆ CONCEPTS

We have repeatedly talked about the importance of problem definition. To accomplish this task successfully, you must define the problem in a way that will allow you to gather information about the problem. This step often requires you to conceptualize and operationalize. The problem must be broken down into concepts that allow measurement. We will discuss measurement in the next chapter. Now, however, we will turn our attention to the subject of political concepts and how you can make them susceptible to measurement through operationalization.

Political scientists use **concepts** to represent political characteristics. They are the basic building blocks in answering political questions. As such, they are a beginning in constructing causal explanations. Concepts pinpoint an essential idea or element that you believe accounts for the entire subject of the study. Concepts summarize the critical aspects in a class of events. Examples of concepts used by political scientists are power, political efficacy, political socialization, and political culture.

Concept Operationalization   Your ultimate goal is to scientifically analyze the concepts you use in your study. To do this, you must operationalize your concepts. Operational means measurable. Measurement and measurable has to do with numbers. Thus, you will need to assign numbers to the concepts you develop. You must determine how you can assign numbers to the concepts of power, political efficacy, political socialization, and political culture, for example. Simply put, you will take steps to translate the concepts you examine into observable and definable events by identifying indicators of your concepts. We call this important process concept operationalization.

Nominal Definitions   Concepts are the premises that provide an answer to your research question. To construct explanations of events or relationships you must define the concepts you intend to use in your study. There are two types of concept definitions: nominal definitions and operational or working definitions.

Nominal definitions are nothing more than the standard dictionary definition of the concept. For example, you may define patriotism as love for one's country. Many define intelligence as an individual's mental capacity. Or, occupation is often defined as the type of work one performs. As you can see from these definitions, you often use your discretion when developing nominal definitions. In order to advance knowledge, however, you should attempt to make definitions as realistic and sensible as possible.

Operational Definitions   **Operational definitions** translate the nominal definition into a form so we can measure the concept empirically. Two examples that come to mind are age and intelligence. We can operationally define age as the number of years the person, object, or law has existed. To operationalize intelligence we might use criteria such as grade point averages and IQ scores.

Operational definitions allow you to assess the extent of empirical support for your theoretical ideas. To clarify our point, recall the first question we posed at the outset of this chapter: Why are social programs in some cities more successful than in others?

As we said before you must assume that such variations are not just random. Cities with successful social programs are different than those with less successful programs. To resolve this research question you need to identify differences in the social, political, and economic activities in the cities that constitute your study. Then you must collect data that, with analysis, will suggest possible explanations.

The concepts you choose to answer this question could include fiscal federalism, political socialization, political efficacy, economic development, and political representation.

To operationalize these concepts, you would collect data concerning levels of federal and state funding, the levels of education and income in the community, the level of unemployment in the community, the structure of the city government, and the composition and voting patterns of the city council. You can possibly collect data for the latter by reviewing the minutes of city council meetings.

In sum, you continue the research process by defining your research problem in terms of nominal and operational concepts. Then you must find ways to collect data that represents the concepts you use to answer your research question. It is not an easy process. Most beginning research students have more difficulty conceptualizing theory and operationalizing concepts than any other stage of the research process. It takes practice and familiarity with the literature on your subject for you to sharpen your skills.

◆ VARIABLES

Variables are concepts that you operationalize and measure in a sample of data. You use variables to move from the conceptual level to the empirical level of research. Variables assign numerical scores or category labels to each item in your sample. For example, if you want to study the extent of political participation of college students, you might gather data for 100 students on the variables of gender, age, grade level, grade point average, major, income, political party identification, voting record, and political campaign activity.

There are two major types of variables—dependent and independent. The **dependent variable** is the variable you are trying to explain. It is the effect variable. For example, voter turnout or party affiliation are variables that change because of the impact of other variables.

The **independent variable** is the variable that contributes to the explanation of the dependent variable. It is the causative variable, or the predictor variable. We use the independent variables to predict the dependent variable. Common examples include age, race, gender, and education. You use these variables to examine their effect on the variable you want to explain. For example, you want to determine the effect of age and education on voter turnout. While the primary purpose of research is to determine the effect that independent variables have on dependent variables, at times you may want to determine how independent variables relate to each other. Antecedent and intervening variables allow you to do this.

An **antecedent variable** is an independent variable that occurs, in time, before another independent variables. Consider this example. You want to identify those variables that explain political party identification (PID). As a result of your literature review and data analysis, you decide that one's attitude about abortion helps to explain why your subjects affiliate with the Republican or Democratic party. In this example, PID is the dependent variable and attitude about legal abortion is the independent variable. That is, attitude helps to explain PID. You may, however, want to know what explains your subject's attitudes towards abortion. As a result, you find that individuals who attended parochial schools have a different attitude than those who attended public schools. This new variable is an antecedent variable because it affects and occurs before the independent variable. As a result, you have enhanced your understanding about the original dependent variable. Your study is a bit more complete.

One last point about antecedent variables. Notice how one's attitude about abortion, the original independent variable, becomes the dependent variable in the relationship involving the antecedent variable. In addition, parochial school attendance has an indirect effect on the original dependent variable, PID, through its impact on attitudes towards legal abortion.

An **intervening variable** occurs between an independent and dependent variable. If we use the example we presented above, attitude about legal abortion (the original independent variable) becomes the intervening variable between parochial education (the antecedent variable) and PID (the dependent variable). In our example, attitude about legal abortion comes between education and PID and helps explain how one variable explains another variable.

Identification of antecedent and intervening variables allows you to develop a more complete understanding about the political question you want to resolve.

◆ HYPOTHESES

Hypotheses are statements that formally propose an expected relationship between independent variables and dependent variables. The key word in this definition of a hypothesis is *expected*. This is a key word because hypotheses are tentative answers to research problems—tentative because you cannot verify a hypothesis until you test it empirically. The components of a hypothesis are a dependent variable, at least one independent variable, and an expected relationship between the variables.

The Purpose of Hypotheses The primary purpose of hypotheses is to account for changes in the dependent variable by linking criteria between independent and dependent variables. The primary virtue of hypotheses is that they allow theoretical ideas and explanations to be tested against actual data. Thus, they provide a means to evaluate theory.

Requirements of Sound Hypotheses In this section we will discuss the requirements of sound hypotheses and offer examples that do not meet the requirements. We will also show you how to reword each hypothesis so that it fulfills the requirements we are about to discuss.

There are several requirements of sound hypotheses. First, the concepts and variables must allow measurement and empirical testing. In other words, you must be able to operationalize them. Remember your goal is to evaluate theory and provide explanations for your research question through the empirical testing of the data you collect.

Second, you must state hypotheses clearly. That is, you must state in precise language the relationship between the independent and dependent variables. For example, what change in the dependent variable can you expect if there is a change in the independent variable? It is not sufficient to state that age affects voting. A proper hypothesis would read, "Older people tend to vote Republican."

Third, you need to make hypotheses specific. In your hypotheses you need to assert that specific variation in the independent variable results in specific variation in the dependent variable. Consider, "The greater the concentration of minorities in a community, the greater the demand for social programs." In short, you need to state the direction of the relationship between the variables in your hypothesis.

Fourth, hypotheses are value free. An example of a normative hypothesis is "Governments should ensure equity in program delivery." While one might agree with the statement, it is value laden. Remember, an important characteristic of scientific knowledge is the fact that it is not normative. We challenge you to prove statements that are value laden.

To summarize our discussion and illustrate the requirements we discussed, consider the following examples of sound hypotheses. "The greater the education level, the greater the level of voter turnout." "The lower the level of federal funding for a program, the less chance of program success." Each statement contains independent and dependent variables. They also depict a relationship between the variables.

These are examples of a positive relationship between the variables. They show how increases or decreases in the independent variable are expected to lead to increases or decreases in the dependent variable. Some hypotheses, however, can be stated as a negative relationship in that an increase, or decrease, in the independent variable will lead to a decrease, or increase, in the independent variable. For example, the higher the degree of federal restrictions on administering a program at the local level, the less is the chance of program success. Positive and negative relationships between variables refers to the direction of a relationship.

Common Errors When Stating Hypotheses   Students engaged in their first attempt at research often make several errors when developing hypotheses. Robert A. Bernstein and James A. Dyer offer some suggestions you should consider when writing hypotheses (Bernstein and Dyer 1984, 12–13). Following are their suggestions accompanied by our examples.

Hypotheses Must Relate Two Variables   Many students develop hypotheses having only one variable in the statement. Consider this example, "Americans are not politically active." There is only one variable in this statement, political activity. You need to relate political activity to another variable to have a sound hypothesis. Perhaps you should state the hypothesis as, "Americans with a low level of political efficacy are less likely to vote than those with a high level of political efficacy."

The Relationship Is Unclear   You must clearly state the relationship between the two variables in your hypotheses. Here is an example of a vague hypothesis, "Political efficacy is related to voting turnout." We cannot tell from this statement whether voting turnout increases or decreases as political efficacy increases or decreases. In sum, we do not know the direction of the relationship in the above example. A sound hypothesis is, "As the level of political efficacy increases in a community, the level of voter turnout tends to increase."

The Statement Lacks Generality   Do not personalize your hypotheses. That is, they should not contain the names of individuals or countries. In addition, do not limit your hypotheses to a specific period of time. The following are examples of hypotheses that lack generality. "The German government is more stable than the government of Czechoslovakia." This statement is too specific. You are merely comparing the governments of Germany and Czechoslovakia. A more general hypothesis is, "Governments based on longstanding democratic and capitalist premises are more stable than former communist regimes."

Now consider the following: "The federal government distributed more funds to the states in 1966 than in 1982." Again, the hypothesis should be more general. A better statement is, "The federal government distributes more funds to the states during Democratic administrations than during Republican administrations."

The Statement Makes a Value Judgement   Avoid hypotheses that make value statements. Remember, a characteristic of scientific research is the fact that it is not normative, or value free. Thus, do not use words such as *should, ought, better,* or *worse.* Hypotheses with these words indicate that you made a value judgement when you wrote the hypothesis. For example, the following is not a sound hypothesis: "All governments in the world should practice democracy." While many of us would prefer such a state of affairs, this hypothesis clearly depicts the values of the researcher. How would you collect data to analyze such a statement? Even with data, are you really proving the statement? If you examine the hypothesis, however, you may see you can write a sound hypothesis from this statement. For example, "Democratic countries have higher levels of economic development than those countries without democratic governments."

In sum, hypotheses establish a relationship between two or more variables. In doing so they demonstrate that there is an association between the independent variable and the dependent variable. You use hypotheses to demonstrate that the results are generally true in the real world. They also enhance your research effort because they reveal whether one phenomenon precedes another in time, and they eliminate as many alternative explanations for a phenomenon as possible.

◆ THE POPULATION AND UNITS OF ANALYSIS

The **theoretical population** is the group of objects you study in order to produce answers or explanations to your research question. To clarify our discussion, let's return to the political questions we introduced at the beginning of this chapter. Why are social programs in some cities more successful than those in other cities? Why are some governments more authoritarian than others? Why do voters belong to different political parties? In these examples, the theoretical populations include American cities, the nations of the world, and political parties.

Within each theoretical population, you will collect data for individual cities, nations, and parties to determine whether your explanation is correct. We refer to these individual objects within the population as **units of analysis.**

When you collect data about social programs in cities, as in our first example, each city is a unit of analysis. San Francisco might be one such unit. Thus, you would collect data about San Francisco that might explain the level of success for their social programs. Chicago might be a second unit of analysis.

For our other two examples, you would use the same procedures. Iraq, Iran, and Cuba might be the units of analysis you would analyze to explain why some nations are more authoritarian than others. To answer the third question, you might gather data about Jerry Perry, Bill Henderson, and Robert Garza, who, as individual voters, make up part of the population you would analyze to determine the characteristics of party membership.

A final comment about populations and units of analysis concerns the scientific goal of generalization. There is a relationship between the range of an explanation and its value to the field of study. An explanation that applies to more people for a greater span of time has more value than one that applies to fewer people for a more limited time.

◆ PERIOD OF THE STUDY

Determining the period of the study seems like a relatively simple task. There are some questions, however, that you need to consider before deciding on the period of your study. For example, what is the time limits for your study? One year? Five years? Ten years? Is the period long enough to reflect a trend, that with analysis, answers your research question? Is the data available for the period you decide to examine? Thus, maybe this task is not so easy after all. Our suggestion is that you decide on a time period to study that will produce reliable and valid data that answers your research question.

◆ CAUSAL RELATIONSHIPS

A relationship in research refers to the association between two or more variables. There is a **causal relationship** between variables when changes in one variable are systematically related to changes in another variable. As we will discuss in subsequent chapters, however, a relationship between variables does not necessarily indicate there is a causal relationship.

As a reminder, direction refers to positive or negative relations between variables. A positive relation means that as values of one variable increase, or decrease, values of the other variable also increase, or decrease. A negative relation means that as values of one variable increase, or decrease, values of the other variable change in the opposite direction.

The magnitude of a relationship between variables is also important when considering causality. The magnitude of a relationship is the extent to which variables change together in one direction or the other. The highest magnitude of relation is a perfect relation, in which knowledge of the value of one independent variables determines the exact value of the dependent variable. On the other hand, the lowest magnitude of relation, the zero relation, occurs when systematic change between the values of an independent variable and a dependent variable is not discernable.

There are four formal criteria that are necessary to establish a relationship of **causation:**—time order, covariance, nonspuriousness, and theoretical justification.

Time Order   A relationship is causal if an action is the result of another action. If A is the cause of B, then A must precede B in time. That is, changes in an independent variable must occur before changes in a dependent variable. This is another way of saying that cause must precede effect.

The notion of time order is probably the most intuitive of the criteria. Most times it is relatively simple to determine time order. For example, gender and age precede political socialization. At times, however, time order is more difficult to determine, for example, job tenure and job satisfaction. Does tenure lead to satisfaction or does satisfaction lead to tenure?

Covariation   When we say that two variables **covary,** we mean that the two variables change, or fluctuate, together. That is, if the independent variable changes and the dependent variable also changes, the independent variable may be the cause of the dependent variable. In other words, if B changes when A changes, there may be a relationship because the two covary. However, if changes in A are never accompanied by changes in B (no covariation), then A cannot be the cause of B.

Consider this hypothesis: "Increases in salary lead to increases in productivity." If salary increases did lead to increases in productivity, then we may have support for the hypothesis. If, on the other hand, salary increases did not lead to productivity increases, we can reject the hypothesis because the variables did not change together.

Nonspuriousness   This criterion of causal relationships is, perhaps, the most difficult to understand. A nonspurious relationship between two variables is an association, or covariation, that you cannot explain with a third variable. A **spurious relationship** results when the impact of a third variable explains the effect on both the independent and dependent variable under analysis.

Consider this example. In her study about the causes of juvenile delinquency, a novice researcher thought she found a causal relationship between ice cream sales and juvenile crime. Those areas having a high level of ice cream sales, also had a high level of juvenile crime. She also discovered that the criteria of time order and covariance applied to her findings. But does a third factor explain both the level of ice cream sales and juvenile crime? In other words, was this a nonspurious relationship? Further research indicated that those areas with a high rate of juvenile crime also had more juveniles living in the neighborhood. Thus, a younger population contributed to both increased ice cream sales and increased levels of juvenile crime. In short, a third variable explained the change in both the independent and dependent variables.

In sum, you will find it difficult to demonstrate the criterion of nonspuriousness. To accomplish this task you must consider all possible intervening variables and their effect on the independent and dependent variables. In statistical analysis we say that you must control for the effects of a third variable. If you find that change in a third variable explains change in the independent and dependent variables, the original relationship is spurious. Conversely, if you find that a third variable does not effect the independent or dependent variable, then the original relationship is nonspurious. As such, you will have satisfied an important criterion of causality. We will discuss the procedures you take to control for the effect of a third variable in Chapter 15.

Theoretical Justification   It is unlikely, but possible, that you will satisfy the first three criterion for causality and still not have causality. That is, your independent variable may precede the dependent variable in time, the two variables may vary together, and you may not find a third variable that explains change in your independent and dependent variables. However, it may just so happen that the relationship does not make sense. Consider our example about ice cream sales and juvenile crime. Does it make sense that ice cream sales cause incidents of juvenile crime? Thus, not every association is a causal one. Demonstrating that there is an association between independent and dependent variables is not sufficient to verify a hypothesis. You need to find a causal association in which variation in one variable influences variation in another variable.

In some cases it may be difficult for you to ascertain whether a relationship makes sense. Thus, you need to make sure that your independent variables have theoretical justification.

A theoretical or substantive justification for the relationship must be provided to support a relationship between variables. A theory interprets the observed covariation while addressing the issue of how and why the relationship occurs. A theory can also serve as an additional check to ensure the relationship you discovered is not spurious. In sum, theory provides support and a substantive justification for observed relationships between two variables.

❖ MULTIPLE CAUSATION

Most times, however, a single variable will not totally account for change in another variable. We live in a very complex and changing environment. Rarely can we explain the behavior of humans and their political institutions through the analysis of a single factor. Similarly, no one hypothesis is apt to provide a complete explanation. That is, there are several independent variables that explain why a dependent variable changes. This is known as **multiple causation.** Age, income, education, race, registration requirements, the type of election, and other variables may influence voter turnout.

Finding a complete explanation, however, is almost impossible. As scholars, we try to add to existing explanations in incremental steps. That is, many research efforts have limits imposed by time and other resources. Therefore most research results in incomplete explanations. According to Bernstein and Dyer, however, "It is the accumulation of those incomplete explanations that advances our knowledge of human behavior" (Bernstein and Dyer 1984, 15).

❖ SUMMARY

In this chapter we discussed ways to identify and specify the various elements of your research project. As such, we talked about concepts, variables, hypotheses, and causation. In the next chapter we introduce you to the idea of measurement, or the assignment of numbers to some phenomenon you are interested in analyzing.

❖ KEY TERMS

antecedent variable	intervening variable
causal relationship	multiple causation
causation	nominal definitions
concepts	operational definitions
covariation	spurious relationship
dependent variable	theory
hypotheses	theoretical population
independent variable	units of analysis

❖ EXERCISES

1. What purposes do concepts serve?

2. What is the difference between nominal and operational definitions of concepts?

3. What is the difference between concepts and variables?

4. What is the difference between dependent and independent variables?

5. Identify the independent and dependent variables in the following statements:

    a. Many theorists assert that a nation's governmental structure will impact the nation's economy.

    b. The scores on the Government 3301 midterm are related to class attendance.

    c. Liberals tend to support welfare programs more than Conservatives.

6. What are the components of a hypothesis?

7. What is the purpose of a hypothesis?

8. What are some of the requirements of a sound hypothesis?

9. What are some common errors made when formulating hypotheses?

10. What is the major weakness (if any) in the following statements:

    a. Americans are apathetic about voting.

    b. The level of education is related to income.

    c. England has a more stable government than China.

    d. Wealthy countries should redistribute their wealth to poor nations.

    e. As the level of education increases the level of voting turnout increases.

11. Identify the four formal criteria necessary to establish that a relationship between variables is causal.

12. Write a hypothesis relating a nation's per capita income with its level of education. What is the independent variable? What is the dependent variable?

13. Write a hypothesis that may partially explain why welfare programs receive more support from some congressional members than from other members.

14. Consider the following hypothesis: "The stricter the voting registration requirements for states, the lower the voting turnout will tend to be for citizens of those states."

   a. What is the theoretical population?

   b. What is the independent variable?

   c. What is the dependent variable?

   d. What is the direction of the proposed relationship?

❖ SUGGESTED READINGS

Bernstein, Robert A., and James A. Dyer. *An Introduction to Political Science Methods*, 2nd ed. Englewood Cliffs, NJ: Prentice-Hall, 1984.

Fox, William. *Social Statistics Using MicroCase*. Chicago: Nelson-Hall, 1993.

Frankfort-Nachmias, Chava, and David Nachmias. *Research Methods in the Social Sciences*, 4th ed. New York: St. Martin's Press, 1992.

Goldenberg, Sheldon. *Thinking Methodologically*. New York: HarperCollins, 1992.

Johnson, Janet Buttolph and Richard A. Joslyn. *Political Science Research Methods*. Washington: Congressional Quarterly Press, 1986.

Kay, Susan Ann. *Introduction to the Analysis of Political Data*. Englewood Cliffs, NJ: Prentice-Hall, 1991.

UNDERSTANDING MEASUREMENT

❖ INTRODUCTION

In this chapter we will expand our previous discussion about variables. Remember, a variable is a characteristic or property that differs in value from one unit of analysis to another. In addition, variables are only useful when they can be measured. That is, we must be able to assign numbers to the characteristics, or variables, of our units of analyses. We may want to determine, for example, a city's per capita income, an individuals's level of education, and a country's level of poverty. Our goal is to determine how much of a characteristic each unit of analysis possesses. We use measurement to develop and use some instrument to assign numbers to the possible characteristics so we can attain our goal. This process will allow you to apply the empirical methods of scientific research that we will discuss in subsequent chapters.

An understanding of this chapter will enable you to:

1. Understand the theory of measurement.
2. Define measurement.
3. Differentiate between measurement validity and measurement reliability.
4. Identify ways to establish measurement validity and measurement reliability.
5. Identify threats to measurement reliability.
6. Identify the levels of measurement.

❖ THE THEORY OF MEASUREMENT

Paul D. Leedy says that "measurement is the quantifying of any phenomenon, substantial or insubstantial, and involves a comparison with a standard" (Leedy 1985, 18). His definition presents several problems, however. For example, what does quantify mean? What is a substantial or insubstantial phenomenon? What does substantial and insubstantial phenomena mean? How do we determine standards for comparison?

Leedy's definition requires us to assign numbers to a concrete observation or a concept, so that we can compare it with some evaluation tool such as a ruler or standardized test. Simply put then, **measurement** is the use of a tool to assign numbers to some political phenomenon that we want to analyze and compare with existing criteria. To aid in the assignment of numbers to our chosen research topic, we will need to use some type of measurement instrument. For our purposes, examples might include standardized tests, surveys, secondary data, and scales and indices.

Measurement theory assumes that a concept representing the phenomenon of concern exists but cannot be directly measured. Educational attainment, level of political participation, and extent of political equality throughout the world, for example, are theoretical concepts that we cannot measure directly. You can, however, measure them indirectly through variables specified by operational definitions. Consider the following examples:

1. *Educational attainment:* you might measure educational attainment by examining students' grade point averages, their scores on standardized achievement tests, or their years in school.
2. *Political participation:* you might measure political participation by determining a citizen's voting record, involvement in political campaigns, and attendance at city council meetings.
3. *Political equality:* you might measure a nation's level of political equality by examining the number of regularly scheduled elections, nominating devices, registration requirements, and the proportion of voting turnout to qualified voters.

Note the similarities in these examples. First, each uses several variables to measure a single concept. Educational achievement, for example, consists of grade point averages and standardized test scores. Second, you can assign numbers to each indicator. To measure political participation you can count the number of times an individual votes, the number of hours he or she spend campaigning, and the number of times he or she attend a city council meeting. Third, each depicts several variables that you can use to measure the concepts of educational attainment, political participation, and political equality.

◆ LEVELS OF MEASUREMENT

In some cases measurement is simpler because the researcher is working with "real" numbers—the percentage of voter turnout, the gross national product of nations, and the number of revolutions throughout the world, for example. In these cases you can calculate averages, percentages, and various measures of deviation. You can also rank, or order, units according to their values. If we are ranking American states according to their voting turnout, for example, there is no question who has the largest and the smallest. We simply compare the values.

Some measures, however, may not be as simple because they lack numerical precision. Consider, for example, race. When you assign a 1 to African Americans, a 2 to Hispanics, and a 3 to Anglos, you do not imply any particular ordering among those classes. They are only convenient labels for each category. How do you measure or calculate the average of these classes? It is meaningless to say that a citizen is more black than white. The citizen is either one or the other.

In measurement theory, you can use numbers several ways. At times you use them as labels for categories of variables. On other occasions you use them to rank or order categories of variables. Last, you use them to specify the interval, or distance, between categories of variables. Thus, there are different levels of measurement. It is important that you understand each level because the various analytic methods we discuss in subsequent chapters apply to specific levels of measurement.

Nominal Level of Measurement　**Nominal measures** merely assign numeric labels to the categories of a variable. While computerized statistical programs are amazing, they require us to assign numbers to variables to facilitate statistical analyses. Some packages can do limited mathematical machinations with symbols other than numbers, but they are more effective and have more meaning for you when they deal with numbers. Race, as discussed above, is an example of a nominal level measure. Each time the program counts a 1, it is also counting an African American. There are many other examples of nominal measures applicable to political research. Gender, political party affiliation, nationality, and college major are common examples that you will probably use in your studies.

While nominal measures are quite simple to use, they also have some shortcomings. Nominal measures are the weakest or least precise level of measurement. You do not have the ability to state how much of a trait or characteristic is possessed by an object or event. In addition, you cannot even determine whether the variable has more or less of the characteristic. Nominal measures lack any sense of relative size or magnitude; they only allow you to say that the classes of a variable are different. There is no mathematical relationship between the classes.

Ordinal Level of Measurement　Ordinal measurement derives from the ordinal numbers—first, second, third, etc. Similar to nominal measures, ordinal measures allow you to classify categories of variables. However, they also enable you to rank the characteristics of variables based on the values you assign. A higher value may indicate "more than" or "greater than" a lower value. It is not possible, however, to say how much more or less. Thus, while the numbers indicate a rank ordering of cases, they do not indicate the exact distances between the objects. For example, in an election, the order of finish of the candidates does not say anything about the number of votes each one received. The order of finish only tells you that the winner received more votes than the other contenders, but not how many more votes.

Interval Level of Measurement   Interval measurement is more precise than either nominal or ordinal measurement. The values assigned to the classes of a variable have meaning. It also allows you to rank the classes of a variable so that the distance between those classes is exact and constant. This level of measurement indicates the precise difference between values. Interval measurements are units or intervals you accept as a common standard—a standard that yields identical results in repeated applications. Examples include number of votes cast, population, age, level of education, and income. With interval-level data it is possible to state that more people voted in 1992 than in 1988. It is also possible to state exactly how many more people voted.

Ratio Level of Measurement   The ratio level of measurement is the most precise of all. With this level of measurement you can rank the classes of a variable, differentiate between the intervals between the classes, and precisely state the relative amounts of the variable represented by the classifications. In short, it is very similar to interval level measures. In fact, the examples of interval measures discussed above are also ratio measures. Then what is the difference between the two types of measurement? Ratio-level measures have a natural "zero" point. With interval-level measurement a zero point is arbitrarily assigned and does not represent the absence of the measured attribute. Temperature is a good example. Zero degrees Celsius is not an absence of heat. It can get colder. It is useful because it is the temperature at which water freezes.

With ratio measures, zero is the lowest possible value. You cannot earn less than zero dollars. No one is less than zero years of age. No one gets less than zero votes. It makes sense to say that someone who received 10,000 votes got twice as many as someone who garnered 5,000 votes. It does not make sense to say that 80 degrees Fahrenheit is twice as hot as 40 degrees Fahrenheit.

When collecting your data, you should try to measure variables at the highest level possible. This will permit enhanced mathematical manipulation and more sophisticated statistical analysis. In political science, however, many measures associated with surveys are of the nominal (race, gender, party affiliation) or ordinal variety (extent of agreement with policy statements). So what do you do? You can use less sophisticated statistical methods, or you can transform your data so that it takes on the qualities of a higher level of measurement.

Suppose a researcher uses five questions in a sample of adults in an effort to get an idea about the ideology of her subjects. Consider this question for example: "When a person has a disease that cannot be cured, do you think doctors should be allowed by law to end the patient's life by some painless means if the patient and his family request it." Possible responses are yes or no. She codes the yes responses to her questions with a 0 and the no responses with a 1. In addition, the yes responses are liberal responses and the no responses are conservative responses. As you can see, she arbitrarily coded the possible responses. She could have just as easily coded conservative responses with a 0 and liberal responses with a 1, for example. The numbers are merely labels used to differentiate the responses and enhance computer input and subsequent analysis.

Our student, however, could transform the measure into a higher level of measurement by creating an index that would measure the ideology of her subjects. She would do this by assigning a score to each respondent by summing the responses to each question. As a result, respondents could score from 0 to 5 based on their responses. The higher the score, the more conservative the respondent.

❖ MEASUREMENT VALIDITY

Assigning numbers to your research concepts seems easy. Alas, measurement is not quite so simple. How do you know you are really measuring what you want to measure? Can you measure political participation by solely analyzing voting turnout?

Measurement validity is concerned with the effectiveness of the measuring instrument and the extent that the instrument reflects the actual activity or behavior you want to study. We say that a measurement tool or variable is a valid measure of a concept if it is an accurate representation of the concept it is intended to measure.

◆ TYPES OF VALIDITY

There are several types of measurement validity. **Content validity** deals with the ability of a measuring tool to truly tap the information we seek. Suppose our project seeks to examine the relationship between unemployment and voting Republican in presidential elections. There are tools that, over time, have demonstrated content validity when determining the number of Republican voters in presidential elections. However, how do we measure unemployment? Does data from the unemployment rolls accurately measure unemployment? What about those unemployed individuals who are not on the rolls because they have exhausted their entitlements? Sole use of this data can lead to content validity problems. Thus, we would need to use other measurement tools, such as surveys, to complement the unemployment rolls.

Discriminate validity answers the question, "Does the tool allow the concept to be distinguished from similar concepts?" For example, using achievement scores on standardized tests may lack discriminate validity if the tests have some cultural bias. That is, are you measuring achievement or equity in educational funding?

Predictive validity means you can use a tool to predict a specified outcome. If scores on a civil service exam accurately predict on-the-job performance, the exam has predictive validity. If income, education, and occupation measurements in a voting district consistently explain voting turnout, they have predictive validity.

◆ SOME CONCLUDING COMMENTS ABOUT MEASUREMENT VALIDITY

Later in this chapter we will discuss how you can use scales and indices to enhance the validity of your measurement instrument. Another way to enhance the validity of your measurement tool is to determine whether the tool meets the above criteria. These are ways to establish measurement validity. They allow you to argue that a variable is a valid measure. While they may not guarantee that the variable is a valid measure of the concept in question, you do have measurement criteria that can withstand critique if you have considered these factors when selecting your variables.

❖ MEASUREMENT RELIABILITY

A variable has **reliability** if it consistently assigns the same numbers to a phenomenon. For example, if we measure a neighborhood's perception of police effectiveness twice and obtain the same results, then the indicator is termed "reliable." Or, if two or more people use an instrument and arrive at the same results, then we say that the instrument is reliable. In sum, an instrument is reliable if the same results are consistently obtained despite different settings, different persons applying the measurement, or any other factors other than variation in the concept being measured.

◆ THREATS TO MEASUREMENT RELIABILITY

There are several potential problems of measurement that threatens the reliability of measurement tools. First, your measure should not rely on the judgment of the measurer or a respondent in a survey. If it does, we say that the measure is subjective. The following question is a good example of a subjective measure: "What is your opinion about the quality of life in your home town?" This question requires a subjective response. What does quality of life mean? Several respondents may have different perceptions about quality of life. As such, their responses will be based on their perceptions. To address this problem you could gather data others have accepted as measurements of quality of life. For example, median education, median income level, number of city parks, the unemployment rate, and statistics that depict the level of crime in the area.

Inexperienced interviewers and misleading questions also detract from the reliability of a measurement tool. One way to control these problems is to test the instrument before you use it in the study. Testing involves administering the survey to several persons and analyzing and correcting any deficiencies that might occur. Other ways to prevent these problems is to train interviewers and ensure they understand the instrument and its purpose.

The respondent can also contribute to the unreliability of the instrument. For example, the respondent may be careless when completing the questionnaire. In addition, the respondent may falsify responses to some questions. You can control these threats by testing the instrument and convincing respondents that you will ensure the privacy of their responses. You might also offer to give respondents a synopsis of your research effort upon its completion.

Finally, data input errors can affect reliability. Despite computer sophistication, human error is a given in most research situations. We used to control for this possibility by reviewing the input or by having two data processors input the data. Fortunately, many modern data analysis packages have edit procedures that will notify you when you input erroneous data.

Before we show you some ways to enhance the validity and reliability of your measurement instrument, we want you to know that while a reliable measure may not be valid, a valid measure will also be reliable, since if it accurately measures the concept in question then it stands to reason that it will do so consistently (Johnson and Joslyn 1986, 77). For example, consider a bathroom scale that always weighs someone 10 pounds light. The scale is a reliable measurement tool. It will always weigh you 10 pounds lighter than your true weight. As such, to determine your true weight you must add 10 pounds to the weight displayed on the scale. The scale, however, is not valid. It is not measuring your true weight. It is erroneous by 10 pounds.

◆ ENHANCING MEASUREMENT VALIDITY AND RELIABILITY

Unfortunately, in the real world of research we have no way to guarantee the validity and reliability of measurement. Proof that your instrument is valid is especially difficult to obtain. But we try to do the best we can.

In establishing validity, your measurement tool should have one or more of the types of validity we previously discussed. For example, it should have content validity in that it measures what it proposes to measure. Or, it should have predictive validity in that you can predict a specified outcome because of your instrument. Ultimately, however, you must use your judgment to determine the validity of the chosen instrument.

A reliable instrument is stable, dependable, and consistent in measurement (Cole 1980, 83). We assume that a respondent's score on some measure is very close to the respondent's actual position on the measured concept. We say close because, as previously discussed, there are several obstacles to reliability that can lead to some error in the results. Unlike validity, you can objectively determine a measure's reliability. There are a number of methods you can use to estimate the reliability of a particular measure.

Test–Retest Method   With this method, you administer the measurement instrument to the same group more than once. Then you examine the two sets of measures. The higher the relationship between the sets of measures, the more reliable the instrument.

The test-retest method has two limitations. First, a second application of the measurement may influence the scores. There may not be a high correlation between scores because the respondents have become familiar with the tool and its purpose. You can partially compensate for this problem by changing the order of your questions and possible responses. Second, scores may change because the respondent's actual attitudes have changed as a function of time and socialization. The first problem results from the unreliability of your instrument. The second problem, however, does not mean your instrument is unreliable. It only gives the appearance of an unreliable measurement. After all, you have measured a change in the respondent's attitudes.

Split–Half Method   This method of estimating reliability requires you to divide your original scale into two or more subscales. You then administer each subscale to a group and determine the average difference among the scores. This average difference helps you determine the reliability of your instrument. If the scores on one subscale deviate from the scores on another subscale by an average of 5 percent, the split-half score is .95 (1.0 – .05). A score of .90 or higher is considered acceptable evidence of a reliable scale (Cole 1980, 83). The scores from the sets may also be correlated, as an estimate of reliability (Frankfort-Nachmias and Nachmias 1992, 165).

Triangulation   Triangulation is an attempt to enhance the reliability and validity of measurement by using multiple and overlapping measurement strategies. There are several types of triangulation. First, data triangulation involves the use of several data sources relative to the concept. For example, if you want to evaluate the effectiveness of public transit systems, you might use the following data sources to gather information for analysis: surveys of mass transit users and nonusers, surveys of public officials, transport authorities, and bus drivers, customer complaint files, and accident reports. Data triangulation enhances the validity and reliability of findings because it taps a variety of information sources.

Second, investigator triangulation involves the use of multiple observers for the same research activity. It reduces potential bias that might come from a single observer. Examples include the use of several interviewers, analysts, and decision makers.

Third, methodological triangulation, combines two or more information collection methods in the study of a single concept. It uses the strengths of various methods. For example, you might use surveys to gather information about a phenomenon. To complement this method, you might discretely observe and chart the activities of your subjects. This method can compensate for the possible bias that could result from interviews and surveys.

Scales and Indices   Indices and scales are similar to each other. You create an **index** when you assign scores based on the combined response of several related questions. You use **scales** to empirically demonstrate a hierarchical ranking of items. An index is a crude form of scaling because you do not rank the items in the index. Scales are more precise measures than indices. In addition, scales involve the principle of unidimensionality that implies that the items comprising the scale reflect a single dimension or concept.

For the most part, you use scales and indices to measure attitudes and knowledge of a particular subject—for example, ideological attitudes, self-esteem concepts, knowledge about the U.S. Constitution, and knowledge about Third World economies. Indices and scales require you to use several questions to measure a concept. Think of scales as tests. Your professor does not ask you a single question to determine your comprehension about a subject such as comparative politics. Likewise, you should not ask a single question to determine one's knowledge about a particular phenomenon or attitude about political parties or ideology. A scale or index measuring ideology, for example, might involve questions about the person's ceonomic, social, and moral beliefs. Several questions will increase the reliability of your measurement tool by reducing possible error. It will also enhance the possibility that you are measuring what you intended to measure.

Scales and indices enable you to transform several questions into a single score that reduces the complexity of the data. Scales and indices provide quantitative measures amenable to greater precision and statistical manipulation. They increase the reliability of measurement. A score on a scale is considered a more reliable indicator of the property being measured than a measure based on a response to one question or item.

When creating a scale or index, you need to define the scale's purpose. What is it you want to measure? You also need to select the sources of data. Will you use census data? Will you use scales designed by other scholars? Or will you use a survey to collect your information? Next, you need to ensure that your scale is unidimensional. The items comprising the scale should reflect a single dimension.

The Composite Index   There are several types of indices or scales we can use. The composite index is the most basic. As with all scales and indices, it uses several questions to measure an attitude or perception. For example, let's consider an index of ideology. You might use ten questions to determine one's attitude about important policy issues. To establish the index you would assign a number to each possible response to each question. You might decide to code liberal responses with a 0 and conservative responses with a 1.

Next you need to compute the minimum and maximum scores. In our example we asked ten questions to measure ideological attitudes. The lowest one could score on your scale is 0, while the highest one could score is 10 (for our purposes, each respondent answered each question). Keeping in mind that you coded conservative responses with a 1, it should be obvious that the higher a respondent's score on the index, the more politically conservative the respondent. You can use your index as an independent or dependent variable. Normally, however, the index is the dependent variable.

There are several advantages to using a composite index. First, it is simple to use. You use several items to measure complex concepts. You can also use the index to develop higher level measures of a particular concept. It is also an efficient way to summarize information.

The index, however, is also somewhat crude. It is difficult to know how to weight the various components of the index. Are all questions equal in describing the concept? Excluding the minimum and maximum scores, how do you interpret the other scores of the index? In addition, some criticize the use of composite indices because respondents may fall into a response-set pattern. They select the same responses for each item without thoroughly considering each question. Last, item selection for the scale is somewhat arbitrary. There is no rational basis for selecting survey items. This could negatively impact the validity of the measurement tool. Therefore, more elaborate types of indices are preferred.

Likert scales are particularly useful in measuring people's attitudes. They differ from indices in that not every individual item score is used to calculate the final score. To design a Likert scale you need to take several steps. First, you need to compile several possible scale items that make up your survey questions. You do this by compiling a series of items that express a wide range of attitudes from extremely positive to extremely negative—several questions about the media's impact on political socialization, for example.

Second, you need to assign numbers to the possible responses. Most Likert scales use the following:

1 = strongly disagree
2 = disagree
3 = undecided
4 = agree
5 = strongly agree

Next, you need to administer the survey to a random sample of respondents. You do this for several reasons. First, you want to test the reliability of your scale. You can accomplish this task by using the test-retest method of estimating reliability or by using the split-half technique of estimating reliability. Second, you want to compute a total score for each respondent. For example, suppose that a respondent "strongly agreed" with three statements and "agreed" with two other statements. Using the above scale, the respondent's score would be 23.

We use the total scores to help us determine the discriminative power (DP) of the scale items. Remember we said that Likert scales differ from indices in that not every individual item score is used to calculate the final score. The DP of an item allows us to readily distinguish those items we want to include in our final scale. The DP enables us to separate those scoring high on an attribute from those scoring low on an attribute in our attitude continuum. We retain those items that allow us to discriminate most readily as a part of the final scale.

One way to determine the DP of our scale is to use item analysis. This method requires us to compare each individual item to the total scale score. If individuals score high on one item, but low on the entire scale, then that item is not measuring the same thing as the other items. Thus, that item should be dropped. Let's consider our political ideology example again. One scale item asked the respondent to show level of agreement with this statement, "The economy is beginning to recover." The respondent strongly agrees and scores a 5 for this item. According to the student's scale, higher scores reflect a liberal ideology. The respondent's total scale score based on other questions however, was only 9 (possible maximum score = 25) which indicates a strong conservative stance. What should you do? Perhaps you should eliminate the economy question. It does not correlate with the total scale score. Thus, it lacks in discriminative power. It may not be measuring the concept of ideology. Common sense tells us this conclusion is correct. Whether the economy is recovering or not has little to do with ideology.

Likert scales have some obvious advantages. They are relatively easy to administer, they provide a more rational basis for item selection, and they provide a range of alternative responses to each question. Several scholars, however, have criticized Likert scales. There is no empirical way to determine if the items finally selected to comprise the scale really do measure the concept of interest. In addition, the scale relies on the selection of extreme items. As a result, some are concerned that the technique can not satisfactorily distinguish between more moderate respondents (Cole 1980, 76). Therefore, many prefer the more precise Guttman scale.

Guttman Scales   Guttman scales have several characteristics. First, they incorporate an empirical test of unidimensionality. They only measure a single dimension or attitude. Second, Guttman scales are cumulative. Potential scale items are ordered according to the degree of difficulty associated with responding positively to each item. Third, the Guttman technique assumes that respondents who answer positively to a difficult item will also respond positively to less difficult items.

As a result of the ordering process, Guttman scales, unlike Likert scales, generally yield scale scores resulting from a single set of responses. That is, to get a 20 on the ideological perception scale, a particular pattern of responses is essential. In a Likert scale different patterns of responses can yield the same scale score.

Because the Guttman scale is more complex than other scales, let's take time to construct one. Assume we asked the following questions about one's tolerance towards members of groups with different political goals. Note the

TABLE 10.1

ILLUSTRATION OF UNIDIMENSIONALITY

More difficult ◄─────────────────────────────► **Less difficult**

Respondent	Marry	Date	Church	Dinner	Talk	Scale Score
1	yes	yes	yes	yes	yes	5
2	no	yes	yes	yes	yes	4
3	no	no	yes	yes	yes	3
4	no	no	no	yes	yes	2
5	no	no	no	no	yes	1
6	no	no	no	no	no	0

order of the questions. You can see that a positive response to each subsequent question requires more tolerance on behalf of the respondent. This is what is meant by "ordering the questions according to difficulty."

1. It is ok for my children to talk to members of a different political party.
2. It is ok for my children to invite members of a different political party to dinner.
3. It is ok for my children to bring members of a different political party to our church.
4. It is ok for my children to date members of a different political party.
5. It is ok for my children to marry members of a different political party.

To continue the illustration, let's assume that we asked six individuals to respond to our survey. Table 10.1 is a possible distribution of answers to these questions. The distribution in Table 10.1 is perfectly unidimensional. We ranked the items on the single underlying dimension of tolerance. In addition, the scale is cumulative in that none of the respondents has a disagreement response before an agreement response or vice versa.

If you examine the table closely, you will see that information on the position of any respondent's last positive response allows the prediction of all of her responses to the other scale items. For example, if a Republican mother allowed her daughter to marry a Democrat (score of 5), she would not mind having this person belong to her social club either.

In addition, with a perfectly unidimensional scale, if you know an individual's total tolerance score, you can accurately predict her response to each tolerance item. Knowing that Respondent 4 received a score of 2 enables you also to know which activities she is tolerant of (coming to dinner and talking to). You also know which activities she does not tolerate. Thus, you are able to reproduce each individual's responses to each question because you know each individual's total score.

However, our simple example has 100 percent reproducibility. In the real research world, this seldom occurs. Reproducibility is the extent to which you can reproduce the total response pattern on a set of items by knowing only the total score. In actuality, you will probably have a number of responses that deviate from the expected pattern. For example, if Respondent 5 (a Democrat) responded yes to inviting a Republican to dinner but no to talking with a Republican, a deviation from the expected unidimensionality has occurred. Hence, it is necessary to establish a criterion for evaluating the unidimensionality and cumulativeness of the scale. We do this by determining the ratio of error responses to the total number of possible responses. This ratio is known as the coefficient of reproducibility. The coefficient of reproducibility (CR) measures the degree of conformity to a perfect scalable pattern such as the one we have in the above example. We calculate it as:

$$CR = 1 - \frac{\text{Number of inconsistencies}}{\text{Total number of responses (number of cases } x \text{ number of scale items)}}$$

Frankfort-Nachmias and Nachmias write that the coefficient you obtain should be .9 or greater to be an acceptable scale (Frankfort-Nachmias and Nachmias 1992).

TABLE 10.2

ILLUSTRATION OF NON-UNIDIMENSIONALITY

More difficult ◄─────────────────────────► Less difficult

Respondent	Marry	Date	Church	Dinner	Talk	Scale Score
1	yes	yes	yes	yes	yes	5
2	no	yes	no	yes	yes	3
3	no	no	no	yes	yes	2
4	no	no	yes	no	yes	2
5	no	no	yes	no	yes	2
6	no	no	no	no	no	0

Total number of inconsistencies = 3
Total number of responses = 30
CR = 1 – 3/30 = .90

TABLE 10.3

ILLUSTRATION OF REVISED SCALE

More difficult ◀──────────────────────────────▶ **Less difficult**

Respondent	Marry	Date	Dinner	Talk	Scale Score
1	yes	yes	yes	yes	4
2	no	yes	yes	yes	3
3	no	no	yes	yes	2
4	no	no	no	yes	1
5	no	no	no	yes	1
6	no	no	no	no	0

Total number of inconsistencies = 0

An examination of Table 10.2 shows that the pattern of true responses you might expect in actual research. Those who agreed with the more difficult questions also agreed with the less difficult ones. Responses to the question concerning bringing other group members to church, however, do not fit the pattern. Respondent 2 agreed with a more difficult question but did not agree with the church question. Respondents 4 and 5, on the other hand, did not agree with a less difficult question and agreed with the church question. Therefore, the question about church accompaniment does not seem to fit the pattern. You should remove it from the scale because it does not measure the concept of tolerance towards other groups. Once the question is removed, the pattern as depicted in Table 10.3 evolves. Notice that the pattern is unidimensional.

❖ SUMMARY

In this chapter we expanded our previous discussion about operational definitions and variables by concentrating on the subject of measurement. We said that you use measurement to answer questions about voting turnout, the governmental structure of other nations, and why people revolt. In addition, we also discussed the theory of measurement while giving you a working definition of measurement. We also spent considerable time differentiating between measurement validity and measurement reliability. Our discussion introduced terms such as content validity, correlation validity, and consensual validity. We also gave you some ways such as triangulation and the use of indices and scales to establish measurement validity and measurement reliability. We also gave you some ways to identify possible obstacles to measurement reliability. Last, we discussed the different levels of measurement and their importance to the research process. In the next chapter we will turn our attention to the next stages of the composite research process, data collection and data input.

❖ KEY TERMS

composite index	measurement validity
content validity	nominal level of measurement
discriminate validity	ordinal level of measurement
Guttman scale	predictive validity
index	ratio level of measurement
interval level of measurement	scales
levels of measurement	split-half method
Likert scales	test-retest method
measurement	threats to measurement
measurement reliability	triangulation

❖ EXERCISES

1. Consider the following characteristics and measures:

   Characteristic: crime

   Measure: FBI crime statistics

   Characteristic: popular sovereignty in other nations

   Measure: voting information from Yugoslavia

   Characteristic: unemployment

   Measure: information from the unemployment office

   a. Are the measures likely to be reliable? Why?

   b. What might increase their reliability?

   c. Are the measures likely to be valid? Why?

   d. What might increase their validity?

2. Discuss the levels of measurement to include the characteristics, advantages, and disadvantages of each level.

3. Identify the following levels of measurement:

   a. Gross national product of different world nations.

   b. Opinion of the way the president is handling the economy (strongly approve; approve; neutral; disapprove; strongly disapprove).

   c. Number of Hispanic representatives in Congress.

   d. Type of government (autocracy, oligarchy, poligarchy).

   e. Ethnicity (African American, Hispanic, Anglo).

   f. Perceived income (very low, below average, average, above average, very high).

   g. Income in dollars.

   h. Interest in politics (low; medium; high).

   i. Political party affiliation (Republican, Democratic, Independent).

   j. Hours of study time per week.

4. Discuss the advantages and disadvantages of indices and scales.

5. The purpose of your study is to ascertain the political ideology of a group of college students. Develop five questions you can use to form a composite index in this area.

6. The purpose of your study is to ascertain the extent of tolerance towards racial groups. Develop five questions you can use to form a scale in this area.

❖ SUGGESTED READINGS

Babbie, Earl R. *The Practice of Social Research,* 3rd ed. Belmont, CA: Wadsworth, 1983.

Bernstein, Robert A., and James A. Dyer. *An Introduction to Political Science Methods,* 2nd ed. Englewood Cliffs, NJ: Prentice-Hall, 1984.

Campbell, Donald, and Julian Stanley. *Experimental and Quasi-Experimental Designs of Research.* Chicago: Rand-McNally, 1966.

Fox, William. *Social Statistics Using MicroCase.* Chicago: Nelson-Hall, 1993.

Frankfort-Nachmias, Chava, and David Nachmias. *Research Methods in the Social Sciences,* 4th ed. New York: St. Martin's Press, 1992.

Freedman, David, Robert Pisani, and Roger Purves. *Statistics.* New York: Norton, 1978.

Goldenberg, Sheldon. *Thinking Methodologically.* New York: HarperCollins, 1992.

Johnson, Janet Buttolph, and Richard A. Joslyn. *Political Science Research Methods.* Washington: Congressional Quarterly Press, 1986.

Kay, Susan Ann. *Introduction to the Analysis of Political Data.* Englewood Cliffs, NJ: Prentice-Hall, 1991.

Leedy, Paul D. *Practical Research: Planning and Design,* 3rd ed. New York: Macmillan, 1985.

Shively, W. Phillips. *The Craft of Political Research,* 3rd ed. Englewood Cliffs, NJ: Prentice-Hall, 1990.

RESEARCH DESIGN

❖ INTRODUCTION

We have discussed the first three stages of the composite research process. We also presented examples and exercises to enhance your comprehension. Hopefully, you realize why it is important to clearly define your research problem, conduct a concise literature review, and understand concepts, variables, and hypotheses. We also hope that you know why measurement and the different levels of measurement are important to the research effort.

Now it is time to learn about the different types of research designs you have at your disposal. Research designs are important. They provide you with a plan to use when collecting, analyzing, and interpreting data you believe provides answers to your research problem. In this chapter we discuss the various research designs, the issues of internal and external validity, and the impact of extrinsic and intrinsic factors on the validity of research designs.

An understanding of this chapter will enable you to:

1. Understand the purpose and importance of research designs.
2. Understand the basics of research designs.
3. Distinguish the difference between internal and external validity as they pertain to research designs.
4. Understand the components and process associated with experimental designs.
5. See the importance of quasi-experimental designs.

❖ THE RESEARCH DESIGN: AN OVERVIEW

Before you test hypotheses you must develop a research design to use when collecting, analyzing, and interpreting observations and data. A research design is a plan specifying how you intend to fulfill the goals of your study. It is a rational plan of verification that guides you through the various stages of your research. Research designs are important because complete designs tend to produce significant and correct conclusions. They contribute to the systematic observation of the research question or problem.

◆ PURPOSE

The research design serves several purposes. First, it suggests the necessary observations you need to make to provide answers to the research question. It outlines the ways you should make your observations. Second, the research design identifies the analytical and statistical procedures you will need to use when analyzing the data. A major purpose of research is to establish that the independent and dependent variables are causally related. The research design consists of three components necessary to establish this purpose: comparison, manipulation, and control (Nachmias and Nachmias 1992, 104). As we will discuss in later chapters, the research design also specifies a model you can use to test the validity and significance of the statistical relationships.

◆ FACTORS AFFECTING THE CHOICE OF DESIGN

There are various types of research designs at your disposal. The one you select depends on the following considerations: First, what is the purpose of your investigation? Is it to explore and describe some political phenomenon? Do you also want to explain what you have discovered? Or, do you want to pursue both purposes? Second, what resources do you have for your research? Are the necessary data available? Are you impeded by time limitations such as the constraints you face when trying to complete a term paper within a school semester? Do you have financial limitations? Is a control group available? Frequently it is expensive to produce hundreds of questionnaires and travel to data sources. Often you will need to find ways to compensate for resource limitations without unduly detracting from your research endeavor. Last, you need to remember our discussion about ethics and research. The privacy of your subjects is supreme. They place their faith in you when they agree to be a part of your research. You should not violate their privacy nor their trust.

There are several factors that affect the type of research design you use. Often they limit your choices to less than the ideal. As a result, your conclusions may be limited and somewhat imperfect.

❖ EXPERIMENTAL DESIGNS

Campbell and Stanley write that experimentation is "that body of research in which variables are manipulated and their effect upon other variables observed" (Campbell and Stanley 1966). This definition implies several things. First, a behavior is studied (the dependent variable). Second, factors impacting that behavior are identified (independent variables). Third, the researcher, through manipulation, determines the effect of the independent variables on the dependent variable. A study about voting behavior, for example, might examine the impact of age, income, and education on voting. In addition, control is essential. We must know whether age, income, and education did impact voting, or did some other factor also impact voting? One way to control for the impact of extraneous factors is to use the classic experimental design.

◆ THE CLASSIC EXPERIMENTAL DESIGN

The development of a classical experimental design involves several important steps. The first step, *selection and assignment*, involves two comparable groups—the test group and the control group. These groups are equivalent except that you expose the test group to the independent variable or treatment. The control group does not receive the stimulus but instead serves as a baseline for evaluating the behavior (dependent variable) of the experimental group. You randomly assign units of analysis to each group. Random assignment means that you base the assignment of units on chance. Each possible unit of analysis has the same probability of assignment to either group. As such, this method posits the notion that incidental factors are the same for each group. It also assumes that each group is equivalent with respect to the dependent variable.

The second step is to **pretest** each group. The pretest enhances the validity of the procedure because it helps you determine the equivalency of the groups. The pretest scores for each group should be similar. You can also consider pretest differences when determining the effect of the independent variable.

The third step is to *treat* the test group. In other words, you subject the group to the independent variable. You do not treat the control group. Next, you **posttest** each group in order to measure the dependent variable. The purpose of this step is to determine the impact of the independent variable on the behavior of the test group.

Last, you *compare* the measurement results to see if there are differences between the two groups. You can also compare measurement differences between pretest and posttest behaviors.

In summary, the classic experimental design requires you to randomly select and assign cases to test and control groups, pretest each group, administer the stimulus, and take post test measurements so that you can compare and make inferences from the results. With this design you can determine whether the groups were equivalent with respect to the dependent variable prior to treatment. A classical experimental design model is illustrated in Figure 11.1.

Let's try to simplify our discussion by applying the classical design to the classroom setting. You enrolled in a special summer school seminar about social policy. During the introductory session you discover that you and the other 49 members of your seminar have some common characteristics such as age, grade point average, and class standing. Then your professor does something strange. She randomly divides the seminar into two comparable

Random Assignment (R)	Pretest (0)	Treatment (X)	Posttest (0)
Experimental group (E)	Yes (01)	Yes	Yes (02)
Control group (C)	Yes (03)	No	Yes (04)

E $\cdots\cdots\cdots\rightarrow$ 01 $\cdots\cdots\cdots\rightarrow$ X $\cdots\cdots\cdots\rightarrow$ 02

R

C $\cdots\cdots\cdots\rightarrow$ 03 $\cdots\cdots\cdots\cdots\cdots\cdots\cdots\rightarrow$ 04

FIGURE 11.1 **Classical Experimental Design**

groups and administers a test to each group. She then gives one group a selection of readings to complete during the semester. She also tells the group not to report to class until the last day of the semester. You, of course, are in the group that must come to class.

The semester is intense but interesting. Your instructor has given you much to think about and, in your opinion, broadened your knowledge about social problems and government attempts to address them. The semester quickly draws to a close and it is soon time to take the final examination. When you come to class to take the exam, however, you notice that the group that was not required to attend the sessions was also sitting for the exam. You also learn that they will take the same exam that you will take. It is obvious to you, however, that your score and the scores of those who attended class will be higher. After all, you had the benefit of your professor's lectures and discussions between members of the class.

Look at this example closely. What is going on? What is the professor trying to do? Which group, if any, will score higher on the exam? While simplistic, this is an example of a classical experimental research design. All the components are present. There is a pretest. There is an experimental group (those who continued to attend class) and a control group (those excused from regular attendance). The professor's lectures represent the independent variable, or treatment. The final exam, of course, is the posttest.

Do the lectures enhance learning? To find out, you need to compare the test results of the two groups. If your group averaged 85 percent on the test compared to 70 percent for the other group, your professor will infer a causal relationship between class attendance and the higher scores.

How safe is the professor when she infers causation between test scores and attendance? Were the groups similar in knowledge about social problems prior to the experiment? The classical design allows your professor to answer these questions. For example, suppose a comparison of pretest scores showed that both groups averaged approximately 55 percent. As a result your professor asserted that the two groups were comparable and equivalent. If the results were different, say 50 percent for the control group and 60 percent for the test group, she would have to admit that the groups, although comparable, were not equivalent.

◆ THE BASICS OF AN EXPERIMENTAL RESEARCH DESIGN

Before we talk about other types of research designs, we want to spend a few moments discussing the components of the experimental research design. As implied by Campbell and Stanley's definition of experimentation, an experimental research design consists of three components: comparison, manipulation, and control. Each one is essential to establish a causal relationship between the independent and dependent variables. In Chapter 9 we said there were four major factors that helped determine causation: covariance, time order, nonspuriousness, and theoretical basis. With an effective research design, comparison allows you to show covariation, manipulation helps establish the time order of events, and control enables you to show that the relationship is nonspurious.

Comparison   The classic research design, through comparison, enables you to show the first requirement of causality; covariation or correlation. In our example above, the professor wanted to demonstrate a correlation between final exam scores in her social policy seminar and class attendance. In other words, class attendance is associated with better exam scores. To test this notion, she compared the final exam scores of those who attended class with those who did not. If her hypothesis was correct, her comparison would reveal higher scores for those who attended class. She can also infer from the results that her lectures enhanced learning and test scores. She could verify this hypothesis by comparing the pretest and posttest scores of those who attended class to see if the lectures made a difference. In sum, to assess covariation in our example, you can evaluate the student's knowledge about social programs before and after the seminar lectures. Or, you can compare the scores of the group who attended the lectures with the scores of the group that did not benefit from the lectures. In one instance you compare a group with itself. In the other example, you compare an experiment group with a control group.

Manipulation   To demonstrate causation, we must also show that a change in one variable causes a change in another variable. Causal relationships are asymmetrical. One variable is the force that determines the response of another variable. The determining, or independent, variable must occur before the response, or dependent, variable. Thus, the time order of events is another important factor when demonstrating a causal relationship.

Let's return to our seminar example. Causality implies that if grade scores (knowledge) are enhanced by seminar attendance, then an induced change in attendance will result in a change in knowledge. You can show this by manipulating the attendance of the group members. You allow the experiment group to come to class and exclude the control group members from the lectures. What you have really done is control the time order of events. The independent variable, lecture attendance, precedes the dependent variable, knowledge about social programs. Based on a comparison of test scores, you can determine whether knowledge increased after application of the independent variable.

Control   A third criterion of causality is to prove that other factors do not explain the observed association between the variables you want to study. In other words, the relationship you find is not spurious. A basic problem in causal analysis is the elimination of alternative causal interpretations. You might satisfy the criteria of time order, however; there are several factors that might account for the fact that two variables demonstrate covariance. X might cause Y, Y might cause X, both might be caused by Z, or causation might not exist. Your task is to show that X caused Y thereby excluding the other possibilities. You want to provide a single causal interpretation of your observed relationship by controlling for the effects of other variables. The classical and other experimental designs will help you eliminate most of these possibilities.

◆ SOLOMON FOUR-GROUP DESIGN

The Solomon four-group design is an extension of the classical research design. It is a very powerful experimental approach that some methodologists believe can be used to counteract short-term changes that may occur no matter whether the treatment is effective or not. This phenomenon is called the Hawthorne effect (Welch and Comer 1988, 22). When you pretest groups, you need to determine the effect the pretest might have on the groups. A pretest may motivate the groups to perform well under experimental conditions. The pretest may amplify the effect of the experimental variable. In sum, the pretest and test stimulus could interact to further change the dependent variable beyond the effects attributable to the pretest and stimulus separately. In sum, while a pretest has advantages such as providing an assessment of the time sequence as well as a basis of comparison, it can have severe reactive effects (Frankfort-Nachmias and Nachmias 1993, 113).

The inclusion of an additional test and control group in the research design addresses this possibility. Figure 11-2 reveals that the additional groups do not take a pretest. This procedure enhances your analysis of the impact of the independent variable on the dependent variable. By examining the posttest scores, you can generalize the results of the experiment on the

Random Assignment (R)	Pretest (0)	Treatment (X)	Posttest (0)
Experimental group (E1)	Yes (01)	Yes	Yes (02)
Control group (C1)	Yes (03)	No	Yes (04)
Experimental group (E2)	No	Yes	Yes (05)
Control group (C2)	No	No	Yes (06)

```
           E1 ·········► 01 ··········► X ··········► 02
           ↑
           ↓
           C1 ·········► 03 ··························► 04
    R ──────┤
           ↑
           ↓
           E2 ·······························► X ······► 05
           ↑
           ↓
           C2 ·····································► 06
```

FIGURE 11.2 **Solomon Four-Group Design**

Random Assignment	Pretest	Lecture	Posttest
Experiment group	70	Yes	85
Control group	70	No	70

FIGURE 11.3 **Lecture and Pretest Impact on Attitudes Towards Welfare Recipients (No Interaction)**

original experiment and control groups to the results experienced by the additional groups. You can also isolate the interaction impact of the stimulus and pretest. A model of the Solomon four-group design is illustrated in Figure 11.2.

Consider this example. You design an experiment to determine the impact a lecture about welfare might have on student attitudes towards welfare recipients. You randomly assign the participating students to two groups. You also pretest each group so that you can determine their attitudes. You then require the test group to attend the lecture. Later, you pretest each group on their attitudes toward welfare recipients. Figure 11.3 depicts the results you might observe if the lecture was the only reason for a change in attitudes. Each group scored the same on the pretest, indicating equivalency between the groups. The posttest scores, however, are different. The test group scored higher than the control group. In addition, the posttest score for the control group is the same as their pretest score. This suggests the group members were not influenced by the pretest. Consequently you can assert that the lecture was the sole reason for change in the experiment group's scores.

Figure 11.4 presents another possibility. Based on the difference between pretest and posttest scores, it shows that the attitudes of the control group

Random Assignment	Pretest	Lecture	Posttest
Experiment group	70	Yes	85
Control group	70	No	75

FIGURE 11.4 **Lecture and Pretest Impact on Attitudes Towards Welfare Recipients (Interaction)**

Random Assignment	Pretest	Lecture	Posttest
Experiment group–1	70	Yes	85
Control group–1	70	No	70
Experiment group–2	0	Yes	85
Control group–2	0	No	70

FIGURE 11.5 **Lecture and Pretest Impact on Attitudes Towards Welfare Recipients (No Interaction) Solomon Four-Group Design**

Random Assignment	Pretest	Lecture	Posttest
Experiment group–1	70	Yes	85
Control group–1	70	No	75
Experiment group–2	0	Yes	75
Control group–2	0	No	70

FIGURE 11.6
Lecture and Pretest Impact on Attitudes Towards Welfare Recipients (No Interaction) Solomon Four-Group Design

also changed. Why? They did not attend the lecture. Is it possible that the pretest influenced their attitudes towards welfare recipients? If the answer is yes, can you assume that the change in the scores experienced by the test group were also impacted by the pretest? In other words, did the lecture and pretest interact to generate the change in attitudes? You use the Solomon four-group design to answer these questions.

You can get several results when you use the Solomon four-group design. Figure 11.5 shows that the changes in attitudes were a result of the lecture. Note that the posttest scores used to determine the occurrence of a change in attitude for the two experimental groups are the same. In addition, the posttest scores for the two control groups are the same. This is what you would expect if the pretest did not interact with the lecture stimulus to impact posttest scores. In other words, lecture attendance is the sole cause of attitude change.

Now consider Figure 11.6. These results occur because of the pretest, the lecture stimulus, and interaction between the pretest and the lecture stimulus.

How much of the attitude change is a result of the pretest, the lecture stimulus, and the interaction between the pretest and lecture? You can use the following formula to determine the extent of change resulting from these factors.

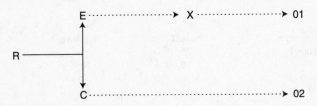

Random Assignment (R)   **Treatment (X)**   **Posttest Measurement (0)**
Experimental group (E)   Yes   Yes (01)
Control group (C)   No   Yes (02)

FIGURE 11.7
Posttest-Only Control Group Design

I = C − P + T

where

I = interaction effect

C = difference in scores of experiment group 1

P = pretest effect (control 1 posttest − control 2 posttest)

T = treatment effect (experiment 2 posttest − control 2 posttest)

Applying our formula to the results depicted in Figure 11.6 we get:

$I = (85 − 70) − (75 − 70) + (75 − 70) = 5$

Thus, we determine that 5 points of the 15 point change resulted from the interaction between the pretest and the lecture stimulus. One last point. Our formula does not consider the impact of "other" factors. To keep things simple, we assume that change is a result of the pretest, the lecture, and any interaction between the pretest and lecture.

◆ THE POSTTEST-ONLY CONTROL GROUP DESIGN

The classical and Solomon four-group designs may be strong experimental designs, but their use is limited because of cost and concern about the reactiveness of the pretest. Thus, some use the post test-only control group design, which is a variation of the classic and Solomon designs. This design requires random assignment of participants/subjects to the experimental and control groups (Johnson and Joslyn 1986, 102). It differs from the other two designs because a pretest is not administered. The design is diagrammed in Figure 11.7.

Political scientists use the posttest-only control group design more than any other type in their research efforts. While it may be the easiest one to use, it can also be used to answer a variety of political questions. Some examples will give you an idea about the broad applicability of this design.

You can use the posttest-only control group design in any political participation study that shows that an individual's (test group) characteristics such as education, gender, income level, etc. (independent variables) causes them to participate (dependent variable) differently than other individuals (control group).

You can also use the design in any policy analysis study that shows that policy output (independent variable) recipients (test group) behave (dependent variable) differently than those (control group) who did not receive output from the policy.

The posttest-only control group design has several benefits. It allows you to make causal inferences because you treated the test group prior to measurement of the dependent variable. You can also argue that differences between the dependent variable for the two groups resulted from exposure to the independent variable. Remember, you randomly assign units to each group to control for the impact of other factors.

The alert student, however, may have some concern about our latter statement. How sure are you that the random assignment of cases to your groups made them identical before you introduced the independent variable? Could the posttreatment differences between the group be a result of pretreatment differences? Unfortunately, this design will not tell you how much of the posttreatment difference results from pretreatment contrasts. This is one reason why some political scientists prefer the classical and Solomon four-group designs.

❖ NONEXPERIMENTAL DESIGNS

While experimental designs enhance comparison, control, and the manipulation of variables, their use is often limited. An important criterion of experimental designs, for example, is the random assignment of cases to the test and control groups. At times, however, it is not possible to randomly select and assign cases to these groups. When it is not possible to guarantee randomness, many political scientists use nonexperimental research designs. We also use these designs when we cannot incorporate some of the other features of experimental designs. In many designs, for example, it is difficult to control exposure to the experimental stimulus. In addition, political scientists are often interested in real-life problems—problems you cannot observe in the confines of a controlled environment. Despite these limitations, however, experimental designs help us understand the logic of all research designs. They are the model we use to evaluate other designs. They also allow us to draw causal inferences about the variables examined in the study. We cannot do this as easily with nonexperimental designs. Thus, if you understand the structure and logic of the experimental designs, you can also understand the limitation of the nonexperimental designs we are about to discuss.

Group	Pretest (0)	Treatment (X)	Posttest (0)
Experimental group	Yes (01)	Yes	Yes (02)
Control group	Yes (03)	No	Yes (04)

01 ————————————→ X ·····················→ 02

03 ···→ 04

FIGURE 11.8 **Nonrandomized Control Group Design**

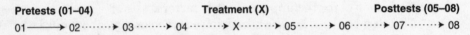

Pretests (01–04)   **Treatment (X)**   **Posttests (05–08)**
01 ———→ 02 ·······→ 03 ·······→ 04 ·······→ X ·······→ 05 ·······→ 06 ·······→ 07 ·······→ 08

FIGURE 11.9 **Time Series Without Control Group Design**

◆ NONRANDOMIZED CONTROL GROUP DESIGN

You use this design when you want to investigate a situation where random selection and assignment are not possible. It is one of the strongest and most widely used quasi-designs and is sometimes called a contrasted group design. It differs from experimental designs because test and control groups are not equivalent. In other words, there is no random selection. You can determine some degree of equivalency between the two groups, however, by comparing the two pretest results. Figure 11.8 is a model of the nonrandomized control group design. The model is very similar to the classical experiment design depicted in Figure 11.2. In addition, if our teacher in the social policy seminar did not divide her groups randomly, her design would be a nonrandomized control group design.

◆ TIME SERIES WITHOUT CONTROL GROUP DESIGN

At times it will not be possible for you to work with an experiment group and a control group. One way for you to compensate is to take a series of initial observations prior to introducing the independent variable. The initial observations establish a baseline. Once we establish the baseline, we introduce the independent variable and perform several postobservations. A substantial change in the behavior of the group, makes the independent variable suspect as to the cause of the behavioral change. You can acquire more validity by repeating the experiment in different places under different conditions. As with the nonrandomized control group design, this design does not randomly assign cases to the group. Figure 11.9 is a model of the time series without control design.

Experimental (E)—Pretests (01–04)	Treatment (X)	Posttests (05–08)
Control (C)—Pretests (01 – 04)	Treatment (X)	Posttests (05–08)

E   01 ——→ 02 ·····➤ 03 ·····➤ 04 ·····➤ X ·······➤ 05 ·····➤ 06 ·····➤ 07 ·····➤ 08

C   01 ········➤ 02 ·····➤ 03 ·····➤ 04 ·····➤ 05 ·····➤ 06 ·······➤ 07 ·····➤ 08

FIGURE 11.10 **Time Series With Control Group Design**

An example of a study using this type of design might be a study where you monitor and attempt to account for time shifts in various economic, social, or political indicators. Changes in the gross national product, unemployment, and public opinion about the president are examples. This study has use because you can make projections based on observed trends.

◆ TIME SERIES WITH CONTROL GROUP DESIGN

This design is similar to the previous design. It differs because you include a parallel set of observations without the introduction of the independent variable. The additional set of observations enhances the validity of the design depicted in Figure 11.9. Like the other quasi-experimental models, random assignment is not a part of this design. In fact, assignment purposely results in nonequivalent groups.

An example might be tracking students in an advanced learning curriculum. Based on several aptitude tests given at different times (pretests), several states separate students by placing some in the advanced curriculum classes (test group) and relegating the others to the normal curriculum classes (control group). School authorities, in addition to local tests, monitor and compare the progress of the students by analyzing a series of state proficiency tests (posttests). If the scores of the advanced children exceed the scores of the other students, school authorities cite the curriculum as the reason.

❖ OTHER TYPES OF RESEARCH DESIGNS

◆ THE CASE STUDY

A case study is an in-depth examination of an event or locale. When you use this type of design you do not assign cases to a test or control group. An example might be an analysis of some public agency where you monitor client satisfaction for a specified period of time. You then consolidate service delivery based on customer recommendations. After some time period, you start to monitor client satisfaction again. You find that their level of satisfaction has significantly increased. The reason? Consolidation of service delivery, of course.

There are some inherent problems with the case study. External validity, for example, is poor. It is difficult to generalize the results of a study that concentrates on a single unit of analysis. What works for one agency might not work for another one. In addition, it is difficult to control the impact of external factors. Service delivery might improve because of new energetic personnel and not because of the consolidation of service delivery.

◆ FIELD RESEARCH

When you study the behavior of a group of people in their natural setting you are doing field research. Field research requires you to participate in the lives of those you want to study so that you can better understand their behavior. As the investigator doing field research, you can act as a complete participant or as a participant observer. In the first role, the research objectives are unknown to those you observe. You try to become a member of the group and conceal your identity and purpose from the group members. In the latter case, you become an active member and participant in the group. You also, however, make your presence known to those you want to study.

Many political science field experiments are somewhat different than the type discussed above. Field research for policy analysts is an extension of the classical design into a natural setting. They are not, therefore, a separate type of design. Analysts attempt to control the selection and assignment of subjects to groups and the manipulation of the independent variable.

An example of a field experiment in political science is the Texas experiment in job placement training for prisoners about to be released from confinement. In 1988, the Texas Departments of Corrections and Employment, with the assistance of Texas A&M University, conducted a field experiment to test the effects of in-prison vocational placement training on the capabilities of parolees to obtain employment upon release from prison. Texas officials thought that the vocational training would give recipients a "head start" in the job market and negatively impact recidivism.

The research design was relatively simple. Parolees living in Dallas, Houston, and San Antonio made up the pool of possible subjects. Those receiving job placement training (the independent variable) made up the experiment group. The control group, those who did not receive the training, consisted of parolees who had similar social and psychological profiles as the members of the experiment group. In addition, researchers tried to interview members of both groups within 72 hours of their release. This was an attempt to control for possible extraneous factors. It also served as a type of pretest. Questions included the number of job contacts made by the parolee, current personal income level, and the income level of anyone else living with the individual. The posttest, conducted six months after the initial interview, was a follow-up interview designed to determine the work history of the parolee since their release. Analysts then compared the work histories of both groups to see if those who received the placement training had a better work history than those who did not receive the training. If there was a significant difference between the two groups, the state of Texas would increase the budget for the job placement program.

There are several problems associated with field experiments. The most obvious deals with the subject's environment. In a true classical experiment design, you have control over the subject's environment. In field research you are not in complete control of the environment. It is very difficult to control, account for, and distinguish between the impact of environmental changes on the subject's behavior and the impact of the experimental stimulus. Can you be sure, for example, that the job placement training was the major reason for a more stable work history? How do you control for the impact of the intervening variables introduced in each parolee's life during the six months between their release and posttest?

The analysts and sponsors of this particular study wanted to know if their program would benefit the citizens of Texas. Therefore, a study about the behavior of parolees in Dallas, Houston, and San Antonio could have application to the entire state. But, can you generalize the results of this study to other parts of the country? It is difficult to generalize the findings of a regional program to a national level. The vocational behavior of a group of parolees in Dallas, Texas, for example, might not represent the vocational behavior of parolees in New York, Chicago, or San Francisco. In other parts of the country the vocational behavior might be impacted by the state of the economy, public transportation opportunities, and political viewpoints of government officials.

Participation in this program was voluntary. Prisoners could apply for the in-prison program. There was not, however, room nor time to give the training to all those who volunteered. Thus an important ethical issue arose. Shouldn't a program intended to enhance the assimilation of prior offenders into the mainstream of society be available to all upon request? After all, analysts measured the success of this program by comparing the employment and recidivism histories of the subjects.

❖ OBSTACLES TO A SUCCESSFUL RESEARCH DESIGN

An effective research design demonstrates causality between variables. It also eliminates, or controls for, as many competing explanations of variable relationships as possible. Competing explanations undermine causality. When this occurs you cannot be sure that the independent variable caused the response or change in the dependent variable. You cannot be sure that your observations are valid.

◆ INTERNAL VALIDITY AND EXTRINSIC OBSTACLES

Internal validity addresses the question of whether the independent variable did, in fact, cause or lead to changes in the dependent variable. Did the manipulation or variation in the independent variable make a difference in the dependent variable? The criteria for assessing internal validity are time order, covariation, nonspuriousness, and theory.

There are several extraneous and innate obstacles to achieving internal validity (Nachmias and Nachmias 1992, 105–12). Some bias can occur because of the way you select and assign individuals to your test and control groups. These extrinsic factors produce differences between the groups before you apply the experimental stimulus. As a result, you are uncertain about the difference between the groups after you apply the independent variable. Is the difference a result of the stimulus or factors related to the selection and assignment procedures? Therefore, you need to be aware of ways to control selection factors.

Matching   The purpose of matching is to enhance the possibility that you assign subjects to test and control groups based on characteristics you know are related to the research study. There are two basic ways to match test and control group participants. Pairwise matching requires you to assign pairs of subjects matched on relevant characteristics to each group. For each person you assign to the test group, you assign an individual with identical characteristics to the control group. The researchers involved in the Texas program dealing with job placement training of Texas prisons used this method of matching. As a means of controlling the effect of education, for example, for every parolee in a specific education category in the test group, a parolee in the same category was placed in the control group. Differences noted between the occupational achievements of members of the test and control groups were attributed to the program and not to education, which was one of many extrinsic factors.

The pairwise procedure has a major limitation. Sometimes it is difficult to identify and match participants on important characteristics. For example, the researchers in the Texas penal study wanted to control for age, gender, race, education, and a psychological profile score calculated by the Texas Department of Corrections. Thus for every 25-year-old Anglo male with eight years of education and a profile score of 4 in the test group, researchers had to find an individual with the same combination of characteristics for the control group. Often, it was a monumental task that required researchers to pore through thousands of parolee records. Thus, while pairwise matching is precise, it is also inefficient and cumbersome.

Frequency distribution matching is another way to assign subjects to test and control groups. Although less precise, it is easier than pairwise matching. You do not match the groups based on one-to-one matching. Instead you match the groups based on the "average" of each extrinsic characteristic. If the average level of education for the test group is ten years, then the average for the control group should be ten years. If you control for race, then each group should have the same proportion of Anglos, Hispanics, and African Americans, for example.

Matching raises another question, how do you know you considered all the relevant factors? By this time we are certain that you know the answer. You must familiarize yourself with the literature in order to discover characteristics others have found important in accounting for differences between individual behavior.

The bottom line, however, is that matching does have some limitations. Thus, random assignment is a better way to select participants for your study.

Random Assignment   Matching helps you control for a limited number of predefined factors—factors you identified through your literature review. As a result, you think you have identified all the characteristics others considered important in explaining differences in behavior. But are you sure you identified all of the important ones? No, you are not sure. There may be other variables that you do not know of that could lead to erroneous causal interpretations. So what do you do? Many political researchers resort to randomization to construct their sample. Randomization controls for the influence of characteristics you might or might not know about. It is a process whereby all cases or subjects in the population have an equal chance of selection and inclusion in the study. It is, perhaps, the foremost method for equating experimental and control groups. We will discuss randomization in more detail in Chapter 12.

◆ INTERNAL VALIDITY AND INTRINSIC THREATS

Researchers have found that, in addition to their experimental stimulus, there are other intrinsic factors that account for changes in their research subjects—factors that pose a threat to the study's internal validity. Campbell and Stanley identified the following intrinsic factors that could nullify causal findings.

History   You want to control your research environment so that exposure to the experimental stimulus is the sole explanation for differences between the test and control groups. Over the period of the study, however, other events might occur that also account for change in the dependent variable. **History** pertains to events that occur throughout the study that might affect your subjects and provide competing explanations for changes in the dependent variable. Did your subjects change their viewpoints about gun control because you exposed them to violent crime statistics? Or, did their viewpoints change because they were a victim of crime during the study period? The longer the period of time between the pretest and posttest, the greater the possibility that external events will taint the study.

Testing   Experimental research requires a comparison of pretest and posttest results to determine the impact of an experimental stimulus. On occasion the pretest could impact the study. A pretest might sensitize your subjects and contribute to better scores on the posttest. As a result, you encounter another threat to the internal validity of your study. What caused a change in the dependent variable, the pretest or application of the independent variable? Consider this example. Your friend took the state bar examination and failed. She then enrolled in a seminar designed to help individuals prepare and take the bar. When she retook the exam she attained a passing score. Why? Was it the seminar? Was it study sessions with friends? Or, did her experience with the first exam prepare her? In any case it is difficult to attribute her success entirely to the seminar.

Regression Artifact   You might assign someone to your test or control group because of a poor score on the pretest. But what if the subject is having a bad day and the score is not indicative of his or her ability? If the individual retook the test, the score might increase. True, you might attribute the increase to testing, but you also might attribute it to the problems the subject experienced at the time of the first test. With both explanations possible, you cannot be sure as to the reason for an enhanced score on a subsequent posttest.

Experimental Mortality   When you assign subjects to control and test groups, you try to make the groups equivalent. Over the course of the study, however, some might drop from the study. As a result the composition of the groups may change enough to bias the results. This threat is most acute during a study that covers several months.

Instrumentation   The problem of instrumentation, or instrument decline, deals with changes in the measuring instrument between the pretest and posttest. To attribute change to the independent variable, you must show that repeated uses of the instrument will produce equivalent results. In other words, you want to make sure the instrument you use to collect data is totally reliable. When applied by different persons, other factors, such as the attitude of the person administering the test, should not influence the results. Additionally, at times your measurement instrument changes during the experiment so that the pretest and posttest measures are not made in the same way. Again, you could taint your results.

Maturation   Over time, people change because of psychological, social, or biological processes. These changes could affect your subjects and create differences between the test and control groups. Therefore your groups will no longer be equivalent. This could cause you to make erroneous inferences. Was the increased racial awareness of your subjects attributed to a government program? Or, was the increase due to increases in the age and experience of your subjects?

◆ EXTERNAL VALIDITY

External validity is the extent you can generalize and apply your findings to larger populations and different settings. You want to know whether a study of American college students at a particular university applies to all college students across America, for example.

Several factors often limit the external validity of experimental designs. The artificial setting of the experiment is one limitation. Often conditions that hold in experimental settings will not hold in real-life settings. The experimental setting is too controlled and too pristine.

Occasionally experimental subjects react differently because they realize they are part of an experiment. This could taint the study results. This possibility occurred during the Hawthorne Electric plant studies. Researchers wanted to analyze the impact of workplace environmental enhancements on productivity. Their findings showed that the productivity of employees exposed to better conditions did increase. The productivity of employees not subjected to the better conditions, however, also increased. What was the answer? The researchers hypothesized that the novelty of participating in an experiment, receiving attention, and increased cohesiveness of study participants contributed to the increased productivity. In sum, the study participants worked hard to make the study a success. They worked so hard that they tainted the results of the study. They also made researchers take steps to address this problem in future studies.

❖ A COMPARISON OF RESEARCH DESIGNS

Table 11.1 shows that experimental designs differ from nonexperimental designs in several ways. The strength of experimental designs is that they meet the requirements of causality. They exert a great deal of control that is manifested through matching and randomization. You can control for the effect of known and unknown extrinsic characteristics or variables. There is also a great deal of control over the introduction of the experimental stimulus. Thus, experimental designs are strong on manipulation. This allows you to establish causal explanations for political behavior more easily than with nonexperimental designs. The classic experiment and Solomon four-group designs are also strong on comparison. You can compare the impact of independent variables by looking at changes in behavior between groups, or within a single group.

In sum, experimental designs are stronger in internal validity than nonexperimental designs. You have more control over the independent variables, the units of analysis, and the environment in which the behavior occurs.

The strong points of the experimental designs are the flaws of the nonexperimental designs. Without random assignment to groups, control over competing explanations is impaired. Difficulties in establishing the time order of events also detracts from your ability to manipulate the independent variables. In addition, the absence of control groups in some of the designs severely limits your ability to compare results. Consequently, your ability to draw clear inferences from your study is reduced.

The experimental designs, however, also have some limitations. A common complaint is that the results attained from experimental designs are tainted and inappropriate for the real world. It is difficult to reproduce a real-world application in the laboratory environment. Because of the sanitized or laboratory setting and the extent of control you use, it is more difficult to generalize the results to other populations. As we previously discussed, political scientists use nonexperimental designs because they deal with real-world situations. Consequently their findings can be generalized. Thus, a strength of non-experimental designs is their external validity.

TABLE 11.1
A COMPARISON OF RESEARCH DESIGNS

Design	Goal	Model	Comparison	Manipulation	Control
Posttest-only design	To evaluate a situation that cannot be pretested	T,R,S,PST C,R,PST	3	5	4
Classic experimental design	To study the effect of an influence on a carefully controlled study	T,R,P,S,PST C,R,P,PST	5	5	5
Solomon four-group design	To minimize the Hawthorne Effect	T1,R,P,S,PST C1,R,P,PST T2,R,S,PST C2,R,PST	5	5	5
Nonrandomized control group design	To investigate a situation where random selection and assignment are not possible	T,P,S,PST C,P,PST	3	3	3
Time series design without a control group	To determine the effect of a variable introduced after initial observations with only one group	T,Pn,S,PSTn	2	3	3
Time series design with a control group	To enhance the validity of the above design with a control group	T,Pn,S,PSTn C,Pn,PSTn	3	3	3

Key

T = test group
P = pretest
R = random assignment
S = stimulus application

C = control group
PST = posttest
n = numerous tests

T1, T2, C1, C2 = test/control group 1 and 2
1 = very low; 2 = low; 3 = moderate; 4 = high; 5 = very high

Many have also pointed out that experimental designs are weak in representation. That is, many experiments include volunteer subjects and as a result are not representative of the population. This problem makes it difficult for you to generalize the results to the public (Frankfort-Nachmias and Nachmias 1992, 144).

While no design is perfect, you can work to improve the findings of your research project. You can enhance experimental results by defining your population and by using a probability sample to select cases for study. You can enhance nonexperimental results by identifying and controlling as many opposing explanations as possible.

❖ SUMMARY

In this chapter we introduced you to the different types of research designs you can use to complete a research study. Research designs provide you with a plan to use when collecting, analyzing, and interpreting phenomena you believe provides answers to your research problem. As such they are an important part of the composite research process.

We discussed several types of designs. We also highlighted the advantages, disadvantages, and differences between the experimental and nonexperimental designs. Experimental designs are stronger in internal validity, but weaker in external validity than the nonexperimental designs. Thus, an experimental design enables you to enhance the comparison, manipulation, and control of your study's components. On the other hand, you cannot generalize the results as readily as you can with a nonexperimental design.

We also discussed several obstacles to the internal and external validity of your study and presented ways to overcome those obstacles. History, maturation, regression artifact, and testing taint the internal validity of your study. A clear definition of your population, probability sampling techniques, and a shorter period of study will help overcome the internal validity threats we discussed. The way you select and assign members to your test and control groups can impact the external validity of your study.

❖ KEY WORDS

comparison	longitudinal design
control	manipulation
control group	matching
experimental mortality	maturation
external validity	nonexperimental design
history	panel study
instrumentation	posttest
internal validity	pretest

regression artifact   time series design
research design

❖ EXERCISES

1. Based on a study of the nations of the world, a researcher finds that wealthier nations generally have a greater percentage of the population employed in the public sector than do less fortunate nations. She claims that this relationship is causal, that is, the wealth of the nation leads to or causes growth in public sector employment. Evaluate this claim with respect to the criteria for assessing causality.

2. Formulate a research hypothesis on one of the following:

   a. The notion that the American two-party system tends to result in non-ideological parties that agree on most important issues since to win the election they must appeal to approximately the same elements of the electorate.

   b. Edmund Burke's classic statement of the trustee theory of representation that "not local purposes, not local prejudices ought to guide, but the general good."

   c. The impact of adult cynicism about politics on adolescents.

3. Design a research project to study the hypothesis you formulated for exercise 2.

4. Discuss ways to enhance the reliability and validity of your design.

5. Use any of the political science journals (Publius, American Political Science Review, etc.), to find and critique an article that uses an experimental design. Do the same for another article that uses a non experimental design.

❖ SUGGESTED READINGS

Bernstein, Robert A., and James A. Dyer. *An Introduction to Political Science Methods*, 2nd ed. Englewood Cliffs, NJ: Prentice-Hall, 1984.

Bowen, Bruce D., and Herbert F. Weisberg. *An Introduction to Survey Research and Data Analysis*. San Francisco: Freeman, 1977.

Campbell, Donald, and Julian Stanley. *Experimental and Quasi-Experimental Designs of Research*. Chicago: Rand-McNally, 1966.

Frankfort-Nachmias, Chava, and David Nachmias. *Research Methods in the Social Sciences*, 4th ed. New York: St. Martin's Press, 1992.

Goldenberg, Sheldon. *Thinking Methodologically*. New York: HarperCollins, 1992.

Johnson, Janet Buttolph, and Richard A. Joslyn. *Political Science Research Methods*. Washington: Congressional Quarterly Press, 1986.

Kay, Susan Ann. *Introduction to the Analysis of Political Data*. Englewood Cliffs, NJ: Prentice-Hall, 1991.

Leedy, Paul D. *Practical Research: Planning and Design*, 3rd ed. New York: Macmillan, 1985.

DATA COLLECTION AND INPUT

❖ INTRODUCTION

Once you have conceptualized theories, operationalized concepts into variables, formulated your hypotheses, and constructed your measurement instruments, you can begin to collect the data pertinent to your research problem so that you can make generalizations. Collecting and inputting your data to statistical packages constitute the fifth stage of the composite systematic research process.

In this chapter we will discuss the various techniques political scientists use to collect data. We will also cover the fundamentals of sampling theory and discuss the aims of sampling. Then, we will discuss the central concepts of sampling—the population, the sampling unit, the sampling frame, and the sample itself. We will also discuss the different types of sampling designs to include procedures of probability and nonprobability. Next, we will discuss the considerations involved in determining the sample size and for estimating nonsampling errors. Last, we will briefly discuss data codification and entering the data to statistical programs.

An understanding of this chapter will enable you to:

1. Understand data collection techniques.
2. Understand the purpose of sampling.
3. Distinguish between population, samples, and sampling units.
4. See the importance of sampling frames when drawing a sample.
5. Identify errors associated with sampling frames.
6. Differentiate between probability and nonprobability sample designs.
7. Draw a random, systematic, stratified, and cluster sample.
8. Design and use a codebook when entering your data to computer statistical programs.

❖ DATA COLLECTION TECHNIQUES

Data collection is one of the more interesting phases of political research. When collecting data you may find yourself in the classroom, in the campus library tracing public issues through the various media resources, or in public depositories examining public records and accounts. You may also find yourself attending legislative sessions, interviewing public officials about political issues, or talking with members of the judiciary about legal procedures and points of law. In short, you may find yourself in the "field," which is the real world of politics. It is during this stage that you begin to sense the excitement that is associated with politics.

Whether you opt to collect your own data—(**primary data**)—or rely on data collected by someone else—(**secondary data**)—the data collection process will be a unique experience because you will have to sort through several sources of information so that you have the data necessary to test your hypotheses. As a result, your final data set may be a compilation of data from several sources. In any event you will need to tailor the data to meet the specific needs of your research problem.

◆ PRIMARY DATA

Direct Observation: Field Research   There are several ways that you can personally collect data. One popular way is to personally observe the behavior of your study group and make notes. For example, you can attend legislative, executive, and judicial proceedings.

One obvious advantage to this method is that you observe the behavior of your study group as it actually happens. As a result, you can control the bias that may be involved with other methods.

This method also has some inherent disadvantages. For example, some phenomena is not directly observable. How do you observe political alienation or efficacy? This method also requires a considerable amount of skill and training in that it may be difficult to quantify observations. In addition, the direct observation of group behavior can be extremely time consuming. Last, direct observation is generally restricted to a small area because you can only be in one place at a time.

The Survey   The survey is an expedient method of data collection. It relies on the verbal report of the respondent. Unlike direct observation, you do not actually observe the subject's behavior.

There are several advantages associated with this method. You can mail surveys to various areas. This expands the scope of your study. This method is also very efficient in terms of time expenditure.

There are also some disadvantages. One obvious disadvantage is the cost of postage. Another disadvantage is the poor return rate of questionnaires. You can enhance the return rate, however, by using a cover letter that explains the importance of the survey and why the addressee should respond.

You should also ensure that the instructions accompanying the survey are clear. Other ways to enhance completion and return include limiting the length of the questionnaire. Only include those questions and items absolutely essential to your investigation. You should also pay attention to the way you word your questions. Take steps to ensure the wording is concise and written so that questions can be understood by those individuals completing the questionnaire. Also include as many close-ended questions as possible. Not only will this enhance completion, but it will also enhance data input and analysis. Another way to enhance completion is to follow up with the individuals you mailed the questionnaires to. In addition, offer to send them the results of your data analyses. Last, enclose a postage paid, self-addressed envelope.

Personal Interview   Many researchers prefer to personally interview their subjects. This method allows you to make face-to-face contact, and, as a result, clarify questions if necessary. This method, however, is also very time consuming. In addition, the clarification of questions can also contribute to interviewer bias when trying to "explain" questions.

Telephone Interview   The telephone interview is less time consuming than the previous methods we discussed. In addition, you have a telephone book available that you can use to select possible respondents. Telephone interviews also enable you to reach more people and reduce travel costs and mailing costs. It also approximates face-to-face contact.

An obvious disadvantage associated with this method is that the interviewee can terminate the interview by hanging up the phone. In addition, you cannot ensure that everyone in your population has an opportunity to be a part of your survey. Individuals without phones or unlisted numbers are often "missed."

◆ SECONDARY DATA

Data Archives   Today many public and private agencies collect, store, and release information at little or no cost. Thus, you should consider making use of available data. Possible general sources include data archives. You need to be familiar with the major social science archives. These organizations that specialize in the distribution of data they collect and store include the Bureau of Applied Social Research at Columbia University. The Opinion Research Center housed at the University of Chicago is another important and often used archive. The Inter-University Consortium for Political and Social Research located at the University of Michigan, however, is one of the most important data archives at your disposal. Since 1962, the Consortium has processed and distributed data such as attitudinal data, census records, presidential election results, legislative records, and international information applicable to over 130 countries. Every year since 1952, dozens of scholars interested in American voting behavior have made use of the Consortium's database on the political attitudes and behavior of the American public.

The Almanac of American Politics   *The Almanac of American Politics*, which is organized by state and published annually, is a summary of the important political issues pertinent to each state of the union. The *Almanac* also includes important state census data, such as the size of the population and median levels of education. In addition, you can find information about voter registration, racial concentrations, employment profiles, the demographics of state and congressional public figures, and the ratings of all members of Congress developed by organizations such as the Ripon Society and Americans for Democratic Action. Thus, the *Almanac* is an exceptional source of information about American politics.

Census Data   The nation's major data collection agency is, of course, the United States Bureau of the Census. One goal of the agency is to make a variety of census reports available to the public and scholars. As a result, you will find extensive data sets about agriculture, the general population, housing, transportation, construction, wholesale and retail trade, and government.

Most of you, however, will find the census of *General Population Characteristics*, *Social and Economic Characteristics*, and *Detailed Characteristics*, to be most useful. The first publication contains detailed information on race, gender, and household characteristics for each state, county, city, and town (with populations in excess of 1,000) within the states. The second publication provides for the same jurisdictions as the general census but also includes information about employment status, school enrollment, income levels, and social status. The last publication contains detailed social and economic data for states, cities with populations exceeding 100,000 people, and metropolitan statistical areas.

Statistical Abstract of the United States   Another data source produced by the Bureau of the Census that may be quite useful to you is the *Statistical Abstract of the United States*. The *Abstract* combines data collected from both public and private organizations as well as from unpublished documents. In addition to population information, the *Abstract* contains data on a wide range of topics such as law enforcement, government finances, and state and local governments. In addition, you will find information about international statistics in the *Abstract*.

Subnational Government Data   There are numerous data publications available that specialize in subnational governments. For example, the *City/County Data Book* is published every five years to update information on all counties and all cities over 25,000. In this publication you will find population data, employment data, and information dealing with all types of government finances. Crime statistics for states and local governments are also published in the *Data Book*.

Other valuable sources of information on subnational governments include the *Municipal Year Book*, the *County Year Book*, the *Book of the States* published by the Council of State Governments, and the *Census of Governments*. This latter publication provides information for counties, municipalities, townships, school districts, and special districts.

Voting and Elections   While there are several data sources dealing with voting and elections, two in particular stand out. The *America Votes* series compiled by Richard Scammon and Alice McGillivray presents data on the results of several national elections. Included are the results of presidential primaries, state election returns for presidential and senate races by county, state congressional election returns by congressional districts, the results of state party primaries and party run-off elections, and historical state voting profiles since 1946.

The *Guide to U.S. Elections* is another major source of election information. The *Guide* presents information on all state-by-state elections for all major political offices. In the *Guide* you will find data on parties, presidential elections, and congressional elections.

Other Sources   A most comprehensive source of public opinion data is *The Gallup Opinion Index*, a monthly publication published by the American Institute of Public Opinion. This publication, while publishing information that may be beyond your interests as a political researcher (UFO sightings), also publishes public opinion responses to questions about the president, capital punishment, and other political questions. In addition, the responses are categorized by demographics such as gender, race, party preference, and education. The *Index* also reports trends associated with those questions that were asked on several occasions.

If your area of expertise is international and comparative politics, there are several publications that may meet your needs. For example, the *Statistical Yearbook* is published each year by the United Nations. The *Yearbook* presents demographic, economic, and political data, on a country-by-country basis. Other annual publications include *The International Year Book and Statesman's Who's Who* and *The Statistical Abstract of Latin America*. Each publication provides economic, demographic, and political information. The *International Yearbook* also provides brief biographical statements about political statesmen.

Content Analysis   **Content analysis** is "the systematic, quantitative analysis of observations obtained from archive records and documents" (Frankfort-Nachmias and Nachmias 1992). Many political scientists use content analysis to systematically reduce a text, such as legislative minutes and media products, so that they can determine the presence and frequency of some characteristic relevant to their study.

While content analysis is not a method extensively used by political scientists, it can be appropriate in some analyses. An interesting application of the technique is Segal and Cover's attempt to "derive independent and reliable measures of the values of all Supreme Court justices from Earl Warren to Anthony Kennedy" (Segal and Cover 1989). They performed a content analysis of the ideological values of all justices from Earl Warren to Anthony Kennedy from editorials published in several of the nation's leading newspapers. They coded the statements made within the editorials as liberal, moderate, and conservative. For example, liberal statements included those professing support for the rights of defendants in criminal cases, women and racial minorities in equality cases, and the individual against the government in privacy and First Amendment cases. Conservative statements were those with an opposite direction. Each justice was then given a score derived from their codification process. Values ranged from a + 1.0 (unanimously liberal) through .0 (moderate) to – 1.0 (unanimously conservative). Segal and Cover found that these values correlated highly with the votes of the justices for cases dealing with the above subject matter (Segal and Cover 1989).

Content analysis has also been used to research the development of international relations (Ithiel de sola Pool 1981) and to identify the authors of several of the Federalist Papers (Mosteller and Wallace 1964). In summary, content analysis is used to enhance the analysis of nonstatistical information found in documentary, newspaper, and archive records.

❖ SAMPLING

◆ INTRODUCTION

Now that you know something about data sources and ways to collect data, you need to understand the notion of sampling. Often, your goal as a researcher is to resolve your research question by observing a group of states, people, or nations. For example, you observe all U.S. congressional persons to understand legislative behavior, or, all nations belonging to the North Atlantic Treaty Organization (NATO) in order to understand international alliances. The entire U.S. congressional body and the entire membership of NATO are known as populations. Each member, or unit, of the population is known as a case. Your goal as a researcher is to generalize about the population from the data you collect.

Typically, however, generalizations are not based on data derived from all the observations, all the respondents, or all the events that are defined by the research problem. Instead, you use a relatively small number of cases (sample) and make inferences about all the cases (population). As an example, pollsters use the responses of a relatively small group of respondents to forecast how the entire population of voters would vote if the election were held at the time the poll was taken. They also use these samples to predict how the population of voters will vote when the actual election is held.

As we mentioned, empirically supported generalizations are usually based on partial information. Why? It may be impossible, impractical, or extremely expensive to collect data from all the potential units of analysis encompassed in the research problem. Yet, you can make precise inferences about the population based on a sample when the sample accurately represent the relevant attributes of the population. For example, in marketing research the preferences of a small sample of households are used to target new products to millions of customers. The Environmental Protection Agency uses a small sample of automobiles of various kinds to obtain data on performance to regulate the performance of all automobiles. In your research efforts you will use a small number of respondents to determine attitudes towards policy, reasons for party identification, and reasons for voter turnout that you can generalize for a larger population.

It is important that you understand what we mean by population, sample, and case. Therefore, we want to spend some more time discussing and presenting examples about these very important concepts in empirical research.

◆ THE POPULATION

As we said, the **population** is the total set of items that you want to analyze; for example, all Third World nations, all members of the U.S. Congress, or all American citizens residing in Texas. In other words, the population is the aggregate of all cases that conform to some designated set of specifications. In the first example, by the specifications "nations" and "Third World," we defined a population consisting of all nations of the Third World. For the second example, by the specifications "members" and "U.S. Congress," we defined a population consisting of all senators and representatives serving in the 104th U.S. Congress located in Washington, D.C. And, for the third example, our population is all American citizens residing in Texas. You can similarly define populations consisting of all households in a given community, all the registered voters in a particular precinct, or all the books in a public library. Thus, a population may be a group of nations, legislators, or people.

Finite and Infinite Populations   A **finite population** is a population that contains a countable number of sampling units, or cases; for example, all U.S. Congress persons serving in the 102nd Congress, or all registered voters in a particular city in a given year. Sampling designed to produce information about particular characteristics of a finite population is usually termed survey sampling.

An **infinite population** is a population that consists of an endless number of sampling units, such as an unlimited number of coin tosses.

◆ THE SAMPLE

A **sample** is a subset of all the observations or cases covered by your research question. It is a portion of the population. For example, a portion of all the nations of the Third World, a portion of all the members of the 102nd U.S. Congress, or a portion of all American citizens living in Texas.

The Sampling Unit   A **sampling unit** is a single member (case) of a sample; for example, Nigeria, Senator Phil Gramm, Bill Henderson, or an American residing in Texas. Sampling units usually need to meet some criteria to be included in your study; for instance, only U.S. congressional members serving during the 102nd Congress.

Sampling Frame   After you have defined the population, you can draw a **sample frame** that adequately represents the population. The actual procedures involve a selection of a sample from a list of sampling units. Your sample frame may be based on congressional records, the census, city directories, or even the telephone book. Every aspect of the sample design—the population coverage, the stages of sampling, and the actual selection process—is influenced by the sample frame.

In an ideal situation your sample frame will include all sampling units in the population. In reality, however, such a list does not always exist. Thus, before you select your sample, you need to evaluate the sample frame for potential problems.

Incomplete Frames   One problem you may encounter is an **incomplete frame.** This problem occurs when sample units included in the population are missing from the sample frame list. An outdated frame could contribute to this problem. You will encounter this problem, for example, if you use a list of senators and representatives who were in the 101st Congress to create a sample of the 102nd Congress. Thus, you need to ensure that your sample frame is current.

Blank Foreign Elements   This problem occurs when the sample units on your sample frame are not a part of the original population. For example, you use a list of the ambassadors who are members of the current United Nations Security Council to select a sample of members who participated in council sessions that met to determine what action should be used against Iraq because of its hostilities towards Kuwait. These cases should be treated as blanks and omitted from the sample.

Clusters of Elements   This problem occurs when the sample units on your frame are listed in clusters, or groups, rather than individually. Your study, for example, may be concerned with individuals residing in a state, county, or city, but your frame consists of aggregate data.

Errors in Sampling Frames   In 1936, the *Literary Digest* conducted a poll to determine who would win the 1936 presidential election—Alf Landon or Franklin Delano Roosevelt. The *Digest* polled almost 2.5 million people. As a result of their poll, the *Digest* predicted that Landon would defeat Roosevelt in a landslide victory—57 to 43 percent. If you know your history, Roosevelt "turned the tables" and won by a huge landslide—62 to 38 percent.

What happened? The *Digest* sampled an adequate number of people to allow prediction. Let's briefly evaluate their methodology and their sample frame in particular. The *Digest* mailed out 10 million questionnaires by obtaining addresses from telephone directories and club membership lists. Roosevelt's supporters, however, were too poor to have phones or belong to private clubs. Thus, the sample frames did not include all possible sample units found in the population. In other words, the frame was incomplete because it excluded those sample units most likely to vote for Roosevelt. As a result, the sample was not representative of the voting public.

◆ Measurement

The population and the sample have measurements you can use to summarize their characteristics. A **parameter** is a measure we use to summarize the characteristics of a population based on all items in the population. For example, the average per capita income of all nations of the Third World, the median age of all the members of the 102nd U.S. Congress, or the median education of all the American citizens residing in Texas.

Because of the reasons we previously discussed, however, we normally use the characteristics of a sample. We call these sample characteristics **statistics.** The major objective of sampling, therefore, is to provide accurate estimates of unknown parameters from the statistics of a subset. In order to accurately estimate unknown parameters from known statistics, however, we need to define the population and collect data from an adequately sized and representative sample.

❖ SAMPLE DESIGNS

When you draw a sample you want to ensure that it represents the population from which it is drawn. You have a representative sample when your analyses of the sample units produce results similar to those you would find had you analyzed the entire population. But how do you go about drawing a representative sample? The answer lies in the distinction between probability sampling and nonprobability sampling.

◆ Probability Sampling

With **probability sampling**, each element in your population has an equal chance to be a part of your sample. The *Literary Digest*'s 1936 poll would have fulfilled the requirements of probability sampling if the poor were included in the frame and had had the same chance as the other prospective voters to be included in the sample. A well-designed sample, therefore, assures that, if you were to analyze several samples drawn from a given population, the findings would not differ from the true population figures by more than some specified amount. A probability sample design makes it possible for you to estimate the extent to which the findings based on one sample are likely to differ from what you would find by studying the entire population. A probability sample design makes it possible for you to estimate the population's parameters from the sample statistics. Thus, you want to use a probability sample design whenever possible.

On occasion, however, you may need to use nonprobability sample designs. Your study may be limited, for example, because of time constraints or funding. Because nonprobability samples are relatively easy to conduct and explain in comparison to probability samples, we are going to discuss several types of nonprobability designs before we turn our attention to probability sample designs.

◆ NONPROBABILITY SAMPLE DESIGNS

When you use a nonprobability design you cannot specify the probability that each unit has of being included in your sample. In addition, you cannot be assured that every unit has some chance of inclusion. In the *Literary Digest*'s 1936 sample, for example, the *Digest* never determined the voting intentions of the poor.

There are three major **nonprobability sample** designs at your disposal— convenience samples, purposive samples, and quota samples.

Convenience Samples   When you use a convenience sample, you select whatever sampling units are at your disposal. Thus, you cannot estimate the representativeness of your sample and the population's parameters. You may, for example, interview the first 50 senators you meet in the halls of Congress who are willing to be interviewed.

Purposive Samples   When you use a purposive sample, you subjectively select your sample units so that your sample appears to represent the population. Purposive samples are often based on some type of trend analysis. Let's say, for example, that you want to predict the results of a particular political event, such as a gubernatorial election. Your resources, however, are limited. You don't have the time nor the money to interview possible voters across the entire state. What do you do?

A purposive nonprobability sample may be the answer. To conduct this type of sample you try to find a particular county or some other geographical division to represent the entire state. That is, you want to find a county, or counties, that consistently votes the way the entire state votes. The underlying assumption that you make is that the subdivisions are representative of their states. Your next step is to interview prospective voters from the subdivisions you determined were representative of the state. The last step is to predict the statewide results based on the interviews you conducted in the subdivisions. While you can see that this is not the ideal way to take a sample, it is not as time prohibitive or costly as a probability sample that would require interviewing voters across an entire state.

Quota Samples   A quota sample is another type of nonprobability sample because every unit of the population does not have the same chance to be included in your sample. The objective of a quota sample is to select a sample that is similar to the sampling population. For example, if you know that the population is 60 percent female, then your sample should be 60 percent female. If the population is 15 percent Hispanic, then the sample should be 15 percent Hispanic.

An obvious limitation to this procedure is that it can be somewhat tedious. You are doing a lot of mixing and matching. In addition, you need to have a good idea about those factors that could influence the dependent variable. Do you have a quota based on religion, occupation, or income level, for example? You also want to make sure that you don't omit an important factor. You do not want to repeat the mistakes made by pollsters who tried to predict the winner of the 1948 election. Basically the pollsters used a form of quota sampling to predict the winner. While they considered variables such as gender, age, ethnicity, income, and residence, they did not establish a quota based on party identification. How could they? This is what they were trying to ascertain. The bottom line was that they must have sampled a disproportionate number of Republicans because several polls predicted Dewey would defeat Truman (Freedman, Pisani, and Purves 1978, 302–7).

◆ PROBABILITY SAMPLE DESIGNS

In contrast to nonprobability sampling, probability designs enable you to specify the probability that each sampling unit has of being included in the sample. There are four major types of probability designs—simple random samples, systematic samples, stratified samples, and cluster samples. We will discuss each one in turn.

Simple Random Samples The simple random sample is the most basic probability design. It is often incorporated into the more elaborate designs we will discuss later. A simple **random sample** is one in which each element of the population has an equal chance of being a part of the sample. In addition, you know the probability of selection and inclusion in the sample. For example, when you toss a perfect coin, you know the probability that it will turn up heads or tails is 50 percent.

The same notion applies to simple random samples. To determine the probability applicable to your study you divide the size of the sample (n) by the size of the population (N). Thus, if your population is 535 U.S. Congress members and you want to survey 300 individuals, the probability of each congressional member being included in the sample is 300/535 or 56.1 percent.

Normally you will use a computer program or a table of random digits to select units to include in your simple random sample. Let's consider this example. You want to conduct a survey of ambassadors to the United Nations. However, you lack the necessary resources to interview each member. So you obtain a sample frame listing each ambassador. There are 600 names (N) from which a simple random sample of 400 (n) is to be drawn.

To start with, you need to number the list, beginning with 001 for the first ambassador and ending with 600 representing the last ambassador on the list. Notice that you have three-digit numbers in your population.

Now refer to the table of random digits (Table A1) in Appendix III. Note that each column has five-digit numbers. You need to drop the last two digits of each number because your sample frame is made up of three-digit numbers (001 through 600). The numbers in the table represent the possible cases that you will include in your sample.

Perusing the first column you will note that the first ten numbers in the column are 104, 223, 241, 421, 375, 779, 995, 963, 895, and 854 (remember to drop the last two digits!). Of these ten numbers, which ones represent cases that you will select from your frame as sample units? We hope you picked numbers 104, 223, 241, 421, and 375. Why these numbers? Remember, your sample frame consists of 600 ambassadors numbered from 001 to 600. So you will only select numbers from the random table within that range. Numbers greater than 600 are outside your range. So far in our example you would interview the 104th, 223rd, 241st, 421st, and 375th ambassador on the sample frame. Carrying this logic through, you need to select 400 numbers from the table until you have your sample.

An often asked question is, where do you start on the random digit table? While we started with the first row and first column, you can select any starting point, such as the first row of the second column. You can also choose to progress in any way you want, down the columns, across them, or diagonally. All you need to do is decide ahead of time on your method of selection and be consistent.

Systematic Samples   A **systematic sample** is a probability sample in which cases are selected from a sample frame at predetermined intervals. For example, suppose you want to select a sample of 200 county administrators from a list of the 2,000 county administrators serving in Texas (hypothetical). With systematic sampling, you first need to calculate the sampling interval. This is accomplished by dividing the number of cases on the list (2,000) by your desired sample size (200). Or, $K = N/n$, where K represents the interval, N represents the population size, and n represents the sample size. Thus, for this example the interval is $K = 2,000 \ (N) \ / \ 200(n) = 10$.

After you determine the sampling interval, you proceed through the sample frame and select every tenth individual until you select 200 names. Basically, you can start with any name on the frame. The first individual, the 1,000th, or whatever. If you want to be somewhat systematic, however, you might want to use a random start. To do this you randomly select a number from 001 to 2,000 from a random numbers table. Thus, if number 20 is randomly selected, administrators 20, 40, 60, etc., would be included in the sample.

Systematic sampling is very useful when dealing with a long list of population elements. Consider the following example. A student has repeatedly read about the liberal viewpoints of college professors. Therefore, he decides to survey 100 professors at a major university and ask them questions that will help to determine their level of liberalism. The student, however, is surprised to find out that this particular institution has over 3,500 professors and employees. Although a simple random sample may be selected, it would involve a great deal of work. Therefore, the student decides to use a systematic random sample. The student's first step is to determine the sampling interval, which he does by dividing the population size ($N = 3,500$) by the size of the desired sample ($n = 100$). This procedure results in a sampling interval of

35. The student then selects the first record at random from the first 35 names listed on the sampling frame (for example, name 20). Next the student selects every 35th record until a sample size of 100 is selected (20, 55, 90, 125, etc.). This method is called a 1-in-35 systematic sample.

Systematic sampling is more convenient than a simple random sample because you do not need a random digits table other than to pick the first case that you will include in the sample. All you need to do is select every kth unit from the sampling frame. In addition, it is more convenient to use with a large population. Unfortunately, there are also disadvantages you need to consider when using this procedure. There may be a systematic pattern in the data that occurs at every kth unit. This could skew or bias your sample. If you are using a personnel list classified by department and position, for example, it is possible that every kth unit is a department head. This might produce a bias because department heads may have more education, income, and other amenities that are not representative of the entire work force.

Stratified Samples   **Stratified samples** are usually used to ensure that different groups of a population are adequately represented in the sample. This procedure enhances the level of accuracy of the sample when estimating parameters. The goal, for example, is to break the population down into homogeneous strata and select from each strata. When combined into the total sample, a more heterogeneous sample should occur. Again, let's use an example to enhance your understanding.

A criminal justice major wants to study the impact of gentrification of crime in an urban neighborhood. To do so, the student decides to examine the attitudes of residents towards crime in the community. The student anticipates that the attitudes of new residents may differ from those of residents who have resided in the neighborhood for an extended period of time. Therefore, as a means of assuring proper representation of both groups, she decides to use a proportional stratified random sample with two strata—new and old-time residents. The population consists of 200 new residents and 300 old-time residents. From this population the researcher wants to sample 100 residents. The first step for our student is to develop separate lists for each strata. Then, she needs to select the proportional sampling fraction by dividing the population by the size of the sample (500/100 = 1/5). Next, she should determine the proportion of new residents and old-time residents to be sampled. She does this by multiplying the proportional sampling fraction (1/5) by the number of new and old-time residents. As a result she will survey 40 newcomers ($200 \times 1/5$) and 60 old-timers ($300 \times 1/5$). Last, our student can use the simple random sampling methodology we previously discussed and apply it separately to both lists.

The example and procedures we discussed above pertain to proportional stratified sampling. There are times, however, when you might want to use a disproportional stratified sample. Disproportional samples allow you to compare two or more particular strata or a single strata more intensively. In addition, they are often used if you are concerned that a proportional sample will not give you enough cases to examine from a particular strata or group. This often occurs when examining race as an impact on some political phenomenon. That is, if you use the other types of sampling we discussed, you may not have a sample that has a sufficient number of African Americans, or some other minority racial group, in your sample. Thus, you would want to use a disproportionate sample.

The steps you take to draw a disproportional sample are similar to those we told you to use with proportional samples. The major exception is that you use several sampling fractions (a different one for each strata). For example, you believe the voting behavior of college students is impacted by their major. To test your notion you decide to survey 600 of 3,000 students. In addition, you stratify your sample as 2,100 liberal arts majors, 600 business majors, and 300 agriculture majors. The problem is you don't think you will get enough agriculture majors if you use a proportional stratified sample. (How many would you sample?) Therefore, you decide to use a disproportional sample and sample 300 liberal arts majors, 150 business majors, and 150 agricultural majors. If you have followed us to this point, you know that your next step is to calculate the sampling interval for each strata. Applying our simple formula (N/n), you find you need to survey every seventh person on the liberal arts sampling frame (2,100/300), every fourth person on the business list (600/150), and every second person on the agriculture frame (300/150).

Do you see anything wrong with this procedure? Well, your sample no longer represents the population. After all, you have a disproportionate number of agriculture majors in the sample which makes it biased. So what do you do? Of course we have an answer—you simply weigh the sample.

Perhaps you are concerned about grade point averages (we have all endured the scores of Aggie jokes haven't we?). As a result of the oversampling of agriculture majors, you are concerned that the sample grade point average is biased downwards from the population grade point average. Consider Table 12.1. The table shows you that the weighted GPA is 3.0 versus the sample GPA of 2.83 that is biased because of the disproportional strata sampling technique.

TABLE 12.1

TABLE OF POPULATION PROPORTION AND AVERAGE GPA

Measure/Statistic	Agriculture	Liberal Arts	Business	Total
Number of individuals	300	2,100	600	3000
Proportion/weight	.1	.7	.2	1.0
Sample GPA	2.0	3.0	3.5	2.83

Calculation:
   Agriculture—.1(2.0) = .20
   Business—.2(3.5) = .70
   Liberal Arts—.7(3.0) = 2.1
   Weighted GPA = .2 + .7 + 2.1 = 3.0

Cluster Samples   **Cluster samples** are frequently used because they are the least expensive way to draw probability samples from a large-scale population. This method requires you to select sample units from several larger groupings called clusters. You initially select the clusters with a simple random sample or stratified sample. Then, you have an option. You can include all the sampling units in each cluster in your sample, or you can select units from the clusters using simple or stratified sampling procedures. In either instance, you will draw from individual population clusters instead of the entire population.

Suppose you are a public administration student who is interested in investigating the relationship between the location of one's residence and support for an economic development initiative. The initiative, a fire fighting school to enhance fire fighter's training, will create several hundred jobs and be a boost to the community's economic development. On the other hand, environmental studies suggest that the smoke from the training exercises could have potential negative effects. You hypothesize that those citizens living closest to the proposed site for the school will be more adverse to its creation.

While designing your study, you discover that there is no single list available that contains the names of every citizen in the community. In addition, it is too expensive to compile such a list. Thus, you decide to use cluster sampling. To use this method, you should take the following steps:

1. Use an up-to-date map to define the area to cover in the study.
2. Define boundaries and exclude those areas that do not include dwelling units. In other words, only use residential areas.
3. Divide each residential area into blocks.
4. Number each block in a nonsymmetrical manner. This will compensate for the possibility of an unforeseen bias being built into your sample.
5. Use a simple random or a systematic sample to select the blocks you will sample from.
6. List and number all of the dwelling units in each of the blocks you select.
7. Use a single random or a systematic sample to select the dwelling units from which you will interview the residents.

Probability Sampling: A Summary   Table 12.2 summarizes the various ways to conduct a probability sample.

❖ DETERMINING THE SAMPLE SIZE

As we have discussed, a sample is a subset or portion of the population you have selected to analyze. But how do you determine the size of a sample? This is one of the most often asked questions in survey research. The answer depends on several factors.

There are numerous suggestions about the necessary size of a sample. For example, the sample size should be a regular proportion (say 5 percent) of the

TABLE 12.2

SUMMARIZATION OF PROBABILITY SAMPLE TECHNIQUES

Type of Sampling	Description
Simple random	Assign to each sampling unit a unique number; select sampling units by use of a table of random digits.
Systematic	Determine the sampling interval (N/n); select the first sample unit randomly; select remaining units according to the interval.
Stratified	Determine strata; select from each stratum a random sample proportionate to the size of the strata in the population.
Cluster	Determine the number of levels of clusters; from each level of clusters select randomly; ultimate units are groups.

Source: Frankfort-Nachmias and Nachmias. *Research Methods in the Social Sciences,* 4th ed. New York: St. Martin's Press, 1992.

population. Or, the sample size should be at least 2,000 cases. No such rule of thumb is adequate. The size of the sample is properly estimated by deciding what level of accuracy is required, and how large an error is acceptable.

◆ POPULATION SIZE

The first factor you need to consider is the size of the population. Common sense suggests that the larger the population, the greater is the needed sample size. A sample of 50 representatives from a legislative body of 55 will probably accurately represent the entire body. On the other hand, a sample of 50 representatives will probably not be representative of legislative body of 435. Thus, when you increase the sample size, you reduce the probability that you will select an unrepresentative sample. It is very important to note that after a point, however, an ever-increasing sample size will have a relatively small impact on the accuracy of your sample. It is possible to achieve a high degree of accuracy for a large population with a relatively small sample. National polling organizations with vast resources, for example, rarely draw a sample size that exceeds 1,500 to 2,000 individuals.

◆ VARIABILITY

The more your population "varies," the larger your sample size needs to be. For example, if everyone in Dallas, Texas is Anglo, female, and a Baptist, how large a sample do you need to draw? We hope you answered one. You know this example is unrealistic because the characteristics of the citizens of Dallas are varied. That is, you will find male and female Baptists, Catholics, and

Jews, who are Anglo, African American, Hispanic, and Asian. Thus, you would need to draw a larger sample so that it could be representative of the population.

◆ SAMPLING ERROR AND CONFIDENCE LEVEL

Sampling error and the level of confidence are important factors in sampling theory and in determining the size of a sample. While the size and extent of heterogeneity of the population are important factors when determining the size of your sample, many consider them constants in the sample-size formula and, as such, will not differ that much from situation to situation (Cole 1980). Therefore, the more important factors you need to consider when determining the size of your sample are the extent of accuracy you want when predicting from the sample to the population and the degree of confidence you have in your prediction. The first factor is known as **sampling error** while the second factor is known as the **level of confidence.**

Of course, you would like to be 100 percent accurate and confident when making predictions about the population from your sample data. Greater accuracy and confidence, however, require an increased sample size, which can be costly in terms of money and time expenditure. Thus, you will find that you may need to accept some error and a reduced level of confidence. You may be willing, for example, to accept a sample size that will vary 5 percent or less from the population 95 times out of 100 than one that will vary one percent or less from the population 99 times out of 100. What you lose in accuracy, you gain in time and money.

Based on our discussion we can use the following formula to calculate the appropriate sample size:

$$n = (CL/SE)^2 [p(1 - p)]$$

where

n = desired sample size

CL = desired level of confidence

SE = sampling error

p = assumed population variance

Before we give you an example using this formula, we need to discuss its components. First, the n represents the sample size you will need to meet certain criteria. Second, the SE is the amount of error you are willing to accept. It usually ranges from 1 percent to 5 percent. Next, the CL represents the level of confidence you want to have when predicting from the sample to the population. The CL is normally a Z score (to be discussed in Chapter 13) which, when used with the concept of the normal curve, represents a certain confidence level. For example, 1.96 represents a confidence level of 95 percent. This means that 95 out of 100 times your sample will not exceed the error range (SE). Last, the p represents the assumed population variance. Because you do not know the actual population variance, you assume maximum variance and uses.[1]

TABLE 12.3

SAMPLE SIZE REQUIREMENTS FOR VARYING DEGREES OF ERROR TOLERANCE AND CONFIDENCE LEVELS

Error Tolerance	Levels of Confidence	
(%)	95%	99%
1	9,604	1,6587
2	2,401	4,147
3	1,068	1,843
4	601	1,037
5	385	664
6	267	461
7	196	339
8	150	260
9	119	205
10	96	166

Source: Richard L. Cole. *Introduction to Political Inquiry.* New York: Macmillan, 1981.

Suppose you want to determine the attitude of a population about ways to reduce the budget deficit. Also assume you are willing to tolerate an error of five percent at the 95 percent level of confidence. What size sample will you need to draw? Using the above formula you calculate that you need a sample size of

$$n = (1.96/.05)^2 [.5(1 - .5)] = 384.16 \text{ or } 385$$

Now let's show you what happens when you want to enhance your predictive capability and the level of confidence. First, if you want to have a confidence level of 99 percent, you will need a sample size of 664. If you only are willing to tolerate an error of 3 percent, you will need a sample size of 1,067. What size sample will you need if you want a confidence level of 99 percent and a tolerable error of 3 percent?

In sum, our examples show you that to enhance your predictive capability and lessen your tolerable error, you will need to increase the size of your sample. If you are working with a very large population, you might want to use Table 12.3, which summarize the various sample sizes you will need as determined by various degrees of error tolerance and confidence levels.

❖ CODING THE DATA

Now that you are familiar with sources of data, we need to spend some time talking about the assembly, storing, and processing of the data you collect. An important step is to assemble your data in a way that will enhance input and analysis. In some instances, you may be able to analyze data directly from the source, for example, the archive or questionnaire. For the most part, however, you will need to Input your data to one of the many statistical packages loaded in mainframe systems or personal computers.

Therefore, before you proceed to the actual analysis stage, you will want to assemble your data in a form amenable to computer processing. As a first step, you will need to code your data. Coding is the process of assigning numbers to all possible responses to all questions or items that will constitute your database. Based on this coding process, you will be able to input and store your data in a mainframe or personal computer.

◆ THE CODESHEET

At one time many political researchers used punch cards to transfer their data to more convenient and permanent modes of storage such as magnetic tape and disk. Today, with the advent of personal computers and the like, many use codesheets.

If you prepare your survey instrument correctly, you can probably input your data into the computer directly from your survey instrument. This will save you much time and effort. Secondary data, however, usually requires the need for a codesheet.

A codesheet is nothing more than a sheet of paper having 80 columns and several rows. The columns contain the information, or variables, you collected about the cases in your sample. Variables such as age, income, and education, for example, will take up several columns. The codesheet has 80 columns to correspond to the number of columns you will find in most statistical packages. Each row corresponds to each case or sampling unit. You will, for example, have 50 rows if the cases in your study are the states of the union.

The amount of column space assigned to any variable is equal to the largest value for that variable. Data should also be entered as "right justified" entries. After the codesheet is finished, it is necessary to develop a codebook and then input the data to the applicable computer program.

◆ THE CODEBOOK

The **codebook** gives you the precise location of each variable in the data set. It will tell you what the numbers in the columns represent. Therefore, you need to take some time when putting your codebook together.

There are several items that you should include in your codebook. First, you want to devise a name for each variable. Most names will be self explanatory (Age = Age). On other occasions you may need to abbreviate the name of the variable because many packages restrict the length of the name to eight to ten characters. For example, you may opt to use PCI to represent "per capita income."

Second, you want to include a variable description. That is, you want to describe the variable so that you will have an idea about the level of measure-

TABLE 12.4

DATA INPUT CODEBOOK: TEXAS COUNTY POLITICAL CHAIRS (DECEMBER 1992)

Variable	Description	CC	Space
The following variables pertain to the impact of early voting on the Democratic political party.			
COUNTY (ALPHA) Name of county		1–15	15
PARTYORD Impact of early voting on party organization (1 = No impact 2 = Some impact 3 = Great impact)		16	1
PHONEBAD Impact of early voting on phone banks and calls (1 = No impact 2 = Some impact 3 = Great impact)		17	1
GRPRALLD Impact of early voting on special group rallies (1 = No impact 2 = Some impact 3 = Great impact)		18	1
IDSURVED Impact of early voting on voter identification surveys (1 = No impact 2 = Some impact 3 = Great impact)		19	1
GETOUTVD Impact of early voting on Get-out-the-vote efforts (1 = No impact 2 = Some impact 3 = Great impact)		20	1

ment and whether the data is a percentage or raw number, for example, median level of education or percent of Hispanic population.

Third, you may want to depict the column length and columnar location of the variable. For example, information about income takes up five columns and is found in columns 5 through 9.

If the data you plan to enter is primary data, that is, survey data, you may want to depict the text of the original question as an entry in your codebook. In addition, you will also want to show the response possibilities and the code value for each response. For example, "How do you rate the president's performance in addressing the budget deficit?" 1 = poor 2 = fair 3 = good 4 = excellent.

Table 12.4 is part of a codebook used by a student who was studying the impact of voting legislation on the county party chairs in Texas counties.

In summary, it is essential that you take time when preparing your codebook. You will find that it is a valuable tool when you are entering and analyzing data at a later time.

❖ **DATA INPUT**

In the past, political scientists would enter and analyze data through one of two ways—the batch mode and the interactive mode. The first method, for the most part, required the use of data input cards. The second method allowed the researcher to directly input data through a computer terminal. Each method, however, was associated with a mainframe computer or mincomputer housed in a computer center. While efficient and cost-effective, these methods have some problems. First, they require you to "wait your turn" for data update and computer printouts. That is, you are sharing the system with other research students across the campus. Second, you may have to wait several hours or even overnight to receive printouts of your input and analysis efforts. Third, many mainframe systems are not "user friendly." That is, you need to be versed in the operations of the system and statistical program.

While the mainframe is an efficient and effective system for the university, it was slow and cumbersome for the individual. As a result, many researchers are using personal computers (PCs) and any of a number of statistical packages to handle their data input and analysis efforts. The major difference between personal computers and the central site computers discussed above is that the PC is self-contained. This means that there is no need to have a computer line linkage between the PC and other units. Although technology may soon render the PC obsolete, for the time being, it is becoming the most popular type of computer used by researchers and students.

With the advancement of PCs, in terms of cost and effectiveness, many statistical software packages can be used with PCs. This innovation has also contributed to the advancement and popularity of the PC. With the PC and appropriate statistical software you can, within a matter of minutes, analyze the results of your data input and analysis efforts. No more time is wasted in sharing or waiting in line for output products. In addition, you can make corrections much quicker with the PC than with the other types of computers. Last, many of the major software packages are user friendly because they provide on-line direction and assistance. If you have ever worked with central mainframes or minicomputers, you will appreciate this feature.

As we said, the manufacturers of several statistical software packages have produced PC versions of their programs. It is not our intent to teach you about the various programs available to you. Such a task is beyond the scope of this book. In fact, you will find entire texts and appendices of texts dealing with individual software packages and their statistical applications.[2] Suffice to say that any of these packages will compliment and enhance your data input and analysis capabilities.

❖ SUMMARY

In this chapter we discussed several techniques political scientists use to collect data. Specifically we discussed the steps applicable to direct observation techniques such as field research; mail, personal and telephone interviewing; and survey research. We also discussed secondary data analysis and content analysis. For each technique we discussed the advantages and disadvantages. For example, while the mail questionnaire has advantages such as low cost and anonymity, its disadvantages include a low response rate. Thus, some prefer to use personal interviews or telephone interviews. The personal interview, however, is extremely time consuming and costly. The telephone interview does not ensure that everyone in a population has the opportunity to be interviewed.

Secondary data analysis is used with data collected by others such as researchers or government agencies such as the U.S. Census Bureau. Secondary analysis is useful because it can be used for comparative purposes and to determine change over a period of time (longitudinal analysis). In addition, the collection of secondary data is somewhat cheaper than the collection of primary data.

We covered the fundamentals of sampling theory and the aims of sampling. We said that the central concepts of sampling were the population, the sampling unit, the sampling frame, and the sample itself. We also discussed the different types of sampling designs to include procedures of probability and nonprobability.

We spent considerable time telling you about ways to determine the sample size. We said that the size of the sample depended on several factors—the size of the population, the variability of the population, the amount of error you were willing to accept when predicting from the sample to the population, and the level of confidence you want to have when making those predictions. To enhance your comprehension we gave you a simple formula and a quick reference table you could use to determine the size of your sample.

Last, we briefly discussed data codification and ways to enter the data into statistical programs. We said that batch processing and the interactive mode of input required the use of punch cards or terminals that were on-line with a central processing unit such as a mainframe or minicomputer. A relatively new innovation used by more and more universities is the personal computer. The PC has become more attractive to researchers and students because they can see the results of their input and analysis efforts in a relatively short period of time. In addition, the statistical software packages used with PCs are more user friendly than those used with central processing units.

❖ KEY TERMS

blank foreign elements	level of confidence
cluster sample	nonprobability sample
cluster of elements	parameter
codebook	population
content analysis	primary data
convenience sample	probability sampling
field research	purposive sample
finite population	quota sample
incomplete frame	random sample
infinite population	sample

sample frame   statistics
sampling error   stratified sample
sampling unit   systematic sample
secondary data   variability

❖ EXERCISES

1. Discuss the various types of data collection techniques and include the advantages and disadvantages of each.

2. Discuss the purpose of sampling.

3. Distinguish between population, samples, and sampling units.

4. Discuss the possible errors associated with sampling frames. What steps would you take to alleviate the possibility of these errors being present in your sample frame?

5. Differentiate between probability and nonprobability sample designs. Make sure you discuss the advantages and disadvantages associated with the various types of designs.

6. From the sources of data discussed in the chapter, select a small number of cases (states, presidents, Supreme Court justices, etc.), and for each case collect information on five variables (age, education, etc.). Develop a codebook based on the data you collect.

7. To study the degree to which Americans are satisfied with the electoral process, a political scientist designs the following sampling procedure. She obtains a list of all political precincts in the United States and randomly selects a number of precincts from that list. She then obtains a list of registered voters for each precinct selected. Finally, from these lists she selects a random sample of individuals and mails each a questionnaire asking them, among other things, how satisfied or dissatisfied they are with the American electoral process.

   a. What type of sampling design is this?

   b. There are two sampling frames in this study. What are they?

   c. Evaluate the adequacy of each frame with respect to meeting the objective of the study.

   d. Specify one way, through sampling techniques, that you could improve the accuracy of the sample estimate of satisfaction with the electoral process.

8. If you were to obtain a systematic sample of size 500 from a population of size 5,000, and you randomly select the number 4 as your initial case, what would be the number of your next case selection?

9. You need a sample of 25 students to interview for a study of attitudes toward intercollegiate athletics, and so you interview the first 25 students

to enter the University Center on a Monday morning. This constitutes a
_____ sample.

❖ SUGGESTED READINGS

Bernstein, Robert A., and James A. Dyer. *An Introduction to Political Science Methods,* 2nd ed. Englewood Cliffs, NJ: Prentice-Hall, 1984.

Blaylock, Hubert M., Jr. *Social Statistics,* 2nd ed. New York: McGraw-Hill, 1979.

Bowen Bruce D., and Herbert F. Weisberg. *An Introduction to Survey Research and Data Analysis.* San Francisco: Freeman, 1977.

Campbell, Donald, and Julian Stanley. *Experimental and Quasi-Experimental Designs of Research.* Chicago: Rand McNally, 1966.

Dometrius, Nelson C. *Social Statistics Using SPSS.* New York: HarperCollins, 1992.

Fox, William. *Social Statistics Using MicroCase.* Chicago: Nelson-Hall, 1993.

Frankfort-Nachmias, Chava, and David Nachmias. *Research Methods in the Social Sciences,* 4th ed. New York: St. Martin's Press, 1992.

Johnson, Janet Buttolph, and Richard A. Joslyn. *Political Science Research Methods.* Washington: Congressional Quarterly Press, 1986.

Kay, Susan Ann. *Introduction to the Analysis of Political Data.* Englewood Cliffs, NJ: Prentice-Hall, 1991.

Leedy, Paul D. *Practical Research: Planning and Design,* 3rd ed. New York: Macmillan, 1985.

Norusis, Marija J. *SPSS/PC+.* Chicago: SPSS, 1988.

❖ NOTES

1. In fact, you do not know any of the actual population parameters. You are analyzing a sample so that you can derive statistics to represent the parameters.
2. See William Fox, *Social Statistics Using MicroCase* (Chicago: Nelson-Hall, 1992); Nelson C. Dometrius, *Social Statistics Using SPSS* (New York: HarperCollins, 1992); Claire L. Felbinger and Stephen F. Schwelgien, "Introduction to SPSS and Introduction to SAS," in Chava Frankfort-Nachmias and David Nachmias. *Research Methods in the Social Sciences,* 4th ed. (New York: St. Martin's Press, 1992).

DATA ANALYSIS: UNIVARIATE STATISTICS

❖ INTRODUCTION

You have now completed several steps in the behavioral research process such as the literature review, the research plan, and data collection and processing. Now you are ready to analyze your data. This procedure, which includes the calculation of different statistics, can be the most exciting part of the entire research process. You begin to convert raw data and indefinable patterns into explanation and understanding. As you begin to receive signs that your data substantiates your initial expectations, your breath shortens and your heart palpitates rapidly. As one noted political scientist commented, "It is here that the political researcher begins to sense the excitement of discovery—a thoroughly invigorating and stimulating intellectual experience shared by all scientists" (Cole 1980).

Thankfully, your computer's statistical program will calculate the statistics for you. The calculation, however, is secondary. The more important task is to interpret the statistics so you can see what your data is trying to tell you. Thus, the next three chapters will give you the tools to interpret statistics so you can revel in the excitement of discovery.

An understanding of this chapter will enable you to:

1. Explain the role of descriptive and inferential statistics.
2. Explain a frequency distribution and describe its characteristics.
3. Interpret measures of central tendency.
4. Interpret the measures of dispersion.
5. Describe the types of frequency distributions.
6. Explain the normal curve.

❖ THE ROLE OF STATISTICS

The role of statistics in political research is a subject of intense debate. Normative theorists see statistics as cold and calculating. They also see the proponents of statistics as more concerned with "what it is versus what it should be." Behavioralists, on the other hand, see statistics as another way to analyze and explain political phenomena. Despite the debate, the role of statistics in the social sciences is important. Statistics enable us to see patterns in the political phenomena we are trying to study. They enable us to organize raw data and to describe and interpret observations in ways that help us test theories and hypotheses. In short, statistics are an invaluable tool for the political scientist who seeks to resolve important political questions.

The empirical analysis of political questions often involves a mass of quantitative data requiring organization before making any analysis and interpretation. Additionally, before examining the relationship between variables, you must describe the typical case of a variable and determine how typical it really is (Kay 1991). Statisticians call this process univariate analysis. Conversely, when we analyze one variable in relation to another variable, we are conducting bivariate analysis.

◆ DESCRIPTIVE STATISTICS

There are two types of statistics that political scientists use—descriptive statistics and inferential statistics. **Descriptive statistics** enable political scientists to organize and summarize data. They provide us with the tools necessary to describe quantitative data. Among these summarizing measures are percentages, proportions, means, standard deviations, and measures of association. Descriptive statistics are especially useful when the researcher finds it necessary to analyze interrelationships among more than two variables.

◆ INFERENTIAL STATISTICS

Inferential statistics deal with sample data. They enable the researcher to infer properties of a population based on data collected from only a sample of individuals. Inferential statistics have value because they offset problems associated with data collection. For example, the time-cost factor associated with collecting data on the entire population may be prohibitive. That is, the population may be immense and difficult to define. In such instances, inferential statistics can prove to be invaluable to the social scientist.

Descriptive and inferential statistics are used in the data analysis process. Data analysis involves noting whether hypothesized patterns exist in the observations. We might hypothesize, for example, that urban legislators are more liberal and supportive of welfare programs than those legislators representing rural constituencies. To test this hypothesis the researcher may ask urban and rural legislators about their views on welfare programs and payments. The researcher then compares the groups and uses descriptive and inferential statistics to find out whether differences between the groups supported expectations.

In sum, a descriptive statistic is a mathematical summary of measurements for one variable. Inferential statistics, on the other hand, use sample data to make statements about the population. Descriptive and inferential statistics provide explanations for complex political phenomena that deal with relationships between variables. As such, they are an important tool in the political scientist's repertoire.

❖ LIMITATIONS OF STATISTICS IN RESEARCH

Statistics cannot resolve every question you have about politics. Therefore, we need to discuss some of the limitations of statistical research.

First, statistics do not provide the means for the researcher to prove anything he or she wants to prove. On the contrary, there are explicit procedural guidelines, rules, and decision-making criteria to follow in the statistical analysis of data. As such, statistics cannot make up for the lack of clear, consistent, logical thinking in the development of a body of theory.

Second, statistics provide little help in understanding political phenomena that we cannot empirically measure. Some contend, for example, that we cannot measure the critical concept of political power (Bacharach and Baratz 1962). Even when measurement is possible, statistics do not always tell us whether we are measuring what we want to measure. There are, for example, several ways to measure the rate of employment. One likelihood is to contact the local unemployment office and find out how many individuals have applied for unemployment benefits. However, what about the few who believe it is beneath them to apply for what they perceive as welfare? And what about those who have dropped out of the job market?

A final principal limitation of statistics is that the techniques tell us something about groups of cases. As such, they do not provide definite predictions about individual cases. Thus, while statistical techniques may provide guidelines, they do not allow us to reach certain conclusions about individuals (Cole 1980). For example, knowing that 64 percent of the respondents in a survey favored gun control does not allow you to say your neighbor favors gun control.

In sum, there are important limits on the value of statistical analysis. There are some political problems you cannot explore statistically. For those questions subject to quantitative analysis, however, statistics may only be a "poor man's" substitute for controlled laboratory, or true experimental research. Statistics in these cases are only valuable when researchers carefully define the problem, develop ways to measure important variables, and use a sound research design to collect data. Then, and only then, are statistics helpful in understanding the research question.

❖ UNIVARIATE STATISTICS

◆ THE FREQUENCY DISTRIBUTION

As a student you have frequently read research papers, articles, and reports that included descriptive statistics. Government textbooks, for example, present displays of voting results, public welfare expenditures, and characteristics of congressional members. Additionally, media headlines read, "President's Popularity Rises by Three Percent," or, "Employment Drops by Four Percent." The media also inundates you with these statistics in the form of public opinion polls. Whatever the source, most of your exposure has usually been with tabular statistics, or frequency distributions.

One step in analyzing and reporting information involves the presentation of frequency distributions of the variables of concern. A frequency distribution is nothing more than a tabulation of raw data according to numerical values and discrete classes. A frequency distribution of party identification, for example, shows the number of individuals belonging to a particular political party. In this chapter you will learn all you need to know about arraying and summarizing single variables.

Table 13.1 is an example of a common display of the values of one variable. In this example the race of individuals elected to Texas county government positions from 1977 to 1987 is shown.

This frequency table is even more simple than some because it does not display measures of central tendency or dispersion. Measures of central tendency, such as the mean, depict the average of the distribution of values. Measures of dispersion, such as the standard deviation, show how values in the distribution cluster about the mean. We will explain these statistics in another section of this chapter.

Before we discuss ways to construct a frequency distribution, let's discuss the following important features of a frequency distribution:

1. *Raw data:* data collected but not summarized into descriptive form.
2. *Variable:* the classification trait of the data, for example, race.
3. *Class:* one of the grouped categories of the variables, for example, county judge and county sheriff.
4. *Class frequency:* the number of items within a given class, for example, 217 Anglo judges.
5. *Total frequency:* the number of items in the table ($N = 226$ and 231).

(NOTE: Other terms that are not applicable to Table 13.1 include class boundary, class midpoint, and class interval. We will explain these terms later in the chapter.)

Now let's turn our attention to the important features of a frequency distribution by examining Table 13.1 in more detail. The presentation of a frequency distribution should have the following:

Table 13.1

Race of Elected Texas County Officials, 1977–1987

| Position | 1977 (N = 226) | | | | 1987 (N = 231) | | | |
| | Anglo | | Hispanic | | Anglo | | Hispanic | |
	No.	%	No.	%	No.	%	No.	%
Judge	217	(96.0)	9	(4.0)	217	(93.9)	13	(5.6)
Comm. Pct 1	207	(91.6)	19	(8.4)	203	(87.9)	26	(11.2)
Comm. Pct 2	209	(92.5)	17	(7.5)	201	(87.4)	22	(9.6)
Comm. Pct 3	207	(92.0)	18	(8.0)	209	(90.0)	18	(7.8)
Comm. Pct 4	209	(92.9)	16	(7.1)	206	(89.2)	22	(9.5)
Clerk	211	(93.4)	15	(6.6)	212	(91.8)	19	(8.2)
Sheriff	216	(95.6)	10	(4.4)	218	(94.4)	13	(5.6)
Treasurer	214	(94.7)	12	(5.3)	207	(92.0)	18	(8.0)
Tax Assessor	216	(95.6)	10	(4.4)	219	(93.9)	14	(6.1)
Totals	1906	(93.8)	126	(6.2)	1890	(91.3)	165	(7.9)

Source: Laurence F. Jones and Delbert A. Taebel. "Hispanic Representation in Texas County Government." *Texas Journal of Political Studies* 16, no. 1 (Fall 1993).

1. *A descriptive title:* researchers must make it clear to the reader what information they are presenting. The title must be as specific as possible. As such, it should include the type of information (race of elected county officials), the time (1977–1987), the location (Texas), and any other pertinent information.

2. *Clear labels:* labels that enable the reader to see the column and row summaries of the table's data are important. In Table 13.1, the reader can quickly see that the columns depict the frequency distribution and the percentage distribution for the period. The row titles are also quite clear because they inform the reader that the researcher classified elected officials according to several positions. You also can see the presentation of the totals of each column.

3. *Appropriate classes:* normally each group should have some entries. Additionally classes should not be so large that they obscure the range and variation in the data. For example, classes that divided cases into less than 20 or 20 or more, may find 85 percent of the cases in a single class. This obscures differences in the data. Conversely, a unit-by-unit breakdown, such as less than 1 or 1 to 2, would be too fine of a classification and leave some classes with few cases. When determining the number of classes, you need to consider the needs of your audience and the nature of your data.

4. *Present frequencies and percentages:* you should always present a percentage summary of frequencies (Welch and Comer 1988). This is important because percentages standardize the data and make it easier for your readers to make comparisons. In Table 13.1, for example, the percentages make it easier to make comparisons between the two years used in the study.

5. *Margins and population:*. always show the number of cases in the distribution (*N*). Presentation of the number of cases in each class (the row margins), however, is optional. (It is preferable to omit these figures when displaying a percentage frequency distribution and when tabulating much data. The reader can calculate them by multiplying the percent for each cell times the total cases presented in the table).

6. *Summary statistics:* as discussed, it is sometimes helpful to depict summary measures such as the mean and the standard deviation with the frequency distribution. We will discuss summary statistics in a later section of this chapter.

7. *Identification of the source:* you must identify the source of your data. This enables your readers to check the reliability of the data. It is also a requirement of ethical academic pursuits.

◆ CONSTRUCTING A FREQUENCY DISTRIBUTION

The general format for presenting a frequency distribution could resemble the one shown in Table 13.2. The format in Table 13.2 gives us a tool to use when collapsing raw data into a frequency distribution. Before we look at this process, however, let's introduce the following definitions:

1. *Class boundary:* the lowest and highest values that fall within the class.

2. *Class midpoints:* the point halfway between the upper and lower class boundaries. Calculate the midpoint by adding the lower and upper class boundaries and dividing by 2. Thus, if a lower boundary is 11 and the upper boundary is 15, the midpoint would be 13 (11 + 15) / 2).

3. *Class interval:* the distance between the upper limit of one class and the upper limit of the next higher class. Thus, if one class is 1–5 and the next class is 6–10, the class interval would be 5 (10 – 5).

To illustrate, let's use the following problem. You are an aide to the congressional representative from San Angelo, Texas. The representative has received some criticism that he does not respond promptly to constituent complaints. He wants you to classify the response times and show him the results. The only information you have is the day your office received the complaint and the day your office mailed the response. From those figures you must calculate the number of days the office took to respond. Your calculations are listed in Table 13.3.

Take the following steps to construct a frequency table that will meet the representative's needs.

TABLE 13.2

GENERAL FORMAT FOR THE FREQUENCY DISTRIBUTION

Category	Frequency	Proportion (or Percent)
A	$f(A)$	$f(A)/N$
B	$f(B)$	$f(B)/N$
C	$f(C)$	$f(C)/N$
D	$f(D)$	$f(D)/N$
E	$f(E)$	$f(E)/N$
	Total N	Total %

where

A,B,C,D,E = categories of the variable

$f(A)$ through $f(E)$ = number of observations in each category

N = sum of frequencies in all categories.

$f(A)/N$ through $f(E)/N$ = number of observations in each category divided by the total number of observations.

Note: The percent is obtained by multiplying the proportion by 100.

Source: Richard L. Cole. *Introduction to Political Inquiry*. London: Macmillan 1981.

TABLE 13.3

NUMBER OF DAYS NECESSARY TO RESPOND TO CONSTITUENT REQUESTS

9	1	6	10	8	12	9	14	15	7
19	8	21	10	50	37	9	4	28	44
9	18	8	39	7	1	4	15	7	28
47	9	6	7	24	10	41	7	9	29
6	4	12	7	9	15	39	24	9	2
20	31	18	9	33	8	6	3	7	16
20	26	9	9	16	5	3	12	36	11
8	6	28	35	8	10	11	20	3	10
16	8	12	4	6	9	10	10	9	16
4	14	11	8	5	8	11	9	7	6
11	9	7	8	10	9	11			

Source: Hypothetical

Step 1: Scan the data to find the lowest and highest values. In our example, 1, the lowest value, is the first value in the second column; 50, the highest value, is the second value in the fifth column.

Step 2: Make a list of the values from the lowest to the highest and mark the number of times each value appears.

1 //	11 //////	21 /	31 /	41 /
2 /	12 ////	22	32	42
3 ///	13	23	33 /	43
4 /////	14 //	24 //	34	44 /
5 //	15 ///	25	35 /	45
6 //////	16 ////	26 /	36 /	46
7 /////////	17	27	37 /	47 /
8 //////////	18 //	28 ///	38	48
9 ////////////////	19 /	29 /	39 //	49
10 ////////	20 ///	30	40	50 /

Step 3: Compress the frequencies into classes. The rule of thumb is to collapse data into no fewer than 4 or no more than 20 classes. Fewer than 4 classes obscures the variation in the data, while more than 20 presents too complex a picture to grasp quickly. We might, for example, create 5 classes divided by weeks: one week, two weeks, three weeks, four weeks, and more than four weeks.

Some other tips to consider when constructing frequency distributions include:

1. Avoid classes so narrow that some intervals have zero observations.
2. Make all the class intervals equal unless the top or bottom class is open-ended.
3. Use open-ended intervals (for example, more than 50) only when closed intervals would result in class frequencies of zero. This usually happens when some values are extremely high or extremely low.
4. Try to construct the intervals so the midpoints are whole numbers.
5. For this example, let's collapse the data into five classes. The results are presented in Table 13.4.

◆ THE PERCENTAGE DISTRIBUTION

Note that the table also depicts the percent of cases that fall within each class. This depiction makes it easier for someone to determine the impact of each class. For example, more than 17 percent of the complaints received by the representative's office took longer than 20 days to answer.

TABLE 13.4

NUMBER OF DAYS NECESSARY TO RESPOND TO CONGRESSIONAL COMPLAINTS, JANUARY–MARCH 1995

Response Time	Number of Complaints	Percent
1–5 days	17	15.4
6–10 days	49	44.6
11–15 days	15	13.6
16–20 days	10	9.1
More than 20 days	19	17.3
Totals	110	100.0

Source: Hypothetical

◆ CUMULATIVE FREQUENCY DISTRIBUTIONS

Frequency distributions and percentage distributions tell us the number or percentage of items that fall in one or more classes. Sometimes the political scientist may want to know how many items (or what percentage of items) fall below or above a certain standard. For instance, the representative in our example above is also concerned about acceptable standards of response times. The representative considers 5 days to be excellent, 10 days to be acceptable, 15 days to be unsatisfactory, and 20 days to be unacceptable. As a result, the representative wants to know the percentage of complaints answered during each of these parameters.

To provide the representative with the necessary information, you must construct a cumulative percentage distribution as shown in Table 13.5. You can satisfy the representative by taking the following steps:

Step 1: Prepare a running total of responses to constituency complaints.

   a. Make another column to the right of the "Number of" column and label it "Running Total."

   b. In this column calculate the number of responses that are less than the upper limit of each interval.

      1. For example, determine the number of complaints responded to in less than five days. The answer is 17. Enter 17 for the first class in the Running Total column.

      2. How many complaint responses were under 10 days? (17 + 49). Enter 66 for the second class in the Running Total column.

      3. Using this logic, fill in the rest of the values.

Step 2: Construct a cumulative percentage column.

TABLE 13.5

NUMBER OF DAYS NECESSARY TO RESPOND TO CONGRESSIONAL COMPLAINTS, JANUARY–MARCH 1995

Response Time	Number of Complaints	Running Total	Cumulative Percent
1–5 days	17	17	15.4
6–10 days	49	66	60.0
11–15 days	15	81	73.6
16–20 days	10	91	82.7
More than 20 days	19	110	100.0
Totals	110	110	100.0

Source: Hypothetical

    a. Divide each frequency in the Running Total column by the total frequency ($N = 110$)

    b. Label a fourth column "Cumulative Percentage" and enter these numbers.

    c. The first entry should be 15.4 (17/110).

    d. The second entry should be 60.0 (66/110).

    e. Fill in the remaining values.

    f. You now have a cumulative frequency distribution for the representative.

◆ GRAPHIC PRESENTATIONS

An extension of the frequency distribution occurs when you present distributions in graphic form. Graphs are a convenient way to present data. That is, one can understand the data without reading a table. We will limit our discussion to three basic types—the bar graph, the histogram, and the frequency polygon.

The Bar Graph   When dealing with nominal or ordinal data, Cole recommends that you use a **bar graph** to present data. As such, bars are drawn for each class of the variable so the height represents the number of cases for each class (Cole 1980). Figure 13.1 presents the data considered in Table 13.4 in bar graph format. The visual advantage of data presented in a bar graph format is obvious. The reader can immediately see that most complaints were in the 6–10 day response class.

The Histogram   A **histogram** differs from a bar graph in that you do not separate the bars in a histogram. The height of the bars of a histogram are

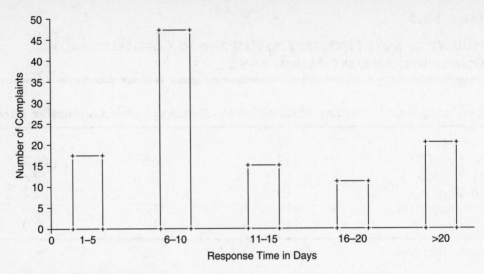

FIGURE 13.1 **Bar Chart**

proportional to the frequencies of each class. Additionally, the widths of the bars are proportional to the size of each interval. Normally one uses a histogram with interval-level data. For purposes of explanation, however, in Figure 13.2 we constructed a histogram of the data presented in Table 13.4 and Figure 13.1.

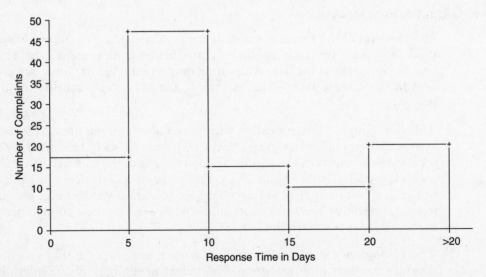

FIGURE 13.2 **Histogram**

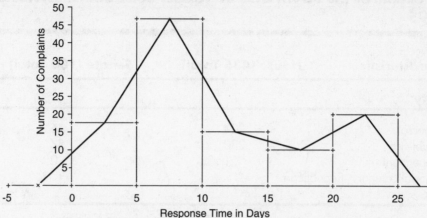

Response Time in Days
Number of Days Necessary to Respond to Congressional Complaints
January–March 1995 (Hypothetical)

NOTE: The frequency polygon line does not need to be extended beyond the range of actual observations, but when extending each end of the frequency polygon to the base line it is best that the graph be extended to intersect the horizontal axis at the midpoints of the vacant intervals on each end of the distribution.

FIGURE 13.3 **Frequency Polygon**

The Frequency Polygon You can also graph interval data by connecting the midpoints of the top of each histogram bar with a solid line. When this is done, you reveal the shape of the distribution. We will talk more about the shape of distributions later in the chapter. The resultant graph, with bars removed, is known as a **frequency polygon.** Figure 13.3 depicts a frequency polygon superimposed on a histogram.

◆ MEASURES OF CENTRAL TENDENCY

While frequency distributions and graphs help to describe and explain variables, political scientists often want to present their findings more conveniently. Reports dealing with several variables would soon become tedious if you relied solely on the depiction of charts and frequency distributions. Therefore, researchers often summarize data with measures of central tendency.

A measure of central tendency is a number that represents the central value of a distribution of data. We commonly refer to these measures as averages. An average you are probably familiar with is your grade point average, or GPA. Your GPA describes and summarizes your academic performance in college classes. Measures of central tendency include the mode, the median, and the mean. In the remainder of this chapter we will discuss these measures and illustrate how to calculate and interpret them.

The Mode The **mode** is a convenient measure to use with nominal data. The mode is the most frequently occurring value in any distribution of data. If

TABLE 13.6

A PORTRAIT OF THE 104TH U.S. CONGRESS: SOME STATISTICS, MARCH 1995

Characteristic	House (435 Total)	Senate (100 Total)
Party		
Democrat	204	46
Republican	230	54
Independent	1	0
Modal category: Republican		
Sex		
Men	386	92
Women	49	8
Modal category: Men		
Race		
Black	39	1
Hispanic	18	0
White and other	378	99
Modal category: White and other		
Average Age	51	58
Religion		
Mainline Protestant	153	47
Evangelical Protestant	72	10
Unspecified Protestant	38	3
Mormon	10	3
Roman Catholic	125	20
Jewish	24	9
Unspecified/Other	13	8
Modal category: Mainline Protestant		
Prior Occupation		
Law	170	54
Business and banking	163	24
Education	76	10
Public service/politics	102	12
Agriculture	19	9
Journalism	15	8
Modal category: Law		

Note: The original table did not depict the mode. Some members specifiy more than one occupation.

Source: *Congressional Quarterly Weekly Report*, November 12, 1994, pp. 9–12.

TABLE 13.7

HYPOTHETICAL DISTRIBUTION OF SCORES TO IDEOLOGY SCALE OF ANGELO STATE STUDENTS, 1995

Student	Score	Student	Score	Student	Score
1	7	10	5	19	3
2	7	11	5	20	3
3	7	12	5	21	2
4	6	13	4	22	2
5	6	14	4	23	2
6	6	15	4	24	1
7	6	16	4	25	1
8	5	17	4		
9	5	18	4		
$N = 25$					

Source: Hypothetical

a distribution has only one mode, we say the distribution is unimodal. If there are two values that appear most frequently, the distribution is bimodal.

As an illustration, Table 13.6 is a portrait of the 104th U.S. Congress.

Table 13.6 shows the modal categories for party identification, gender, race, religion, and prior occupation. It also depicts the average age of members in each chamber of Congress. Close scrutiny shows that the prior occupations of law (170) and business and banking (163) were the most common prior occupations of members of the 104th Congress. While not equal, this latter distribution approximates a bimodal distribution.

The Median   The **median** is the middle item of a set of numbers after ranking the items according to their size. The median is a measure of central tendency used with ordinal data. For a ranked distribution the median is the score of the middle case if there are an odd number of cases. If there are an even number of cases, the median is the value halfway between the two middle cases. Thus, you divide the two middle cases by 2.

As an example, assume that a political science student used a scale to determine the ideological views of 25 respondents. The distribution of scores ranging from 1 (liberal) to 7 (conservative) might appear as shown in Table 13.7. Determining the median in the above example is a simple process if you take the following steps:

1. Rank the numbers.
2. Determine the number of items in the set. 25
3. Add 1 to the number of items. 25 + 1 = 26
4. Divide the result by 2 to determine the middle item. 26/2 = 13
5. The median is 4, or the response of the 13th respondent.

This value is no greater than half the distribution (those 12 students whose scores range from 5 to 7). Additionally, it is no smaller than half the distribution (those 12 students whose scores range from 4 to 1).

If student 25 was not in this sample, there would be no middle case. For a data set having an *even* number of items the same steps are taken.

1. Rank the numbers.
2. Determine the number of items in the set. 24
3. Add 1 to the number of items. 24 + 1 = 25
4. Divide the result by 2. 25/2 = 12.5

Thus, the 12 1/2 item is the median. To determine the value you calculate the average of the values of the 12th and the 13th items 5 + 4 / 2 = 4.5). This value represents the median.

Before we leave our discussion about the median, we need to discuss several of its characteristics. First, extreme values do not affect the median. When we discuss the arithmetic mean, we will see how extreme values can detract from the interpretive value of the statistic. Second, although we use every item to determine the median, we do not use their actual values in the calculations. At most, we only use the values of the two middle items to calculate the median. Third, if items do not cluster near the median, the median may not be a good measure of the group's central tendency. Last, medians usually do not take on values that are not realistic. The median number of children per American families, for example, is 2.

The Mean   The **mean,** used with interval level data, is the average of a set of numbers. With ungrouped data we calculate the mean by summing the observations in a data set divided by the number of cases.

To illustrate how we use the mean in political science, let's analyze the following problem. For the current budget year, a school district board has limited the grade school to serve school lunches to a monthly average of 34 children. For the first nine months of 1994 the serving figures were 32, 36, 35, 35, 37, 33, 36, 37, and 34.

1. Is the school meeting its monthly average target?
   a. Calculate the mean: 32 + 36 + 35 + 35 + 37 + 33 + 36 + 37 + 34 / 9 months = 315/9 = 35
   b. Since the mean of 35 exceeds the school board goal of 34 children, it does not appear that the school can meet the board's target.
2. How many children must the school average over the next three months to meet the target?
   a. Determine the number of children the school would have to feed for the year if they adhered to the board's edict. 34 × 12 = 408
   b. Determine the number of children the school is feeding to date. 35 × 9 = 315

TABLE 13.8

HYPOTHETICAL NUMBER OF VIOLENT CRIMES PER PRECINCT IN DALLAS, TEXAS, 1994

Number of Crimes	Number of Precincts	Class Midpoints
0–50	5	25
50–100	10	75
100–150	15	125
150–200	4	175
200–250	3	225
Totals	37	

Source: Hypothetical

c. Determine the number of children the school can feed over the last three months of the year without exceeding the goal. 408 – 315 = 93

d. Determine the number of children the school can feed for each month for the remainder of the year. 93/3 = 31.

The mean has several important characteristics. First, we use every item in a group to calculate the mean. Second, unlike the mode, every group of data has one and only one mean. Third, the mean may take on a value that is not realistic. For example, the average American family has exactly 1.7 children. Fourth, an extreme value may have a disproportionate influence on the mean and thus may affect how well the mean represents the data.

◆ MEASURES OF CENTRAL TENDENCY AND GROUPED DATA

So far, we calculated the measures of central tendency for ungrouped data. You can also calculate these statistics for grouped data. Grouped data are classes of observations. For example, 1 to 5 years of age and 6 to 10 years of age, are age data groups. Because grouped data collapse frequencies, information is lost. Thus, statistics calculated for grouped data are less accurate than statistics calculated for ungrouped data. As a result, never calculate statistics for grouped data if the ungrouped data are available.

The mode for data grouped into a frequency distribution is the midpoint of the class having the most frequencies. The mode for the distribution in Table 13.4 is 8 days, which is the midpoint of the 6–10 class. You also can calculate medians for grouped data. The logic is similar to that used with ungrouped data. For grouped data, the median is the middle value.

Using the hypothetical data presented in Table 13.8, let's calculate the median by using steps similar to those we used above.

1. Determine the median precinct in order of size. 37 + 1 / 2 = 19.

TABLE 13.9

NUMBER OF CLAIMS PROCESSED BY STATE WELFARE AGENCIES, JANUARY–MARCH 1995

Number of Claims	Number of Agencies	Midpoint	Midpoint Times Number of Agencies
1–25	2	13	26
26–50	19	38	722
51–75	17	63	1071
76–100	8	88	704
101–125	4	113	452
Totals			2975

$N = 50$
Mean = 2975/50 = 595 claims

Source: Hypothetical

2. Determine the class for the 19th Precinct (the middle item). There are 15 precincts with less than 100 crimes and 15 with 100–150 crimes. This means that the 19th item is in the third class. In fact, it is the 4th item in the third class.

3. Calculate how far the median item goes into the class. (When working with grouped data, statisticians assume equal distribution of the items throughout the class interval.) Since there are 15 items in the third class the median is 4/15ths of the distance into the class.

4. Calculate how far 4/15ths is into the third class. To do this simply multiply this fraction by the class interval of 50. Add the resulting number to the lower limit of the class (4/15 × 50 = 13.33). In this case the lower limit is 100, for a median of 113.33.

In sum, the median is 100 + 4/15ths of the interval of the third class. Thus, the median number of violent crimes in Dallas, Texas for 1994 was 113.33.

As with the other measures of central tendency, we can calculate the mean from grouped data. When calculating a mean for grouped data, multiply the midpoint of each interval by the frequency of the interval. Next, sum these numbers and divide the result by the total frequency.

As an illustration, let's examine the distribution in Table 13.9. It shows the number of claims processed by state welfare agencies during the first quarter of 1995. The midpoint of each interval is as shown. The product of each frequency and midpoint is also as shown. The mean of the distribution equals 2975/50 (states), or 595 claims per state welfare agency during the quarter.

◆ COMPARISON OF THE MODE, MEDIAN, AND MEAN

The three measures of central tendency that we just discussed represent univariate distributions. Each, however, has its own characteristics that prescribe and limit its use. The mode is the most common value in any distribution of data. The median is nothing more than the middle item of a set of numbers when one ranks the items in order of size. Last, the mean is the average of a set of numbers.

How does one know, however, when to use the mode, the median, or the mean? Alas, there is not an easy answer to this question. Most statisticians agree, however, that the application of any measure of central tendency depends on the measurement level of the analyzed variable (Cole 1980). The mode can represent nominal variables such as the distribution of ideology or party affiliation. We apply the median, on the other hand, with ordinal variables such as classes of attitudes and income ranges. The political researcher uses the mean with interval variables such as income and age.

Last, it is permissible to use the measures appropriate for lower levels of measurement with higher level data. However, it is not appropriate to use higher level measures with lower level data. For example, the mode can represent income, but the mean cannot represent the distribution of ideology.

Let's illustrate the appropriateness for using measures of central tendency. To do this, let's consider the Government grades made by Jerry Perry during one agonizing semester. (The grades have been arrayed in descending order.)

75

75

61

50 Total of all grades = 342.

40 Number of grades = 9.

25

10

5

1

We used the interval level of measurement for these grades. Thus, according to our discussion, the appropriate measure of central tendency is the arithmetic mean. When we calculate the mean our answer is 38 (342/9). Additionally, the median score, the value that occupies the middle position in an array of values, is also very low (40). Thus, neither Jerry nor his professor is very happy.

Additionally, Jerry knows his father will be unhappy about his course grades. Jerry does not want to tell his father about the low mean and median values. So he decides that if his father asks about his Government average, he will give his father the modal value, the most commonly occurring value in an array of data. In this example the mode is 75, which appeals to Jerry. Therefore, his father will be happy and Jerry will not incur his father's wrath. In sum, this example illustrates how the different measures of central tendency can be misleading if used in the wrong context.

◆ MEASURES OF DISPERSION

Measures of central tendency are helpful in identifying important characteristics among distributions of data. They accurately reflect the actual values of distributed data when the data closely group about the measures. Conversely, measures of central tendency are less likely to reflect the actual values of all members of a distribution when the data have extreme values. For example, the mean for Jerry Perry's Government grades was 38. However, the high score was 75 and the low score was 1. Thus, there is much dispersion between the mean and the two extreme scores. Therefore, we need some measure of the deviation from the average value to tell us how well the measure of central tendency summarizes the data.

Political scientists use measures of dispersion to gain a clearer understanding of a distribution of data. In short, measures of dispersion are ways to communicate other differences in a set of data. They tell how much the data cluster about the various measures of central tendency. We will discuss several measures of dispersion for the various levels of data in the following sections.

The Variation Ratio (v)   The variation ratio is useful when analyzing nominal data. It is simple to calculate and easy to understand. Specifically, the variation ratio tells the political scientist the degree to which the mode satisfactorily represents a particular frequency distribution. The formula for v is:

$$v = 1 - \frac{\text{Number of cases in the modal category}}{\text{Number of cases}}$$

By analyzing the formula, one can see that if all cases in a distribution fell into the modal class, the value of v would be 0. Thus, the lower the v score, the more representative is the mode of all cases in the distribution.

As an illustration, let's examine the distribution of ideology and party identification as shown in Table 13.10. The variation ratio for Republicans suggests that the mode is a better representation of ideology for Republicans than for the other groups. The variation ratio also shows that the mode is a less satisfactory summary of ideology for those respondents that considered themselves to be Independent. Put another way, the Independent respondents varied more in their ideological orientations. Thus, one should be cautious in reporting the mode as representative of the ideological orientation of all Independents in this example.

The Range   The range is a useful measure when the researcher is working with ordered or ranked data. Thus, it is useful with ordinal data and when

TABLE 13.10

DISTRIBUTION OF IDEOLOGY AND PARTY IDENTIFICATION, 1995

	Party Identification		
Ideology	Democrat	Independent	Republican
Liberal	240	160	80
Moderate	220	260	180
Conservative	180	280	540
Not considered	360	300	200
Totals	1,000	1,000	1,000
$v =$	$1 - 360/1000$	$1 - 300/1000$	$1 - 540/1000$
$v =$	0.640	0.700	0.460

Source: Hypothetical

considering the accuracy of the median. The **range** is the difference between the largest value and the smallest value in a distribution. The smaller the range, the more accurate or representative is the median score of all values in the distribution.

In our example of the median, we presented a hypothetical distribution of scores of 25 Angelo State University students on a scale of ideological orientation in Table 13.7. The median in our example is 4 and the range is 6 $(7 - 1)$.

The responses to another sample of 25 students using the same seven-point scale appear in Table 13.11. In this example the median is still 4, but the range is 4. As such, the measures show that there is greater homogeneity in the responses of the second group of students.

The range is easy to calculate and has utility as a measure of dispersion. However, extreme values in a distribution can influence the range. In those instances when one or a few cases have the highest or lowest possible values, the range may give a misleading impression of variation. Therefore, researchers use a variety of measures of the range to drop extreme cases from consideration. Some researchers, however, contend that these statistics have little statistical value (Meier and Brudney 1981). Therefore, for a discussion of these statistics you should consult any elementary statistics book.

The Mean Deviation   The mean deviation is useful when the data are interval. Simply put, the **mean deviation** is the average difference between the mean and all other values in the distribution. The mean deviation makes use of every observation in the distribution. One computes this measure by taking

TABLE 13.11

HYPOTHETICAL DISTRIBUTION OF SCORES TO IDEOLOGY SCALE ANGELO STATE STUDENTS, 1995

Student	Score	Student	Score	Student	Score
1	6	10	5	19	3
2	6	11	5	20	3
3	6	12	5	21	2
4	6	13	4	22	2
5	6	14	4	23	2
6	6	15	4	24	2
7	6	16	4	25	2
8	5	17	4		
9	5	18	4		

$N = 25$
Median = 4
Range $(6 - 2) = 4$

Source: Hypothetical

the difference between each observation and the mean. Summing these deviations is the next step. (Note: when summing, ignore negative signs. Otherwise, the sum would always be zero. Try it if you do not believe us.) Finally, divide the sum by the number of observations. Arithmetically, the mean deviation is expressed as

$$\text{Mean deviation} = \frac{|X_i - \bar{X}|}{N}$$

where

X_i = each observation

$\bar{X}$ = mean of all observations

N = number of observations

$|\ |$ = absolute difference (ignoring signs)

Table 13.12 illustrates the calculation of the mean deviation for the 1992 presidential voting turnout (hypothetical) for the southeastern states. The results show that, on the average, the registered voter turnout in each southeastern state in 1992 deviated from the mean turnout for all southeastern states by 3.09 percent.

The Variance   The mean deviation is a helpful measure of dispersion because of its ease in calculation and interpretation. Absolute values, however, are not amenable to mathematical manipulations. Thus, many do not use the mean deviation with other mathematical calculations. Therefore, there are other tests that are more useful as measures of dispersion of interval data.

TABLE 13.12

PERCENT OF REGISTERED VOTERS IN SOUTHEASTERN STATES VOTING IN THE 1992 PRESIDENTIAL ELECTION

State	Percent Voting, X	$\overline{X}$	$|X_i - \overline{X}|$
Louisiana	51.3	46.2	5.1
Mississippi	49.9	46.2	3.7
Kentucky	48.2	46.2	2.0
Alabama	45.8	46.2	.4
Florida	44.7	46.2	1.5
Tennessee	44.7	46.2	1.5
Georgia	38.8	46.2	7.4
Totals			21.6
Mean deviation = 21.6/7 = 3.09			

Source: Hypothetical

One such tool is the variance. Similar to the mean deviation, the **variance** uses the mean variation in its calculation. However, when you calculate the variance, you square the absolute differences between each observation and the mean. Next, you sum the squares and divide the result by the number of cases. Thus, the formula for the calculation of the variance looks very much like the formula for the calculation of the mean deviation:

$$\text{Variance } (s^2) = \frac{\Sigma (X_i - \overline{X})^2}{N}$$

where

X_i = each observation

$\overline{X}$ = mean of all observations

N = total number of observations

Table 13.13 is similar to Table 13.12 in that it depicts the voting turnout in the southeastern states (hypothetical) during the 1992 presidential election. It differs, however, in that it illustrates the calculation of the variance for the same data set. For this example, the variance is 14.73. The lower the variance, the more accurately does the mean represent all the scores of all cases in a distribution of interval level data.

The Standard Deviation   The standard deviation is probably the most common measure of dispersion for interval data. The basis for **standard deviations** is the squared differences between every item in a data set and the mean of that set. The smaller the standard deviation in a set of data, the more closely the data cluster about the mean. The standard deviation is a stable measure of dispersion from sample to sample. Political scientists use standard deviations with the normal curve to determine where scores or observations

TABLE 13.13

PERCENT OF REGISTERED VOTERS IN SOUTHEASTERN STATES VOTING IN THE 1992 PRESIDENTIAL ELECTION

State	Percent Voting, X	$\overline{X}$	$(X_i - \overline{X})$	$(X_i - \overline{X})^2$
Louisiana	51.3	46.2	5.1	26.01
Mississippi	49.9	46.2	3.7	13.69
Kentucky	48.2	46.2	2.0	4.00
Alabama	45.8	46.2	.4	.16
Florida	44.7	46.2	1.5	2.25
Tennessee	44.7	46.2	1.5	2.25
Georgia	38.8	46.2	7.4	54.76
Totals			21.6	103.12

Variance = 103.12/7 = 14.73

Source: Hypothetical

cluster about the mean and to determine standard scores. In sum, it is a useful summary statistic and is the square root of the variance.

$$\text{Standard deviation } (s) = \sqrt{\frac{\Sigma (X_i - \overline{X})^2}{N}}$$

where

X_i = each observation
$\overline{X}$ = mean of all observations
N = number of observations

To see the usefulness of the standard deviation, let's use our example of the percent of registered voter turnout in southeastern states in the 1988 presidential election. The standard deviation calculated for this example is 3.84. The lower the standard deviation, the more homogeneous is the group. Additionally, the mean is more representative of all values in the data set.

Unlike the mean deviation, the standard deviation is not easy to interpret. Its usefulness becomes clearer when it is used with other statistics and the normal curve. Before discussing the normal curve, however, let's consider how the standard deviation is used with the mean to interpret data. Table 13.14 depicts the means and standard deviations computed on an index of satisfaction with the electoral system in five states.

The table shows that the means for each state are similar. This suggests that satisfaction with the electoral system is similar in the states studied. However, there are differences in the standard deviations. The low scores in

TABLE 13.14

MEAN AND STANDARD DEVIATION ON AN INDEX OF ELECTORAL SATISFACTION IN FIVE STATES

	Statistic	
State	Mean	Standard Deviation
Texas	6.7	1.0
Colorado	6.7	1.2
Florida	6.6	3.2
New York	6.5	1.3
California	6.6	1.1

Source: Hypothetical

Texas, Colorado, New York, and California suggest that these states are homogeneous. That is, people have a satisfaction score close to their group's mean score. In Florida, however, the dispersion is greater. This suggests the degree of satisfaction reflected by the mean is not common to all the Floridians in the study. Thus, when we use the standard deviation with the mean, we begin to appreciate the statistic's application.

The Coefficient of Variation (V)   A last measure of dispersion that has usefulness when analyzing interval level data, is the **coefficient of variation** (*V*). Political scientists use *V* when they want to compare the dispersion of two or more groups about their respective means. Of course, if the mean score for each group were exactly the same, the standard deviation would serve the purpose. If the means are different, however, a comparison of standard deviation scores alone could be misleading. For example, a standard deviation of 2.5 for groups with means of 4.0 and 20.0 would have different interpretations. For the first example, the standard deviation of 2.5 shows a large amount of dispersion, or spread, about the mean. In the second example, however, the standard deviation of 2.5 shows more homogeneity within the group because their scores cluster more about the mean. The coefficient of variation is used to compare differences such as this and is symbolized by:

$$V = s/\overline{X}$$

where

V = coefficient of variation

s = standard deviation

$\overline{X}$ = mean

TABLE 13.15

MEAN, STANDARD DEVIATION, AND COEFFICIENT OF VARIATION ON AN INDEX OF ELECTORAL SATISFACTION IN FIVE STATES

		Statistic	
State	Mean	Standard Deviation	Coefficient of Variation
Texas	6.7	1.0	0.149
Colorado	6.7	1.2	0.179
Florida	6.6	3.2	0.485
New York	6.5	1.3	0.200
California	6.6	1.1	0.167

Source: Hypothetical

The coefficient of variation for the first group discussed above (mean of 4.0, standard deviation of 2.5), is 0.625. For the second group (mean of 20.0, standard deviation of 2.5), the V score is 0.125. Once again, the lower the coefficient of variation, the greater is the homogeneity of the group.

As another example, let's calculate and interpret the V scores for the data presented in Table 13.14. Table 13.15 shows the results. Remember, lower V scores suggest more homogeneity within groups. Thus, the scores for electoral satisfaction suggest there is much agreement within four of the five states in the study. In Florida, however, the V score suggests there is some divisiveness between the survey respondents.

❖ SHAPE OF THE DISTRIBUTION

Up to this point we have discussed measures of central tendency and measures of dispersion as ways to consider data distributions. Political scientists also analyze distributions when they consider the shape of the distribution. Recall that we said that researchers determine the shape of a distribution when they construct a frequency polygon. To do this, one must connect the midpoints of the top of each bar of a histogram with a solid line (see Figure 13.3). The shape is a function of the original frequency distribution. Those distributions having most of their case scores above the mean will have a different shape from those having a large proportion of scores below the mean.

◆ SKEWED DISTRIBUTIONS

Three possible shapes can result when drawing frequency polygons of data distributions. Figure 13.4 shows these shapes. The first two shapes represent **skewed distributions.** This means that in both cases there are more scores in

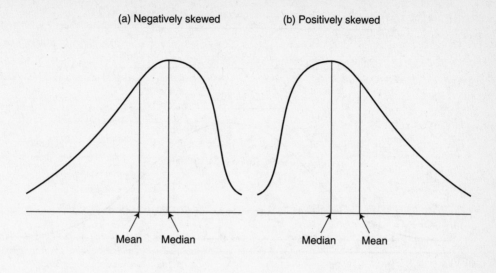

(a) Negatively skewed   (b) Positively skewed

Mean Median   Median Mean

(c) Symmetrical

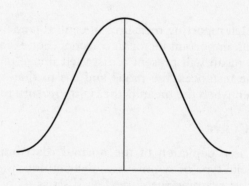

Mean and Median

FIGURE 13.4   **Some Possible Shapes of Frequency Distributions**

one direction or the other. In the first instance, there are more low scores. This is a negatively skewed distribution. Additionally, the lower scores pull the mean in their direction. The second shape shows the impact of the many high scores in the distribution. In this example, they pull the mean in their direction. This shape shows a positively skewed distribution.

◆ SYMMETRICAL DISTRIBUTIONS

The third shape is a symmetrical distribution in that an equal number of cases fall to each side of the curve. Additionally, the various measures of central tendency coincide.

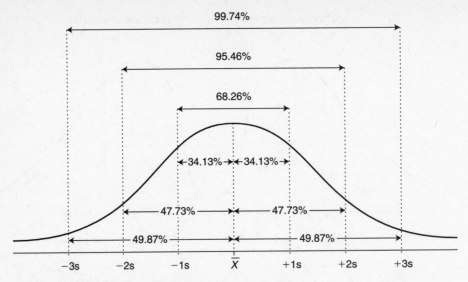

FIGURE 13.5 **Areas Under the Normal Curve**

Thus, when reporting measures of central tendency, the shape of the distribution is an important factor to consider. For example, with skewed distributions, the mean will present a distorted image of the distribution. Therefore, in these instances, the mode and the median may be a more accurate measure, even when the mean is the right measure to use.

◆ THE NORMAL CURVE

Figure 13.5 is a depiction of the **normal distribution curve.** The normal curve, a special type of symmetrical distribution, is very important in statistics. Before we examine the curve let's discuss its principal properties. First, the curve is symmetrical and bell-shaped. Second, the measures of central tendency coincide at the center of the distribution. The last property of the normal curve that we will discuss, however, is probably its most distinctive characteristic. In any normal distribution, a fixed proportion of the observations lies between the mean and fixed units of standard deviations. To help you understand why this property is so important, let's examine figure 13.5.

The proportions can be seen in Figure 13.5. The mean of the distribution divides the curve exactly in half. Note that 34.13 percent of all cases fall within an area one standard deviation (+1s) greater than the mean. Additionally, 34.13 percent of all cases fall within one standard deviation less than the mean (−1s). Thus, slightly more than 68 percent of all cases in a normal distribution lie within one standard deviation (plus or minus) of the mean. Similarly, more than 95 percent of all cases lie within a plus or minus two standard deviations of the mean. Last, most cases (99.73 percent) will fall within a plus or minus three standard deviations of the mean.

Thus, the standard deviation used with the normal curve can be a very important tool in the political scientist's repertoire. It is important because the researcher can determine the proportion of observations included within fixed distances of the mean.

For example, assume that the public's rating of a particular welfare program rated on a scale of 0 to 100 has a normal distribution. Additionally, the distribution has a mean of 50 and a standard deviation of 10. Based on this information we can conclude that more than 68 percent of the public assigns the program a rating between 40 and 60 (±1 standard deviations from the mean). Additionally, more than 95 percent assigned the program a rating between 30 and 70 (±2 standard deviations from the mean). Last, most everyone in the survey assigned the program a rating between 20 and 80 (±3 standard deviations from the mean).

◆ STANDARD SCORES (THE Z SCORE)

When rating the proportion of observations within a desired interval, the political scientist should express observations in units of standard deviation. For example, to determine the proportion of cases rating the welfare program from 50 to 75, you have to determine how many standard deviations the rating of 75 lies from the mean. Political scientists calculate the Z score to accomplish this task. The formula for Z is:

$$Z = \frac{X - \overline{X}}{s}$$

where

Z = the standard score

X = any proportionate distance, or score, of any observation we want to estimate

$\overline{X}$ = the mean

s = the standard deviation

The Z score tells us the number of standard deviations that the score lies above or below the mean. If we apply the formula to the example discussed above, the Z score is:

$$Z = \frac{75 - 50}{10} = 2.50$$

In our example, we find that the score of 75 is 2.5 standard deviation units above the mean. Intuitively, this should make sense. Recall that we showed that a score of 70 lied 2 standard deviation units above the mean, and a score of 80 lied 3 standard deviation units above the mean. Thus, a score of 75 had to fall between 2 and 3 standard deviation units.

To carry our analysis further, recall that 47.43 percent of the cases lie between the mean and 2 standard deviations above the mean. We also said that 49.87 percent of the cases lie between the mean and 3 standard deviations above the mean. Thus, if a 75 rating is 2.5 standard deviation units above the mean, somewhere between 47.43 and 49.87 percent of the public assigned the program a score between 50 and 75.

Table A2 in Appendix III enables you to interpret the Z value. Take the following steps to use this table:

1. Scan the far left column to find the first two digits of the Z value. In our case, 2.5.
2. Under the numerical column headings find the third digit of the Z value. In our case, 0.
3. Extend both the column and the row until they intersect. The value that you find at the point of intersection is the proportion of cases that lie between the mean and 2.5 standard deviations above the mean. In our case 4938, which lies between 47.43 percent and 49.87 percent.

Thus, for a Z score of 2.5 we find the value to be 4938. This means that 49.38 percent of the public assigned the welfare program a rating between 50 and 75.

To conclude our discussion about the normal curve and Z scores, let's look at a final illustration. Suppose you want to determine the proportion of the public assigning the program a rating of from 0 to 75? Before you begin to plug figures into the above formula, there is a quicker way to determine the proportion. Simply add 0.50 to the Z value calculated above (4938). We do this because the normal curve assumes that 50 percent of the population will lie on either side of the mean. Thus, we conclude that 99.38 percent of the public would rate the program from 0 to 75.

❖ SUMMARY

In this chapter we examined some important tools to use in the preliminary stage of data analysis. For example, sophisticated computer programs summarize data as frequency distributions. These distributions depict number of cases (N) and number of cases by class, percentages, and proportions. These techniques help the political scientist assess the weight of a single class in relation to other classes of a distribution or distributions.

Additionally, political scientists use measures of central tendency to describe the distribution's main characteristics. These measures help the researcher answer questions such as, "What is the typical party identification of respondents?" or "What is the average level of income of the group?"

Measures of central tendency, however, can be misleading if not accompanied by measures that describe the amount of dispersion in the distribution. While measures of central tendency reflect a group's typical characteristic, measures of dispersion depict the extent of variance from the typical value, or average. The dispersion measures show how many members of the group deviate from the typical and the extent of their deviation. A small deviation shows that most responses cluster around the measure of central tendency, and thus, a homogeneous group. Large deviations, on the other hand, suggest that the measure of central tendency is a poor representation of the distribution.

Another important step in examining a distribution is the identification of its general form. For example, the shape of frequency polygons may show that extreme scores in the distribution may affect the measure of central tendency. Or, the form may be symmetrical, or even normal because there are no extreme scores affecting the shape of the distribution. If this is the case, there is a fixed proportion of observations lying between the mean and fixed units of standard deviations.

The measures discussed throughout this chapter help the political scientist understand data distributions. These descriptive statistics, however, are only a first step in data analysis. Once summarized, researchers often want to discover relationships between variables. We turn to this issue in the next chapter.

❖ KEY TERMS

bar graph	mean deviation
coefficient of variation	median
descriptive statistics	mode
frequency polygram	normal distribution curve
histogram	range
inductive statistics	skewed distribution
inferential statistics	standard deviation
mean	variance

TABLE 13.16

Category	Number
Complete activists	110
Campaigners	150
Communalists	200
Voting specialists	210
Contacters	40
Inactives	220
Unclassifiable	70

TABLE 13.17

Rating		Responses
(Very poor job)	0	100
	1	44
(Poor job)	2	406
	3	364
(Fair job)	4	1,525
	5	370
(Good job)	6	670
	7	75
(Very good job)	8	51

Source: Hypothetical

❖ EXERCISES

1. In a survey respondents showed their extent of political participation according to categories Sidney Verba and Norman Nie developed in "Participation in America." The Table 13.16 depicts the results.

   a. Prepare a frequency distribution that shows the number of cases in the distribution and the proportion and percent of cases falling in each class.

   b. What is the most appropriate measure of central tendency to use with this distribution? Why? What is the value of the measure?

   c. What is the most appropriate measure of dispersion to use with this distribution? Why? What is the value of the measure?

   d. Discuss this distribution by referring to the measures of central tendency and dispersion you calculated above. How do these measures help in understanding the distribution?

2. A survey concerned about the Texas State Legislature's performance showed the results found in Table 13.17.

   a. Prepare a frequency distribution that shows the number of cases in the distribution and the proportion and percent of cases falling into each class.

   b. Calculate the proper measures of central tendency and dispersion. Why do you consider them appropriate?

   c. Discuss the distribution by referencing the measures you calculated. How do these measures help you to understand this distribution?

3. Suppose you collect a set of scores of attitudes about capital punishment from a group of respondents. The standard deviation for the set is zero. What does this say about the group?

TABLE 13.18

Group	Mean	Standard Deviation
Male	50	9
Female	70	4
Democrat	65	6
Republican	15	3

Source: Hypothetical

TABLE 13.19

Nation	Percent
Norway	95.8
United States	40.1
Britain	89.2
Netherlands	80.3
Sweden	90.2
Switzerland	67.4
Japan	73.4
France	80.0
New Zealand	79.8
Germany	77.9
Australia	73.8
Canada	76.1

Source: Hypothetical

4. Table 13.18 presents statistics based on a survey that asked respondents to show their feelings about legal abortion. The higher the score, the more inclined the respondent was to be supportive of legal abortion. (Note: the statistics are from normal distributions.)

   a. What do the mean scores and standard deviations say about the comparative evaluation of legal abortion by males and females? By Democrats and Republicans?

   b. For the Democrat sample, what proportion of cases has a score between the mean and 80? What proportion has a score less than 25?

   c. For the female sample, what proportion of cases has a score ranging from 55 to 85?

   d. For each sample, what is the range of scores for 68.26 percent of the sample? For 95.46 percent? For 99.74 percent?

5. The data in Table 13.19 pertains to government spending as a percent of total health spending in selected democracies.

   a. Construct a bar graph for this distribution.

b. Construct a frequency polygon for the distribution.

c. What are the proper measures of central tendency and dispersion to use for this distribution? Why? What are the values of these measures?

d. What do the graphs you prepared and the statistics you calculated reveal about the distribution? Discuss.

❖ SUGGESTED READINGS

Bernstein, Robert A., and James A. Dyer. *An Introduction to Political Science Methods,* 2nd ed. Englewood Cliffs, NJ: Prentice-Hall, 1984.

Blaylock, Hubert M., Jr. *Social Statistics,* 2nd ed. New York: McGraw-Hill, 1979.

Bowen, Bruce D., and Herbert F. Weisberg. *An Introduction to Survey Research and Data Analysis.* San Francisco: Freeman, 1977.

Dometrius, Nelson C. *Social Statistics Using SPSS.* New York: HarperCollins, 1992.

Fox, William. *Social Statistics Using MicroCase.* Chicago: Nelson-Hall, 1993.

Frankfort-Nachmias, Chava, and David Nachmias. *Research Methods in the Social Sciences,* 4th ed. New York: St. Martin's Press, 1992.

Freedman, David, Robert Pisani, and Roger Purves. *Statistics.* New York: Norton, 1978.

Johnson, Janet Buttolph, and Richard A. Joslyn. *Political Science Research Methods.* Washington: Congressional Quarterly Press, 1986.

Kay, Susan Ann. *Introduction to the Analysis of Political Data.* Englewood Cliffs, NJ: Prentice-Hall, 1991.

Leedy, Paul D. *Practical Research: Planning and Design,* 3rd ed. New York: Macmillan, 1985.

DATA ANALYSIS: BIVARIATE STATISTICS

❖ INTRODUCTION

In the previous chapter we discussed measures useful for summarizing and describing a single variable. You should be interested in information such as the proportion of Supreme Court justices that support state legislative efforts to dilute the impact of *Roe v. Wade,* the number of minorities and women in the U.S. Congress, and the number of voters who supported Ross Perot in the 1992 general election. This type of information enhances the systematic research process.

As you progress in your scholarly efforts, however, you will become more interested in analyzing relationships among variables. You will want to determine those factors associated with judicial voting behavior, change in the number of minorities and women in Congress, and support for a third-party presidential candidate. In other words, you want to know the degree to which knowledge of one variable helps you understand another variable.

In this chapter, we will examine some useful ways to analyze the relationships among two variables. We will examine ways to analyze variables measured at the nominal, ordinal, and interval levels of measurement. Because we only analyze two variables at one time, we call this **bivariate analysis.**

An understanding of this chapter will enable you to:

1. Understand the nature of association.
2. Construct tables that depict the association between two variables.
3. Understand the tests of association for nominal, ordinal, and interval data.
4. Select the most appropriate statistic for explaining an association.
5. Take the appropriate steps to determine statistical significance and to test hypotheses.

❖ THE RUDIMENTS OF ASSOCIATION

When we say that two variables are associated, we mean that knowledge of one variable (the independent variable) helps us understand, or predict, another variable (the dependent variable). The greater our ability to predict a dependent variable by knowing something about an independent variable, the stronger the relationship, or **association,** between the variables.

Some independent variables have greater explanatory power than others when predicting a dependent variable. How do we know which variables contribute more to the explanation of a dependent variable? Fortunately for us, mathematicians have developed several statistics we can use to determine the extent of a relationship between two variables, called a **bivariate relationship.**

These statistics answer five basic questions. First, they show that there is a relationship between the independent and dependent variables. Second, they indicate the direction of the relationship. Third, they reveal the strength of the relationship. Fourth, they let us know whether the relationship is statistically significant. Fifth, as we will discuss in Chapter 15, they help us determine whether the relationship is causal.

◆ RANGE OF SCORES

The range of scores for tests of association for straight-line (linear) relationships depends upon the level of measurement. For nominal-level data the relationship values range from a score of 0.0 to 1.0. In the case of ordinal and interval level data the scores range from –1.0 to 1.0. In all instances the closer to 1.0 (in either a positive or a negative direction) the stronger the relationship. A score of 1.0 would indicate what is called a **perfect positive relationship;** knowledge of the values of the independent variable enables you to predict, without error, values of the dependent variable. A score of –1.0 indicates a **perfect negative relationship.** Again, knowledge of the values of the independent variable enables you to predict, without error, values of the dependent variable. Last, the closer the value is to zero, the weaker the relationship.

You will see in Chapter 15 that even strong relationships between two variables can be misleading. On occassion what seems to be a strong relationship between two variables is the result of the influence of one or more additional variables. You must control for these influences before concluding there is a causal relationship between the two variables. Our concern for the time being, however, is to establish the initial relationship between the independent and dependent variables.

◆ CONTINGENCY TABLE OR CROSSTABULATION

Political scientists often use contingency tables, or **bivariate tables,** to analyze the relationship between variables that are measured at the nominal or ordinal level of measurement. In practice the independent variable is symbolized as X and the dependent variable is symbolized as Y. When constructing the table you should display the dependent variable (Y) horizontally or in rows. The independent variable (X) should be displayed vertically or in columns across the top of the table. You should present the data so that the categories of the independent variable sum to 100 percent. Thus, a fundamental rule is to compute percentages within categories of the independent variable. This will enhance your ability to interpret the possible relationship. You will be able to see how each category of the independent variable impacts the dependent variable. We want to make one additional point before we examine a model of a contingency table. Statisticians refer to the totals of each column as column marginals. The sums of each row are called row marginals.

Table 14.1 is a model of a bivariate, or contigency, table that depicts the relationship between two variables. Notice that both variables have only two values, low and high. The table is called a 2-by-2 table because it has two rows and two columns. Tables can be larger, for example 3-by-4 and 2-by-3. In addition, the first number represents the number of rows (r) while the second number represent the number of columns (c). Thus, some refer to contingency tables as r-by-c tables (Fox 1993, 114).

If you have really been keeping up with us, you know that each row is a category value of the dependent variable and each column is a category value of the independent variable. Table 14.1 also presents the format conventions you should use when presenting data in tabular fashion. Study the model carefully because it presents a general format for contingency table presentations.

This example depicts ordinal-level data because the responses for each variable are either "low" or "high." For nominal level data the values could possibly be yes or no, or gender, racial, or political categories. In addition, when data are ordinal, it is conventional to assign the lowest numerical codes to the lowest values (1 = low; 2 = high).

Cells A through D represent all the possible combinations of lower and higher values of the two variables. Cell A depicts all those cases having low scores on both variables (LL). Cell B depicts all those cases having high scores on the X variable and low scores on the Y variable (HL). Cell C depicts all those cases scoring low on the X variable and high on the Y variable (LH). Last, cell D depicts all those cases scoring high on both variables (HH). The total number of cases in each cell, as well as the total marginal figures, sum to the total number of cases in the table (n).

Table 14.1 also implies that the greater the proportion of cases that fall in the diagonal cells (AD and BC), the stronger the relationship between the two variables. We call the AD diagonal the **main diagonal** while the BC diagonal is referred to as the **off diagonal.** The main diagonal represents those cases that scored low on both variables and those cases that scored high on both variables. Conversely, the off diagonal represents those cases that scored low on one variable and high on the other variable. If a higher proportion of cases fall in the A and D cells than in cells B and C, a positive relationship exists. As the independent variable increases in value, so does the dependent variable. On the other hand, if a higher proportion of cases fall in the off diagonal cells than in cells A and D, a negative relationship exists. If this occurs the higher

TABLE 14.1

TABULAR PRESENTATION

Dependent Variable (Y) by Independent Variable (X)			
Dependent Variable, Y	**Low X Value**	**High X Value**	**Row Marginals**
	Cell A (LL)	Cell B (HL)	
Low Y value	Cases scoring **low** on **both** X and Y variables (# & %).	Cases scoring **high** on X variable and **low** on Y variable (# & %).	Total **value** cases scoring **low on Y** variable cells (A + B)
	Cell C (LH)	Cell D (HH)	
High Y value	Cases scoring **low** on X and **high** on Y variable (# & %).	Cases scoring high on X and Y variables (# & %).	Total cases scoring **high on Y** variable cells (C + D)
Column marginals	Total cases scoring **low on X** variable (cells A + C) **(100%)**	Total cases scoring **high on X** variable (cells B + D) **(100%)**	Total cases in table (cells A + B + C + D) (n)

Source: Richard L. Cole. *Introduction to Political Inquiry.* New York: Macmillan, 1981, p. 112.

values of the independent variable are associated with lower values of the dependent variable. The greater the proportion of cases falling on either diagonal, the stronger the relationship. If the cases are evenly apportioned among all the cells, we say that there is little relationship between the variables. In other words, it would be difficult to predict values of the dependent variable based on our knowledge of the independent variable.

◆ FORMAT CONVENTIONS FOR BIVARIATE TABLES

Before we look at an example to help clarify the points we just made, let's summarize the format conventions for bivariate tables:

1. Number your tables with Arabic numerals if you are presenting more than one table.

2. Use a clear, straightforward title that describes the contents of the table. Use this form:

   a. Dependent Variable by Independent Variable (for example, Congressional Vote by Party).

   b. The title should also give information that describes the data, for example: Congressional Vote on Abortion Bill by Party, 101st Congress, 1991.

3. Label the leftmost column with the *name or description* of the dependent variable.

4. Label the other columns with the *values* of the independent variable.

5. Enter the name of the independent variable above the independent variables's values.

6. Include a Total row to depict marginal distributions.

7. Show the number of cases and percentage of cases for each cell.

8. Round percentages to either whole numbers or one decimal place.

9. Keep the same number of decimal places throughout your table.

10. Don't put percent (%) signs after cell entries.

11. Do not draw vertical lines in a table.

Now let's look at an example to support our discussion. Assume that a researcher is interested in examining the relationship between political party identification and the vote on HR2707, a U.S. House of Representatives vote to lift the ban on the use of federal money for abortion counseling. The researcher hypothesizes that Republican representatives will vote to maintain the ban while Democratic representatives will support the bill. Relying on data collected from the *Congressional Record,* the resulting frequency distributions for party identification (coded as Republican or Democratic) and the vote cast by the representative (coded as "yes" to indicate support, or "no" to maintain the ban) are presented in Table 14.2.

You can see from the frequency distributions that a larger proportion of the representatives supported the proposed legislation. The distributions also show you that the Republicans are outnumbered in the House by 23 percent. The table, however, says nothing about the possible relationship between party identification and the votes cast for the bill.

Frequency distributions by themselves may not reveal relationships. A contingency table, however, might reveal a relationship between the representatives' political party and their votes. Before we construct a contingency table from the above distributions, however, let's briefly look at how to read a contingency table.

You can analyze relationships by comparing and examining differences between the percentages depicted across categories of the independent variable. Fox offers a "very rough rule" of thumb you can use when ascertaining the extent of difference. First, differences of less than 10 percent indicate that there is a weak relationship between the variables. Differences ranging from

TABLE 14.2

FREQUENCY DISTRIBUTIONS OF VOTE ON HR2707 AND PARTY IDENTIFICATION

Variable	Frequency	Percent
Party Identification		
Republican	164	38.5
Democratic	262	61.5
Total	426	100.0
Vote on HR 2707		
Yes	270	63.4
No	156	36.6
Total	426	100.0

NOTE: This table depicts the actual number of representatives that voted for the bill.

TABLE 14.3

VIEWPOINT ON CAPITAL PUNISHMENT BY GENDER (IN PERCENTAGES)

Capital Punishment OK?	Gender	
	Males	**Females**
Yes	53	55
No	47	45
Total	100	100
(n)	(425)	(510)

10 to 30 percentage points indicate that there is a moderate relationship between variables. Last, differences greater than 30 percentage points indicate a strong relationship between variables (Fox 1993, 117). Consider the following hypothetical examples.

Table 14.3 shows virtually no difference between the percentages of males and females who believe that capital punishment is a viable alternative for capital offenses. Thus, you would conclude that there is no relationship between gender and one's viewpoint on capital punishment. Both genders, in this hypothetical distribution, tend to have the same level of support for the policy.

TABLE 14.4

VOTING BY RACE (IN PERCENTAGES)

Vote in 1992 General Election?	Race	
	Anglo	**Non-Anglo**
Yes	61	44
No	39	56
Total	100	100
(*n*)	(451)	(275)

TABLE 14.5

VIEWPOINT ON PRAYER IN PUBLIC SCHOOLS BY POLITICAL PARTY (IN PERCENTAGES)

Organized Prayer in Public Schools OK?	Political Party	
	Republican	**Democratic**
Yes	81	20
No	19	80
Total	100	100
(*n*)	(400)	(450)

Table 14.4 shows a 17 percentage point difference between Anglos and non-Anglos who report that they voted in the 1992 general election. Using our rule of thumb, we can say that there is a moderate relationship between race and voting in this election.

In our last example, Table 14.5, there is a difference of 61 points between Republicans and Democrats and their viewpoint on organized prayer in public schools. Thus, there is a strong relationship between political party affiliation and this heated topic.

Now let's return to our example about congressional support for HR2707, the proposed U.S. House legislation to lift the ban on the use of federal funds

TABLE 14.6

SUPPORT FOR HR2707 BY POLITICAL PARTY U.S. HOUSE OF REPRESENTATIVES VOTE—101ST CONGRESS NOVEMBER 6, 1991

	Political Party		
Vote on HR2707	Democratic	Republican	Total
Yes	219 (83.6)	51 (31.1)	270 (63.4)
No	43 (16.4)	113 (68.9)	156 (36.6)
Total	262 (100)	164 (100)	426 (100)

for abortion counseling. Table 14.6 is a contingency table of the frequencies depicted in Table 14.2.

Before we analyze the relationship between the political party of the representatives and the vote cast, let's briefly discuss the tabular format conventions. There is a clear, straightforward title that describes the content of the table. The leftmost column depicts the name of the dependent variable, support for HR2707. The other columns are labeled with the values of the independent variable, political party identification. Above these value labels is the name of the independent variable. There are also row totals to depict the marginal distributions. Each cell shows the number of cases and percentages of cases for each cell. For example, 219 Democrats, or 83.6 percent of all Democratic representatives who voted, supported lifting of the ban. In addition, the decimal places for the percentage figures were consistent throughout the table. Note also that percentage signs were not used and the columnar percentage totals add to 100 percent.

By presenting the data in this manner, you see that there is a difference of over 52 percent between Democratic and Republican support for the legislation. Thus, there is a strong relationship between the representatives' political party and their vote. You can also see that most of the cases lie on the main diagonal (cells A and D). Most Democrats supported the bill (83.6 percent), while most Republicans opposed the legislation (68.9 percent).

The table also illustrates another point important to political research. The relationship between party identification and support for the bill is not perfect. Some Democrats opposed the bill (16.4 percent) while 51 (31.1 percent of the Republicans cast affirmative votes. Thus other factors must be related to the vote; party identification is only one determinant.

TABLE 14.7

PERFECT RELATIONSHIP: SUPPORT FOR HR2707 BY POLITICAL PARTY U.S. HOR VOTE—101ST CONGRESS NOVEMBER 6, 1991

	Political Party		
Vote on HR2707	Democratic	Republican	Total
Yes	262 (100)	0 (0)	262 (61.5)
No	0 (0)	164 (100)	164 (38.5)
Total	262 (100)	164 (100)	426 (100)

Before we move on, let's see if you understand our discussion so far. What would the table look like if there was a perfect relationship between the political party of the representatives and their votes? We hope that you suggest something like Table 14.7.

As you can see each Democratic representative would support lifting the ban, while each Republican would cast an opposing vote. In the real world, however, this rarely happens.

❖ MEASURES OF ASSOCIATION

◆ INTRODUCTION

So far we have measured the relationship between two variables by analyzing a crosstabulation. Crosstabulations can, at times, be so large that we need some simpler way to summarize the information. Thus, we use measures of association that efficiently summarize the following:

1. The *existence* of a relationship.
2. The *direction* of a relationship.
3. The *strength* of a relationship.
4. The *statistical significance* of a relationship.

Measures of association mathematically summarize the distribution of cases in the cells. As we said earlier, the range of values for these measures range from 0 to 1.0 for nominal-level data and from −1.0 to 1.0 for ordinal-

and interval/ratio-levels of data. Again, the stronger the relationship, the higher the value of the measure.

As you will see, there are several measures you can use. So which ones do you use to determine relationships in your data? To select the best measure, you need to consider several factors. First, there are different measures for each level of measurement. Second, the size of the table is important. Some measures are appropriate for smaller tables, for example. Last, you use some measures when you make an assumption about the direction of the relationship between two variables. With measures appropriate for **asymmetrical** relationships, you must posit which variable is the independent variable and which one is the dependent variable. With these measures we assume that variation in the independent variable is at least one possible cause of variation in the dependent variable. The value of the statistic depends on which variable is dependent and which variable is independent. You do not need to make an assumption about the direction of causation between two variables with **symmetrical** measures. These measures yield the same value regardless of which variable is considered the dependent or independent variable.

◆ Tests of Association for Nominal Data

There are numerous measures of association. As discussed in the introduction to this part, each measure has its own application. The level of measurement, size of the table (2 by 2, 2 by 3, etc.), and the direction of the relationship, dictate which measure you should use. In addition, each measure has its own interpretation, advantages, and disadvantages.

The Phi Coefficient   If the independent and dependent variables in a particular contingency table are nominal and dichotomous (2-by-2 table), a measure often used by political scientists is the **phi coefficient.** Because you use this statistic with data measured at the nominal level, the range of scores is 0 to 1.0. The closer phi is to 1.0, the greater the relationship between the variables. Phi is a symmetric measure of association which means that its value does not depend on which variable is the independent variable and which variable is the dependent variable.

Recalling the cell labels shown in Figure 14-1, the formula for the phi coefficient is:

$$\text{phi} = \frac{AD - BC}{\sqrt{(A + B)(C + D)(A + C)(B + D)}}$$

Cells labelled as:

A = B

C = D

The phi coefficient measures the concentration of observations on either diagonal. To enhance this discussion, let's reexamine the relationship presented in Table 14.6. You will recall that the table showed a relationship between the political party of U.S. House members and their vote in support of lifting

TABLE 14.8

SUGGESTED VERBAL INTERPRETATIONS OF MEASURES OF ASSOCIATION

Correlation Values	Appropriate Phrases
+.70 or higher	Very strong positive association
+.50 to +.69	Substantial positive association
+.30 to +.49	Moderate positive association
+.10 to +.29	Low positive association
+.01 to +.09	Negligible positive association
0.00	No association
−.01 to −.09	Negligible negative association
−.10 to −.29	Low negative association
−.30 to −.49	Moderate negative association
−.50 to −.69	Substantial negative association
−.70 or lower	Very strong negative association

the ban on the use of federal dollars for abortion counseling. The table showed that most of the cases were concentrated on the main diagonal (A − D). You could imply from this that there is a substantial relationship. You could also report the strength of this relationship by comparing the percentage of each party that voted for the legislation (83.6 percent of those Democrats who voted supported the legislation, while only 31.1 percent of the Republicans cast supporting votes). Or, you could calculate the phi statistic to summarize the relationship. For this example, you calculate phi as follows:

$$\text{phi} = \frac{\overset{A\quad D}{(219)(113)} - \overset{B\quad C}{(51)(43)}}{\sqrt{\underset{(270)\ (156)\ (262)\ (164)}{A+B\ \ C+D\ \ A+C\ \ B+D}}} = \frac{22554}{42541.88} = 0.53$$

Based on the phi statistic, you can conclude that a relationship exists between the political party of the representative and his or her vote. Phi, however, does not have an operational interpretation. Thus, how do you interpret the observed relationship? How do you know whether .53 is a weak, moderate, or strong relationship? What words do you use to describe this relationship? Fortunately James Davis offered some phrases you can use to describe the various ranges of values for Yule's Q. Richard Cole adopted these descriptions to fit all measures of association that lack an operational interpretation (Davis 1967, 49; Cole 1980, 156). We also believe they can help you describe relationships relying on such measures of association.

Using these suggested phrases we can say that there is a substantial positive association between the political party of U.S. representatives and their vote on the abortion counseling legislation.

Cramer's V **Cramer's V** (*V*) is a variation of the phi coefficient. However, you can use this measure with any sized table depicting variables measured at the nominal level of measurement. When you calculate this statistic for a 2-by-2 table, the result is the same as phi. Thus, the *V* value for our example is also .53. Similar to phi, its values range between 0 and 1, and there is no operational definition.

Pearson's Coefficient of Contingency (C) Pearson's C is more appropriate for larger tables (4 by 4, etc.). Why? Because its upper limit depends on the number of rows and columns. Therefore, the range of values is 0 to something less than 1. In fact, the upper limit for a 2-by-2 table is .71. In our example, the value of this statistic is .468. How would you interpret this value? You could not use the table we gave you because it is based on values ranging from −1.0 to 1.0. As we just said the upper limit for *C* for a 2-by-2 table is only .71. So, what does our example of .468 mean? Thus, this limitation is a distinct disadvantage of Pearson's C.

◆ Lambda Asymmetric and Symmetric Coefficients

While the statistics we just discussed help us to interpret the strength of a particular relationship, they have several limitations. For example, you can only use phi to examine a dichotomous relationship. In addition, the statistics do not have an operational definition. With a *V* of .70 for example, you can only say that it is stronger than a *V* of .69 and weaker than a *V* of .71. You cannot say that it is 1 percent higher or lower.

Lambda coefficients, on the other hand, are **proportionate reduction of error (PRE)** statisitics. **Lambda** is interpreted as a percentage. A lambda value of .29, for example, is interpreted as 29 percent. Thus, unlike phi, *V*, and *C*, it has an operational definition. Lambda coefficients enable us to answer the question, how much can the error in predicting values of the dependent variable be reduced, knowing the values of the independent variable? Like the phi coefficient, lambda values range from 0 to 1.0. Unlike phi, however, you can use the lambda statistic with any size table. In addition, you can use lambda when you predict the direction of the relationship (asymmetric). You can also use the statistic when the direction is unknown or you cannot predict a direction (symmetrical). Thus, lambda has more uses and an intrinsic meaning that makes it somewhat more useful than phi, *V*, or *C*.

Remember we said that lambda coefficients enable us to answer the question, how much can the error in predicting values of the dependent variable be reduced, knowing the values of the independent variable? Therefore, the formula for lambda is:

$$\text{lambda} = \frac{L - M}{L}$$

where

L = number of prediction mistakes without considering IV

M = number of prediction mistakes when considering IV

To illustrate, let's return to our example concerning members of the U.S. House and the vote on HR2707. Our research question is "Can you use a representatives political party affiliation to predict his/her vote for HR2707?" If you were asked to individually predict the vote for each of the 426 representatives, knowing no other information but the distribution presented above, you would predict yes for each representative. You know from the distribution that there were 270 yes votes versus 156 no votes. Thus, you would predict that a representative voted with the majority if for no other reason than the odds are in your favor. In other words, your best predictor of how representatives voted is yes.

Yes, however, is only your best predictor. You could also be wrong 156 times because that many representatives voted against the legislation. Applying the above formula, then, the L is 156, which is the number of mistakes you would make without having knowledge about the impact of an independent variable.

Now let's consider the impact of the independent variable, political party affiliation. Knowing the impact of party affiliation you would predict that each representative would vote for the *modal* choice in each category (Democratic = yes; Republican = no). Even with this knowledge, however, you would be wrong on occasion. How many times would you be wrong? Of the 262 Democrats that voted, 43 opposed the legislation. Of the 164 Republicans that voted, 51 supported the resolution. Therefore, even knowing their party identification and knowing that it related to the vote, you would still be wrong 94 times. Thus, $M = 94$. Your error rate without considering the political party, however, was 156. You improved your predictive capability by reducing your errors from 156 to 94. When we insert these figures into the lambda formula we get:

$$\text{lambda} = \frac{L - M}{L} = \frac{156 - 94}{156} = .397$$

When you interpret this lambda result, you could say something like "Knowledge of the representative's political party (the independent variable) reduces by almost 40 percent the error in predicting the representative's vote on HR2707 (the dependent variable)." This operational meaning gives lambda a distinctive advantage over a measure of association such as phi, C, and V.

◆ TESTS OF ASSOCIATION FOR ORDINAL DATA

General   Similar to nominal-level data, there are several tests appropriate when analyzing ordinal-level data. Unlike the nominal measures, however, ordinal measures range in value from −1 to +1. You use the ordinal measures of association when both of the variables in a contingency table you are analyzing are ordinal. If one variable is nominal, then you should use the nominal measures of association.

Ordinal measures rely upon a comparison of paired relationships in the data. To enhance our discussion, let's look at Table 14.9, which presents a hypothetical relationship between two dichotomous ordinal variables. While

TABLE 14.9

HYPOTHETICAL RELATIONSHIP BETWEEN TWO DICHOTOMOUS ORDINAL VARIABLES

	Independent Variable X		
Dependent Variable, Y	**Education**		**Total**
Income	Low	High	
	A	B	
Low	1	1	2
	C	D	
High	1	1	2
Total	2	2	4

Source: Richard L. Cole. *Introduction to Political Inquiry.* New York: Macmillan, 1981, p. 122.

the figure is simplistic because it only depicts four cases, it will make our explanation of pairs clearer. In any table, the possible combinations of paired relationships is determined by the following formula:

Total number of pairs = $N(N - 1)/2$

Where N is the total number of observations. In Table 14.9, the total number of possible pairs of observations is 6, as calculated by:

$4(4 - 1)/2 = 6$

As in previous examples, the cells in the figure are labeled A through D. We also still have our main (AD) and off diagonals (BC). Keeping this in mind, we can examine the possible types of pairs found in a contingency table.

Concordant Pair   A concordant pair of cases is one in which one case is higher on *both* variables than the other case. The case in cell D has a higher level of education and income than the case in cell A. This pair also represents the main diagonal. The product of the cases along the main diagonal yield the number of concordant pairs. Thus, if cell A has 4 observations and cell D has 3 observations, there are 12 concordant pairs in the table. The greater the proportionate number of concordant pairs in any table, the stronger the relationship in a positive direction.

Discordant Pair   A discordant pair of cases is one in which one case is higher on one variable than the other case but lower on the other variable. The case in cell B has a higher level of education than the case in cell C. On the other hand, the case in cell C has a higher level of income than the case in cell B. This pair also represents the off diagonal. The product of the cases along the off diagonal yields the number of discordant pairs. The greater the proportionate number of discordant pairs in any table, the stronger the relationship in a negative direction.

Tied Pair   A tied pair of cases is one in which both observations are tied on at least one of the variables. The cases in cells A and C both have lower levels of education. The cases in cells B and D both have higher levels of education. We call these tied pairs the X pairs. (Education is the independent variable which is denoted as X.) The cases in cells A and B both have lower levels of income. The cases in cells C and D both have higher levels of income. We call these tied pairs the Y pairs. The greater the proportionate number of tied pairs in any table, the weaker the relationship between the variables. In other words, the appropriate measures of association will have values close to zero.

All of this may seem confusing at first, but the ordinal tests of associations are based on paired relationships and are important for determining relationships and association. Now let's turn our attention to some specific ordinal measures of association.

Gamma   You can use the gamma statistic with any size table. It is used as a symmetrical (nondirectional) measurement. Similar to the lambda statistic, gamma is a PRE statistic. Hence, it has an operational definition. Unlike the other ordinal measures we will discuss in the following passages, gamma does not consider tied pairs in its calculation, so its value will be higher than other ordinal measures of association. The following formula is used to calculate the gamma statistic:

$$\text{gamma} = \frac{\text{concordant pairs } (P) - \text{discordant pairs } (Q)}{\text{concordant pairs } (P) + \text{discordant pairs } (Q)}$$

Let's look at another example to illustrate the use of the gamma statistic. Suppose you are concerned about the number of bad checks written by members of the U.S. House of Representatives. Therefore, you collected data that shows the number of bad checks written by each representative and his or her level of education. Your hypothesis is "The more education a representative has, the lower the number of bad checks he or she wrote." Because of the number of representatives and the number of bad checks written, you collapsed data into the following categories: low number of bad checks written (includes no bad checks), high number of bad checks, no graduate degree, and graduate degree. (You can see that some specificity of information is lost by collapsing the data. However, this is just an example to illustrate the use of the gamma statistic.) Table 14.10 is the contingency table you constructed.

TABLE 14.10

NUMBER OF BAD CHECKS BY LEVEL OF EDUCATION U.S. HOR—101ST CONGRESS JANUARY 16, 1992

	Level of Education		
Number of Bad Checks	No Graduate Degree	Graduate Degree	Total
Low	93 (35.1)	79 (47.6)	172 (39.9)
High	172 (64.9)	87 (52.4)	259 (60.1)
Totals	265 (100)	166 (100)	431 (100)

Source: Hypothetical

Analysis of the percentages show that there is a moderate relationship between the level of education and the number of bad checks written by our representatives. As in our previous examples that examined the relationship between nominal-level variables, we can calculate a measure of association that will enhance our ability to interpret the relationship. For this example we want to calculate the gamma statistic. The calculation of gamma is

$$\frac{P-Q}{P+Q} = \frac{8091 - 13588}{8091 + 13588} = \frac{-5497}{21679} = -.254$$

Because gamma is a PRE statistic, it has an operational definition. Thus we can say that our knowledge of a representative's level of education enhances our ability to predict whether he or she wrote a low number of bad checks or a high number of bad checks by 25 percent. You will also note that the direction of the relationship is negative. That is, as the level of education for a representative increases, the number of bad checks written by the representative decreases.

Tau Statistics: Tau b and Tau c   You only use the tau *b* statistic for square tables (2 by 2; 3 by 3). Why? This statistic will only achieve a maximum value of −1 or +1 for perfectly symmetrical tabular dimensions. It will not reach a maximum value with any other shape of table. The tau *c* statistic corrects for this deficiency. Thus you can use tau *c* with any size table. In practice, however, the magnitude of difference between the values of the two statistics is slight. These measures differ from gamma because they consider the impact of the tied pairs in their calculations. Thus, their values are usually less than the gamma statistic calculated for the same contingency table. The formulas for tau b and tau c are:

$$\text{tau } b = \frac{P - Q}{\sqrt{(P + Q + Y)(P + Q + X)}}$$

$$\text{tau } c = \frac{(P - Q)}{1/2^2 N\,[(m - 1)/m]}$$

where

N = the total number of cases

m = smaller of rows or columns in the table (in a 4 by 3 table, m = 3)

When we calculate the tau b and tau c coefficients for our example the results are tau b = −.124 and tau c = −.118. The tau statistics are also PRE statistics. Therefore, based on these statistics, we can say that our knowledge of a representative's level of education enhances our ability to predict whether they wrote a low number or high number of bad checks by almost 12 percent.

Sommer's DYX and DXY   Gamma and the tau coefficients are symmetric in their treatment of the variables because no direction of the relationship is made. Sommer's DYX and DXY, however, are asymmetric in interpretation. Therefore, when you hypothesize a direction in a relationship, or specify causality, you should use one of these statistics in lieu of gamma and the tau coefficients. These statistics are also helpful because you can use them with any size table. In addition, the DYX statistic considers those pairs that are tied on the dependent variable (Y pairs) in its calculation. The DXY statistic, on the other hand, considers those pairs that are tied on the independent variable (X pairs) in its calculation. You will recall that gamma does not consider the tied pairs in its calculation. As a result, the gamma statistic is often larger than the Sommer's statistics. The formula for these statistics are similar to the gamma formula:

$$DYX = \frac{\text{concordant pairs } (P) - \text{discordant pairs } (Q)}{\text{concordant pairs } (P) + \text{discordant pairs } (Q) + Y}$$

$$DXY = \frac{\text{concordant pairs } (P) - \text{discordant pairs } (Q)}{\text{concordant pairs } (P) + \text{discordant pairs } (Q) + X}$$

When we calculate the DYX and DXY coefficients for our example the results are DYX = −.125 and DXY = −.123. These are PRE statistics. Again we can say that knowledge of a representatives level of education enhances our ability to predict whether he/she wrote a low or high number of bad checks by a little over 12 percent. Although slight, based on our preliminary analysis, it looks like your hypothesis may have some support.

◆ SUMMARY: SELECTING THE APPROPRIATE STATISTIC

We have just covered quite a bit of information—information about a confounding array of nominal and ordinal level measures of association. As a result of this inundation of information, you might ask, which statistic do I use? Remember we said that selection depends on the level of measurement, the size of the table, and the substantive nature of the theory you are testing. In other words, does your model specify a one-way causal relationship? If so, you should use an asymmetrical test such as DXY. Confusing, right? The purpose of Table 14.11 is to alleviate some of your confusion by giving you some help in selecting the appropriate measure of association.

❖ STATISTICAL SIGNIFICANCE AND HYPOTHESIS TESTING

◆ INTRODUCTION

Before we talk about measures of association and interval-level data, we want to introduce you to the notion of statistical significance. At the outset of this chapter we said that mathematicians have developed several measures we can use to determine the extent of a relationship between two variables. The measures we have just discussed tell us whether there is a relationship between the independent and dependent variables, the direction of the relationship, and the strength of the relationship for nominal- and ordinal-level variables. In short, they enhance your ability to predict the values of a dependent variable based on your knowledge of an independent variable.

When you work with **sample** data, however, there is another question you must address. How confident are you that the relationship you found in the sample data actually depicts a relationship in the population from which you drew the sample cases? This question is important because it is the population, not the sample, that is of interest to you. You only took a sample because it was impractical or impossible to gather data about the entire population. Thus the sample is only important to the extent that it allows you to make meaningful predictions about the entire population. In the words of statisticians, you want to know whether the relationship is statistically significant, and whether the relationship is causal (see Chapter 15).

You use a test of statistical significance in conjunction with hypothesis testing to infer properties of the population based on the analysis of sample data. These tools help you decide whether you can generalize an observed relationship between variables in your probability sample to the population from which you took the sample.

Statistical significance tests are premised on probability theory. You should only use a statistical significance test when analyzing the data from a probability sample. It is inappropriate to use these tests to examine relationships from convenience or quota samples.

It is also inappropriate to use statistical significance tests when you work with the entire population in lieu of a sample of the population. If you have data about all the cases in a population, for example, census data for the 50 states, or demographic data about all members of the U.S. Congress, there is no population you need to generalize. Thus, tests of statistical significance

TABLE 14.11

CHOOSING THE APPROPRIATE MEASURE OF ASSOCIATION

Measure of Association	Level of Measurement	Table Size	Asymmetric/ Symmetrical	General Comments
Lambda	1	Any size	Both	PRE statistic. Can underestimate the degree the of relationship.
Cramer's V	1	Any size	Symmetric	Preferable to C. Use when dependent variables are skewed.
Phi coefficient	1	2×2	Symmetric	Limited by size of table.
Contingency Coefficient (C)	1	Larger tables	Symmetric	Upper limit is less than 1.0
Gamma	2	Any size	Symmetric	PRE statistic. Can overestimate the degree of relationship.
Tau b	2	Square tables	Symmetric	Limited by shape of table.
Tau c	2	Any size	Symmetric	More useful than tau b.
Somer's DYX/DXY	2	Any size	Assymetric	Use when you you know the direction of the relationship.

1 = two nominal variables or one nominal and one ordinal variable
2 = two ordinal variables

have little purpose. You already know about the population. Why generalize to it?

◆ THE STEPS IN DETERMINING STATISTICAL SIGNIFICANCE

The application of tests of significance involves a number of steps: specifying a null and a research hypothesis, choosing the appropriate statistical test, specifying a significance level, computing the statistic, and deciding whether to accept or reject the hypotheses. After we briefly discuss each step, we will apply our discussion to an example that examines opinion about prayer in public schools.

Specification   Earlier we defined hypotheses as "testable statements relating two or more concepts or variables." As a reminder when writing a hypothesis, as a minimum, you should state the direction of an expected relationship between a dependent variable and at least one independent variable.

There are several types of hypotheses. The first hypothesis we will discuss is the research or alternative hypothesis (Ha). The research hypothesis makes an assertion. For example, "Republicans are more likely than Democrats to support a pro-life agenda." A relationship is asserted to exist between party identification and the abortion issue.

A **null hypothesis (Ho),** however, assumes that a relationship does not exist. For example, "No difference exists between Republicans and Democrats and their views about abortion." A null hypothesis is necessary because it is never possible to prove that an assertion is true beyond any doubt. Thus, you can prove a research hypothesis if you can show that a null hypothesis is false. Therefore, it is actually the null hypothesis that you test. When you fail to reject the null hypothesis you can conclude that whatever difference that occurs in the sample could have occurred just by chance. In other words, the relationship is not statistically significant. Rejecting the null hypothesis is to conclude that whatever difference that occurs in the sample probably did not occur just by chance and is therefore statistically significant.

Selection   The second step you take when testing hypotheses is to choose the appropriate statistical test. One criterium is the level of data. There are different tests for different levels of data. Z scores, for example, are used with interval data. They are also used with a sample that is normally distributed, when you know the standard deviation of the population, and when you have more than 30 cases. Z scores measure deviations from the means in terms of standard deviation units. They can be used with a single sample or two samples.

You use the Student's T or the t-test when the standard normal curve is inappropriate, when your sample size is 30 cases or less, and when your data are measured at the interval level. Additionally, it may not be possible to know the standard deviation of the population. In such cases you would use the t-distribution. In addition, you use the standard deviation of the sample to estimate the standard deviation of the population. The t-test is also commonly used to test the significance of Pearson's C and whether independent variables are significant for explaining variance in a dependent variable in regression models.

Other measures of statistical significance include the chi square statistic and the F ratio. The **chi square** statistic is used with nominal data. The **F ratio** is commonly used to test the statistical significance of simple, partial, and multiple correlation coefficients—tools that are normally used with interval-level data. We will provide you with an in-depth discussion of these statistics in the coming passages.

Determining the Level of Significance   Our next step in deciding whether you can generalize a relationship to the overall population is to select a **level of statistical significance.** Statistical significance is the exact probability of error that you are willing to accept in making an inference from the sample to the population. A significance level tells you the likelihood that a relationship found in a probability sample occurred as a result of sampling error. In other words, the relationship does not exist in the population. Put a bit differently, the level of significance gives you the probability that there is no real relationship between the independent and dependent variables in the study population you used to draw your sample from.

You know that if you took repeated samples they would not always produce exactly the same results. You should expect the same from a single sample. You will experience some error. But you want to minimize that error. You want to increase the probability that your sample results reflect the population and did not occur just by chance. That is why you take random probability samples. You want to have a sample as representative of the population as possible.

How sure do you want to be that your sample results did not occur because of sampling error? Do you want to be right 90 percent of the time? Or do you want to be right 95 or 99 percent of the time? Just what level of acceptance political scientists are willing to take is a matter of some debate. Most of us, however, want to be sure that our sample results would occur by chance no more than 5 percent of the time. Therefore the most often used level of significance is .05. This means, that there is a probability of 5 percent that an incorrect inference will be made that a relationship exists in the population when in fact it does not.

Making the Decision   To determine the statistical significance of an observed relationship, you need to compare the calculated value of the statistic with values that relate to the different levels of significance. To do this, tables of statistic distributions developed by statisticians are printed in the appendices of most statistics books. For example, a table of the chi square distributions is in Appendix III (Table A3). You can use the table to determine whether the value you calculate is statistically significant. If it is, then you reject the null hypothesis and accept the research hypothesis that there is a statistically significant relationship between the independent and dependent variables. (We will discuss how to use this table later in the chapter.)

Errors   When testing null hypotheses, two types of errors can occur. First it is possible that you erroneously reject the null hypothesis when it is, in fact, true. As a result, you will infer the existence of a relationship when one does not exist. Statisticians call this type of error a *Type I error*. When you erroneously accept a null hypothesis, however, you make a *Type II error*. As a result, you will erroneously infer no relationship when one actually does exist.

So what do you do? If you are concerned about inferring a relationship when one does not exist, you can minimize this error by making the level of significance as low as possible. Type I and Type II errors, however, are inversely related. A decrease in the probability that you will reject a true hypothesis leads to an increase in the probability of retaining a false one. Thus, the decision then is based on the type of problem you are investigating and the consequences of rejecting a true hypothesis versus retaining a false one.

Statistical Significance and the Chi Square Statistic   Although your analysis of a bivariate table shows a relationship between an independent and a dependent variable in a sample, you need to know whether the observed relationship resulted from sampling error, or whether it is an accurate reflection of a relationship that exists in the population. Thus, you need a statistic that allows you to draw inferences about the likelihood of sampling error. One statistic you can use is the chi square statistic. It is a statistic that compares the actual frequencies in a bivariate table with the frequencies you would expect if there was no relationship between the variables in the population. Chi square is also used when both variables are nominal or if one is nominal and the other is ordinal.

To understand the logic of chi square, we start by asking what data in a contingency table would look like if there was no relationship between the independent and dependent variables. To help us with our task, let's return to our example concerning the relationship between one's viewpoint on prayer in public schools and ones' political party in Table 14.5.

Notice that the cell frequencies are blank. We did this to help you understand the logic of statistical significance and the chi square statistic. Remem-

TABLE 14.12

Organized Prayer in Public Schools OK?	Political Party		
	Republican	Democratic	Total
Yes			414 (48.7)
No			436 (51.3)
Total	400 (100)	450 (100)	850 (100)

Source: Hypothetical

ber, you use measures of statistical significance with probability sample data. For our example, chi square compares the actual frequencies in a bivariate table with the frequencies you would expect to find if there were no relationship between one's political party and one's viewpoint on prayer in public schools in the larger population. Thus, the question is if political party and the viewpoint about organized prayer in public schools were independent, or not related, what numbers would you expect to find in each cell? That is, how would the 400 Republicans and the 450 Democrats in each column be distributed over the two categories of the dependent variable?

To answer this question you might decide to distribute the Republicans and Democrats equally across the prayer responses. For example, 200 Republicans for each response code and 225 Democrats for each response code. Simple mathematics, however, shows that this is the wrong approach. While the cell entries add up to the column marginals, they do not equal the row marginals. No relationship between the variables means the pattern of responses on the dependent variable should be essentially the same for all categories of the independent variable. In other words, there should be no difference between Republicans and Democrats for each category of the dependent variable. Thus, if the overall distribution of opinion is such that approximately 49 percent of the respondents support organized prayer in our public schools, we would expect that 49 percent of the Republicans and 49 percent of the Democrats would give the same response if political party does not explain a respondent's viewpoint about the issue. Similarly, we would expect that the row representing no responses should contain a little over 51 percent of each political party.

The cell entries that we expect to find if there is no relationship are called the expected frequencies. You use the following formula to calculate the expected frequencies for the cells of a contingency table:

Expected frequency (FE) = column N * row %

Thus, the expected cell frequency is the number of cases in each column times the percent of cases in each row. Using this formula, the expected frequencies for the above table are shown in Table 14.13.

Notice that the cell frequencies now sum to the row and column marginals. In addition, there is no difference between the party identification and support for public school prayer: 48.7 percent of each party are in support, while 51.3 percent of each party are opposed. Hence, based on our expected frequencies, there does not appear to be any difference between the two groups. An equal percentage of both parties support and oppose school prayer. In other words, based on expected frequencies, political party affiliation is not related to the school prayer issue. In sum, we just answered the question we posed about the distribution of Republicans and Democrats over the two categories of the dependent variable if there was not a relationship between the two variables.

Table 14.14 depicts the observed, or actual, observations for the two political parties. When you compare these frequencies and percentages, it appears that a relationship between the two variables does exist. Republicans seem to

TABLE 14.13

EXPECTED FREQUENCIES

Organized Prayer in Public Schools OK?	Political Party		
	Republican	Democratic	Total
Yes	195 (48.7)	219 (48.7)	414 (48.7)
No	205 (51.3)	231 (51.3)	436 (51.3)
Total	400 (100)	450 (100)	850 (100)

Source: Hypothetical

TABLE 14.14

OBSERVED FREQUENCIES

Organized Prayer in Public Schools OK?	Political Party		
	Republican	Democratic	Total
Yes	324 (81)	90 (20)	414 (48.7)
No	76 (19)	360 (80)	436 (51.3)
Total	400 (100)	450 (100)	850 (100)

Source: Hypothetical

be more supportive of school prayer (81 percent) than do Democrats (20 percent). This is in sharp contrast to Table 14.13.

We determine whether a relationship is statistically significant by comparing the actual frequencies in a bivariate table with the frequencies you would expect to find if there were no relationship between ones' political party and one's viewpoint on prayer in public schools. Table 14.15 compares the cell entries from the two previous figures.

If a relationship did not exist, we would expect to find 195 Republicans who supported prayer in public schools and 205 who did not support the issue. The observed, or actual numbers, however, were 324 for the measure and 76 opposed to the measure. Similarly, we would expect 219 Democrats to

TABLE 14.15

OBSERVED/EXPECTED FREQUENCIES

| Organized Prayer in Public Schools OK? | Political Party | | | | Total |
| | Republican | | Democratic | | |
	FO	FE	FO	FE	
Yes	324	195	90	219	414 (48.7)
No	76	205	360	231	436 (51.3)
Total	400	400	450	450	850 (100)

Source: Hypothetical

support school prayer and 231 to oppose the measure. Our observed frequencies were 90 and 360, respectively. Small differences between the observed and expected frequencies would lead us to believe that differences could be the result of sampling error. Large differences, however, would indicate that there was a relationship between the two variables. That is, political party affiliation does explain one's attitude about prayer in public schools.

The chi square statistic uses the comparison between expected and observed frequencies to determine whether there is a statistically significant relationship between variables. It tells us whether we can expect our sample (850 respondents) to display this degree of dependency if party identification and support for prayer in public schools in the entire population is not related. In short, it helps us determine whether we can generalize a relationship between variables in our hypothetical probability sample to the population that was the source of our sample.

Before we calculate the chi square statistic so that we can complete our analysis of our sample data, let's look at the formula:

$$x^2 = \text{Sum of } \frac{(FO - FE)^2}{FE}$$

where

FO = observed frequency for each cell

FE = expected frequency for each cell

The first step is to determine the expected value of each cell—expected frequency (FE) = column n * row %. Next, subtract the expected frequency for each cell from the actual observed frequency for each cell. The third step is to square the results obtained from step 2. Fourth, you divide the squared value by the expected value for each cell (a process that standardizes for different size cell entries). Last, you sum the values. Following these steps we come up with a chi square value of 314.55. These steps are summarized in Table 14.16.

TABLE 14.16

CALCULATION OF THE CHI SQUARE STATISTIC

Cell	FO	FE (1)	FO – FE (2)	$(FO – FE)^2$ (3)	$(FO – FE)^2$ / FE (4)
A	324	195	129	16641	85.34
B	90	219	–129	16641	81.18
C	76	205	–129	16641	75.99
D	360	231	129	16641	72.04

(5) $x^2 = 85.34 + 81.18 + 75.99 + 72.04 = 314.55$

To summarize to this point, your analysis of a bivariate table constructed from probability sample data showed a relationship between political party affiliation and support for prayer in public schools. You reached this conclusion by examining the differences in percentages across the columns and several measures of association. Now you need to know whether the observed relationship resulted from sampling error, or whether it is an accurate reflection of a relationship that exists in the population. Thus, you calculated the chi square statistic that allows you to draw inferences about the likelihood of sampling error. This test of statistical significance allows you to decide if the observed relationship in your sample is also found in the population from which you drew the sample. If the answer is yes, we have a statistically significant relationship. If the answer is no, we do not have a statistically significant relationship. The relationship we found between the variables in the sample occurred just by chance or because of sampling error.

To determine whether the statistic you calculated is significant, you need to take the following steps: First, you must calculate the **degrees of freedom** associated with the table. Degrees of freedom are a correction or safety factor and are used in many statistical tests. For example, suppose you had two variables (x and y) where the values were unknown. You could assign any value to x and y. Thus, you have two free choices or two degrees of freedom. Suppose, however, you know $x + y = 30$. In this case, you have only one degree of freedom. Once you assign a value to x, the value of y is determined. For example, if $x = 10$, then $10 + y = 30$, thus $y = 20$ (Welch and Comer 1988, 211).

To further enhance this discussion, let's look at the following analogy. Suppose the contractors building your dream house determine that each beam needs to withstand 2,000 pounds of pressure. They would not use beams manufactured exactly to that specification. Errors in quality control can occur. Occasionally a beam will be manufactured that will only withstand 1,900 pounds of pressure. To compensate your contractors add a safety factor and use beams built to withstand 2,200 pounds of pressure. This will allow them to use an occasional weak beam that would still be strong enough to support your dream house.

The same is true in calculating sample statistics. Our sample is a tool we use to study the population. Based on the sample, we want to draw reliable conclusions about that population. In sum, the power of the statistics we calculate is affected by the size of our sample. Therefore, the net effect of the degrees of freedom is to give us a safety factor when estimating population characteristics (Dometrius 1992, 128–29).

Well, now that we have explained why we use degrees of freedom, we need to tell you how to calculate them for a given contingency table. The formula is very straight forward. It is: $(c - 1)(r - 1)$, where c = the number of columns and r = the number of rows in the table. For our table the degrees of freedom are $(2 - 1)(2 - 1) = 1$.

Our next step in deciding whether our relationship can be generalized to the overall population is to select a *level of statistical significance*. As a reminder, statistical significance is the exact probability of error that you are willing to accept in making an inference from the sample to the population. A significance level tells you the likelihood that a relationship found in a probability sample occurred as a result of sampling error. As we previously stated the most often used level of significance is .05, or there is a 5 percent probability that you will make an incorrect inference that a relationship exists in the population when in fact it does not (Type I error).

So, we now have a chi square value of 314.55, one degree of freedom, and a significance level of .05. We can now determine the statistical significance of our relationship. To do this we can turn to a table of the chi square distribution to determine whether the value we calculated is statistically significant (see Table A3 in Appendix III). The table gives us the probability of attaining a chi square of a given size even if there is no relationship between two variables in the larger population from which the sample was drawn.

The top row of the chi square table depicts several levels of significance. The left hand column shows the degrees of freedom. The table also shows the minimum value of chi square needed to achieve statistical significance.

Before we continue with our example, take a few minutes to examine the chi square distribution table. You will notice that as the levels of probability increase (.001 to .05) the table values decrease. In addition, as the degrees of freedom increase, so do the table values. What does this suggest to you?

First, if you want to minimize the probability of sample error by using a .01 level of significance in lieu of a higher level, the minimum value to attain significance is greater. You may infer from this discussion that you will always want to select a more stringent level of significance in your analyses. This decision, however, could lead to other problems. It is possible that you could reject a real relationship because of this notion (Type II error). In addition, a less stringent level of significance could result in the acceptance of a false relationship (Type I error). This is the matter of debate we referred to earlier in the chapter.

Second, more degrees of freedom, (which you will recall are based on the number of variable categories), imply greater opportunity for false results. Thus, the minimum chi square values are greater as the number of degrees of freedom, or variable categories, increase.

When using the table, you first need to select the degrees of freedom applicable to your table (1 for our example). Then you select the level of significance you want to use. For our example .05 (95 percent level). Next, you need to determine the applicable table value. This value is found at the intersection of the appropriate degrees of freedom and the level of significance you selected. The table value at one degree of freedom and at the .05 level of significance is 3.841. This is the minimum chi square value needed to show that our sample results did not occur by chance. Last, we compare the table value (3.841) with the value we calculated (314.55). If the calculated value is equal to, or greater than, the table value, we reject the null hypothesis and conclude that there is a statistically significant relationship between the variables. Thus, we can conclude that the difference in the level of support for organized prayer in public schools due to political party identification are statistically significant at the .05 level of significance. They are probably indicative of real differences in our population. Put another way, 95 samples of 100 will produce chi square values of 3.84 or more for tables with one degree of freedom.

Now let's apply what we know. We found a substantial positive relationship between respondents' political party identification and their support of prayer in public schools ($V = .61$). We also calculated a chi square value. Then, we determined that the minimum chi square value needed to show that our sample results did not occur by chance was 3.841. Our calculated chi square value of 314.55 is far greater than this *critical value*. Thus, we can say there is a statistically significant relationship between party identification and support for prayer in public schools.

We must make one last point before we look at the measures of association we use when working with interval-level data. A test of statistical significance determines whether an observed relationship between variables in a sample is real. In other words, we would also find the relationship in the population from which the sample was drawn. These tests, however, do not tell you the strength of the relationship. The measures of association we previously discussed provide you with that information.

❖ BIVARIATE TESTS FOR INTERVAL DATA

Data analysis and interpretation is enhanced when you use interval-level data and statistics. Interval-level data permit a degree of precision in stating relationships that is not possible with nominal or ordinal data. Statistical techniques designed for use with interval data indicate the magnitude and the direction of the relationship between two variables. When you use these techniques, you can predict with a certain degree of accuracy the effect of unit changes in the independent variable on changes in the dependent variable.

TABLE 14.17

FREQUENCY DISTRIBUTION

Years of Education	Index Score
7	42
8	46
9	52
10	63
11	70
12	75
13	80
14	82
15	85
16	90

Thus, the major purpose of bivariate tests for interval data is to increase your ability to predict the dependent variable based on what you know about the independent variable.

◆ DETERMINING RELATIONSHIPS

The Frequency Distribution   There are several steps you need to take when determining relationships between two interval-level variables. Initially, you should analyze the data you collect in a frequency table. As before, an example will enhance our discussion. You hypothesize that education influences one's viewpoint about the purpose, value pursuits, and scope of government. To test your hypothesis, you design a simple questionnaire and randomly administer it to ten individuals. (We use ten individuals to simplify our example). Your questionnaire asks several background questions, including level of education (an independent variable), and several questions to ascertain one's knowledge about government (the dependent variable). Later, you use these latter questions to design an index in order to test your hypothesis. Table 14.17 is a frequency distribution of the data you collected.

The Scattergram   A preliminary analysis of your data suggests that there may be a relationship between one's level of education and their index score. You can see that individuals with more education also attained higher index scores. When analyzing relationships between interval data, they are often displayed graphically in the form of a **scattergram,** which depicts the relationship between two variables by plotting on intersecting axes the points representing the dependent (Y) and independent variable (X) observations for

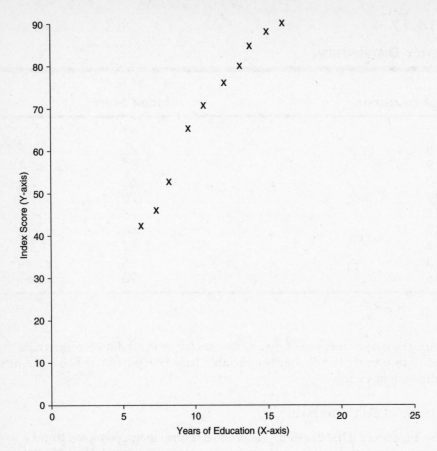

FIGURE 14.1 **Scattergram**

each case in the database. You use a scattergram to visually summarize a relationship. Figure 14.1 is a scattergram, or plot, of the data presented in Table 14.17.

A scattergram depicts the relationship of two variables by plotting the points representing the variable observations for each case, or respondent in the survey. The X-coordinates depict the level of education, or the independent variable, for the respondents in the sample. The Y-coordinates depict the index score, or the dependent variable, for the respondents. The intersection of the X and Y observations are plotted on the graph to help you see a possible relationship between the two variables. Thus the scattergram provides a rough indication of the *nature* of the relationship. If the general flow of the plotted points is upward and to the right, the relationship is positive. As one variable increases in value, so does the other. If the general flow is downward and to the right, the relationship is negative. As one variable increases in value, the other will decrease in value. If the plotted points appear to be randomly spread, there is little or no relationship between the variables.

The scattergram also indicates the *shape* of the relationship. If the plotted points are distributed so that the values of the dependent variable appear to increase or decrease in relation to the independent variable at a more-or-less consistent and constant rate, a **linear relationship** is said to exist. If a nonlinear relationship is discovered, the techniques that we are discussing are inappropriate.

Predictive Capability   One of the major purposes of bivariate interval-level statistics and analysis is to enhance our ability to predict the value of a dependent variable based on our knowledge about the independent variable. Without this knowledge you would estimate the value of any interval level dependent variable for an individual case to be equal to the mean of all the cases. Recall that when examining nominal data and the lambda statistic, you use the modal response as the best prediction for any value of the dependent variable. If most of your respondents in a sample of 1,200 are Protestant, the best guess of any case's religion in your distribution is Protestant. The same rationale is used with interval-level variables. Thus, without any knowledge about the level of education of the students, we would predict that the index score of any student in our sample to be the mean for the respondents, or 68.5. However, with additional information regarding each student (level of education), we can enhance our ability to explain the index scores in the sample. That is, we can compute measures of association (correlation coefficients) and use a statistical procedure called **regression analysis** to accomplish this task.

Assumptions of Regression   To this point we examined a frequency distribution and a scattergram to see if there was a possible relationship between two interval variables. As a result we determined that a relationship may exist. The regression procedure, however, summarizes a relationship more concisely with a straight line that best describes the relationship. Figure 14.2 is the scattergram we discussed previously. However, we drew a straight line through the data points to enhance our description of the relationship. You can see that the line we drew appears to fit the pattern of the scatter points. But what does this line represent? In short, it minimizes the sum of the squared distances between the line and the index score (dependent variable score) for each case, or respondent. The purpose of regression is to give you the best linear estimate to use when predicting the value of the dependent variable. Sure, we could draw other lines through the scatter points. No other line, however, would minimize the sum of the squared distances between the line and the dependent variable score as well as the one we drew for Figure 14.2. In other words, we are minimizing our variance or dispersion in the data set. The closer the values of the dependent variable to the line, the more the regression line explains the dependent variable values, or simply put, the stronger the relationship. There is less dispersion. Statisticians call this summary line the *linear regression line*. The linear regression line is very important in statistics.

Based on our discussion, there are several requirements we need in place before regression is the appropriate statistical tool to use. First, there must be

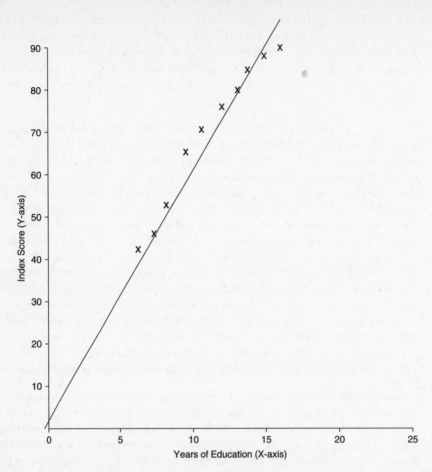

Figure 14.2 **Scattergram with Linear Regression Line**

a linear relationship between the variables. A linear relationship is one where the relationship between two variables when graphed results in a straight line. Second, the variables should be measured in interval data. While some political scientists use ordinal-level data and even nominal-level data, purists believe that any level of measurement below the interval level will not produce the best linear estimate of the dependent variable.

The Regression Model and Equation   Summarizing a relationship between variables with a straight line is defined by the following formula (a formula you may recall from your high school algebra class):

$$Y = a + bX$$

In this formula, Y refers to the *predicted* values of the dependent variable and X refers to the *actual* values of the independent variable. In our example, the X values are the actual levels of education for each respondent. The Y values are the predicted index score for each respondent for each value of X. The

TABLE 14.18

CALCULATING THE SIMPLE REGRESSION EQUATION

	Years of Education and Index Score		
Education (X)	**Score (Y)**	**XY**	**X²**
7	42	294	49
8	46	368	64
9	52	468	81
10	63	630	100
11	70	770	121
12	75	900	144
13	80	1040	169
14	82	1148	196
15	85	1275	225
16	90	1440	256
Totals 115	685	8333	1405

a represents the Y-intercept. It defines the location where the regression line should intercept with the Y-axis. It is also the value of the dependent variable when the value of the independent variable is 0. Thus if *a* was equal to 28, we would predict that even someone without any formal education would attain a score of 28 on the index.

The symbol *b* represents the **slope** of the regression line. It is also called the regression coefficient. It is interpreted as the average change in the dependent variable associated with a single unit change in the independent variable. A *b* value of 2, for example, would mean that every unit increase in the independent variable corresponds to an average increase of 2 units in the dependent variable. In our example, a *b* value of 2 would imply that each additional year of education results in a higher average index score of 2. Before we show you how to use this line to predict one's score on the index, let's calculate the slope and Y-intercept for the data we presented about the relationship between one's level of education and one's viewpoint about government activity.

Calculating the Slope   The formula for calculating the slope (*b*) is:

$$b = \frac{N\left(\sum XY\right) - \left(\sum X\right)\left(\sum Y\right)}{N\left(\sum X^2\right) - \left(\sum X\right)^2}$$

The formula for calculating the Y-intercept (*a*) is:

$$a = \frac{\sum Y - b\left(\sum X\right)}{N}$$

For the data on level of education and the index score presented in the above figures, b and a are calculated as presented in Table 14.18.

To calculate the slope you need to take the following steps:

1. Obtain the sum for the independent variable (X). 115
2. Obtain the sum for the dependent variable (Y). 685
3. Multiply the value of the dependent variable for each case by the value of the independent variable for each case (XY).
4. Obtain the sum for the products obtained in step 3. 8333
5. Square the value of the independent variable (X) for each case (X^2).
6. Obtain the sum of the squared independent variables. 1405
7. Substitute the results from steps 1–6 into the formula.

$$b = \frac{10(8333) - (115)(685)}{10(1405) - (13225)} \quad \frac{83330 - 78775}{1450 - 13225} = \frac{4555}{825} = 5.521212$$

The slope (b) for our data equals 5.521212.

When you calculated the slope you produced all the information you need to calculate the Y-intercept.

$$a = \frac{685 - 5.52(115)}{10} = \frac{685 - 634.8}{10} = 5.02$$

The Y-intercept (a) for our data equals 5.02. When you substitute these values into the regression line equation, you get

predicted index score = 5.52 + 5.02 (actual level of education)

An Application   We have now determined the constants (a and b) that we use in the regression formula. For linear relationships, these constants provide our *"best guess"* of values of the dependent variable (score on the scale) given values of the independent variable (level of education). Thus, the regression routine gives us a powerful predictive tool. We use information on one variable (level of education) to predict expected scores on another variable (scale score). Of course we know the precise scale score in our group of ten students, but the regression routine allows us to state the effect on the score associated with changing levels of education. We can say, for example, that an increase of one year of education is associated with an increase of approximately 5 points on the scale score. Further, if this sample of students were assumed to be representative of all students, you can use this information to predict the expected scale score of all students in the population. For example, if a student has seven years of education, what would you predict her score would be on the ideological scale? Using our regression formula we find the following:

predicted score = 5.52 + 5.02(7) = 40.66.

TABLE 14.19

CALCULATION OF THE SIMPLE CORRELATION COEFFICIENT

Years of Education and Index Score

Education (X)	Score (Y)	XY	X²	Y²
7	42	294	49	1764
8	46	368	64	2116
9	52	468	81	2704
10	63	630	100	3969
11	70	770	121	4900
12	75	900	144	5625
13	80	1040	169	6400
14	82	1148	196	6724
15	85	1275	225	7225
16	90	1440	256	8100
Totals 115	685	8333	1405	49527

The Correlation Coefficient (r)   Just how accurate is our prediction equation? That is, how good will our prediction of the scale score be based on our knowledge about the level of education? To answer this question we use a statistic called the correlation coefficient or Pearson's product moment correlation coefficient (*r*). The **correlation coefficient** gives us an idea of the strength of the relationship between the two variables. Similar to ordinal measures of association the correlation coefficient has a range of values from −1 to +1. The closer a value is to −1 or 1, the stronger the relationship in a negative or positive direction. A value of zero implies the absence of a linear relationship between the two variables. A positive coefficient indicates that as one variable increases (or decreases) in value, so does the other. A negative coefficient indicates that as one variable declines in value the other increases. The formula for *r* is

$$r = \frac{N(\sum XY) - (\sum X)(\sum Y)}{[N \sum X^2 - (\sum X)^2][N \sum Y^2 - (\sum Y)^2]}$$

As we did before, let's enhance our explanation by computing the correlation coefficient for our hypothetical data dealing with education and the government perception scale scores (as in Table 14.19).

Follow these steps to calculate the correlation coefficient (*r*)

1. Sum the values of *X* and the values of *Y*. 115 and 685
2. For each case, calculate the products of the *X* and *Y* values.
3. Sum the products. 8333

4. Square each *X* and each *Y* value.

5. Sum the *X* and *Y* squared values. 1405 and 49527

6. Substitute the values into the formula for *r* and calculate.

$$r = \frac{10(8333) - (115)(685)}{\sqrt{[10(1405) - (13225)][10(49527) - 469225]}} = .98 \text{ (rounded)}$$

Similar to phi and the lower level data statistics we discussed, *r* does not have an operational value. You cannot say, for example, that the *r* value is equal to a certain percent. It just depicts a "strength of association" between variables. For example, the correlation coefficient value of .98 that we computed, tells us that there is a very strong positive association, or strong correlation, between the two variables. A common question then is "How do I interpret the magnitude of a correlation coefficient?" This is not so difficult for those reduction of error and variance tests such as lambda, gamma, and *r* square (discussion to follow), which have intrinsic meaning of their own. For *r* though, it is more difficult. Thus, you need to use Table 14.8.

Some Cautions When Using the Correlation Coefficient   When using the correlation coefficient you need to examine all of your data, not just the correlation coefficient. Because the correlation coefficient is a summarizing statistic, some may be tempted to rely solely on its value to determine associations. This could result in overlooking important deviations from the major trend. Thus, you should examine the data distribution and consider as much information as possible.

An advantage of correlation techniques is their precision. They allow you to take a large set of data and clarify underlying relationships. A disadvantage, however, is the fact that you may end up with a false sense of precision (Cole 1980). The coefficient is the product of many factors including the actual relationship between the variables. However, other factors may also influence the coefficient. For example, if you make errors in the recording and reporting of information, you will end up with a misleading coefficient. Sampling errors could also impact its calculation and the subsequent interpretation. In addition, missing values for some cases and using an inappropriate level of data in the computation will impact the results. But mistakes do happen. Therefore, you should remember that the correlation coefficient is an approximation of the actual relationship.

You should also beware of ecological and individualistic fallacies. Ecological fallacy refers to the possibility of incorrectly reaching conclusions about the behavior of individuals based on aggregate data. For example, data collected at the state level that shows that states with higher levels of education are more likely to have a higher voting turnout rate cannot be interpreted to mean better educated individuals in each state would always be more likely to vote. To make inferences about individuals, one needs to collect information at the individual level.

Individualistic fallacy occurs when inferences of group behavior are made on the basis of information collected from individuals. Data collected from individual voters that show that a person with a higher level of education is more politically active should not be used to conclude that the states with lower education levels will have lower voting turnout rates. If you want to make a statement about states, you need to collect data at the state level.

You should not confuse correlation with causation. Determining correlation is only one step in determining causation. Remember our previous discussions about causation. To determine **causation,** time order, nonspuriousness, and theoretical importance need to be demonstrated when determining causation. Correlation only supports the notion of covariance. Thus, high correlation results do not mean that changes in the independent variable causes changes in the dependent variable. Statistical associations that are not causal relationships are called spurious relationships. We will spend more time talking about causation in Chapter 15.

The Coefficient of Determination (r²)   The **coefficient of determination** (r^2) is very helpful when you want to explain the variance in a dependent variable. The range of values for this statistic is from 0 to 1. What makes this statistic useful is the fact that its value is expressed as a percentage of the variation in the dependent variable that is explained, or accounted for, by the dependent variable. For example, a value of .76 would be expressed as explaining 76 percent of the variance in the dependent variable. The coefficient of determination value in our example is approximately .96. We interpret this value by saying, "The education level of students accounts for approximately 96 percent of the variance in the scores attained by students on the profile scale." The level of education of students is a very good predictor of scale scores for these students. Thus, interpretation of this statistic is similar to the interpretation of lambda with nominal data and the gamma statistic that we use with ordinal data.

Test of Significance for the Correlation Coefficient   When we were working with nominal and ordinal data, we wanted to know whether our observed relationships were statistically significant. That is, could we generalize our sample findings to the population? For these lower levels of data, you will recall that we used the chi square statistic to give us this information. For the correlation coefficient we use the F test.

The test of significance for r requires us to make several assumptions. First, there is a linear relationship. Second, our sample is random. Last the variables are normally distributed in the population. This latter assumption is especially important when our sample is made up of less than 30 cases. We can relax this assumption somewhat for larger samples. The formula for the F test is

$$F = \frac{r^2(N-2)}{1-r^2}$$

where

r = the correlation coefficient

N = the number of cases (observations)

When we use the F test we also need to compute two types of degrees of freedom. The first one is equal to the number of independent variables minus 1. The second is the number of cases minus 2 ($N - 2$). For our hypothetical example the degrees of freedom are 1 and 8. The F ratio for the example is

$$F = \frac{.96(8)}{.04} = 192$$

After you calculate the statistic you need to use a table of F values. Go to Table A5 in Appendix III. Notice for 1 and 8 degrees of freedom, a value of 5.32 is needed to conclude statistical significance at the .05 level and a value of 11.26 is needed to conclude significance at the .01 level. What value is needed to conclude statistical significance at the .001 level? Since our calculated value of 192 is greater than the table value, we can conclude that our relationship is statistically significant. In other words, we can generalize our findings to the population from which our sample was drawn.

❖ SUMMARY

We covered quite a bit of ground in this chapter. We examined some useful ways to analyze the relationship among two variables measured at the nominal, ordinal, and interval levels of measurement. Because we only analyze two variables at one time, we call this type of analysis bivariate analysis.

Our major purpose in this chapter was to introduce you to the notion of association and show you some ways to determine whether there was a relationship between two variables. We also said that there are several questions we need to answer to determine causation. First, is there a relationship between the variables we are analyzing? Second, what is the strength of the relationship? Third, what is the direction of the relationship? Is it positive, or is it a negative relationship? Fourth, is the relationship statistically significant? What are the odds that the relationship we observe in our sample will also be present in the population? In other words, can we generalize the relationship to the population from which the sample was drawn? Last, is the relationship nonspurious, or can it be explained by a third variable?

Bivariate tabular analysis is one of several ways to determine whether two variables are related. Careful scrutiny of a properly constructed table will answer our first three questions. We compare the columnar percentages to determine whether there is a relationship. We assess the magnitude of the percentage differences to determine the strength of our relationship. We also examine the pattern of the percentages to determine the direction of the relationship we observe.

Measures of association, however, enhance this process for us. We have an array of measures that not only answer these questions (phi, lambda, tau *c*, gamma, correlation coefficient) but also tell us if the relationship is statistically significant (chi square). How do we know which statistic to use? It depends on the level of data for our variables, the size of the table, and whether we have a symmetrical or assymetrical relationship.

But what about our last question, is the relationship nonspurious, or can it be explained by a third variable? The next chapter presents statistical procedures for answering this question.

❖ KEY TERMS

association	measures of association
assymetrical statistic	null hypothesis (Ho)
bivariate analysis	off diagonal
bivariate relationship	perfect relationship
bivariate table	phi coefficient
causation	population
chi square	proportionate reduction in error (PRE)
coefficient of determination	range of values
correlation coefficient	regression analysis
Cramer's V	research hypothesis
degrees of freedom	sample
F ratio	scattergram
gamma	slope
lambda	Sommer's D
level of significance	symmetrical statistic
linear equation	tau statistic
linear relationship	weak relationship
main diagonal	Y-intercept

❖ EXERCISES

1. Review Table 14.20. Then complete the questions.
   a. What is the independent variable?
   b. What is the dependent variable?
   c. Interpret the above table.
   d. How many males and how many females believe in capital punishment?
   e. How many males and how many females oppose capital punishment?
2. Review Table 14.21. Then complete the questions.
   a. What is the independent variable?
   b. What is the dependent variable?
   c. Interpret the above table.
   d. How many Anglos and how many non-Anglos voted in the 1992 general election?

TABLE 14.20

VIEWPOINT ON CAPITAL PUNISHMENT BY GENDER (IN PERCENTAGES)

	Gender	
Capital Punishment OK?	Males	Females
Yes	55	53
No	45	47
Total	100	100
(n)	(525)	(410)

Source: Hypothetical

TABLE 14.21

VOTING BY RACE (IN PERCENTAGES)

	Race	
Vote in 1992 General Election?	Anglo	Non-Anglo
Yes	59	42
No	41	58
Total	100	100
(n)	(400)	(325)

Source: Hypothetical

TABLE 14.22

VIEWPOINT ON PRAYER IN PUBLIC SCHOOLS BY POLITICAL PARTY (IN PERCENTAGES)

	Political Party	
Organized Prayer in Public Schools OK?	Republican	Democratic
Yes	83	18
No	17	82
Total	100	100
(n)	(425)	(475)

Source: Hypothetical

TABLE 14.23

SUPPORT FOR NATIONAL HEALTH LEGISLATION BY POLITICAL PARTY

	Political Party	
Vote on Health Bill	**Democratic**	**Republican**
Yes	229	41
No	33	123
Total	262	164

Source: Hypothetical

TABLE 14.24

Gender	Harrassed	Gender	Harrassed	Gender	Harrassed
Male	No	Female	No	Female	Yes
Male	Yes	Male	Yes	Female	Yes
Female	Yes	Female	Yes	Female	Yes
Female	Yes	Male	Yes	Female	No
Female	No	Male	No	Female	Yes
Male	No	Male	No	Male	Yes
Female	Yes	Female	Yes	Male	No
Female	Yes	Male	No	Male	No
Female	No	Male	No	Female	Yes
Male	No	Female	Yes	Female	Yes

    e. How many Anglos and how many non-Anglos did not vote in the 1992 general election?

3. Review Table 14.22. Then complete the questions.

    a. What is the independent variable?

    b. What is the dependent variable?

    c. Interpret the above table.

    d. How many Republicans and how many Democrats believe in organized prayer in public schools?

    e. How many Republicans and how many Democrats oppose organized prayer in public schools?

4. Review Table 14.23. Then complete the questions.

    a. What is the independent variable?

    b. What is the dependent variable?

    c. Interpret the above table.

    d. Calculate and interpret the most appropriate measure of association.

    e. Calculate and interpret the chi-square statistic.

5. Consider the following hypothetical data in Table 14.24 pertaining to gender and whether a respondent has ever been sexually harrassed.

    a. What is the independent variable?

    b. What is the dependent variable?

    c. Construct a bivariate table depicting frequencies and percentages. Make sure the table is in accordance with the chapter discussion.

    d. Calculate and interpret the appropriate measure of association.

    e. Calculate and interpret the chi square statistic.

6. Discuss the components of the simple regression model.

7. Review the following regression model. Then complete the questions.

$$VT = .44 + .5(E)$$
$$F = 35 \ (prob = .001)$$

where

    VT = percent voting turnout in the state

    E = median level of education in the state

    a. What is the dependent variable?

    b. What is the independent variable?

    c. What is the value of the Y-intercept? Interpret the Y-intercept.

    d. What is the value of the slope? Interpret the slope.

    e. Interpret the F ratio.

    f. What is the predicted voting turnout for a state with a median level of education equal to 10 years? 15 years?

❖ SUGGESTED READINGS

Bernstein, Robert A., and James A. Dyer. *An Introduction to Political Science Methods,* 2nd ed. Englewood Cliffs, NJ: Prentice-Hall, 1984.

Blaylock, Hubert M., Jr. *Social Statistics,* 2nd ed. New York: McGraw-Hill, 1979.

Bowen Bruce D., and Herbert F. Weisberg. *An Introduction to Survey Research and Data Analysis.* San Francisco: Freeman, 1977.

Dometrius, Nelson C. *Social Statistics Using SPSS.* New York: HarperCollins, 1992.

Fox, William. *Social Statistics Using MicroCase.* Chicago: Nelson-Hall, 1993.

Frankfort-Nachmias, Chava, and David Nachmias. *Research Methods in the Social Sciences,* 4th ed. New York: St. Martin's Press, 1992.

Johnson, Janet Buttolph, and Richard A. Joslyn. *Political Science Research Methods.* Washington: Congressional Quarterly Press, 1986.

Kay, Susan Ann. *Introduction to the Analysis of Political Data.* Englewood Cliffs, NJ: Prentice-Hall, 1991.

Leedy, Paul D. *Practical Research: Planning and Design,* 3rd ed. New York: Macmillan, 1985.

Wang, Chamant. *Sense and Nonsense of Statistical Inference.* New York: Morrel Dekker, 1992.

DATA ANALYSIS: MULTIVARIATE ANALYSIS

❖ INTRODUCTION

To this point, our data analysis discussions have concentrated on the characteristics of a single variable (univariate analysis) and the isolated impact of one independent variable on a dependent variable (bivariate analysis). Political scientists, however, are also interested in assessing the relative and combined impacts of a number of independent variables on a dependent variable. They want to know, for example, the relative and combined impacts of all variables related to the voting behavior of American legislators, the power of governments in other nations, and the civic culture of other democratic nations. The classification of techniques useful for such analyses is called **multivariate analysis.**

An understanding of this chapter will enable you to:

1. Understand the nature of control.
2. Understand the ways we control for the impact of other independent variables on a dependent variable.
3. Interpret the effects of introducing a control variable.
4. Understand the advantages and disadvantages of the various methods of control.
5. Understand and interpret the components of the multiple regression model.
6. Understand and interpet beta weights.

❖ ON THE NATURE OF CONTROL

Research would be simpler if we could always explain phenomena by only one other factor. Unfortunately this is rarely the case. It is unusual for one variable to provide a satisfactory and complete explanation of another variable. Thus, to thoroughly understand a particular variable, we often examine that variable in reference to several independent variables. In so doing, we may find that an original bivariate relationship that appeared to be strong may be quite weak, stronger, or unchanged. Thus, accounting for the influence of additional independent variables can affect an original relationship in many ways.

The researcher uses the concept of **control** to amplify and focus the research effort. Control is the next logical step after you find a relationship between an independent and dependent variable. Controlling techniques are important because they help you to clarify the critical issue of causation. Controlling techniques address the notion of nonspuriousness. Hopefully you will recall from Chapter 9 that a nonspurious relationship between two variables is an association, or covariation, that you cannot explain with a third variable. If, for example, the original correlation vanishes or the original correlation is significantly reduced when accounting for the third factor, we say that the original relationship was spurious. In short, there was not a causative relationship between the two original variables.

Recall our example about the causes of juvenile delinquency. A novice researcher thought she found a causal relationship between ice cream sales (X1) and juvenile crime (X2). Those areas of the city having a high level of ice cream sales also had a high level of juvenile crime. She also discovered that the criteria of time order and covariance applied to her findings. Correlating the two variables, the researcher found a fairly high positive correlation. This suggested that areas of the city with high juvenile crime rates also had higher levels of ice cream sales.

$$X1\overset{}{\underset{.80}{\rule{3cm}{0.4pt}}}\rightarrow X2$$

But is this a valid correlation? Or, does a third factor explain both the level of ice cream sales and juvenile crime? In other words, was this a nonspurious relationship?

Further research indicated that those areas with a high rate of juvenile crime also had more juveniles living in the neighborhood (X3). The correlations produced from her efforts showed that there was a strong correlation between a younger population and increased ice cream sales and increased levels of juvenile crime, as illustrated in Figure 15.1.

Based on these statistics, our researcher concluded that a younger population contributed to both increased ice cream sales and increased levels of juvenile crime. In short, a third variable explained the change in both the independent and dependent variables. Additionally, the original correlation vanished. If this is the case, then we say that a spurious relationship existed between juvenile crime and ice cream sales.

Determining causality and identifying spurious relationships is a difficult and trying phase of scientific research. To accomplish this task, you must consider all possible intervening variables and their effect on the independent and dependent variables. In statistical analysis we say that you must control for the effects of a third variable. If you find that change in a third variable

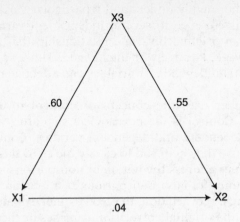

FIGURE 15.1 **Three-Variable model**

explains change in the independent and dependent variables, the original relationship is spurious. Conversely, if you find that a third variable does not affect the independent or dependent variable, then the original relationship is nonspurious. In either case, you will have satisfied an important criterion of causality.

We have briefly discussed the nature of control and presented an example to give you an idea about what we are talking about. Now we need to turn our attention to the various statistical methods we have at our disposal to control for the impact of a third variable.

❖ METHODS OF CONTROL

◆ MULTIVARIATE CROSSTABULATION

As with bivariate analysis, you use crosstabulation to analyze the impact of a control variable on the observed relationship between two variables measured at the nominal or ordinal level. This procedure requires you to reexamine the original relationship between the independent and dependent variables for each category of the control variable. The original correlation (gamma, Cramer's V, etc.) is compared with the correlation for each category of control. Any changes you observe are said to result from the influence of the third variable. Consider the following example. On June 24, 1993, the U.S. House of Representatives took a vote to determine the future of the Superconducting Super Collider, a scientific project underway near Waxahachie, Texas. Concerned about the cost of the project and the country's budget deficit, many wanted to terminate the project. A political science undergraduate student wanted to analyze the vote by the representative's region of the country. She hypothesized that legislators whose districts were near Texas would vote to continue the project, which was perceived by many to be an economic boost to the region. Table 15.1 depicts the vote by region of the country.

TABLE 15.1

SUPER COLLIDER VOTE: U.S. HOUSE OF REPRESENTATIVES BY REGION OF THE COUNTRY

	Region of the Country				
Vote	Northeast	Midwest	South	West	Total
Discontinue	54 (79)	101 (77)	67 (47)	58 (63)	280
Continue project	14 (21)	30 (23)	74 (53)	32 (34)	150
Did not vote	0	1	1	3 (3)	5
Total	68	132	142	93	435
Cramer's V = .29					

Table 15.1 depicts a low positive relationship between the representative's region and the vote for the Super Collider project. Even without the 30 supportive votes cast by the Texan representatives, however, 44 other southern representatives supported the project. This number is higher than any other region. In sum, almost half of the votes in support of the project came from the southern region. Thus, the student's hypothesis has some preliminary support. At this point you may be asking, What about statistical significance? Well, what about it? We have the voting results of the entire membership of the U.S. House of Representatives. Therefore, statistical significance is not a concern because we are not working with a sample.

Our student, however, suspects that the legislators' political party affiliation (PID) will also influence their vote. In other words, perhaps it is the representatives' PID, not the location of their constituency, that is the more important factor in predicting legislative vote on this project. To test for this possibility, she prepares a distribution that depicts the vote by PID seen in Table 15.2.

Six percent more Republicans than Democrats voted to continue the project. Although there is a relationship between PID and support for the project, the association is negligible. Therefore, there does not seem to be a substantial difference between PID and support for the project. It would be difficult, in other words, to predict a representative's vote based on party affiliation. Because there is a relationship between PID and the Super Collider vote, our student creates a table to reexamine the original relationship between region and the vote while controlling for the political party of the representative. This technique divides the original table into two tables. One table represents the voting patterns of Republican legislators from the various regions and one represents the voting patterns of Democrat legislators from the regions. In this manner, our student can assess the influence of partisanship on legislative vote under conditions in which the location of the constituency does not vary. Table 15.3 depicts the results of her efforts.

TABLE 15.2

SUPER COLLIDER VOTE: U.S. HOUSE OF REPRESENTATIVES BY POLITICAL PARTY

| | Political Party | | |
Vote	Republican	Democratic	Total
Discontinue	105 (61)	175 (67)	280
Continue project	65 (38)	83 (32)	150
Did not vote	2 (1)	3 (1)	5
Total	172	263	435
Cramer's V = .07			

TABLE 15.3

SUPER COLLIDER VOTE: U.S. HOUSE OF REPRESENTATIVES BY REGION OF THE COUNTRY CONTROLLING FOR POLITICAL PARTY

| | Republican | | | | | Democratic | | | | |
Vote	NE	MW	S	W	Total	NE	MW	S	W	Total
Discontinue	23	2	23	17	105	30	59	44	41	174
Continue	5	13	27	20	65	9	17	47	12	85
Did not vote	0	1	0	1	2	0	0	1	2	3
Total	28	56	50	38	172	39	76	92	55	262
	Cramer's V = .33					Cramer's V = .31				

Before we continue we need to introduce you to an important term—
partial tables. When you use crosstabular methods to control for the effect of
another variable, a table is produced for each category of the control variable.
Statisticians call these tables partial tables.

As you can see by the Cramer's V scores for each partial table, there was
little change. In fact the original relationship is somewhat stronger. Regardless of the representative's party allegiance, representatives from the southern
region were still more likely to suport the project while representatives from
the other regions were still more likely to oppose the project. The student can
conclude that controlling for party has not affected the original relationship.
Thus, the representative's region continues to explain legislative voting behavior even when we control for the effect of party. In this case, Fox says the orig-

inal relationship was replicated (Fox 1993, 232). That is, each partial table is almost identical to the original table.

Before we move on, let's discuss some other possibilites that could occur for our budding researcher. First, assume she attained Cramer's V scores of .00 when controlling for the Republican party and .04 when controlling for the Democratic party. In this example, when she controlled for the influence of party, the original relationship of .29 virtually disappears. Hence, controlling for party justifies the conclusion that there is no relationship between the legislator's region and vote for this particular scientific project. Thus, the original relationship is said to be spurious. Partisanship explains the vote, not regionalism. In this case, the control variable explained the relationship.

Now let's consider another possibility. Suppose the student attained a Cramer's V of .53 when controlling for the Republicans and a Cramer's V of .03 when controlling for the Democrats. This possibility illustrates an instance in which the association for one category of the control variable was greatly reduced. For the other category, however, the original relationship increased. How is this to be interpreted? PID is a differentiating factor in voting on this bill for Democratic legislators. Despite the location of their constituency, Democrats oppose the project. Thus, for Democratic legislators, party identification is a very important factor. Partisanship and region, however, are both important factors for explaining the Republican vote on the bill. Republicans from the southern and western regions, for example, are more supportive than the Democrats and more supportive than those Republicans representing the Northeast and Midwest.

◆ SUMMARY

You can see from these examples that controlling for the influence of a third factor can have any number of possible effects on the original relationship between variables. Crosstabulation control procedures are very useful in that they allow us to examine the correlation between two variables for each level of the control variable. Thus we are able to observe factors in the relationships that would otherwise remain undetected. This procedure, however, can produce some confounding results that will tend to confuse you. Therefore, we suggest that you use Table 15.4 as a guide when working with partial tables.

◆ DISADVANTAGES OF CROSSTABULATION PROCEDURES

When you use crosstabulation control procedures you may find that there are several disadvantages. First, the procedure can be somewhat cumbersome. The example we presented above only dealt with one control variable having only two categories of control. Yet you had to compare the original measure of association with the measures generated for two partial tables and interpret the change in measures. We're somewhat sure this was confusing for you. Now imagine working with three or four control variables, each having several categories. A dozen or more partial tables might be generat-

TABLE 15.4

EFFECT AND INTERPRETATION OF INTRODUCING A CONTROL VARIABLE

Empirical Effect of Introduction of Control Variable	Substantive Interpretation	Implications for Further Analysis
Relationship between independent and dependent variables virtually unchanged.	Evidence that the independent variable is related to the dependent variable and that the control variable is not related to the dependent variable.	Eliminate control variable from further analysis. Continue analysis of relationship between independent and dependent variables.
Relationship between independent and dependent variables virtually disappears (spurious).	Evidence that the independent variable is not related to the dependent variable and that the control variable is related to the dependent variable.	Eliminate independent variable from analysis. Control variable becomes new independent variable in further analysis.
Relationship between independent and dependent variables changes markedly depending upon the category of the control variable (interaction).	Relationship between the three variables is interactive.	Both independent and control variables must be considered in further analysis.
Relationship between independent and dependent variables is weakened but persists in each of the control tables.	Evidence that both independent and control variables are related to the dependent variable.	Both independent and control variables must be considered in further analysis.

ed. This would really confound the analysis and interpretation processes for you.

Crosstabulation procedures are also limited by the size of the sample. Crosstabulation divides the sample into smaller and smaller subsamples for each category of control. It does not take long to exhaust all cases. Unless the number of cases is very large, it is difficult to apply more than two or three crosstabulation controls at the same time.

◆ PARTIAL CORRELATION

You use **partial correlation** procedures with interval/ratio-level data. This procedure is not limited by sample size. In addition, it is not as cumbersome as cross-tabulations. The method extends the logic of simple regression in that knowledge of an independent variable helps us to predict values of a linear dependent variable. However, seldom does regression explain all the variance in a dependent variable. Some error in prediction remains. This error in prediction is called the "unexplained variance," or the **residuals.** Residuals represent those deviations in the dependent variable left unaccounted for by variations in the independent variable $(1 - r^2)$. They also help us to understand the concept of the partial correlation coefficient. For example, assume that we are interested in the relationship between two interval-level variables but believe that a third variable may also affect this relationship. We suspect that the original relationship observed between the two variables may really result from the fact that the two are related to the third variable. One way to test this is to perform regressions between the two original variables (X1 and X2) and the third variable (X3). That is, two regression equations are generated: one predicting the values of X1 based on X3 $(Y < X1 > = a + bX3)$ and one predicting the values of X2 based on X3 $(Y < x2 > = a + bX3)$. The residual values that result represent the variation in both X1 and X2 that is unexplained by X3. The correlation of these residuals represents the correlation of X1 and X2 controlling for the effect of X3 on each. The result is the partial correlation between X1 and X2 controlling for X3. Following is the formula:

$$r_{12.3} = r_{12} - \frac{(r_{13})(r_{23})}{\sqrt{1 - r_{13}^1}\sqrt{1 - r_{23}^2}}$$

where

1 and 2 = dependent and independent variables

3 = control variable

Let's look at the following hypothetical illustration to enhance our discussion. We sampled 2,000 adults and collected data dealing with levels of income and support for limited government intervention in the economy. From our sample we find a simple correlation of .45. Those with higher levels of income were found to be more supportive of limited governmental intervention. But we suspect that some other factor may be responsible for this apparent correlation. Having also collected information on education, we find the following correlation matrix for the three variables:

	X1	X2	X3
X_1 (limit government)	1.0	.45	.55
X_2 (income)	.45	1.0	.65
X_3 (education)	.55	.65	1.0

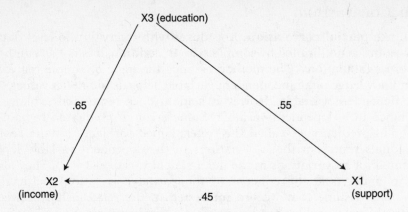

FIGURE 15.2 Proposed Three-Variable Model

We see that education is related to both variables, so we may be dealing with a possible spurious situation. In this instance the model we are testing might be as shown in Figure 15.2.

Applying the formula, we see that the partial correlation between income and support for a decreased role for government in the economic arena is:

$$r_{12.3} = r_{12} - \frac{(r_{13})\,(r_{23})}{\sqrt{1 - r_{13}^2}\,\sqrt{1 - r_{23}^2}} = \frac{.45 - (.55)\,(.65)}{\sqrt{1 - .55^2}\,\sqrt{1 - .65^2}} = \frac{.0925}{.634669} = .146$$

The partial correlation is .146. In this example, we have reduced the original correlation between income and support substantially (.146 versus .45). Therefore, we can conclude that the relationship between income and support for limiting the government's role in the economic policy arena is spurious. Education is the important factor in each instance. Those with higher education levels have higher incomes and are more supportive of efforts to reduce big government.

◆ **SUMMARY**

Partial correlations determine the correlation between the residuals produced by a regression model. Original results produced between two variables are compared with the results produced by a third variable in separate interactions with both variables. If the original results are altered or disappear, the original relationship is spurious.

There are several advantages that partial correlation has over partial crosstabulation procedures. First, unlike crosstabulations, a single statistic is used to determine relationships. Second, there is not a need for numerous tables. Third, more than one variable can be controlled for simultaneously.

A disadvantage is that partial correlations involves the 631 "averaging" of residual impacts and partials. Thus, some essential information could be obscured.

◆ MULTIPLE REGRESSION

The general regression equation for multivariate analysis is an extension of the simple regression equation. The following is the general form of the linear **multiple regression** model:

$$Y = a + B_1 X_1 + B_2 X_2 + B_3 X_3 + B_i X_i + e$$

Let's take some time to examine the components of this equation. The Y represents the dependent variable, or effect variable. It is the variable that the researcher is trying to explain. The X1, X2, X3, and Xi components represent the independent variables, or cause variables. They are the variables used to explain variations in the Y dependent variable. Each subscript identifies the separate independent variable. The i subscript represents the last variable in the model.

As in the simple regression model, the a represents the Y-intercept. It is also called the "constant" and is represented as such in computer printout results. It estimates the average value of Y (dependent variable) when the independent variables are equal to zero.

The B1, B2, B3, and Bi, are known as **partial slopes** with their computed values reflected as "coefficients" on the computer printout. Interpretation of the partial slope B1 represents the average change in the dependent variable, Y, 632 associated with a unit change in the independent variable X1, when the other independent variables are held constant. Thus, the values of the coefficients determine the contribution of the independent variables on the dependent variable. With this means of statistical control, you can isolate the effect of the X1 variable itself, free of any distorting influences from the other independent variables. Thus, the reason B1 is called a partial slope, or partial regression coefficient. Bi represents the last coefficient in the equation.

The e represents the **random error** term. Without a random error term, the model would be deterministic in that the values of the dependent variable can always be determined exactly when the value of the independent variables and intercept are known. However, with the inclusion of the random error term, the model becomes probabalistic in that there is an allowance for error in the predictive capabilities of the model. Thus, the values of the independent variables, by themselves, do not determine the value of the dependent variable.

The random error term is used to account for errors that may arise because of the omission of pertinent independent variables in the model or because of errors in the collection and measurement of the data (values of X's).

Again let's examine an example to enhance our discussion. A student studying international politics developed a model to explain a nation's status as a world military power. His model shows:

$$PR = 24 + 10P + 9M + 2AF + 12MB + 23N + e \quad R^2 = 0.78$$

$N = 50$

where

PR = power rating

P = population (in millions)

M = persons in uniform (in thousands)

AF = persons in the Air Force (in thousands)

MB = military budget (in millions)

N = nuclear weaponry (estimated number of nuclear warheads)

The above regression model is a probabalistic model since there is an error term (e) included. This implies that you cannot determine exactly the value of the dependent variable when the values of the independent variables are known. There is some allowance for error in this model. There are some other variable(s) we have not discovered that may also explain the perception of a nation's military might. The components of the model are these: PR represents the dependent variable, or effect variable. It is the variable that the researcher is trying to explain (the nation's military power rating). The symbols P, M, AF, MB, and N represent the independent variables, or cause variables. They are the hypothesized variables used to explain variations in the dependent variable. In this example, the researcher is trying to determine if the independent variables explain variation in the nation's military power rating.

The value 24 is the value of the Y-intercept. As with simple regression, it is called the intercept because it indicates the point where the regression line "intercepts" the Y-axis in a graphical depiction of the equation. It estimates the average value of the dependent variable, military power rating, when the independent variables equal zero.

This example highlights a problem when interpreting the intercept. That is, at times the intercept can present misleading information. For example, if the intercept has a negative value, and the independent variables equal 0, the predicted value of the dependent variable would equal the negative value. In this example it would be difficult to have a negative power rating. This is the intercept, or constant, is added to the other components in order for the dependent variable to be properly estimated. In economic terms the constant represents a "fixed cost" that must be included along with the "varying costs" (independent variable values) in order to calculate total cost.

The figures 10, 9, 2, 12, and 23, are known as partial slopes with their computed values reflected as "coefficients" on the computer printout. Interpretation of the partial slope 10 represents the average change in the dependent variable, PR, associated with a unit change in the independent variable, P, when the other independent variables are held constant. With this means of statistical control, one is able to isolate the effect of the P variable itself, free of any distorting influences from the other independent variables. This is the reason figure 10 is called a partial slope, or partial regression coefficient.

In the above example, the partial slope for the P independent variable estimates that for every million people in the country, the power rating of the nation will increase by 10 points. The partial slope for the M independent variable estimates that for every million people in the military, in the country, the power rating will increase by 9 points.

The R-squared (R^2) in this model is known as the **coefficient of multiple determination.** Researchers use this statistic to assess the goodness of fit of the multiple regression, or least squares prediction equation. The R-square for the equation indicates the proportion of variation in the dependent variable, PR, explained by all of the independent variables. In other words, R-squared represents the fraction of the sample variation of the dependent variable values that is explained by the least squares prediction equation. In our example, the R-squared of .78, indicates that the nation's population, armed forces, Air Force, military spending, and nuclear warheads, explains 78 percent of the nation's variation in their military power rating.

Thus, an R-square of 0 implies a complete lack of fit of 636 the model to the data. On the other hand, an R-squared of 1 implies a perfect fit with the model passing through every data point. In general, the larger the R-squared value, the better the model fits the data. Therefore, R-squared is a sample statistic that tells us how well the model fits the data and thereby represents a measure of the usefulness of the entire model.

◆ DETERMINING THE RELATIVE IMPORTANCE OF COEFFICIENTS

As discussed above, B coefficients reflect the net effect of each independent variable on the dependent variable. You can also use them to denote the relative importance of the independent variables. However, because each variable is often measured on a different scale and in different units, (that is, dollars versus years), the coefficient should be standardized to truly be comparable.

Beta Weights   The standardized equivalent of the B coefficient is called the **beta weight,** or the beta coefficient. The mathematical process to obtain beta weights is to subtract the mean for the variable and divide by its standard deviation. As a result, the standardized variables have a mean of 0 and a variance of 1. Once the variables all have the same variance, new regression coefficients are calculated. Thus, beta weights are standardized measures and their values are not distorted by comparing one variable measured in dollars to another variable measured in percentages, or some other unit of measurement. Therefore, they allow you to see the relative importance of each independent variable in the model.

Beta weights are important because they measure how many standard deviation units the dependent variable in a multiple regression equation changes with a change of one standard deviation unit in the independent variable, while controlling for other independent variables. For example, if education has a beta weight of .765 and tenure has a beta weight of .125, and the dependent variable is income, the model shows that for every increase of one standard deviation in education, income increases by .765 standard deviations, and with an increase of one standard deviation in tenure, income increases by .125 standard deviations. Thus, it allows you to ascertain the relative importance of particular variables while controlling for other variables.

In sum, beta weights are standardized coefficients in the regression equation that have been translated to a uniform scale and can easily be used to compare the relative strength of the variables. For instance, in the above example, it is clear that education explains more of the variation in income than does the tenure variable.

Statistical Significance   Although not applicable for this example because we have information about a population (all states) versus a sample, another way to judge the relative importance of each of the independent variables is to determine if the coefficients associated with each variable are significant. To accomplish this we set up a null hypothesis and use the t-test as the test statistic. For example, Ho: B = 0. If the null is not rejected, then we can say that the independent variable has no impact on the variation in the dependent variable. To obtain the t-statistic, you divide the B coefficient by its standard deviation. (Computer programs routinely print out the t-score or t-ratio.) Then we determine the rejection region by choosing a level of significance, say .05, determine whether we need to use a one- or two-tailed test (two-tailed for this example), and calculate the degrees of freedom. To determine the degrees of freedom, we subtract the number of B parameters in the model (4), plus 1 from the number of observations (29 as an example), which equals 24. Then, we determine the tabulated t-statistic for a rejection region at $a = .05$, two-tailed test, and 24 df which is 2.064. We will reject the null hypothesis if the calculated t-statistic is greater than 2.064. If we reject the null hypothesis, then we say that the variable is significant and does explain variation in the dependent variable. We do this for each variable. Those variables having the highest absolute t-value are usually considered to be the best predictors of the dependent variable.

◆ MAGNITUDE OF THE PARTIAL SLOPES

Lastly, we can compare the magnitude of the partial slopes to determine which independent variable is most important for explaining change in the dependent variable. However, this procedure is not accurate if the independent variables are measured in different terms (dollars versus years). In this case the "unstandardized" coefficients should be "standardized" into beta weights.

❖ SUMMARY

In this chapter we spent much time on the notion of control. We saw from several real and hypothetical examples that controlling for the influence of a third factor can have any number of possible effects on the original relationship between variables. Crosstabulation control procedures, for example, are very useful in that they allow us to examine the correlation between two variables for each level of the control variable. Thus we are able to observe factors in the relationships that would otherwise remain undetected.

If we do not find a bivariate relationship in the partial tables that control for the effect of a third variable, the original bivariate relationship is spurious because it is explained by the third variable. On the other hand, if we also find a bivariate relationship in the partial tables that control for the third variable, the bivariate relationship is genuine.

Often, however, a control for a third variable reduces but does not completely eliminate a relationship between two 640 variables. Thus, the control variable explains only part of the relationship. In this instance, you should retain both variables because they both explain the dependent variable.

A partial correlation coefficient describes the strength and direction of a relationship between two variables after you eliminate the effects of one or more other variables. A partial correlation coefficient is the correlation between the residuals of the regressions of the dependent variable on the control variable and the independent variable on the control variable.

Multiple regression extends the bivariate regression model by including additional independent variables. It produces a multiple correlation coefficient that describes the strength of the relationship between a dependent variable and a set of two or more independent variables. The square of the multiple correlation coefficient is the proportion of variation in the dependent variable explained by the set of independent variables considered at the same time. In multiple regression, a standardized beta coefficient is the standard deviation change in the dependent variable produced by one standard deviation change in the independent variable, controlling for the other independent variables.

We have covered quite a bit throughout this text. In the next chapter we will try to put it altogether by summarizing the steps in the research process and by examining and critiquing the efforts of other political science scope and methods students—students just like many of you.

❖ KEY TERMS

beta weight	partial correlation
coefficient of multiple determination	partial slopes
control	partial tables
multiple regression	random error
multivariate analysis	replication
multivariate crosstabulation	residuals

TABLE 15.5

CONGRESSIONAL VOTING PATTERNS BY REGION (IN PERCENTAGES)

| | | | | | Region of the State | | | | | |
Rate of Change (%)	PAN	WEST	NE	EAST	NC	GULF	SO	SW	CEN	Total
Less than 0	44	45	65	30	40	44	67	38	37	44
.001–9.99	24	23	29	45	34	37	33	19	37	30
More than 10	32	32	6	25	26	19	0	43	26	26
Totals	100	100	100	100	100	100	100	100	100	100
(N)	25	64	17	20	43	16	18	21	30	254
Cramer's V = .204										

❖ **EXERCISES**

1. Discuss the nature of control.

2. Discuss the ways an original relationship can be impacted after controlling for the effects of another variable(s).

3. Discuss the advantages and disadvantages of the various methods political scientists use to control for the effects of another variable(s).

4. Discuss ways you would determine the magnitude of the partial slopes produced by a multiple regression model you produced.

5. A student interested in the impact of legislation passed to enhance voting turnout in Texas created the following tables from data she collected. Table 15.5 depicts U.S. congressional voting patterns by region of the state. The independent variable is region of the state. The dependent variable is the rate of change between the 1980 congressional election, which was prior to enactment of the legislation, and the 1990 congressional election held after enactment of the legislation.

Table 15.6 depicts U.S. congressional voting patterns by the rate of urbanization of the county. The independent variable is urbanization of the country. The dependent variable, once again, is the rate of change between the 1980 congressional election, which was prior to enactment of the legislation, and the 1990 congressional election held after enactment of the legislation.

Table 15.7 depicts the change in the association between region and the rate of change in congressional voting patterns after the effects of urbanization were controlled.

TABLE 15.6

CONGRESSIONAL VOTING PATTERNS BY MSA (IN PERCENTAGES)

Rate of Change (%)	MSA Status		
	Non-MSA County	MSA County	Total
Less than 0	42.7	50.0	44.1
.001–9.99	31.1	27.1	30.3
More than 10	26.2	22.9	25.6
Totals	100	100	100
(N)	(206)	(48)	(254)
Cramer's V = .06			

TABLE 15.7

RATE OF CHANGE IN VOTING TURNOUT BY REGION CONTROLLING FOR URBANIZATION (MSA STATUS)

Election	Category of Urbanization		
	Region	Non-MSA	MSA
Congressional	$V = .204$	$V = .20$	$V = .42$

a. Discuss and interpret the data presented in Table 15.5 and Table 15.6.

b. Discuss and interpret the statistics resulting after the student controlled for the effects of urbanization.

c. What are the implications for further analysis?

6. $I = 20 + .10AA + .09H + .02F + 12I + e$

$R^2 = 0.77$

$N = 50$

where

AA = percent of African Americans in the population

H = percent of Hispanic Americans in the population

F = percent of foreign born in the population

I = per capita income level of the state

The following pertain to the above model:

    a. Define the components of the model.

    b. What are the hypotheses the model is testing?

    c. Interpret the statistics associated with the model.

❖ SUGGESTED READINGS

Bernstein, Robert A., and James A. Dyer. *An Introduction to Political Science Methods*, 2nd ed. Englewoods Cliffs, NJ: Prentice-Hall, 1984.

Blaylock, Hubert M., Jr. *Social Statistics*, 2nd ed. New York: McGraw-Hill, 1979.

Bowen, Bruce D., and Herbert F. Weisberg. *An Introduction to Survey Research and Data Analysis*. San Francisco: Freeman, 1977.

Dometrius, Nelson C. *Social Statistics Using SPSS*. New York: HarperCollins, 1992.

Fox, William. *Social Statistics Using MicroCase*. Chicago: Nelson-Hall, 1993.

Frankfort-Nachmias, Chava, and David Nachmias. *Research Methods in the Social Sciences*, 4th ed. New York: St. Martin's Press, 1992.

Johnson, Janet Buttolph, and Richard A. Joslyn. *Political Science Research Methods*. Washington: Congressional Quarterly Press, 1986.

Kay, Susan Ann. *Introduction to the Analysis of Political Data*. Englewood Cliffs, NJ: Prentice-Hall, 1991.

Leedy, Paul D. *Practical Research: Planning and Design*, 3rd ed. New York: Macmillan, 1985.

PUTTING IT ALL TOGETHER

❖ INTRODUCTION

Political scientists often investigate a phenomenon, distinguish and measure its attributes, identify systematic patterns, and then construct a theory. In other words, they perform research based on inductive reasoning. In this book, however, we posit the use of deductive reasoning to guide a research effort. That is, you select a proposition derived from existing theory for empirical investigation. Then you design a research project and collect empirical data to test the proposition. Next you input and analyze the data to determine support for the proposition. These steps take you through the first seven stages of the composite research process—problem identification, element clarification, research design, measurement, data collection, data input, and data analysis. This brings us to the last stage of the process—generalization of the results through theory and policy implications.

❖ THEORETICAL IMPLICATIONS

When you consider the **theoretical implications** resulting from your study, you want to discuss the links you discovered between the conceptual world and the empirical world. In other words, does the data support the theoretical proposition you tested? If the answer is no, you need to change the theory, the design, or measurement you used and perhaps select another proposition to test. If the data supports the proposition, you can test other propositions as one way to improve the theory. In any case you advance scientific knowledge through the acceptance or refutation of theoretical propositions.

Let's consider the following research question: "Why is the United States better off economically than China?" While several factors account for America's wealth and China's poverty, there are two important ones: China is heavily populated with scant natural resources. America, on the other hand, is not as populated as China and has abundant natural resources. Capitalism contributes to a higher GNP and healthier economy than communism.

To test these propositions you would collect data about each nation's GNP, population, and level of natural resources. You may also compare the economic vitality of other capitalist and communist countries. Then you would perform statistical manipulations to test your hypotheses. If you found statistical significance for your propositions, then you would have support for your theories. In other words, the theories you tested explain the difference between the wealth of America and China. In sum, you can advance the theories you tested to your research problem and the international scene.

❖ POLICY IMPLICATIONS

While the advancement of theory is important, it is equally important to determine the **policy implications** of your research efforts. Although the results of your study tell you whether the theory you tested does apply to your sample and therefore to the population you are studying, the composite research process requires you to address ways to put the results into practice through the policy-making process. In other words, you need to discuss the policy implications resulting from your study.

Suppose, for example, you analyzed Edward Banfield's notion that crime depends primarily upon two sets of variables. The first set relates to one's class culture and personality and collectively determines an individual's propensity to commit crime. The second set consists of several situational factors, such as the number of police on patrol. This set determines the individual's inducement to commit crime (Banfield 1968). As a result of your analyses, you discover that you can refute the proposition dealing with an individual's propensity to commit crime. On the other hand, you find support for the second proposition.

Based on these findings, what are the policy implications? It may be a suggestion to expand the police force or increase patrols in high crime areas. In other words, your study, which was an evaluation of Banfield's theory, should suggest ways to improve the policy. This is what we mean by policy implications.

❖ WRITING THE REPORT

◆ INTRODUCTION

You have spent a great deal of time identifying a problem to examine, reviewing literature, developing hypotheses, collecting, coding, and inputting data to computer systems, analyzing an array of data, and determining the theoretical and policy implications of your efforts. The good news is that these steps are finally complete. The bad news, however, is it is time for you to prepare the final report.

Many believe that the hard work is over and, for the most part, it is. All that most readers know about your research efforts, however, will be gleaned from your final report. Thus, you want to prepare a professional report. You want to ensure that your report clearly delineates each stage of the composite research process. You do not want to detract from your efforts by producing a sloppy and haphazard report.

We would like to give you a concise set of instructions that guarantee a professional final report. Unfortunately, we can only give you some general guidance that will assist you.

◆ RESOURCES

There are several manuals that deal with the format and presentation of research papers addressing general topics and political science. Some of the better ones are:

Chicago Manual of Style, 14th ed. (Chicago: University of Chicago Press, 1993).

Farlow, Daniel. *Writing a Research Paper in Political Science.* Glenview, IL: Scott, Foresman, 1989.

Fowler, H. Ramsey, and Jane Aaron. *The Little Brown Handbook,* 4th ed. Glenview, IL: Scott, Foresman, 1989.

Lester, James D. *Writing Research Papers: A Complete Guide.* Glenview, IL: Scott, Foresman, 1990.

Schmidt, Diane E. *Expository Writing in Political Science: A Practical Guide.* New York: HarperCollins, 1993.

Strunk, William, Jr., and E. B. White. *The Elements of Style,* 3rd ed. New York: Macmillan, 1979.

Turabian, Kate L. *A Manual for Writers of Term Papers, Theses, and Dissertations,* 3rd ed. Chicago: University of Chicago Press, 1987.

Each of these manuals helps you to footnote, prepare bibliographies, display quoted material, and prepare and depict tables, charts, and figures. These manuals will also help you with your grammar and punctuaton.

In addition to the guidance you will find in these publications, you may also want to consider the follwing suggestions dealing with report length, format, and style.

◆ LENGTH OF THE REPORT

Inevitably our students ask us the following question: "How long should our final paper be?" Often, we answer, "Long enough to adequately present the findings." At the doctoral level this amounts to, on the average, 225 pages.

Additionally, Master's theses often exceed 100 pages while undergraduate research papers seldom exceed 20 pages. Thus, it becomes a question of depth, brevity, precision, and level of education. Regardless of the latter requirement, however, you can attain these objectives if you carefully consider what you want to say, edit your work, and rewrite your paper after completing your first draft.

◆ FORMAT OF THE REPORT

As a minimum, your report should contain sections that address the problem statement, review the related literature, succinctly discuss the research design, present the data analysis, results, and interpetations, and present the theoretical and policy implications and conclusions. In other words, the format of your paper should, for the most part, follow the stages of the composite research process.

In addition, most professors will want you to prepare a title page that includes the title of your paper, your name, the professor's name, the course number, course name, and date. Some will also require an abstract and table of contents. Finally, most will require a bibliography.

◆ WRITING STYLE OF THE REPORT

Your paper should succinctly address the salient points. Having said this, we suggest that you use some of the manuals we listed earlier in the chapter. Strunk and White's manual, for example, will give you several suggestions to improve your writing style. For example, they stress the importance of revising and rewriting your paper. Schmidt presents several checklists that you can use to enhance your paper. For example, each paragraph should be at least three sentences long. Each paragraph in the body of the paper should have at least two references, except for the original information. Limit the number of quotes you use in your paper (in other words paraphrase) (Schmidt 1993, 250). In addition, Schmidt, Shelley, and Bardes offer the following summary of rules on how to write a successful research paper (Schmidt, Shelley, and Bardes 1993).

1. Use a plan when deciding on a topic.
2. Develop a research plan.
3. Develop an outline before you begin writing.
4. Use a word processor, if possible.
5. Write a first draft.
6. Revise your first draft.
7. Define your terms.
8. Consider your reader/audience.
9. Paraphrase and use your own words.
10. Eliminate extraneous phrases such as "it should be noted. . . ."

11. Be succinct.

12. Be convincing and avoid the use of qualifiers such as "it seems,"

13. Be attentive to grammar and style.

❖ A SAMPLE RESEARCH PROPOSAL AND RESEARCH PAPER

We have spent a considerable amount of time talking about political questions and ways to resolve them through systematic research. Appendix I presents you with an example research proposal, and a research paper prepared by government students at Angelo State University. Our goal is to show you the quality of research that you can accomplish in a one-semester course.

You should carefully examine the proposal and paper. We believe they provide some useful guidelines about research methodology, format, and style. When evaluating the proposal and paper we want you to consider the following questions:

1. Were the problems clearly stated?

2. Was the literature succinctly reviewed?

3. Were the research elements clarified?

4. Were the research designs clearly presented?

5. Were testable hypotheses developed?

6. Were the data appropriate for the testing of the hypotheses?

7. Were the appropriate statistical techniques used?

8. Were the findings clearly presented?

9. Were the conclusions reached appropriate to the findings?

10. Were the theoretical and policy implications appropriate?

❖ A FINAL THOUGHT

As we said in Chapter 1, we wrote this book for several reasons. Our main reason, however, was to give you the basic tools to carry out rigorous and sensible political science research and data analyses. We told you about the importance of defining your problem, doing a thorough review of the pertinent literature, developing a sound research design, and creating an instrument and tool to collect your data and then input it to a statistical computer program. We then spent much time telling you ways to analayze one variable at a time (univariate analysis), two variables (bivariate analysis), and several variables (multivariate analysis). In the process, we also showed you how to summarize information and test its generalizability to a larger population.

For many of you when you reviewed the first chapters of our book a deep feeling of anxiety may have set in. You were convinced that its contents would be beyond your comprehension. But you persevered and worked through the book. We know our efforts may not have made you an expert in the rigors of political science research. That was not our intent. Our intent was to enable you to know more—more about political science, more about the statistics used by political scientists, and more about the political world around you. As another political scientist once said, "Ignorance may be bliss, but it is also dangerous" (Fox 1993).

In sum, the purpose of this book was to show you that political research can be an enjoyable academic experience. As our way to enhance your satisfaction, we spent considerable time introducing you to a systematic research process—a process designed to alleviate your frustration, contribute to the reliability and validity of your results, and make your research more effective. Thus, we wanted to show you that although political research was an exacting and discriminating investigation undertaken by political scientists to discover and interpret new political knowledge, it can be, for the most part, "fun."

❖ KEY TERMS

policy implications   theoretical implications

❖ EXERCISES

1. Select a recent issue of a political science journal and examine any study using an empirical approach as its methodology. Then, report on the following:

    a. What problem did the author address?

    b. What theory did the author examine?

    c. How did the author conceptualize, operationalize, and measure the theory he or she was testing?

    d. What hypotheses did the author test?

    e. Discuss the research design used by the author.

    f. Discuss the results of the study as they pertain to the hypotheses that were tested.

    g. What were the theoretical, and if applicable, policy implications resulting from the study?

2. Using one of the manuals of style discussed in this chapter, critically examine the study you reviewed above. Include in your analysis a discussion of the following:

    a. Did the author clearly state the hypotheses at the outset of the paper?

    b. Could the hypotheses have been stated more precisely? How?

 c. Was the research design adequate and clearly defined? How could it have been improved?

 d. Were the statistics appropriate for the data and hypotheses? If not, what statistics should have been used?

 e. Were the conclusions appropriate based on the analysis and findings? If not, why not?

 f. What suggestions do you have to improve the study?

❖ SUGGESTED READINGS

Bowen, Bruce D., and Herbert F. Weisberg. *An Introduction to Survey Research and Data Analysis.* San Francisco: Freeman, 1977.

Johnson, Janet Buttolph, and Richard A. Joslyn. *Political Science Research Methods.* Washington: Congressional Quarterly Press, 1986.

Leedy, Paul D. *Practical Research: Planning and Design* 3rd ed. New York: Macmillan, 1985.

Appendix I

◆ ◆ ◆

SAMPLE RESEARCH STUDIES

❖ **EXAMPLE ONE: A RESEARCH PROPOSAL**

◆ AN ANALYSIS OF SUPREME COURT DECISION MAKING BEGINNING
WITH THE WARREN COURT: A RESEARCH PROPOSAL

Background of Study   The power of judicial review, claimed by the Supreme
Court in the *Marbury v. Madison* case of 1803, placed the judiciary on an
equal footing with Congress and the president (Janda, Berry, and Goldman
1992, 527). While the principle of checks and balances can restrain judicial
power through several means, such as constitutional amendment and removal
from office through impeachment, there were infrequent restrictions on that
power. As a result, the federal courts exercise considerable influence through
judicial review and statutory construction. Consequently, the federal courts,
and the Supreme Court of the United States in particular, inevitably shape
policy that impacts each of the states and the nation.

The way that they shape policy has intrigued political scientists, sparked
intense scholarly debate, and generated important questions. Has the judiciary exceeded its intended U.S. constitutional authority? Has it taken some of
the law-making power from legislatures (Patterson 1993, 649)? There are two
schools of thought concerning these issues that help to clarify the opposing
philosophical positions on the Court's proper role: the notions of judicial
restraint and judicial activism (Halpern and Lamb 1982).

The doctrine of judicial restraint holds that the judiciary should respect
precedent and defer to the judgment of legislatures (Patterson 1993, 649).
This notion places a high value on the consistency of law and on rule through
elected institutions. In short, "the job of judges is to work within the confines
of legislation and precedent, seeking to discover their application to specific
cases, rather than searching for new principles that essentially change the
meaning of law" (Patterson 1993, 649). Proponents of judicial restraint, therefore, would oppose the decisions rendered by the Supreme Court concerning
reform movements and the constitutionality of abortion. As Justice John

Harlan argued: "The Constitution is not a panacea for every blot upon the public welfare; nor should this Court, ordained as a legal body, be thought of as a general haven for reform movements" (*Reynolds v. Sims*, U.S. 533 1964).

The doctrine of judicial activism, on the other hand, holds that the courts should involve themselves extensively in interpreting and enlarging the law. While proponents of this doctrine accept the principles of precedent and majority rule, they claim that the courts should not be overly respectful to existing legal principles or to the judgments of elected officials. In addition, they believe that natural law gives justices greater leeway when rendering opinions. They believe there are universal standards of right and wrong that one can discover through reason. Thus, judicial power is appropriate for upholding such standards. Proponents also point out that the theory of sociological jurisprudence holds that man-made law contains fallible rules made by the majority to resolve conflicts between competing values. This theory emphasizes that justices can consider information about society provided by multiple and varying sources and need not base their decisions exclusively on narrow legal considerations (Patterson 1993, 652).

These perceptions have an ideological basis. Proponents of these views have conflicting opinions about the role, scope, and value pursuits of government. Conservatives, for example, believe in judicial restraint. Thus, they look for limited government, the pursuit of social order, and decisions that enhance the capitalist system. Liberals, on the other hand, believe in judicial activism. In other words they believe that the Court does have a role in reversing the fallible rules often made by elected bodies. Thus, the notion of equity is important to them.

Supreme Court justices and nominees to the Court also have their ideas about their roles as justices. Robert H. Bork, a conservative nominated by President Reagan to be a Supreme Court justice, advocated judicial restraint during the Senate Judiciary hearings held to gather information about his perception of his role on the Court. Some believe his stance contributed to not being confirmed by the Senate. As a result, succeeding nominees demonstrated ideological moderation during their hearings which netted them places on the Supreme Court (Janda, Berry, and Goldman 1992, 519).

Purpose Statement   There is a preoccupation with the way Supreme Court justices should act when reviewing cases. Should Supreme Court justices, for example, practice judicial restraint or should they practice judicial activism? While this is an interesting question, it cannot be satisfactorily answered. Therefore, the major purpose of this research effort is to answer the following question: **Do Supreme Court justices practice judicial restraint or judicial activism after their appointment to the Court?** In other words, do the votes of Supreme Court justices reflect their attitudes, values, and personal policy preferences? A subordinate purpose of this research project is to identify those factors contributing to the way justices vote when rendering opinions on the cases they review.

Methodology

The Dependent Variable   The primary purpose of this study is to determine whether Supreme Court justices practice judicial restraint or judicial activism after their appointment to the Supreme Court. But how does one operationalize concepts such as judicial restraint and judicial activism? Although the Court's position is constrained by the facts of a case, by the U.S. Constitution, by statutes and government regulations, and by legal precedent, the vagueness of existing legal guidelines gives justices some discretion when rendering their decisions. Thus, "the state of the law narrows a judge's options in a particular case, but within these confines there is room for considerable discretion" (Patterson 1993, 655). This study asserts that this "considerable discretion" is demonstrated through judicial activism. This assertion is predicated on the notion that proponents of judicial activism emphasize the Court's obligation to protect civil rights and liberties and find justification for their position in the U.S. Constitution's strong moral language and Amendments (Abraham 1974, 13). As previously mentioned, a liberal ideological stance is associated with judicial activism while a conservative ideological stance is associated with judicial restraint.

To determine the judicial role practiced by a justice, this study will examine the votes of all justices appointed since 1953 in all formally decided civil liberties cases from 1953 through 1992. Civil liberties issues are those involving criminal procedure, the First Amendment, civil rights, and privacy. Examples of judicial activism decisions are pro-citizen accused or convicted of crime, pro-civil liberties or civil rights claimant, and antigovernment in due process and privacy (Segal and Cover 1989, 561). Cases concerned with these examples include *Gideon v. Wainwright* (1963) (pro-citizen accused of crime), *Roe v. Wade* (1973) (antigovernment in privacy), and *Johnson v. Texas* (1989) (pro-civil liberties claimant).

The dependent variable will be operationalized in accordance with the following formula:

$$\frac{\text{Number of Liberal votes} - \text{Number of Conservative votes}}{\text{Total cases rendering a vote}}$$

The range of values will be from –1.0 (extreme judicial restraint/conservative stance) to +1.0 (extreme judicial activism/liberal stance). A score close to zero will demonstrate a balanced judicial role and moderate ideological stance.

The Independent Variables   The subordinate purpose of this study is to identify variables that explain the judicial role demonstrated by the justices. While studies have suggested there are "outside" influences impacting Court decisions, such as the expectations of interest groups (Puro 1981), personal policy preferences (Rohde and Spaeth 1976), and elected officials, particularly the president and members of Congress (Abraham 1974). In addition, Wasby theorized that Supreme Court justices are responsive to public opinion and strived to stay close enough to avoid serious eroding of public support for their decisions (Wasby 1978, 53). As Patterson asserts, however, "the precise impact of these outside pressures cannot be measured, but judicial experts agree that the courts are affected by them" (Patterson 1993, 640).

Since it is difficult to measure the precise impact of outside pressures, this study will concentrate on the socialization pressures that contribute to the opinions rendered by justices. Socialization pressures include those identified and used in the studies of C. Neal Tate (1981) and Jeffrey Segal and Albert Cover (1989).

Tate used information on the justices' personal attributes from sources such as biographical directories, (*Who's Who in America*), and the data collections of scholars such as Schmidhauser (1959), Krislov (1972), and Abraham (1974, 1975). Examples include background information such as birth, religion, education, tenure on the Court, career characteristics and partisanship measures (Tate 1981, 359).

While it is difficult to operationalize the ideological values of a justice prior to installation on the Court, Segal and Cover (1989) used a unique way to attempt to do so. They performed a content analysis of the ideological values of all justices from Earl Warren to Anthony Kennedy from newspaper editorials in several of the nation's leading newspapers. They coded the statements made within the editorials as liberal, moderate, and conservative. Each justice was given a score derived from their codification process. Values ranged from a +1.0 (unanimously liberal) through .0 (moderate) to −1.0 (unanimously conservative). The values of their dependent variable correlated highly with the votes of the justices, which was their dependent variable. This study will make use of their information. It will also derive similar measures for David Souter and Clarence Thomas.

Statistical Methods   This study will examine each variable in a multivariate analysis to determine the independent impact of each of the variables on the voting records of each justice included in the study. This analysis will include several steps. First, Pearson product-moment correlation coefficients will be calculated to determine the magnitude and direction of relationship between the dependent and independent variables and between each independent variable. The analysis of correlations between independent variables is to determine whether multicollinearity possibly exists. Multicollinearity could impact the reliability of the results. Second, beta weights will be calculated to compare the impact and relative importance of the independent variables on the justices' vote. Third, multiple regression will be used to determine the amount of relationship between the vote on civil liberties issues and the independent variables.

◆ EXPECTED RESULTS

After applying the above procedure it is expected that a model will exist that can be used to determine the amount of variance in Supreme Court voting based on changes in the various independent variables. Additionally, the model can be used to predict future Supreme Court voting behavior. Following is an example of a possible model:

$$JRS = BC1 + \ldots + BCn + CC1 + \ldots + CCn + TC1 + \ldots + TCn + PC1 + \ldots PCn$$

where

    JRS = judicial role score of justice

    BC $1, n$ = background characteristics

    CC $1, n$ = career characteristics

    TC $1, n$ = tenure characteristics

    PC $1, n$ = partisan characteristics

Furthermore, the theoretical implications of this study are many. For example, it is expected that the theories of those who believe that justices are important policy-making officials as a result of socialization (Tate 1981) will be supported. It is also expected that Segal and Cover's (1989) finding that the justices' bring their political baggage with them to the Court will be expanded to include the new members of the Court. Last, it is expected that this study will identify additional factors that can be used to predict the decision-making and voting behavior of the justices.

◆ Bibliography

Abraham, Henry J. 1974. *Justices and Presidents.* New York: Oxford University Press.

Halpern, Stephen C., and Charles M. Lamb, eds. 1982. *Supreme Court Activism and Restraint.* Lexington, Mass: Lexington Books.

Janda, Kenneth, Jeffrey M. Berry, and Jerry Goldman. 1992. *The Challenge of Democracy: Government in America,* 3rd ed. Boston: Houghton Mifflin.

Krislov, Samuel. 1972. *Judicial Process and Constitutional Law: A Laboratory Manual.* Boston: Little, Brown.

Marshall, Thomas R. 1989. *Public Opinion and the Supreme Court.* Boston: Unwin Hyman.

Patterson, Thomas E. 1993. *The American Democracy,* 2nd ed. New York: McGraw-Hill.

Puro, Steven. 1981. "The United States as Amicus Curiae." In *Courts, Law, and Judicial Processes,* ed. S. Sidney Ulmer. New York: Free Press.

Rohde, David, and Harold Spaeth. 1976. *Supreme Court Decision Making.* San Francisco: W.H. Freeman.

Schmidhauser, John R. 1959. "The Justices of the Supreme Court: A Collective Portrait." *American Journal of Political Science* 3:1–50.

Segal, Jeffrey A., and Albert D. Cover. 1989. "Ideological Values and the Votes of U.S. Supreme Court Justices." *The American Political Science Review* 83:557–65.

Tate, C. Neal. 1981. "Personal Attribute Models of Voting Behavior of U.S. Supreme Court Justices: Liberalism in Civil Liberties and Economics Decisions, 1946–1978." *American Political Science Review* 75:355-67.

Wasby, Stephen L. 1978. *The Supreme Court in the Federal Judicial System.* New York: Holt, Rinehart and Winston.

❖ EXAMPLE TWO: A RESEARCH PAPER

◆ NO EXCUSE VOTING COMES TO TEXAS: AN ANALYSIS OF EARLY VOTING ON ELECTIONS

Introduction   The voting turnout rate (calculated as a percentage of the voting age population who cast votes) in presidential election years has dropped from approximately 62 percent in 1952 to a little over 50 percent in 1988 (America Votes series). In addition, voter turnout in American presidential elections ranks at the bottom of voting rates for 27 countries with competitive elections (Janda, Berry, Goldman 1993). This low voting turnout, as a result, has become an embarrassment to a nation that considers itself the arch democracy in the world. To further confound those who believe that free elections are the cornerstone of democracy is the fact that studies have shown that Americans are much more likely to vote in national elections than state and local elections. As support, the voting turnout based on voting age population in state elections from 1980 to 1990 was only 44.24 percent (the percentage based on registered voters was 62.46) (*The Book of the States*, vols. 24 and 29). Voter turnout in local contests was even lower (approximately 30 percent), even though the impact of individual votes is much greater (Patterson 1993).

Scholars have offered several explanations for low voter turnout. One school focuses on individual factors, such as the enfranchisement of 18-year-olds (Shaffer 1981; Abransom and Aldrich 1981), the growing belief that government is not responsive to citizens (Teixeira 1987), the efficacy of the electorate (Berman 1991), the saliency of elections (Cole and Taebel 1987), voter apathy and alienation (Berman 1991), and socioeconomic factors such as education and income (Verba and Nie 1972). In addition, some have suggested that nonparticipation in the election process is an indication of satisfaction with the status quo (Schattschneider 1960). Last, some cite the inability of political parties to mobilize the vote of particular social groups, especially lower-class and less-educated people, as a contributor to low turnout. American parties, skeptics contend, do not make an effort to get out the vote. This is regretful because comparative studies have shown that strong party-group linkages significantly increase voter turnout (Powell 1986).

Another school argues that low turnout is a function of structural requirements. Many of these "structural" critics believe American voting laws and election procedures deter voting (Piven and Cloward 1989). As support, they point to the liberal voting practices in European countries such as weekend voting and voting on more than one day. In addition, several nations have election holidays to encourage people to vote and even impose a fine for not voting (Glass, Squire, and Wolfinger 1984). For the most part, the United States does none of these things. In contrast, voting in American elections is usually restricted to a 12-hour period on a given day, and by our Constitution that happens to be a work day. Further, most democratic nations place the burden of registration on the government rather than the voter (Janda, Berry and Goldman 1993). In fact, only 3 of 14 democratic nations having a voter turnout in excess of 67 percent require their citizens to register (Glass, Squire and Wolfinger 1984). Thus, one structural requirement that has received much attention lately, is the requirement to register.

Voting in the United States is a two-step process: one must register before one can vote. To complicate matters the burden of registration is placed on the individual. In many American states, the registration process is usually weeks in advance of the election and at a location different from the polling place. Further, people who move must reregister. Hence, voter registration requires more initiative than going to the election booth to cast a vote (Janda, Berry and Goldman 1993). Although most states adopted registration around the turn of the twentieth century to prevent corruption associated with ballot stuffing, procedures differ greatly from state to state. This also hinders election studies because there is no official record of total registered voters in the United States (Federal Election Commission release, January 14, 1993). Registration, for the most part, is easiest and least restrictive in the upper Great Plains states and the Northwest. North Dakota and Wisconsin have no registration requirements, while Minnesota and Maine allow their citizens to register just prior to voting on election day. As a result, their turnout rates averaged 73.2 percent compared to the nation's average of 55.9 percent for the 1992 election (Federal Election Commission 1993).

In summary, many argue that low voter turnout results from onerous state registration requirements. Consequently, they use voting age as the basis for computing voter turnout rather than registered voters. If you reject this rationale, however, and compute voter turnout on the basis of those registered to vote, then America's voting turnout rate in presidential contests averaged 72.49 percent from 1980 to 1990. This figure moves America closer to the median of all democratic nations (*The Book of the States*, vols. 24–25; Federal Election Commission 1993).[1]

Although the differential between the number of voting age residents, that is, those 18 years and older, and the number of registered voters may be a function of restrictive registration practices in some states, it may well be a cultural and legal problem in others. Voter registration in Texas, for example, is quite simple. In addition, activist groups have worked long and hard to register minority voters. Yet, among Hispanics there is a long-standing suspicion that voter registration subjects them to jury duty (Fukurai, Butler, and Krooth 1990). Many also believe that jury duty and voting takes them away from their jobs and livelihood (Starr and McCormick 1985).

What, then, does one do to enhance voter turnout? Some governments have mailed ballots to registered voters. In 1992, for example, San Diego voters, voted by mail on whether to build a new convention center. Approximately 500,000 ballots were mailed out on April 20 to voters with over 261,000 valid ballots returned by the May 5 deadline. Never had a higher percentage of eligible voters participated in a San Diego city election (Lorch 1992).

To this point, this discussion implies that states should alleviate registration requirements, declare voting holidays, and provide a multiday voting period. Texas, however, has taken an additional step. While most states permit some form of absentee voting before election day, their rules were quite restrictive with severe penalties for violators. But Texas has softened those restrictions. In fact, in 1987 the state legislature took steps to practically eliminate restrictions associated with absentee voting. Their legislation allowed voters, beginning with the 1988 elections, to cast their votes in person and by mail 20 days before a first primary or general election and 10 days before a run-off primary or run-off election. The early voting period ends four days prior to any primary or election. The legislation also authorized several counties to set up numerous election sites, use mobile voting facilities, and establish voting sites at retail outlets. The legislature confirmed its intentions by officially changing what was called "absentee" voting to "early" voting.[2]

The gravity of the 1987 extension of the no-excuse voting law was initially demonstrated in the 1989 Tarrant County run-off election to elect a replacement for U.S. Representative Jim Wright. Election day results had Republican Bob Lanier in front of Democrat Pete Geren by almost 1,400 votes. In the 16 days of early voting, however, Geren had more than 3,000 votes than Lanier and consequently won the election (Jones et al. 1992).

The purpose of this study is to examine the effect of this law on voter turnout in Texas. In this examination, two major sets of data are used. First, for comparative purposes, voter turnout in the 50 states is examined as a way to determine the extent changes in the Texas law contributed to increased voter turnout. Then, a longitudinal design is used to examine voter turnout in each of the 254 counties in Texas.

In the following section, data collection methodology and the problem one faces in comparative analyses of this type are discussed. Then the various issues raised above are analyzed. The analysis is concluded with an assessment of the overall impact of early voting in Texas elections.

◆ RESEARCH METHODOLOGY

Comparing Voter Turnout in Texas and the Nation The data collection efforts were extensive. One of the databases consists of National Presidential and Congressional Election data from 1980 through 1992. These data were collected so that the change in Texas voter turnout with the change in national voter turnout could be compared. This will also provide a control to assess the impact of the early voting legislation. Table 1 compares presidential voting turnout data between Texas and the rest of the United States.

The table shows the numbers of voters and the turnout rate for the presidential elections contested from 1980 through 1992. In 1980 a little less than 82,000,000 voters turned out across the nation. This represents the lowest turnout, in numbers, for the study period. In 1988, almost 71 percent of registered voters cast ballots. This percentage was bettered by more than 3 percent in the 1980 election. In 1992, more than 98,000,000 voters voted for a presidential candidate in states outside of Texas. This represents more than

TABLE 1

PRESIDENTIAL VOTING PARAMETERS, TEXAS AND THE UNITED STATES, 1980–1992 (MILLIONS)

	Year				
	1980	1984	1988	1992	Average
National					
Voters	81.9	87.3	86.2	98.4	88.5
Turnout Rate	73.9	73.0	70.8	77.3	73.8
Texas					
Voters	4.5	5.4	5.4	6.2	5.4
Turnout Rate	68.2	67.2	65.8	70.8	68.0

77 percent of the registered voters in the population. It also exceeded the average for the entire study period by 3.5 percent. Texas, on the other hand, was consistently below the nation. During the study period, 68 percent of registered voters in Texas turned out to vote. This is more than 5 percent below the average turnout rate for the rest of the country. Perhaps even more surprising is the fact that 6.5 percent more Americans voted in the other states than in Texas for the volatile 1992 election—surprising because Ross Perot, a leader in Texas politics and economics, was running for president. Voting turnout for the 1992 election, however, was 5 percent higher than the 1988 turnout and 2.8 percent higher than the average for the 12-year period. We would like to attribute this increase to the early voting legislation, however, turnout across the nation was higher in this election than for any other presidential election in the study. Political scientists posited many reasons for the high turnout including the electorate's lack of faith in the Bush administration to alleviate our economic concerns, the emergence of Ross Perot as a viable presidential candidate, and the perceived need for a change by many voters.

Table 2 compares congressional voting data between Texas and the rest of the nation. Table 2 supports what many studies have shown; fewer Americans vote in nonpresidential elections than in presidential contests. In fact, over the study period only a scant 58.2 percent of the registered voters voted across the nation. In Texas, the turnout was even less, a paltry 51.4 percent. The table also shows that there was a 1.9 percent increase in voter turnout in Texas in 1990 over the 1986 rate. This rate also slightly exceeded the turnout during the 1982 election.

Table 3 is similar to Table 1 and Table 2. It differs, however, because it compares voting data prior to, and after, enactment of the Texas legislation

TABLE 2

CONGRESSIONAL VOTING PARAMETERS, TEXAS AND THE UNITED STATES, 1982–1990 (MILLIONS)

	Year			
	1982	**1986**	**1990**	**Average**
National				
Voters	64.5	61.5	62.5	62.8
Turnout Rate	60.8	58.0	55.8	58.2
Texas				
Voters	3.2	3.4	3.9	3.5
Turnout Rate	51.5	50.5	52.4	51.4

TABLE 3

VOTER AND TURNOUT CHANGE, TEXAS AND THE UNITED STATES, 1980–1992 (MILLIONS)

National						
Presidential Elections			**Congressional Elections**			
	Pre	**Post**	**Chg**	**Pre**	**Post**	**Chg**
Voters	83.3	84.6	1.3	63.0	62.5	−.5
Turnout	73.5	74.1	.6	59.4	55.8	−3.6
Texas						
Presidential Elections			**Congressional Elections**			
	Pre	**Post**	**Chg**	**Pre**	**Post**	**Chg**
Voters	5.0	5.8	.8	3.3	3.9	.6
Turnout	68.4	68.5	.1	48.5	50.6	2.1

that enhanced early voting. The data represents the average presidential and congressional elections turnout for the two periods of analysis.

Table 3 shows that while there was an increase in the number of voters voting in presidential races after enactment of legislation, the turnout rate of change was slight for both Texas (.2 percent) and the other states (.8 percent). For congressional races outside of Texas, there was an overall 6.2 percent decrease in the voting turnout rate. Texas, however, experienced an increase exceeding 2 percent, which is approximately 8.3 percent higher than the rest of the nation.

In sum, while more voters turned out in Texas to vote in presidential elections after enactment of the early voting legislation, the turnout percent decreased. For congressional elections, however, there was an increase in voter turnout—an increase bettered by only 11 other states.

A Comparison of Texas Counties   Since 1988, Texas voters could vote in person up to 20 days before election day. In addition, early voting in Texas is available to any eligible voter in that one does not need a state-sanctioned reason to vote early. Other states, on the other hand, restrict absentee balloting to individuals that cannot, for one reason or another, go to the polls on election day. In this section voting turnout in the 254 counties in Texas is examined. The 1992 presidential election data were furnished by the Texas Secretary of State. Other data were collected from the *Texas Almanac* and the America Votes publications. Data for nonpresidential elections were for Texas United States Senate seats.

Before looking at the voting data for Texas counties, a recap of the overall turnout in the state from 1980 to 1992 for presidential and U.S. congressional races may be in order. A cursory review of Tables 1 and 2 showed that the average turnout for presidential elections was 68 percent of the registered voters with the highest turnout recorded in 1992 (70.8 percent). The average turnout for congressional races was 51.4 percent, with the highest turnout occurring in 1990 (52.4 percent).

As stated above, in this section voting turnout in the 254 counties in Texas is examined. Specifically, early voting results in the largest 15 counties is examined and compared with changes in voting turnout between counties within and outside metropolitan statistical areas (MSAs), and according to the county's geographical location.

Early Voting in the 15 Largest Counties   The voting turnout rate of change in presidential and congressional races for the 15 largest counties in Texas is depicted in Table 4. Presidential change is the percent difference in voting turnout between the 1992 and 1980 presidential elections. Congressional change is the percent difference in voting turnout between the 1990 and 1982 congressional elections.

TABLE 4

A COMPARISON OF VOTING RATE CHANGE IN THE 15 LARGEST TEXAS COUNTIES IN PRESIDENTIAL AND CONGRESSIONAL ELECTIONS, 1980–1992

County	Presidential Elections	Congressional Elections	Average Rate of Change
Bexar	3.21	−3.83	1.30
Cameron	−.31	−8.11	−4.37
Collin	12.05	11.85	17.98
Dallas	6.36	2.62	7.67
Denton	11.32	4.62	13.63
El Paso	−1.31	−16.93	−9.78
Galveston	11.41	2.67	12.75
Harris	5.72	1.91	−6.68
Hidalgo	−.63	−18.47	−9.87
Jefferson	6.64	.74	7.01
Lubbock	.90	−5.55	−1.88
McLennan	4.14	7.77	8.03
Nueces	5.33	−8.79	.94
Tarrant	4.84	−2.11	3.79
Travis	9.93	13.87	16.87
Average rate of change	5.31	−1.18	4.72

Table 4 depicts mixed voter turnout results for the larger counties in Texas. On the one hand, there was an increase of 5.31 percent in the average turnout rate for presidential elections. On the other hand, there was a decrease of 1.18 percent in the average turnout rate for congressional elections. Overall, however, there was an increase of 4.72 percent in the average turnout rate for presidential and congressional elections for these counties. The table also shows that more voters turned out in the 1982 congressional election than the 1990 congressional election for these counties (−1.18 percent change). This is somewhat surprising because Table 3 showed that, for all Texas counties, there was a 4.3 percent rate of increase for these two elections. Perhaps even more surprising, however, is the fact that these 15 counties reflected a 5.31 percent rate of increase for the two presidential elections, while Table 3 depicts a slight .2 percent increase for all Texas counties. In short, urban residents in Texas reacted differently to early voting than did the citizens in the rural parts of the state.

TABLE 5

RATE OF CHANGE IN VOTING TURNOUT FOR TEXAS PRESIDENTIAL AND CONGRESSIONAL ELECTIONS, 1980–1992

	Presidential		Congressional	
	#	%	#	%
≤ 0	70	27.6	112	44.1
.001 to 9.99	129	50.8	77	30.3
≥ 10	55	21.7	65	25.6
Totals	254	100.0	254	100.0

These results generate two interesting questions. First, is there a difference between the voting turnout rates between the larger and smaller counties in Texas? Second, is there a difference between the voting turnout rates between counties in the different regions of Texas?

The Dependent Variables: Change in Voting Turnout   Before regional and urban/rural voting patterns are examined, a brief explanation of how the dependent variables were operationalized is called for. First, the percent of voting turnout, based on registered voters, for each county, for all presidential elections between 1980 and 1992 was computed. Second, the percent of voting turnout for the U.S. Senate races held in 1982, 1986, and 1990 were computed. Next, the differences between the 1980 and 1992 presidential elections and the 1982 and 1990 senatorial elections were determined. Then the rate of change for each county was computed. Last, the turnout rates were collapsed into the following categories: voting turnout rate of change less than or equal to 0; voting turnout rate of change ranging from .001 to 9.99; and voting turnout rate of change greater than 10. This was done for both the presidential and congressional elections. The results are depicted in Table 5.

In Martin county, the voting turnout rate of change was a -25.9 percent for presidential elections. This was the largest decrease. The largest increase, 82.3 percent, was experienced in Maverick county. The mean for the study period was 4.4 percent and the standard deviation was 9.4. Kent county experienced a voting turnout rate of change of -64.3 percent in congressional elections. Pecos county, on the other hand, experienced a 54.7 percent rate of change increase for the same period. The average rate of change in turnout for congressional elections was 2.5 percent while the standard deviation was 14.2. This indicates that there was more diversity in the rate of change for congressional voting turnout than in the rate of change for presidential elections.

TABLE 6

TEXAS COUNTIES BY REGION

Region	Number	Percent	Cumulative %
Panhandle	25	9.8	9.8
West	64	25.2	35.0
Northeast	17	6.7	41.7
East	20	7.9	49.6
North Central	43	16.9	66.5
Gulf Coast	16	6.3	72.8
South	18	7.1	79.9
Southwest	21	8.3	88.2
Central	30	11.8	100.0
Total	254	100.0	

The table also shows that a majority of the counties experienced a change between 0 and 9.99 percent in the rate of voting turnout for presidential elections. On the other hand, more counties experienced a decrease in the rate of voting turnout change for congressional elections (44.1 percent). After we computed our dependent variables, we computed several contingency tables to see if there were differences in regional voting patterns. We used the same methodology to ascertain differences in the voting patterns of MSA and non-MSA county residents.

Regional and MSA Voting Patterns   Texas counties were categorized into nine regions: the panhandle, west, northeast, east north central, gulf coast south, southwest, and central. Table 6 depicts the distribution of counties according to their region.

Most of the counties in Texas are located west of Austin, north of San Antonio, and south of Canyon (25.2 percent). The fewest counties are located along the Gulf Coast (6.3 percent) and the Arkansas border (6.7 percent). The western counties, however, account for over 28 percent of the 48 counties outside of metropolitan statistical areas. Conversely, more than 50 percent of the MSA counties are located in the north central, central, and Gulf Coast regions of the state. Thus, while most of the counties are in the western portion of the state, most of the population is concentrated between Interstate 35 and Interstate 45.

Table 7 depicts regional voting patterns for the presidential elections conducted in 1980 and 1992. Table 7 shows that a greater percentage of the counties in the western part of Texas experienced a decrease in the rate of change

TABLE 7

PRESIDENTIAL VOTING PATTERNS BY REGION (IN PERCENTAGES)

						Region				
Category	PAN	WEST	NE	EAST	NC	GULF	SOUTH	SW	CEN	Total
<0	32	43.8	0	10	14	18.8	38.9	33.3	30	27.6
.001–9.9	60	43.8	70.6	50	58.1	37.5	50	52.4	43.3	50.8
>10	8	12.4	29.4	40	27.9	43.7	11.1	14.3	26.7	21.7
Totals	100	100	100	100	100	100	100	100	100	100
(N)	25	64	17	20	43	16	18	21	30	254
Cramer's V = .265										

in voting turnout for presidential elections than any other region (43.8 percent). Almost 44 percent of the counties along the Gulf Coast, on the other hand, experienced a rate of change greater than or equal to 10 percent. In addition, none of the counties in the northeast part of the state experienced a decrease.

To help determine the extent of the relationship between the variables a comparison of percentages across categories of the region of the state is required[3]. This will also help to assess the strength of the relationship more succinctly by examining various measures of association. The V value of .265, for example, tells us that there is a low positive association between the two variables. In other words, the voting rate change in presidential elections varied across the state.

Table 8 depicts regional voting patterns for the congressional elections conducted in 1982 and 1990. Table 8 depicts that a greater percentage of the counties in the southern and northeastern parts of Texas experienced a decrease in the rate of change in voting turnout for congressional elections than any other region (66.7 percent and 64.7 percent, respectively). The data for the northeastern counties is somewhat surprising because none of these counties experienced a decrease in presidential elections. Almost 45 percent of the eastern experienced a rate of change greater than or equal to 10 percent. Almost 43 percent of the southwestern counties saw an increase of 10 percentage points or more in the congressional elections. In addition, none of the counties in the southern part of the state experienced an increase of 10 percentage points or more.

Table 8 also tells us that there is a low positive relationship between region of the state and the voting rate change for congressional elections. Additionally, the relationship is not as strong for congressional turnout than it was for presidential elections.

TABLE 8

CONGRESSIONAL VOTING PATTERNS BY REGION (IN PERCENTAGES)

					Region					
Category	PAN	WEST	NE	EAST	NC	GULF	SOUTH	SW	CEN	Total
<0	44	45.3	64.7	30	39.5	43.8	66.7	38.1	36.7	44.1
.001–9.9	24	23.4	29.4	45	34.9	37.5	33.3	19.1	36.7	30.3
>10	32	31.3	5.9	25	25.6	18.7	0	42.8	26.6	25.6
Totals	100	100	100	100	100	100	100	100	100	100
(N)	25	64	17	20	43	16	18	21	30	254
Cramer's V = .204										

TABLE 9

PRESIDENTIAL VOTING PATTERNS BY MSA (IN PERCENTAGES)

	MSA Status		
	Non-MSA County	**MSA County**	**Total**
<0	30.6	14.6	27.6
.001–9.9	48.5	60.4	50.8
>10	20.9	25.0	21.7
Totals	100	100	100
(N)	206	48	254
Cramer's V = .14			

Tables 9 and 10 depict MSA voting patterns for the presidential elections conducted in 1980 and 1992, and the congressional elections conducted in 1982 and 1990. Table 9 shows that a greater percentage of the counties experienced a rate of change in voting turnout for presidential elections in the .001 to 9.99 category. For congressional races, however, most counties regardless of their MSA status experienced a decrease in voting turnout.

Although there is a relationship between the rate of change in voter turnout for presidential elections and MSA status, it is quite low. In addition, based on Table 10, there is a very low relationship between the MSA status of a county and change in the congressional voting turnout rate. In sum, it

TABLE 10

CONGRESSIONAL VOTING PATTERNS BY MSA (IN PERCENTAGES)

	MSA Status		
	Non-MSA County	MSA County	Total
<0	42.7	50.0	44.1
.001–9.9	31.1	27.1	30.3
>10	26.2	22.9	25.6
Totals	100	100	100
(N)	206	48	254
Cramer's V = .06			

TABLE 11

RATE OF CHANGE IN VOTING TURNOUT BY REGION CONTROLLING FOR URBANIZATION (MSA STATUS)

		Category of Urbanization	
Election	Region	Non-MSA	MSA
Presidential (Table 7)	V = .27	V = .26	V = .56
Congressional (Table 8)	V = .20	V = .20	V = .42

appears that the region of the state may explain more about voting change in Texas as the result of the early voting legislation than does the MSA status of the county.

To enhance this analysis, it was decided to examine the relationship between region of the state and the percent change in voting turnout for presidential and congressional elections after the effects of urbanization (MSA status) were controlled for.[4]

Perusal of Table 11 shows that we have virtually replicated the statistics applicable to Tables 7 and 8 for the rural counties in Texas. That is, the original relationship is virtually unchanged. For MSA counties, however, the original relationship for both types of elections is stronger. There is an interactive effect between region and urbanization in the explanation of change in voting turnout. Thus, in addition to the region of the state, the MSA status is also important for explaining the change in voting turnout for presidential and congressional elections.

◆ CONCLUSION

In 1987, legislation was introduced in the Texas legislature to eliminate absentee voting requirements and associated penalties. A goal of the legislation was to enhance voting turnout in Texas state and general elections. The purpose of this research paper was to determine the impact of the legislation on voting turnout in Texas. To do this, voting turnout between Texas and the rest of the United States was compared. Then the rate of change in voting turnout in Texas counties for the presidential and congressional elections conducted before and after implementation of the early voting legislation was compared. There are several conclusions that can be drawn from this study.

First, despite legislation to enhance the voting process, Texas still trails many other states in voting turnout. The turnout rate of change for presidential and congressional elections, for example, was bettered by 13 and 11 states, respectively. Second, voting turnout has not increased as much in the western and southern counties as in counties located in other parts of the state, such as the north central region. It is possible that the traditional political culture of these regions is working to limit voting turnout. Third, the rate of change for voting turnout was greater in the urban counties. This may be due to the mobilization and cohesion of ethnic groups in the inner city and the fact that urban counties may have taken greater steps to implement the provisions of the legislation.

This research effort also suggests other studies. This paper, did not, for example, try to identify those factors contributing to the changes that were observed. Therefore, further research should commence to identify those social, economic, and political characteristics having a causative effect on the change in voting turnout. In addition, an in-depth study should begin that looks at the impact of the early voting legislation on the campaign strategies of the major parties and the campaign efforts of political candidates. The results of these studies, coupled with the results discussed in this research paper, will provide some insight into the substantive impact of early voting in Texas.

❖ NOTES

1. The voter turnout rates depicted in the tables were calculated as a percentage of registered voters in the population. This method was chosen in lieu of calculating percentages based on voting age for several reasons. First, registration often requires more initiative than going to the polls to vote. Thus, registration implies concern about the political process. Second, Garcia, Stein, and Ward (1993) report that registration figures reported by

individual states often overreport the number of registered voters because they do not purge the names of deceased individuals and those who leave the state on a timely basis. One could argue, however, that these lists are still more current than census information. Third, the election data received from the Texas Secretary of State were based on registered voters.

2. In accordance with the early voting statute, the number of early voting sites, days, and hours of operation, varies with the population of each county. Subsequently, larger counties must provide more sites, more days, and more hours of operation. Days of operation, however, are limited to a three-week period preceding the third day prior to the scheduled election. For a comprehensive discussion, one should read "The New Early Voting Law," published in 1992 by the Office of the Texas Secretary of State.

3. Differences of less than 10 percentage points depict a small relationship, differences between 10 and 30 percentage points are moderate, and differences greater than 30 percentage points are large. Thus, the larger the differences between percentages across categories of the independent variable, the stronger the relationship.

4. The statistics in Table 11 were produced using the crosstabulations statistical procedure. Specifically, the relationship between region and voting turnout was examined by controlling for the effect of urbanization.

❖ BIBLIOGRAPHY

Abramson, Paul R., and John H. Aldrich. 1981. "The Decline of Electoral Participation in America," *American Political Science Review* 76 (September): 603–20.

America Votes Series 1980–1992.

Berman, David R. *State and Local Politics*, 6th ed. Dubuque, IA: William C. Brown.

Cole, Richard E., and Taebel, Delbert A. 1987. *Texas: Politics and Public Policy*. New York: Harcourt Brace Jovanovich.

Council of State Governments. 1982. *The Book of the States, vol 24*. Lexington, KY: Council of State Governments.

Council of State Governments. 1984. *The Book of the States, vol 25*. Lexington, KY: Council of State Governments.

Fukurai, H., E. W. Butler, and R. Krooth. 1990. *Race and the Jury*. New York: Plenum Press.

Garcia, Patricia A., Robert M. Stein, and Daniel S. Ward. 1993. "Registration and the Cost of Voting: Early Voting in Texas." Unpublished paper prepared for the 1993 Annual Meeting of the Southwestern Political Science Association, March 18–20, 1993, New Orleans, LA.

Gibson, L. Tucker, Jr., and Clay Robison. 1993. *Government and Politics in the Lone Star State*. Englewood Cliffs, NJ: Prentice-Hall.

Glass, David, Peverill Squire, and Raymond Wolfinger. 1984. "Voter Turnout: An International Comparison." *Public Opinion* 6 (December–January): 52.

Janda, Kenneth, Jeffrey M. Berry and Jerry Goldman. 1993. *The Challenge of Democracy: Government in America,* 3rd ed. Boston: Houghton Mifflin.

Jones, Eugene W., Joe E. Ericson, Lyle C. Brown, and Robert S. Trotter, Jr. 1993. *Practicing Texas Politics,* 8th ed. Boston: Houghton Mifflin.

Lorch, Robert S. 1992. *State and Local Politics: the Great Entanglement,* 4th ed. Englewood Cliffs, NJ: Prentice-Hall.

Powell, G. Bingham, Jr. 1986. "American Voter Turnout in Comparative Perspective." *American Political Science Review 80* (March): 25.

Schattschneider, E. E. 1960. *The Semi-Sovereign People.* New York: Holt, Rinehart and Winston.

Shaffer, Stephen D. 1981. "A Multivariate Explanation of Decreasing Turnout in Presidential Elections, 1960–1976," *American Journal of Political Science 25* (February): 68–95.

Starr, V. H., and M. McCormick. 1985. *Jury Selection: An Attorney's Guide to Jury Law and Methods.* Boston: Little, Brown.

Teixeria, Ruy A. 1987. *Why Americans Don't Vote: Turnout Decline in the United States, 1960–1984.* New York: Greenwood Press.

Verba, Sidney, and Norman H. Nie. 1972. *Participation in America: Political Democracy and Social Equality.* New York: Harper & Row.

1992 Official Presidential General Election Results. 1993. Washington D.C.: Federal Election Commission January.

1992 Texas General Election Results. 1992. Austin: Texas Secretary of State.

Appendix II

SAMPLE DATA SETS AND SELECTED VARIABLES

TABLE
Database 1

VOTE IN THE 1992 PRESIDENTIAL ELECTION (HYPOTHETICAL)

Respondent	Gender	Race	Age	Educ	Income	Religion	Vote
1	1	3	1	2	2	1	1
2	1	3	2	1	1	1	1
3	1	3	2	2	2	1	1
4	2	3	2	2	2	1	1
5	1	2	2	1	1	2	1
6	2	2	3	2	2	2	2
7	2	1	3	2	2	1	2
8	1	3	1	2	2	1	1
9	1	3	4	4	5	3	1
10	1	3	4	3	5	3	2
11	2	1	2	2	1	1	2
12	1	1	2	2	1	1	2
13	2	2	3	2	2	2	2
14	2	3	2	3	4	3	2
15	1	3	2	3	4	2	1
16	1	2	2	2	2	2	1
17	1	2	2	1	1	2	1
18	2	2	3	1	2	2	2
19	2	3	3	2	2	1	2
20	1	3	4	4	5	3	1
21	1	1	4	2	2	1	2

TABLE *(Continued)*

Database 1

VOTE IN THE 1992 PRESIDENTIAL ELECTION (HYPOTHETICAL)

Respondent	Gender	Race	Age	Educ	Income	Religion	Vote
22	2	3	1	1	1	2	1
23	2	3	1	2	2	2	2
24	2	2	2	2	2	2	2
25	1	1	2	2	1	1	2

Notes:

Gender: 1 = MALE; 2 = FEMALE.

Race: 1 = BLACK; 2 = HISPANIC; 3 = WHITE.

Age: 1 = < 20; 2 = 20–29; 3 = 30–39; 4 = > 40.

Educ: 1 = < 12; 2 = HIGH SCHOOL; 3 = SOME COLLEGE; 4 = 16+

Income: 1 = < 10K; 2 = 10–20K; 3 = 20–30K; 4 = 30–40K; 5 = > 40K.

Religion: 1 = PROTESTANT; 2 = CATHOLIC; 3 = JEWISH; 4 = OTHER.

Vote: 1 = CLINTON 2 = BUSH

◆ **TASKS**

1. Enter data into computer program.
2. Produce a code book.
3. Produce the following statistics for each variable:
   a. Measures of central tendency.
   b. Measures of dispersion.
4. Discuss the statistics for each variable.
5. Produce a crosstabulation for several variables with "VOTE" as the dependent variable. Discuss the results.

TABLE

Database 2

SELECTED CASES DECIDED BY THE REHNQUIST COURT, 1992–1993 SESSION

Variables 1–7

Justice	Age at Confirm	Time on Court	Religion	Class	Ideol Score*	Apptg Pres
Rehnquist	48	21	Protestant	Middle	−.91	Nixon
Blackmun	62	23	Protestant	Middle	−.77	Nixon
Kennedy	52	5	Catholic	Upper	−.27	Reagan
O'Connor	51	12	Protestant	Lower	−.71	Reagan
Scalia	50	7	Catholic	Lower	−1.00	Reagan
Souter	51	3	Protestant	Middle	−.47	Bush
Stevens	55	18	Protestant	Upper	−.50	Ford
Thomas	43	2	Catholic	Lower	−.70	Bush
White	45	31	Protestant	Upper	0.00	Kennedy

Variables 8–17

Justice	Judicial Experience	Number of Republican Senators at Confirmation	Cases 1 2 3 4 5 6 7 8
Rehnquist	3	46	C C C C C C C C
Blackmun	12	42	C L L L L C L L
Kennedy	13	45	C L L L C C L C
O'Connor	8	54	C L C L L C L C
Scalia	9	53	C C C C C C L C
Souter	12	45	C L C L L C L C
Stevens	9	39	C L L L L C L L
Thomas	2	44	C C C C C C C C
White	2	36	C C C C C C C C

Variables 18–34

Justice	Cases 9 10 11 12 13 14 15 16 17 18 19 20 21 22 23 24 25
Rehnquist	C C C L L L L L C C L C L C L C C C C L
Blackmun	C L L L L L L L L L L C L L L C L L
Kennedy	C C C L L L L L L C L C L C L C C C C L
O'Connor	C L C L L C L C L C C L C L C L L L C C L

Scalia	C	C	C	C	L	L	L	C	C	C	C	L	C	C	C	C	L
Souter	C	C	L	L	L	L	L	L	L	C	L	C	L	L	L	C	C	L
Stevens	C	L	L	L	L	L	L	L	L	L	L	C	L	L	L	C	L	L
Thomas	C	C	C	L	L	L	L	C	C	C	C	L	C	C	C	C	L
White	C	C	C	L	L	L	L	C	C	C	L	C	L	C	L	C	C	C	C	L

Ideology based on analyses of newspaper editorials from time of nomination until the start of Senate confirmation hearings. Negative scores denote conservative ideology while positive scores denote a liberal ideology. See Jeffrey A. Segal and Albert D. Cover. 1989. "Ideological Values and the Votes of U.S. Supreme Court Justices." *The American Political Science Review* 83:557–65.

TABLE

Case #	Case Description
1	*Wright v. West* (1992)
2	*Forsyth Co. v. Nationalist Movement* (1992)
3	*Burdick v. Takushi* (1992)
4	*Lee v. Krishnas* (1992)
5	*Graham v. Collins* (1993)
6	*U.S. v. Dunnigan* (1993)
7	*Crosby v. U.S.* (1993)
8	*Arave, Warden v. Creech* (1993)
9	*Parke, Warden v. Raley* (1992)
10	*Deal v. U.S.* (1993)
11	*Herrera v. Collins* (1993)
12	*Richmond v. Lewis* (1992)
13	*Soldal v. Cook County* (1992)
14	*Edenfield v. Fane* (1993)
15	*Church of Lukini Babalu Ave v. Hialeah* (1993)
16	*Alexander v. U.S.* (1993)
17	*Gilmore v. Taylor* (1993)
18	*Helling v. McKinney* (1993)
19	*Minnesota v. Dickerson* (1993)
20	*Lamb's Chapel v. Center Moriches Union Free* (1993)
21	*Zobrest v. Catalina Foothills S.D.* (1993)
22	*Hiller v. Doe* (1993)
23	*Wisconsin v. Mitchell* (1993)
24	*Godinez v. Moran* (1993)
25	*Sullivan v. Louisiana* (1993)

C = Conservative vote
L = Liberal vote

◆ TASKS

1. Enter data into the computer program. (Hint: assign numbers to the applicable alpha variables).
2. Produce a code book.
3. Produce the following statistics for each variable:
   a. Measures of central tendency.
   b. Measures of dispersion.
4. Discuss the statistics for each variable.
5. Construct an index using the opinions rendered for the court cases.
6. Assign the label "IDINDEX" to the index you created.
7. Produce a crosstabulation for several variables with "IDINDEX" as the dependent variable. Discuss the results.

Appendix III

STATISTICAL TABLES

TABLE A1
RANDOM DIGITS

```
10 09 73 25 33    76 52 01 35 86    34 67 35 48 76    80 95 90 91 17    39 29 27 49 45
37 54 20 48 05    64 89 47 42 96    24 80 52 40 37    20 63 61 04 02    00 82 29 16 65
08 42 26 89 53    19 64 50 93 03    23 20 90 25 60    15 95 33 47 64    35 08 03 36 06
99 01 90 25 29    09 37 67 07 15    38 31 13 11 65    88 67 67 43 97    04 43 62 76 59
12 80 79 99 70    80 15 73 61 47    64 03 23 66 53    98 95 11 68 77    12 17 17 68 33

66 06 57 47 17    34 07 27 68 50    36 69 73 61 70    65 81 33 98 85    11 19 92 91 70
31 06 01 08 05    45 57 18 24 06    35 30 34 26 14    86 79 90 74 39    23 40 30 97 32
85 26 97 76 02    02 05 16 56 92    68 66 57 48 18    73 05 38 52 47    18 62 38 85 79
63 57 33 21 35    05 32 54 70 48    90 55 35 75 48    28 46 82 87 09    83 49 12 56 24
73 79 64 57 53    03 52 96 47 78    35 80 83 42 82    60 93 52 03 44    35 27 38 84 35

98 52 01 77 67    14 90 56 86 07    22 10 94 05 58    60 97 09 34 33    50 50 07 39 98
11 80 50 54 31    39 80 82 77 32    50 72 56 82 48    29 40 52 42 01    52 77 56 78 51
83 45 29 96 34    06 28 89 80 83    13 74 67 00 78    18 47 54 06 10    68 71 17 78 17
88 68 54 02 00    86 50 75 84 01    36 76 66 79 51    90 36 47 64 93    29 60 91 10 62
99 59 46 73 48    87 51 76 49 69    91 82 60 89 28    93 78 56 13 68    23 47 83 41 13

65 48 11 76 74    17 46 85 09 50    58 04 77 69 74    73 03 95 71 86    40 21 81 65 44
80 12 43 56 35    17 72 70 80 15    45 31 82 23 74    21 11 57 82 53    14 38 55 37 63
74 35 09 98 17    77 40 27 72 14    43 23 60 02 10    45 52 16 42 37    96 28 60 26 55
69 91 62 68 03    66 25 22 91 48    36 93 68 72 03    76 62 11 39 90    94 40 05 64 18
09 89 32 05 05    14 22 56 85 14    46 42 75 67 88    96 29 77 88 22    54 38 21 45 98

91 49 91 45 23    68 47 92 76 86    46 16 28 35 54    94 75 08 99 23    37 08 92 00 48
80 33 69 45 98    26 94 03 68 58    70 29 73 41 35    53 14 03 33 40    42 05 08 23 41
44 10 48 19 49    85 15 74 79 54    32 97 92 65 75    57 60 04 08 81    22 22 20 64 13
12 55 07 37 42    11 10 00 20 40    12 86 07 46 97    96 64 48 94 39    28 70 72 58 15
63 60 64 93 29    16 50 53 44 84    40 21 95 25 63    43 65 17 70 82    07 20 73 17 90
```

Table A1 (Continued)

Random Digits

---

61 19 69 04 46   26 45 74 77 74   51 92 43 37 29   65 39 45 95 93   42 58 26 05 27
15 47 44 52 66   95 27 07 99 53   59 36 78 38 48   82 39 61 01 18   33 21 15 94 66
94 55 72 85 73   67 89 75 43 87   54 62 24 44 31   91 19 04 25 92   92 92 74 59 73
42 48 11 62 13   97 34 40 87 21   16 86 84 87 67   03 07 11 20 59   25 70 14 66 70
23 52 37 83 17   73 20 88 98 37   68 93 59 14 16   26 25 22 96 63   05 52 28 25 62

04 49 35 24 94   75 24 63 38 24   45 86 25 10 25   61 96 27 93 35   65 33 71 24 72
00 54 99 76 54   64 05 18 81 59   96 11 96 38 96   54 69 28 23 91   23 28 72 95 29
35 96 31 53 07   26 89 80 93 54   33 35 13 54 62   77 97 45 00 24   90 10 33 93 33
59 80 80 83 91   45 42 72 68 42   83 60 94 97 00   13 02 12 48 92   78 56 52 01 06
46 05 88 52 36   01 39 09 22 86   77 28 14 40 77   93 91 08 36 47   70 61 74 29 41

32 17 90 05 97   87 37 92 52 41   05 56 70 70 07   86 74 31 71 57   85 39 41 18 38
69 23 46 14 06   20 11 74 52 04   15 95 66 00 00   18 74 39 24 23   97 11 89 63 38
19 56 54 14 30   01 75 87 53 79   40 41 92 15 85   66 67 43 68 06   84 96 28 52 07
45 15 51 49 38   19 47 60 72 46   43 66 79 45 43   59 04 79 00 33   20 82 66 95 41
94 86 43 19 94   36 16 81 08 51   34 88 88 15 53   01 54 03 54 56   05 01 45 11 76

98 08 62 48 26   45 24 02 84 04   44 99 90 88 96   39 09 47 34 07   35 44 13 18 80
33 18 51 62 32   41 94 15 09 49   89 43 54 85 81   88 69 54 19 94   37 54 87 30 43
80 95 10 04 06   96 38 27 07 74   20 15 12 33 87   25 01 62 52 98   94 62 46 11 71
79 75 24 91 40   71 96 12 82 96   69 86 10 25 91   74 85 22 05 39   00 38 75 95 79
18 63 33 25 37   98 14 50 65 71   31 01 02 46 74   05 45 56 14 27   77 93 89 19 36

74 02 94 39 02   77 55 73 22 70   97 79 01 71 19   52 52 75 80 21   80 81 45 17 48
54 17 84 56 11   80 99 33 71 43   05 33 51 29 69   56 12 71 92 55   36 04 09 03 24
11 66 44 98 83   52 07 98 48 27   59 38 17 15 39   09 97 33 34 40   88 46 12 33 56
48 32 47 79 28   31 24 96 47 10   02 29 53 68 70   32 30 75 75 46   15 02 00 99 94
69 07 49 41 38   87 63 79 19 76   35 58 40 44 01   10 51 82 16 15   01 84 87 69 38

09 18 82 00 97   32 82 53 95 27   04 22 08 63 04   83 38 98 73 74   64 27 85 80 44
90 04 58 54 97   51 98 15 06 54   94 93 88 19 97   91 87 07 61 50   68 47 66 46 59
73 18 95 02 07   47 67 72 52 69   62 29 06 44 64   27 12 46 70 18   41 36 18 27 60
75 76 87 64 90   20 97 18 17 49   90 42 91 22 72   95 37 50 58 71   93 82 34 31 78
54 01 64 40 56   66 28 13 10 03   00 68 22 73 98   20 71 45 32 95   07 70 61 78 13

08 35 86 99 10   78 54 24 27 85   13 66 15 88 73   04 61 89 75 53   31 22 30 84 20
28 30 60 32 64   81 33 31 05 91   40 51 00 78 93   32 60 46 04 75   94 11 90 18 40
53 84 08 62 33   81 59 41 36 28   51 21 59 02 90   28 46 66 87 95   77 76 22 07 91
91 75 75 37 41   61 61 36 22 69   50 26 39 02 12   55 78 17 65 14   83 48 34 70 55
89 41 59 26 94   00 39 75 83 91   12 60 71 76 46   48 94 97 23 06   94 54 13 74 08

TABLE **A1** *(Continued)*

RANDOM DIGITS

```
77 51 30 38 20   86 83 42 99 01   68 41 48 27 74   51 90 81 39 80   72 89 35 55 07
19 50 23 71 74   69 97 92 02 88   55 21 02 97 73   74 28 77 52 51   65 34 46 74 15
21 81 85 93 13   93 27 88 17 57   05 68 67 31 56   07 08 28 50 46   31 85 33 84 52
51 47 46 64 99   68 10 72 36 21   94 04 99 13 45   42 83 60 91 91   08 00 74 54 49
99 55 96 83 31   62 53 52 41 70   69 77 71 28 30   74 81 97 81 42   43 86 07 28 34

33 71 34 80 07   93 58 47 28 69   51 92 66 47 21   58 30 32 98 22   93 17 49 39 72
85 27 48 68 93   11 30 32 92 70   28 83 43 41 37   73 51 59 04 00   71 14 84 36 43
84 13 38 96 40   44 03 55 21 66   73 85 27 00 91   61 22 26 05 61   62 32 71 84 23
56 73 21 62 34   17 39 59 61 31   10 12 39 16 22   85 49 65 75 60   81 60 41 88 80
65 13 85 68 06   87 64 88 52 61   34 31 36 58 61   45 87 52 10 69   85 64 44 72 77

38 00 10 21 76   81 71 91 17 11   71 60 29 29 37   74 21 96 40 49   65 58 44 96 98
37 40 29 63 97   01 30 47 75 86   56 27 11 00 86   47 32 46 26 05   40 03 03 74 38
97 12 54 03 48   87 08 33 14 17   21 81 53 92 50   75 23 76 20 47   15 50 12 95 78
21 82 64 11 34   47 14 33 40 72   64 63 88 59 02   49 13 90 64 41   03 85 65 45 52
73 13 54 27 42   95 71 90 90 35   85 79 47 42 96   08 78 98 81 56   64 69 11 92 02

07 63 87 79 29   03 06 11 80 72   96 20 74 41 56   23 82 19 95 38   04 71 36 69 94
60 52 88 34 41   07 95 41 98 14   59 17 52 06 95   05 53 35 21 39   61 21 20 64 55
83 59 63 56 55   06 95 89 29 83   05 12 80 97 19   77 43 35 37 83   92 30 15 04 98
10 85 06 27 46   99 59 91 05 07   13 49 90 63 19   53 07 57 18 39   06 41 01 93 62
39 82 09 89 52   43 62 26 31 47   64 42 18 08 14   43 80 00 93 51   31 02 47 31 67

59 58 00 64 78   75 56 97 88 00   88 83 55 44 86   23 76 80 61 56   04 11 10 84 08
38 50 80 73 41   23 79 34 87 63   90 82 29 70 22   17 71 90 42 07   95 95 44 99 53
30 69 27 06 68   94 68 81 61 27   56 19 68 00 91   82 06 76 34 00   05 46 26 92 00
65 44 39 56 59   18 28 82 74 37   49 63 22 40 41   08 33 76 56 76   96 29 99 08 36
27 26 75 02 64   13 19 27 22 94   07 47 74 46 06   17 98 54 89 11   97 34 13 03 58

91 30 70 69 91   19 07 22 42 10   36 69 95 37 28   28 82 53 57 93   28 97 66 62 52
68 43 49 46 88   84 47 31 36 22   62 12 69 84 08   12 84 38 25 90   09 81 59 31 46
48 90 81 58 77   54 74 52 45 91   35 70 00 47 54   83 82 45 26 92   54 13 05 51 60
06 91 34 51 97   42 67 27 86 01   11 88 30 95 28   63 01 19 89 01   14 97 44 03 44
10 45 51 60 19   14 21 03 37 12   91 34 23 78 21   88 32 58 08 51   43 66 77 08 83

12 88 39 73 43   65 02 76 11 84   04 28 50 13 92   17 97 41 50 77   90 71 22 67 69
21 77 83 09 76   38 80 73 69 61   31 64 94 20 96   63 28 10 20 23   08 81 64 74 49
19 52 35 95 15   65 12 25 96 59   86 28 36 82 58   69 57 21 37 98   16 43 59 15 29
67 24 55 26 70   35 58 31 65 63   79 24 68 66 86   76 46 33 42 22   26 65 59 08 02
60 58 44 73 77   07 50 03 79 92   45 13 42 65 29   26 76 08 36 37   41 32 64 43 44
```

TABLE A1 *(Continued)*

RANDOM DIGITS

```
53 85 34 13 77   36 06 69 48 50   58 83 87 38 59   49 36 47 33 31   96 24 04 36 42
24 63 73 87 36   74 38 48 93 42   52 62 30 79 92   12 36 91 86 01   03 74 28 38 73
83 08 01 24 51   38 99 22 28 15   07 75 95 17 77   97 37 72 75 85   51 97 23 78 67
16 44 42 43 34   36 15 19 90 73   27 49 37 09 39   85 13 03 25 52   54 84 65 47 59
60 79 01 81 57   57 17 86 57 62   11 16 17 85 76   45 81 95 29 79   65 13 00 48 60

03 99 11 04 61   93 71 61 68 94   66 08 32 46 53   84 60 95 82 32   88 61 81 91 61
38 55 59 55 54   32 88 65 97 80   08 35 56 08 60   29 73 54 77 62   71 29 92 38 53
17 54 67 37 04   92 05 24 62 15   55 12 12 92 81   59 07 60 79 36   27 95 45 89 09
32 64 35 28 61   95 81 90 68 31   00 91 19 89 36   76 35 59 37 79   80 86 30 05 14
69 57 26 87 77   39 51 03 59 05   14 06 04 06 19   29 54 96 96 16   33 56 46 07 80

24 12 26 65 91   27 69 90 64 94   14 84 54 66 72   61 95 87 71 00   90 89 97 57 54
61 19 63 02 31   92 96 26 17 73   41 83 95 53 82   17 26 77 09 43   78 03 87 02 67
30 53 22 17 04   10 27 41 22 02   39 68 52 33 09   10 06 16 88 29   55 98 66 64 85
03 78 89 75 99   75 86 72 07 17   74 41 65 31 66   35 20 83 33 74   87 53 90 88 23
48 22 86 33 79   85 78 34 76 19   53 15 26 74 33   35 66 35 29 72   16 81 86 03 11

60 36 59 46 53   35 07 53 39 49   42 61 42 92 97   01 91 82 83 16   98 95 37 32 31
83 79 94 24 02   56 62 33 44 42   34 99 44 13 74   70 07 11 47 36   09 95 81 80 65
32 96 00 74 05   36 40 98 32 32   99 38 54 16 00   11 13 30 75 86   15 91 70 62 53
19 32 25 38 45   57 62 05 26 06   66 49 76 86 46   78 13 86 65 59   19 64 09 94 13
11 22 09 47 47   07 39 93 74 08   48 50 92 39 29   27 48 24 54 76   85 24 43 51 59

31 75 15 72 60   68 98 00 53 39   15 47 04 83 55   88 65 12 25 96   03 15 21 92 21
88 49 29 93 82   14 45 40 45 04   20 09 49 89 77   74 84 39 34 13   22 10 97 85 08
30 93 44 77 44   07 48 18 38 28   73 78 80 65 33   28 59 72 04 05   94 20 52 03 80
22 88 84 88 93   27 49 99 87 48   60 53 04 51 28   74 02 28 46 17   82 03 71 02 68
78 21 21 69 93   35 90 29 13 86   44 37 21 54 86   65 74 11 40 14   87 48 13 72 20

41 84 98 45 47   46 85 05 23 26   34 67 75 83 00   74 91 06 43 45   19 32 58 15 49
46 35 23 30 49   69 24 89 34 60   45 30 50 75 21   61 31 83 18 55   14 41 37 09 51
11 08 79 62 94   14 01 33 17 92   59 74 76 72 77   76 50 33 45 13   39 66 37 75 44
52 70 10 83 37   56 30 38 73 15   16 52 06 96 76   11 65 49 98 93   02 18 16 81 61
57 27 53 68 98   81 30 44 85 85   68 65 22 73 76   92 85 25 58 66   88 44 80 35 84

20 85 77 31 56   70 28 42 43 26   79 37 59 52 20   01 15 96 32 67   10 62 24 83 91
15 63 38 49 24   90 41 59 36 14   33 52 12 66 65   55 82 34 76 41   86 22 53 17 04
92 69 44 82 97   39 90 40 21 15   59 58 94 90 67   66 82 14 15 75   49 76 70 40 37
77 61 31 90 19   88 15 20 00 80   20 55 49 14 09   96 27 74 82 57   50 81 69 76 16
38 68 83 24 86   45 13 46 35 45   59 40 47 20 59   43 94 75 16 80   43 85 25 96 93
```

TABLE A1 *(Continued)*

RANDOM DIGITS

25 16 30 18 89	70 01 41 50 21	41 29 06 73 12	71 85 71 59 57	68 97 11 14 03
65 25 10 76 29	37 23 93 32 95	05 87 00 11 19	92 78 42 63 40	18 47 76 56 22
36 81 54 36 25	18 63 73 75 09	82 44 49 90 05	04 92 17 37 01	14 70 79 39 97
64 39 71 16 92	05 32 78 21 62	20 24 78 17 59	45 19 72 53 32	83 74 52 25 67
04 51 52 56 24	95 09 66 79 46	48 46 08 55 58	15 19 11 87 82	16 93 03 33 61
83 76 16 08 73	43 25 38 41 45	60 83 32 59 83	01 29 14 13 49	20 36 80 71 26
14 38 70 63 45	80 85 40 92 79	43 52 90 63 18	38 38 47 47 61	41 19 63 74 80
51 32 19 22 46	80 08 87 70 74	88 72 25 67 36	66 16 44 94 31	66 91 93 16 78
72 47 20 00 08	80 89 01 80 02	94 81 33 19 00	54 15 58 34 36	35 35 25 41 31
05 46 65 53 06	93 12 81 84 64	74 45 79 05 61	72 84 81 18 34	79 98 26 84 16
39 52 87 24 84	82 47 42 55 93	48 54 53 52 47	18 61 91 36 74	18 61 11 92 41
81 61 61 87 11	53 34 24 42 76	75 12 21 17 24	74 62 77 37 07	58 31 91 59 97
07 58 61 61 20	82 64 12 28 20	92 90 41 31 41	32 39 21 97 63	61 19 96 79 40
90 76 70 42 35	13 57 41 72 00	69 90 26 37 42	78 46 42 25 01	18 62 79 08 72
40 18 82 81 93	29 59 38 86 27	94 97 21 15 98	62 09 53 67 87	00 44 15 89 97
34 41 48 21 57	86 88 75 50 87	19 15 20 00 23	12 30 28 07 83	32 62 46 86 91
63 43 97 53 63	44 98 91 68 22	36 02 40 09 67	76 37 84 16 05	65 96 17 34 88
67 04 90 90 70	93 39 94 55 47	94 45 87 42 84	05 04 14 98 07	20 28 83 40 60
79 49 50 41 46	52 16 29 02 86	54 15 83 42 43	46 97 83 54 82	59 36 29 59 38
91 70 43 05 52	04 73 72 10 31	75 05 19 30 29	47 66 56 43 82	99 78 29 34 78

SOURCE: The RAND Corporation, *A Million Random Digits*, Free Press, Glencoe, Ill., 1955, pp. 1–3, with the kind permission of the publisher.

TABLE A2

THE STANDARD NORMAL DISTRIBUTION

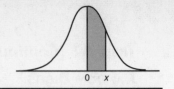

z	.00	.01	.02	.03	.04	.05	.06	.07	.08	.09
0.0	.0000	.0040	.0080	.0120	.0160	.0199	.0239	.0279	.0319	.0359
0.1	.0398	.0438	.0478	.0517	.0557	.0596	.0636	.0675	.0714	.0753
0.2	.0793	.0832	.0871	.0910	.0948	.0987	.1026	.1064	.1103	.1141
0.3	.1179	.1217	.1255	.1293	.1331	.1368	.1406	.1443	.1480	.1517
0.4	.1554	.1591	.1628	.1664	.1700	.1736	.1772	.1808	.1844	.1879
0.5	.1915	.1950	.1985	.2019	.2054	.2088	.2123	.2157	.2190	.2224
0.6	.2257	.2291	.2324	.2357	.2389	.2422	.2454	.2486	.2517	.2549
0.7	.2580	.2611	.2642	.2673	.2703	.2734	.2764	.2794	.2823	.2852
0.8	.2881	.2910	.2939	.2967	.2995	.3023	.3051	.3078	.3106	.3133
0.9	.3159	.3186	.3212	.3238	.3264	.3289	.3315	.3340	.3365	.3389
1.0	.3413	.3438	.3461	.3485	.3508	.3531	.3554	.3577	.3599	.3621
1.1	.3643	.3665	.3686	.3708	.3729	.3749	.3770	.3790	.3810	.3830
1.2	.3849	.3869	.3888	.3907	.3925	.3944	.3962	.3980	.3997	.4015
1.3	.4032	.4049	.4066	.4082	.4099	.4115	.4131	.4147	.4162	.4177
1.4	.4192	.4207	.4222	.4236	.4251	.4265	.4279	.4292	.4306	.4319
1.5	.4332	.4345	.4357	.4370	.4382	.4394	.4406	.4418	.4429	.4441
1.6	.4452	.4463	.4474	.4484	.4495	.4505	.4515	.4525	.4535	.4545
1.7	.4554	.4564	.4573	.4582	.4591	.4599	.4608	.4616	.4625	.4633
1.8	.4641	.4649	.4656	.4664	.4671	.4678	.4686	.4693	.4699	.4706
1.9	.4713	.4719	.4726	.4732	.4738	.4744	.4750	.4756	.4761	.4767
2.0	.4772	.4778	.4783	.4788	.4793	.4798	.4803	.4808	.4812	.4817
2.1	.4821	.4826	.4830	.4834	.4838	.4842	.4846	.4850	.4854	.4857
2.2	.4861	.4864	.4868	.4871	.4875	.4878	.4881	.4884	.4887	.4890
2.3	.4893	.4896	.4898	.4901	.4904	.4906	.4909	.4911	.4913	.4916
2.4	.4918	.4920	.4922	.4925	.4927	.4929	.4931	.4932	.4934	.4936
2.5	.4938	.4940	.4941	.4943	.4945	.4946	.4948	.4949	.4951	.4952
2.6	.4953	.4955	.4956	.4957	.4959	.4960	.4961	.4962	.4963	.4964
2.7	.4965	.4966	.4967	.4968	.4969	.4970	.4971	.4972	.4973	.4974
2.8	.4974	.4975	.4976	.4977	.4977	.4978	.4979	.4979	.4980	.4981

TABLE A2 (Continued)

THE STANDARD NORMAL DISTRIBUTION

z	.00	.01	.02	.03	.04	.05	.06	.07	.08	.09
2.9	.4981	.4982	.4982	.4983	.4984	.4984	.4985	.4985	.4986	.4986
3.0	.4987	.4987	.4987	.4988	.4988	.4989	.4989	.4989	.4990	.4990
3.1	.4990	.4991	.4991	.4992	.4992	.4992	.4992	.4992	.4993	.4993

Note: An entry in the table is the proportion under the entire curve which is between $Z = 0$ and a positive value of Z. Areas for negative values of Z are obtained by symmetry.

SOURCE: P. G. Hoel, *Elementary Statistics*, 2d ed. (New York: John Wiley & Sons, 1966). Copyright © 1966 by John Wiley & Sons. Reprinted by permission of John Wiley & Sons.

TABLE A3

THE CHI SQUARE DISTRIBUTION

						Probability								
df	.99	.98	.95	.90	.80	.70	.50	.30	.20	.10	.05	.02	.01	.001
1	.0²157	.0²628	.00393	.0158	.0642	.148	.455	1.074	1.642	2.706	3.841	5.412	6.635	10.82
2	.0201	.0404	.103	.211	.446	.713	1.386	2.408	3.219	4.605	5.991	7.824	9.210	13.81
3	.115	.185	.352	.584	1.005	1.424	2.366	3.665	4.642	6.251	7.815	9.837	11.341	16.268
4	.297	.429	.711	1.064	1.649	2.195	3.357	4.878	5.989	7.779	9.488	11.668	13.277	18.465
5	.554	.752	1.145	1.610	2.343	3.000	4.351	6.064	7.289	9.236	11.070	13.388	15.086	20.517
6	.872	1.134	1.635	2.204	3.070	3.828	5.348	7.231	8.558	10.645	12.592	15.033	16.812	22.457
7	1.239	1.564	2.167	2.833	3.822	4.671	6.346	8.383	9.803	12.017	14.067	16.622	18.475	24.322
8	1.646	2.032	2.733	3.490	4.594	5.527	7.344	9.524	11.030	13.362	15.507	18.168	20.090	26.125
9	2.088	2.532	3.325	4.168	5.380	6.393	8.343	10.656	12.242	14.684	16.919	19.679	21.666	27.877
10	2.558	3.059	3.940	4.865	6.179	7.267	9.342	11.781	13.442	15.987	18.307	21.161	23.209	29.588
11	3.053	3.609	4.575	5.578	6.989	8.148	10.341	12.899	14.631	17.275	19.675	22.618	24.725	31.264
12	3.571	4.178	5.226	6.304	7.807	9.034	11.340	14.011	15.812	18.549	21.026	24.054	26.217	32.909
13	4.107	4.765	5.892	7.042	8.634	9.926	12.340	15.119	16.985	19.812	22.362	25.472	27.688	34.528
14	4.660	5.368	6.571	7.790	9.467	10.821	13.339	16.222	18.151	21.064	23.685	26.873	29.141	36.123
15	5.229	5.985	7.261	8.547	10.307	11.721	14.339	17.322	19.311	22.307	24.996	28.259	30.578	37.697

TABLE A3 *(Continued)*
THE CHI SQUARE DISTRIBUTION

Probability

df	.99	.98	.95	.90	.80	.70	.50	.30	.20	.10	.05	.02	.01	.001
16	5.812	6.614	7.962	9.312	11.152	12.624	15.338	18.418	20.465	23.542	26.296	29.633	32.000	39.252
17	6.408	7.255	8.672	10.085	12.002	13.531	16.338	19.511	21.615	24.769	27.587	30.995	33.409	40.790
18	7.015	7.906	9.390	10.865	12.857	14.440	17.338	20.601	22.760	25.989	28.869	32.346	34.805	42.312
19	7.633	8.567	10.117	11.651	13.716	15.352	18.338	21.689	23.900	27.204	30.144	33.687	36.191	43.820
20	8.260	9.237	10.851	12.443	14.578	16.266	19.337	22.775	25.038	28.412	31.410	35.020	37.566	45.315
21	8.897	9.915	11.591	13.240	15.445	17.182	20.337	23.858	26.171	29.615	32.671	36.343	38.932	46.797
22	9.542	10.600	12.338	14.041	16.314	18.101	21.337	24.939	27.301	30.813	33.924	37.659	40.289	48.268
23	10.196	11.293	13.091	14.848	17.187	19.021	22.337	26.018	28.429	32.007	35.172	38.968	41.638	49.728
24	10.856	11.992	13.848	15.659	18.062	19.943	23.337	27.096	29.553	33.196	36.415	40.270	42.980	51.179
25	11.524	12.697	14.611	16.473	18.940	20.867	24.337	28.172	30.675	34.382	37.652	41.566	44.314	52.620
26	12.198	13.409	15.379	17.292	19.820	21.792	25.336	29.246	31.795	35.563	38.885	42.856	45.642	54.052
27	12.879	14.125	16.151	18.114	20.703	22.719	26.336	30.319	32.912	36.741	40.113	44.140	46.963	55.476
28	13.565	14.847	16.928	18.939	21.588	23.647	27.336	31.391	34.027	37.916	41.337	45.419	48.278	56.893
29	14.256	15.574	17.708	19.768	22.475	24.577	28.336	32.461	35.139	39.087	42.557	46.693	49.588	58.302
30	14.953	16.306	18.493	20.599	23.364	25.508	29.336	33.530	36.250	40.256	43.773	47.962	50.892	59.703

For larger values of df, the expression $\sqrt{2\chi^2} - \sqrt{2df - 1}$ may be used as a normal deviate with unit variance, remembering that the probability for χ_2 corresponds with that of a single tail of the normal curve.

SOURCE: Table A3 is reprinted from Table IV of R. A. Fisher and F. Yates, *Statistical Tables for Biological, Agricultural and Medical Research* (1948 ed.), published by Oliver & Boyd Ltd., Edinburgh and London, by permission of the authors and publishers.

TABLE A4

LEVELS OF SIGNIFICANCE FOR STUDENT'S T

	Level of significance for one-tailed test					
	.10	.05	.025	.01	.005	.0005
	Level of significance for two-tailed test					
df	.20	.10	.05	.02	.01	.001
1	3.078	6.314	12.706	31.821	63.657	636.619
2	1.886	2.920	4.303	6.965	9.925	31.598
3	1.638	2.353	3.182	4.541	5.841	12.941
4	1.533	2.132	2.776	3.747	4.604	8.610
5	1.476	2.015	2.571	3.365	4.032	6.859
6	1.440	1.943	2.447	3.143	3.707	5.959
7	1.415	1.895	2.365	2.998	3.499	5.405
8	1.397	1.860	2.306	2.896	3.355	5.041
9	1.383	1.833	2.262	2.821	3.250	4.781
10	1.372	1.812	2.228	2.764	3.169	4.587
11	1.363	1.796	2.201	2.718	3.106	4.437
12	1.356	1.782	2.179	2.681	3.055	4.318
13	1.350	1.771	2.160	2.650	3.012	4.221
14	1.345	1.761	2.145	2.624	2.977	4.140
15	1.341	1.753	2.131	2.602	2.947	4.073
16	1.337	1.746	2.120	2.583	2.921	4.015
17	1.333	1.740	2.110	2.567	2.898	3.965
18	1.330	1.734	2.101	2.552	2.878	3.922
19	1.328	1.729	2.093	2.539	2.861	3.883
20	1.325	1.725	2.086	2.528	2.845	3.850
21	1.323	1.721	2.080	2.518	2.831	3.819
22	1.321	1.717	2.074	2.508	2.819	3.792
23	1.319	1.714	2.069	2.500	2.807	3.767
24	1.318	1.711	2.064	2.492	2.797	3.745
25	1.316	1.708	2.060	2.485	2.787	3.725

TABLE A4 (Continued)

LEVELS OF SIGNIFICANCE FOR STUDENT'S T

	Level of significance for one-tailed test					
	.10	.05	.025	.01	.005	.0005
	Level of significance for two-tailed test					
df	.20	.10	.05	.02	.01	.001
26	1.315	1.706	2.056	2.479	2.779	3.707
27	1.314	1.703	2.052	2.473	2.771	3.690
28	1.313	1.701	2.048	2.467	2.763	3.674
29	1.311	1.699	2.045	2.462	2.756	3.659
30	1.310	1.697	2.042	2.457	2.750	3.646
40	1.303	1.684	2.021	2.423	2.704	3.551
60	1.296	1.671	2.000	2.390	2.660	3.460
120	1.289	1.658	1.980	2.358	2.617	3.373
∞	1.282	1.645	1.960	2.326	2.576	3.291

SOURCE: Table A4 is abridged from Table III of R. A. Fisher and F. Yates, *Statistical Tables for Biological, Agricultural and Medical Research* (1948 ed.), published by Oliver & Boyd, Ltd., Edinburgh and London, by permission of the authors and publishers.

TABLE A5

CRITICAL VALUES OF F

n_2\\n_1	1	2	3	4	5	6	8	12	24	∞
1	161.4	199.5	215.7	224.6	230.2	234.0	238.9	243.9	249.0	254.3
2	18.51	19.00	19.16	19.25	19.30	19.33	19.37	19.41	19.45	19.50
3	10.13	9.55	9.28	9.12	9.01	8.94	8.84	8.74	8.64	8.53
4	7.71	6.94	6.59	6.39	6.26	6.16	6.04	5.91	5.77	5.63
5	6.61	5.79	5.41	5.19	5.05	4.95	4.82	4.68	4.53	4.36
6	5.99	5.14	4.76	4.53	4.39	4.28	4.15	4.00	3.84	3.67
7	5.59	4.74	4.35	4.12	3.97	3.87	3.73	3.57	3.41	3.23
8	5.32	4.46	4.07	3.84	3.69	3.58	3.44	3.28	3.12	2.93
9	5.12	4.26	3.86	3.63	3.48	3.37	3.23	3.07	2.90	2.71
10	4.96	4.10	3.71	3.48	3.33	3.22	3.07	2.91	2.74	2.54
11	4.84	3.98	3.59	3.36	3.20	3.09	2.95	2.79	2.61	2.40
12	4.75	3.88	3.49	3.26	3.11	3.00	2.85	2.69	2.50	2.30
13	4.67	3.80	3.41	3.18	3.02	2.92	2.77	2.60	2.42	2.21
14	4.60	3.74	3.34	3.11	2.96	2.85	2.70	2.53	2.35	2.13
15	4.54	3.68	3.29	3.06	2.90	2.79	2.64	2.48	2.29	2.07
16	4.49	3.63	3.24	3.01	2.85	2.74	2.59	2.42	2.24	2.01
17	4.45	3.59	3.20	2.96	2.81	2.70	2.55	2.38	2.19	1.96
18	4.41	3.55	3.16	2.93	2.77	2.66	2.51	2.34	2.15	1.92
19	4.38	3.52	3.13	2.90	2.74	2.63	2.48	2.31	2.11	1.88
20	4.35	3.49	3.10	2.87	2.71	2.60	2.45	2.28	2.08	1.84
21	4.32	3.47	3.07	2.84	2.68	2.57	2.42	2.25	2.05	1.81
22	4.30	3.44	3.05	2.82	2.66	2.55	2.40	2.23	2.03	1.78
23	4.28	3.42	3.03	2.80	2.64	2.53	2.38	2.20	2.00	1.76
24	4.26	3.40	3.01	2.78	2.62	2.51	2.36	2.18	1.98	1.73
25	4.24	3.38	2.99	2.76	2.60	2.49	2.34	2.16	1.96	1.71
26	4.22	3.37	2.98	2.74	2.59	2.47	2.32	2.15	1.95	1.69
27	4.21	3.35	2.96	2.73	2.57	2.46	2.30	2.13	1.93	1.67
28	4.20	3.34	2.95	2.71	2.56	2.44	2.29	2.12	1.91	1.65
29	4.18	3.33	2.93	2.70	2.54	2.43	2.28	2.10	1.90	1.64
30	4.17	3.32	2.92	2.69	2.53	2.42	2.27	2.09	1.89	1.62

$p = .05$

TABLE A5 (Continued)

CRITICAL VALUES OF F

p = .05

n_1 n_2	1	2	3	4	5	6	8	12	24	∞
40	4.08	3.23	2.84	2.61	2.45	2.34	2.18	2.00	1.79	1.51
60	4.00	3.15	2.76	2.52	2.37	2.25	2.10	1.92	1.70	1.39
120	3.92	3.07	2.68	2.45	2.29	2.17	2.02	1.83	1.61	1.25
∞	3.84	2.99	2.60	2.37	2.21	2.09	1.94	1.75	1.52	1.00

Values of n_1 and n_2 represent the degrees of freedom associated with the larger and smaller estimates of variance respectively.

Source: Table AJ is abridged from Table V of R. A. Fisher and F. Yates, *Statistical Tables for Biological, Agricultural and Medical Research* (1948 ed.), published by Oliver & Boyd, Ltd., Edinburgh and London, by permission of the authors and publishers.

TABLE A5 (Continued)

CRITICAL VALUES OF F

p = .01

n_2 ＼ n_1	1	2	3	4	5	6	8	12	24	∞
1	4052	4999	5403	5625	5764	5859	5981	6106	6234	6366
2	98.49	99.01	99.17	99.25	99.30	99.33	99.36	99.42	99.46	99.50
3	34.12	30.81	29.46	28.71	28.24	27.91	27.49	27.05	26.60	26.12
4	21.20	18.00	16.69	15.98	15.52	15.21	14.80	14.37	13.93	13.46
5	16.26	13.27	12.06	11.39	10.97	10.67	10.27	9.89	9.47	9.02
6	13.74	10.92	9.78	9.15	8.75	8.47	8.10	7.72	7.31	6.88
7	12.25	9.55	8.45	7.85	7.46	7.19	6.84	6.47	6.07	5.65
8	11.26	8.65	7.59	7.01	6.63	6.37	6.03	5.67	5.28	4.86
9	10.56	8.02	6.99	6.42	6.06	5.80	5.47	5.11	4.73	4.31
10	10.04	7.56	6.55	5.99	5.64	5.39	5.06	4.71	4.33	3.91
11	9.65	7.20	6.22	5.67	5.32	5.07	4.74	4.40	4.02	3.60
12	9.33	6.93	5.95	5.41	5.06	4.82	4.50	4.16	3.78	3.36
13	9.07	6.70	5.74	5.20	4.86	4.62	4.30	3.96	3.59	3.16
14	8.86	6.51	5.56	5.03	4.69	4.46	4.14	3.80	3.43	3.00
15	8.68	6.36	5.42	4.89	4.56	4.32	4.00	3.67	3.29	2.87
16	8.53	6.23	5.29	4.77	4.44	4.20	3.89	3.55	3.18	2.75
17	8.40	6.11	5.18	4.67	4.34	4.10	3.79	3.45	3.08	2.65

TABLE A5 (Continued)

CRITICAL VALUES OF F

					p = .01					
n_2 \ n_1	1	2	3	4	5	6	8	12	24	∞
18	8.28	6.01	5.09	4.58	4.25	4.01	3.71	3.37	3.00	2.57
19	8.18	5.93	5.01	4.50	4.17	3.94	3.63	3.30	2.92	2.49
20	8.10	5.85	4.94	4.43	4.10	3.87	3.56	3.23	2.86	2.42
21	8.02	5.78	4.87	4.37	4.04	3.81	3.51	3.17	2.80	2.36
22	7.94	5.72	4.82	4.31	3.99	3.76	3.45	3.12	2.75	2.31
23	7.88	5.66	4.76	4.26	3.94	3.71	3.41	3.07	2.70	2.26
24	7.82	5.61	4.72	4.22	3.90	3.67	3.36	3.03	2.66	2.21
25	7.77	5.57	4.68	4.18	3.86	3.63	3.32	2.99	2.62	2.17
26	7.72	5.53	4.64	4.14	3.82	3.59	3.29	2.96	2.58	2.13
27	7.68	5.49	4.60	4.11	3.78	3.56	3.26	2.93	2.55	2.10
28	7.64	5.45	4.57	4.07	3.75	3.53	3.23	2.90	2.52	2.06
29	7.60	5.42	4.54	4.04	3.73	3.50	3.20	2.87	2.49	2.03
30	7.56	5.39	4.51	4.02	3.70	3.47	3.17	2.84	2.47	2.01
40	7.31	5.18	4.31	3.83	3.51	3.29	2.99	2.66	2.29	1.80
60	7.08	4.98	4.13	3.65	3.34	3.12	2.82	2.50	2.12	1.60
120	6.85	4.79	3.95	3.48	3.17	2.96	2.66	2.34	1.95	1.38
∞	6.64	4.60	3.78	3.32	3.02	2.80	2.51	2.18	1.79	1.00

Values of n_1 and n_2 represent the degrees of freedom associated with the larger and smaller estimates of variance respectively.

TABLE A5

CRITICAL VALUES OF F

					p = .001					
n_2 \ n_1	1	2	3	4	5	6	8	12	24	∞
1	405284	500000	540379	562500	576405	585937	598144	610667	623497	636619
2	998.5	999.0	999.2	999.2	999.3	999.3	999.4	999.4	999.5	999.5
3	167.5	148.5	141.1	137.1	134.6	132.8	130.6	128.3	125.9	123.5
4	74.14	61.25	56.18	53.44	51.71	50.53	49.00	47.41	45.77	44.05
5	47.04	36.61	33.20	31.09	29.75	28.84	27.64	26.42	25.14	23.78
6	35.51	27.00	23.70	21.90	20.81	20.03	19.03	17.99	16.89	15.75
7	29.22	21.69	18.77	17.19	16.21	15.52	14.63	13.71	12.73	11.69

TABLE A5 *(Continued)*

CRITICAL VALUES OF *F*

p = .001

$_{n_2}^{\ n_1}$	1	2	3	4	5	6	8	12	24	∞
8	25.42	18.49	15.83	14.39	13.49	12.86	12.04	11.19	10.30	9.34
9	22.86	16.39	13.90	12.56	11.71	11.13	10.37	9.57	8.72	7.81
10	21.04	14.91	12.55	11.28	10.48	9.92	9.20	8.45	7.64	6.76
11	19.69	13.81	11.56	10.35	9.58	9.05	8.35	7.63	6.85	6.00
12	18.64	12.97	10.80	9.63	8.89	8.38	7.71	7.00	6.25	5.42
13	17.81	12.31	10.21	9.07	8.35	7.86	7.21	6.52	5.78	4.97
14	17.14	11.78	9.73	8.62	7.92	7.43	6.80	6.13	5.41	4.60
15	16.59	11.34	9.34	8.25	7.57	7.09	6.47	5.81	5.10	4.31
16	16.12	10.97	9.00	7.94	7.27	6.81	6.19	5.55	4.85	4.06
17	15.72	10.66	8.73	7.68	7.02	6.56	5.96	5.32	4.63	3.85
18	15.38	10.39	8.49	7.46	6.81	6.35	5.76	5.13	4.45	3.67
19	15.08	10.16	8.28	7.26	6.61	6.18	5.59	4.97	4.29	3.52
20	14.82	9.95	8.10	7.10	6.46	6.02	5.44	4.82	4.15	3.38
21	14.59	9.77	7.94	6.95	6.32	5.88	5.31	4.70	4.03	3.26
22	14.38	9.61	7.80	6.81	6.19	5.76	5.19	4.58	3.92	3.15
23	14.19	9.47	7.67	6.69	6.08	5.65	5.09	4.48	3.82	3.05
24	14.03	9.34	7.55	6.59	5.98	5.55	4.99	4.39	3.74	2.97
25	13.88	9.22	7.45	6.49	5.88	5.46	4.91	4.31	3.66	2.89
26	13.74	9.12	7.36	6.41	5.80	5.38	4.83	4.24	3.59	2.82
27	13.61	9.02	7.27	6.33	5.73	5.31	4.76	4.17	3.52	2.75
28	13.50	8.93	7.19	6.25	5.66	5.24	4.69	4.11	3.46	2.70
29	13.39	8.85	7.12	6.19	5.59	5.18	4.64	4.05	3.41	2.64
30	13.29	8.77	7.05	6.12	5.53	5.12	4.58	4.00	3.36	2.59
40	12.61	8.25	6.60	5.70	5.13	4.73	4.21	3.64	3.01	2.23
60	11.97	7.76	6.17	5.31	4.76	4.37	3.87	3.31	2.69	1.90
120	11.38	7.31	5.79	4.95	4.42	4.04	3.55	3.02	2.40	1.56
∞	10.83	6.91	5.42	4.62	4.10	3.74	3.27	2.74	2.13	1.00

Values of n_1 and n_2 represent the degrees of freedom associated with the larger and smaller estimates of variance respectively.

SOURCE: Table A5 is abridged from Table V of R. A. Fisher and F. Yates, *Statistical Tables for Biological, Agricultural and Medical Research* (1948 ed.), published by Oliver & Boyd, Ltd., Edinburgh and London, by permission of the authors and publishers.

GLOSSARY

abstract: A summary of an article usually found at the beginning of the article.

administrative ethics: The rules or standards governing the moral conduct of the members of a public administrative organization.

adverse personnel actions: Personnel activities such as reprimands and dismissals taken against an employee because of incompetency or violation of established agency policies or practices.

agenda setting: The stage of the policy-making process during which problems get defined as political issues.

alternative-form: Calculating reliability by repeating different but equivalent measures at two or more points in time.

analysis of variance: A technique for measuring the relationship between one nominal or ordinal-level variable and one interval or ratio-level variable.

analytical budgeting: An alternative to the traditional incremental, line-item approach to public budgeting. Examples include *management by objectives, zero-based budgeting,* and *planning programming and budgeting.*

antecedent variable: An independent variable that precedes other independent variables in time.

applied research: Research designed to produce knowledge useful in altering a real-world condition or situation.

assignment at random: Random assignment of subjects to experimental and control groups.

association: The statistical relation between two or more variables, either by covariation or joint occurrence.

assymetrical statistic: A directional measure of association that is used when the direction of a relationship is being predicted—the lambda statistic, for example.

authority: The ability to affect the actions or predispositons of others to act because people feel obliged to comply because compliance is right or correct.

bar graph: A type of graphic display of frequency or percentage distribution of data.

behavioralism: The study of politics that focuses on political behavior and embraces the scientific method.

beta weight: A statistic used to assess the relative importance of predictive variables in a single regression equation. Also known as the standardized partial regression coefficient.

bivariate relationship: The association between two variables.

bivariate table: A table showing the relationship between two variables by displaying all the combinations of categories of the variables.

blank foreign elements: A threat to the usefulness of a sample frame. This problem occurs when the sample units of a sample frame are not a part of the original population.

bureaucracy: A system of authority relations defined by rationally developed rules. Bureaucracy in today's world refers primarily to government agencies that are characterized by day-to-day policy functions.

case study design: Comprehensive and in-depth study of a single case or several cases. Nonexperimental design in which an investigator has little control over events.

causal relationship: When the variation in one variable independent of variation in other variables causes variation in a second variable.

causation: Involves three distinct operations: establishing the time order of the occurrences, demonstrating covariation, and eliminating spurious relations. (See *causal relationship*.)

causal hypothesis: A hypothesis in which the independent variable is thought to be a cause of the dependent variable.

central tendency: The most frequent, common, or central value in the distribution of values of a variable.

chi square: A measure used with crosstabulation to determine if a relationship is statistically significant.

Civil Service Reform Act of 1978: A major act that reformed the federal personnel system. It assigned the functions performed by the Civil Service Commission to two new and separate agencies: the Merit Systems Protection Board and the Office of Personnel Management. Also provided for an appeal's procedure for employees to use to address grievances.

classic experimental design: Experiment with random assignment of subjects to experimental and control groups with pretest and post-test for both groups.

closed-ended question: A question with response alternatives provided.

cluster of elements: A threat to the usefulness of a sample frame. This problem occurs when the sample units of a sample frame are listed in groups rather than individually.

cluster sample: A probability sample used when no list of elements exists. Sampling frame initially consists of clusters of elements.

codebook: A book that identifies observations and the numbers assigned to describe the categories of the observations.

coefficient of determination: Symbolized as r^2, it is a reduction of variance ratio. It refers to the amount of variance in one variable that is accounted for by the variation in another variable. Commonly used to depict the explained variance in a bivariate regression equation.

coefficient of multiple determination: Symbolized as R^2. Similar to a coefficient of determination. It is used, however, in a multiple variate regression equation.

comparative politics: A subfield of political science where different political systems are examined for likenesses and differences.

coefficient of variation: A measure of dispersion used by political scientists to compare the dispersion of two or more groups about their respective means.

comparison: The operational process required to demonstrate that two variables are correlated.

compensation plans: A plan that outlines the types of payment to employees for their services.

composite index: An index developed by using several items (questions) to measure complex concepts. Although somewhat crude, it is an efficient way to summarize information.

composite political research: A research approach that combines elements of behavioralism and postbehavioralism in the study of political phenomena.

concept: The definition or meaning of a phenomenon used in empirical research.

confidence level: The probability that the population parameter actually falls within the margin of error of a sample statistic.

consensual validity: The acceptance of the validity of a measurement instrument based on the acceptance of experts in the field. For example, the recidivism rate has been accepted as a valid measurement to determine the success of programs designed to place criminals back in society as contributing citizens.

consent: The political theory that governments should exist and operate only with the approval of the governed.

construct validity: Demonstrating validity for a measure by showing it is related to the measure of another concept.

content analysis: A procedure by which verbal, nonquantitative records are transformed into quantitative data.

content validity: Demonstrating validity by ensuring that the full domain of a concept is measured.

control: A procedure designed to eliminate alternative sources of variation that may distort the research results.

control by grouping: A form of statistical control in which observations identical or similar to the control variable are grouped together.

control group: A group of subjects that does not receive the treatment or test stimulus.

convenience sample: A nonprobability sample in which the selection of elements is determined by the researcher's convenience.

correlation coefficient: A linear measure of association between two interval/ratio variables that measures the direction and strength (extent) of the relationship.

correlation matrix: A table showing the relationships among a number of discrete measures.

correlative hypothesis: A hypothesis that proposes a relationship between two variables without indicating the nature of that relationship.

correlational validity: Refers to the congruence between results obtained from the measure and some other evidence of the phenomenon being analyzed.

covariation: The situation where a unit change in one variable is paralleled with some degree of regularity by a comparable change in another variable, for example, education and income.

covert observation: The observer's presence or purpose is kept secret from those being observed.

Cramer's V: A variation of the phi statistic. It is designed for use with a crosstabulation of any size. It has no operational definition and is used with nominal-level data.

critique: A critical evaluation of a piece of literature.

crosstabulation: A technique for measuring the relationship between nominal and ordinal-level measures.

cross-sectional design: Research design in which measurements of independent and dependent variables are taken at same time; naturally occurring differences in independent variable are used to create quasi-experimental and quasi-control groups; extraneous factors are controlled for by statistical means.

curvilinear relationship: A relationship between two variables that may best be described by a curved, rather than a straight, line.

decision makers: Those people in government that confront issues and make public policy.

deduction: A process of reasoning from a theory to specific observations.

degrees of freedom: A measure used in conjunction with chi square and other measures to determine if a relationship is statistically significant.

democracy: A system of government in which, in theory, the people rule, either directly or indirectly.

dependent variable: The phenomenon thought to be influenced, affected, or caused by some other phenomenon.

descriptive statistics: Mathematical summary of measurements for one variable.

deterrence: The defense policy of American strategists during the Eisenhower administration, who believed the Soviets would not take aggressive action knowing they risked nuclear annihilation.

difference of means test: A technique for measuring the relationship between one nominal or ordinal-level variable and one interval or ratio level variable.

direct observation: A data collection method in which the researcher directly observes a behavior or physical traces of the behavior.

direct relationship: A relationship in which the values of one variable increase as the values of another variable increase.

direction of a relationship: An indication of which values of the dependent variable are associated with which values of the independent variable.

directional hypothesis: A hypothesis that specifies the expected relationship between two or more variables.

dispersion: The distribution of data values around the most common, middle, or central value.

disproportionate sample: A stratified sample in which elements sharing a characteristic are underrepresented or overrepresented in a sample.

distributive policy: Policy involving the provision of benefits to citizens, groups, or corporations—for example, tax abatements and farm subsidies to promote economic development.

document analysis: Data collection based on records kept by institutions or individuals.

double-barreled question: A question that is really two questions in one.

ecological fallacy: When the attributes or behavior of groups is a misleading indication of the attributes or behavior of individuals.

economic security: Having a relatively strong economy within a nation-state.

element: An entity about which information is collected or the unit of analysis.

elite interviewing: Interviewing respondents in a nonstandardized, individualized manner.

elite theory (elitism): The theory that follows the idea that despite the procedural characteristics of majoritarian democracy and the presence of different groups, a very small minority makes all the important governmental decisions.

empirical generalization: A statement that summarizes the relationship between individual facts while communicating general knowledge.

empirical research: Based on actual, "objective," observation of phenomena.

empirical theory: Theory relying on perceptions, experience, and behavior.

empirical verification: Demonstration by means of objective observation that a statement is true.

epistemology: The study of the foundations of knowledge.

equality: The principle that all individuals have moral worth and are entitled to fair treatment under the law.

eta-squared: A measure of association used with the analysis of variance that indicates the proportion of the variance in the dependent variable explained by the variance in the independent variable.

experimental control: Assessing the impact of a third variable by manipulating the exposure of experimental groups to experimental stimuli.

experimental effect: Effect of independent variable on the dependent variable.

experimental group: A group of subjects receiving treatment or test stimulus.

experimental mortality: A differential loss of subjects from experimental and control groups that affects equivalency of groups.

experimentation: Research using an experimental research design in which the researcher has control over the independent variable, the units of analysis, and their environment; used to test causal relationships.

explanation: A systematic, empirically verified understanding of why a phenomenon occurs as it does.

explained variance: That portion of the variation in a dependent variable that is accounted for by the variation in the independent variable(s).

external validity: The ability to generalize from one set of research findings to other situations.

extraneous factors: Other factors besides the independent variable that may cause change in the dependent variable.

F ratio: A measure used with the analysis of variance to determine if a relationship is statistically significant.

face validity: Asserting validity by arguing that a measure corresponds closely to the concept it is designed to measure.

field research: Experimental designs applied in a natural setting. Observation in a natural setting.

filter question: A question used to screen respondents so that subsequent questions will be asked only of certain respondents for whom the questions are appropriate.

finite population: The aggregate of all cases that conform to some designated set of specifications where the number of cases is known; for example, the population of the U.S. Congress, which is 535 members, is a finite population.

frequency curve: A line graph indicating frequency distribution.

frequency distribution (f): The number of observations per value or category of a variable.

frequency distribution control: When frequency distribution of a characteristic is the same in the experimental group as in the control group.

gamma: A coefficient of association indicating the magnitude and direction of the relationship between ordinal variables.

general: Applicable to many rather than a few cases.

government: The legitimate use of force to control human behavior within territorial boundaries.

guttman scale: A multi-item measure in which respondents are presented with increasingly difficult measures of approval for an attitude.

hierarchy: An administrative organizational system in a bureaucracy based on the principle of interlocking responsibility and control that integrates all personnel.

histogram: The type of bar graph used to depict interval and ratio-level measures.

history: Change in a dependent variable due to changes in environment over time; threat to internal validity.

hypothesis: A statement proposing a relationship between two or more variables.

incomplete frame: A sample frame that does not include all elements of the population.

incremental decision making: A major approach to problem solving that suggests a conservative and practical view to administrators in order for them to meet new challenges slowly and progressively.

independent variable: The phenomenon thought to influence, affect, or cause some other phenomenon.

index: A multi-item measure in which individual scores on a set of items are combined to form a summary measure.

indirect observation: Observation of physical traces of behavior.

induction: The acquisition of scientific knowledge where observation precedes theory. A theory is developed based on repeated observations.

inductive statistics (inferential statistics): Statistics that enable the researcher to make decisions (inferences) about characteristics of a population based on observations from a probability sample taken from the population.

infinite population: The aggregate of all cases that conform to some designated set of specifications where the number of cases is unknown.

influence: The use of political resources to affect the actions or predispositions to act of others.

input functions: The process where the wants and desires of the relevant public get placed on the policy agenda.

instrumentation: A process that designates changes in the measuring instrument between the pretest and the posttest.

instrument decay: Change in a measurement device used to measure dependent variable producing change in measurements.

interaction effect: Reaction of subjects to combination of pretest and test stimulus.

internal validity: The ability to show that manipulation or variation of the independent variable causes the dependent variable to change.

international organizations: Organizations made up of two or more sovereign states. They usually meet regularly and have a permanent staff.

international relations: The interactions, rules, and processes that exist between sovereign states and other international actors.

international system: Any collection of independent political entities which interact with considerable frequency and according to regularized processes.

interquartile range: The middle 50 percent of observations.

interval level of measurement: A measure for which a one-unit difference in scores is the same throughout the range of the measure.

intervening variable: A variable coming between an independent and dependent variable in an explanatory scheme.

interviewer bias: Interviewer influence on a respondent's answers; an example of reactivity.

interview data: Observations derived from written or verbal questioning of respondent by researcher.

inverse relationship: A relationship in which the values of one variable increase as the values of another variable decrease.

journals: Records of events, meetings, visits, and other activities of an individual(s) or group, over a given period of time.

Kendall's tau: A measure of association between ordinal-level variables.

lambda: A measure of association between two nominal-level variables or between an ordinal level variable and one nominal-level variable.

leading question: A question that leads respondent to choose a particular response.

level of significance: The probability that a relationship could have occurred by chance. It is also the probability of rejecting a true null hypothesis or making a Type I error. Most researchers are willing to accept a 5 percent chance that a relationship could have occurred by chance.

levels of measurement: The extent to which typical numbers describe characteristics of a variable. We distinguish nominal, ordinal, interval, and ratio levels. The higher the level of measurement, the greater the number of applicable statistics and statistical methods.

liberty: The principle that the people are the ultimate source of governing authority and that their general welfare is the only legitimate purpose of government.

Likert scale: A multi-item measure in which the items are selected based on their ability to discriminate between those scoring high and those scoring low on the measure.

limited government: A government that is subject to strict limits on its lawful uses of powers, and thus on its ability to deprive the citizen of their liberty.

line positions: Employee positions within a bureaucratic organization that are a part of the chain of command.

linear relationship: A relationship between two variables that when displayed on a graph forms a straight line.

linkage institutions: Institutions such as the media, interest groups, and political parties that communicate the demands of the citizen (public opinion) to those who can act on them.

literature review: A part of the research process whereby researchers examine existing publications to familiarize themselves with the topic and the ways others have examined the topic.

logarithmic relationship: A mathematical relationship in which increasing amounts of one variable have less and less effect on another variable.

longitudinal design: A research design whereby observations are made of a unit over a period of time, for example, the study of a legislative body over a number of years.

mailed questionnaire: Survey instrument mailed to respondents for completion and return.

main diagonal: The diagonal in a bivariate crosstabulation where most of the units of analysis (cases) lie. The more cases that lie on the diagonal, the stronger the relationship in a positive direction.

mainframe: A large computer that controls and coordinates activities of a entire computer system.

majoritarian model of democracy: The classical theory of democracy in which government by the people is interpreted as government by the majority of the people.

management by objectives (MBO): A process whereby organizational goals and objectives are set through the participation of organizational members in terms of expected results. It was proposed by analytical budgeting advocates as an alternative to the typical line-item, incremental approach to public budgeting.

manipulation: A procedure that allows the researcher in experimental settings to have some control over the introduction of an independent variable. It satisfies the time-order criterion of causality.

margin of error: The range around a sample statistic within which the population parameter is likely to fall.

matching: A control method that involves making the experimental and control groups equal in accordance with extrinsic variables that are presumed to relate to the research question.

maturation: Change in subjects over time that affects dependent variable.

mean: The sum of the values of a variable divided by the number of values.

mean deviation: A measure of dispersion of data points for interval- and ratio-level data.

measurement: The process by which phenomena are observed systematically and represented by scores or numerals.

measures of association: Statistics that summarize the relationship between two variables.

measurement reliability: The degree to which measures yield the same results when applied by different researchers to the same units under the same circumstances. The consistency of a measurment tool.

measurement validity: The degree to which a measurement tool measures what it is supposed to measure.

median: The category or value above and below which one-half of observations lie.

mixed-scanning: An approach to decision making that attempts to integrate the incremental and the rational-comprehensive models. It involves the collection and evaluation of general data on a broad range of topics and detailed analysis of particular issues.

mode: The category with the greatest frequency of observations.

multinational corporations: Business corporations with headquarters in one nation-state that owns and operates subsidiaries in other nation-states.

multiple causation: An instance when a dependent variable is produced by two or more independent variables.

multiple regression: A technique for measuring the mathematical relationships between more than one independent variable and a dependent variable, while controlling for all other independent variables in the equation.

multivariate crosstabulation: A procedure by which crosstabulation is used to control for a third variable.

multivariate data analysis: Data analysis techniques designed to test hypotheses involving more than two variables.

national prestige: The way others perceive a nation-state. It is, many times, associated with military and/or economic power.

national security: Protection against military threats on a nation. There are two types of security: territorial security and political independence.

nation-states: Self-ruling political entities established first with the Treaty of Westphalia. A state whose residents consider themselves a nation.

negatively skewed: A distribution of values in which more observations lie to the left of the middle value.

negative relationship: When high values of one variable are associated with low values of another variable.

nominal definition: The dictionary definition of a concept.

nominal level of measurement: A measure for which different scores represent different, but not ordered, categories.

nonexperimental design: Research design characterized by presence of a single group or lack of researcher control over assignment of subjects to control and experimental groups.

nongovernmental organizations: Organizations not associated with governments. They play a subsidiary role in the international arena, the American Red Cross, for example.

nonnormative knowledge: Concerned not with evaluation or prescription but with factual or objective determinations.

nonprobability sample: A sample for which each element in the total population has an unknown probability of being selected.

normal distribution curve: A frequency curve showing a symmetrical, bell-shaped distribution in which the mean, mode, and median coincide and in which a fixed proportion of observations lies between the mean and any distance from the mean measured in terms of the standard deviation.

normative knowledge: Evaluative, value-laden, concerned with prescribing what ought to be.

null hypothesis: A hypothesis that proposes no relationship between two variables.

off diagonal: The diagonal in a bivariate crosstabulation where many of the units of analysis (cases) lie. The more cases that lie on the diagonal, the stronger the relationship in a negative direction.

open-ended question: A question with no response alternatives from which respondent may choose.

operational definition: The rules by which a concept is measured and scores assigned.

order: The rule of law and custom or the observance of prescribed procedure.

ordinal level of measurement: A measure for which the scores represent ordered categories that are not necessarily equally distant from each other.

output functions: Refers to the different types of government actions. For example, public policy, judicial decisions, executive action.

overt observation: Those being observed are informed of the observer's presence and purpose.

panel study: A cross-sectional study in which measurements of variables are taken on the same units of analysis at multiple points in time.

parameter: A specified value of the population (mean, standard deviation).

partial correlation: A mathematical adjustment in the relationship between two variables, designed to control for the effect of a third.

partial slopes: Coefficients generated by the multiple regression routine. They represent the amount of change in the dependent variable associated with each independent variable, holding all other independent variables constant.

partial tables: Crosstabulation tables measuring the extent of association between two nominal, two ordinal, or one nominal and one ordinal, measured variables while controlling for the effects of another variable.

participant observation: Observation in which an observer becomes a regular participant in the activities of those being observed.

participatory democracy: The Jeffersonian and Jacksonian notions of democracy where the government should be open to most of the people. This includes participation as voters, candidates, and service as elected and appointed officials.

Pearson product-moment correlation: The statistic computed from a regression analysis that indicates the strength of the relationship between two interval- or ratio-level variables.

percentage distribution: The percent of observations per category of variable.

perfect relationship: The relationship that exists when two variables are paired in such a way that the absolute value of one variable can be perfectly predicted by knowing the absolute value of another variable.

personal interview: Face-to-face questioning of a respondent.

phi coefficient: A measure of association used if both independent and dependent variables are nominal and dichotomous.

pie graph: A type of graphic display of frequency distribution.

planning, programming, and budgeting system (PPBS): An analytical budgeting method that quantifies goals, programs, and projects. It was proposed by analytical budgeting advocates as an alternative to the typical line-item, incremental approach to public budgeting.

pluralist model: An interpretation of democracy in which government by the people is taken to mean government by people operating through competing interest groups.

policy adoption: The stage of the policy-making process during which proposals are accepted by the decision-making body.

policy analysis: The evaluation of public policy to determine whether it is meeting the goals of the decision makers. Today, more and more policy analysts use surveys and empirical methods to evaluate policy. (See *policy evaluation.*)

policy agenda: The list of activities public decision makers pay attention to at any given time. It is used to bring new issues into the political limelight.

policy evaluation: The analysis of public policy.

policy formulation: The stage of the policy-making process during which formal proposals are developed and adopted.

policy implementation: The primary function of the public bureaucracy. It refers to the process of carrying out the authoritative decisions of Congress, the president, and the courts. Also applicable to subnational levels of government.

policy implications: The predicted effect that the findings of policy evaluation and analysis will have on public policy.

policy termination: The stage of the policy-making process whereby public policy is discontinued when it has attained the goals of the policy.

policy triggering devices: Events or activities that generate the demand for public policy.

political decay: The gradual deterioration and downfall of a political system.

political development: The way political systems evolve over time. Includes the process of coping with crises that all nations experience.

political resources: Any attribute(s) that an individual, group, or nation can use to influence others.

political science: The application of the methods of acquiring scientific knowledge to the study of political phenomena.

political system: A set of interrelated institutions that link people with government. Any persistent pattern of human relationships that involves, to a significant extent, control, influence, power, or authority.

politics: The process that determines who gets what, when, and how.

population: All of the cases or observations covered by a hypothesis; all the units of analysis to which a hypothesis applies.

population parameter: The incidence of a characteristic or attribute in a population (not a sample).

position classification: The clustering of government jobs according to their nature, qualifications required, duties performed, and responsibilities assumed.

positively skewed: A distribution of values in which more observations lie to the right of the middle value.

positive relationship: When high values of one variable are associated with high values of another variable.

postbehavioralism: A way to study politics that not only focuses on political behavior using the scientific method, but also allows researchers to use their values when presenting policy implications. It could also involve the use of advanced mathematical techniques such as calculus to analyze behavior.

posttest: Measurement of dependent variable after manipulation of independent variable.

power: The ability in politics to control or change the behavior of human beings in a way favored by the power-wielder.

precision matching: Matching of pairs of subjects with one of the pair assigned to experimental group and the other to control group.

prediction: The application of explanation to events in the future. The ability to correctly anticipate future events.

predictive validity: Validation of a measure by prediction to an external criterion.

pretest: Measurement of dependent variable prior to administration of treatment or manipulation of independent variable.

primary data: Data that is collected by the researcher versus by someone else (secondary data), for observations, or surveys.

probabalistic explanation: An explanation that does not explain or predict events with 100 percent accuracy.

probability sample: A sample for which each element in the total population has a known probability of being selected.

problem recognition: The first step in a research process involving the identification of a phenomenon worthy of study. Also applicable to the first step in the policy-making process whereby an item is recognized as requiring the attention of public policy makers.

problem statement: A succinct statement of the phenomenon that is being analyzed.

progressive movement: A movement in American politics that had an important influence on the development of American public administration. The primary goals of the Progressives were to make government more efficient and businesslike through the professionalization of public agencies and functions.

proportionate reduction in error (PRE): A method used to measure the magnitude of the relationship between two variables where one is used to predict the values of another.

provisional: Subject to revision and change.

public administration: The process by which the government delivers common goods and services to members of a community be it at the national, state, or local level of government.

public opinion: The beliefs, wants, and desires of the people.

public policy: Can be any broad course of governmental action. In a more narrow sense, it can be a specific government program or initiative.

purposive sample: A nonprobability sample in which a researcher uses discretion in selecting elements for observation.

pure research: Research design to satisfy one's intellectual curiosity about some phenomenon. (Also referred to as theoretical or recreational research.)

questionnaire design: The physical layout of a questionnaire.

quota sample: A nonprobability sample in which elements are sampled in proportion to their representation in the population.

random digit dialing: A procedure used to improve the representativeness of telephone samples by giving listed and unlisted numbers a chance of being selected.

random numbers table: A list of random numbers.

random sample: A subset of the population where each unit in the population has an equal chance of being selected. In addition the selection of any one unit has no effect on the selection of any other unit.

random start: Selection of a number at random to determine where to start selecting elements in a systematic sample.

range: The distance between highest and lowest values or the range of categories into which observations fall.

ratio level of measurement: A measure for which the scores possess the full mathematical properties of the numbers assigned.

rational decision making: A systems analysis approach based on principles of scientific investigation and scientific problem solving. It involves value clarification, means-ends analysis, choosing the most appropriate means to achieve desired ends, comprehensive analysis, and analysis that is theory-based.

reactivity: The effect of data collection on the phenomenon being observed.

redistributive policy: Occurs when the government redistributes the wealth from one group in our society to another group; involves the direct provision of benefits to citizens through social programs such as welfare.

regression analysis: A technique for measuring the relationship between two interval- or ratio-level variables.

regression artifact: A problem that occurs when individuals have been assigned to the experimental group based on their extreme scores on the dependent variable. When this occurs, and measures are unreliable, individuals who scored below average on the pretest will appear to have improved upon retesting. The opposite may also occur.

regression coefficient: Another name for the slope of a regression equation.

regression equation: The mathematical formula describing the relationship between two interval- or ratio-level variables. $(y = a + bx)$

regulatory policy: Policy designed to maintain order and prohibit behaviors that endanger society. Examples include attempts to control criminal activities and to protect economic activities and business markets.

relationship: The association, dependence, or covariance of the values of one variable with the values of another variable.

reliability: The extent to which a measure yields the same results on repeated trials.

replication: The repetition of an investigation in an identical way as a safeguard against unintentional error or deception. Also used to describe the results of statistical controlling in crosstabulation analysis where the results duplicate the original relationship between the dependent and independent variables.

research design: A plan specifying how the researcher intends to fulfill the goals of the study; a logical plan for testing hypotheses.

research ethics: The moral considerations/implications of research.

research hypothesis: A tentative answer to a research problem. It is expressed in the form of a relationship between independent and dependent variables.

residual: In a regression analysis, the difference between the observed and predicted values of Y (the dependent variable).

response rate: The proportion of respondents selected for participation in a survey who actually participate.

response set: The pattern of responding to a series of questions in a similar fashion without careful reading of each question.

sample: A subset of all the observations or cases covered by a hypothesis; a portion of a population.

sample bias: The bias that occurs whenever some elements of a population are systematically excluded from a sample. It is usually due to an incomplete sampling frame or a nonprobability method of selecting elements.

sample statistic: The estimate of a characteristic or attribute in a sample.

sampling error: The confidence level and the margin of error taken together.

sampling fraction: The proportion of the population included in a sample.

sampling frame: The population from which a sample is drawn. Ideally it is the same as the total population of interest to a study.

sampling interval: The number of elements in a sampling frame divided by the desired sample size.

sampling unit: The entity listed in a sampling frame. It may be the same as an element, or it may be a group or cluster of elements.

satisficing: The process of finding a decision alternative that meets the decision maker's minimum standard of satisfaction. Coined by James G. March and Herbert A. Simon.

scale: A combined measure used to operationalize abstract concepts such as racial prejudice that cannot be adequately measured by a single indicator.

scattergram: A technique for displaying graphically the relationship between two interval- or ratio-level variables.

scientific knowledge: Knowledge that is obtained through verification, rigorous reasoning, and empirical observation.

secondary data: Data collected by someone else, for example, public records data such as the United States Census.

simple random sample: A probability sample in which each element has an equal chance of being selected.

skewed distribution: A data distribution in which more observations fall to one side of the mean than the other. Thus, the mean is "pulled" towards the extreme low (negative skew) or extreme high (positive skew).

slope: The part of a regression equation that shows how much change in the value of Y (the dependent variable) corresponds to a one-unit change in the value of X (the independent variable.)

snowball sample: A sample in which respondents are asked to identify additional members of a population.

Somer's DYX and DXY: A measure of association between ordinal-level variables.

specified relationship: A relationship between two variables that varies with the values of a third.

split-half method: Calculating reliability by comparing the results of two equivalent measures made at the same time.

spurious relationship: A relationship between two variables caused entirely by the impact of a third.

staff position: Employee positions within a bureaucratic organization that are not a part of the chain of command. They are usually advisory positions to the head of the organization, auditors for example.

standard deviation: The measure of dispersion of data points about the mean for interval- and ratio-level data.

standard error: The standard deviation of sample means about the mean of sample means.

standard normal distribution: Normal distribution with a mean of 0 and standard deviation and variance of 1.

standard score: An individual observation that belongs to a distribution with a mean of 0 and a standard deviation of 1.

statistic: A characteristic of a sample as opposed to a characteristic (parameter) of a population. Statistics are used to infer properties, or parameters, of the population.

statistical control: Assessing the impact of a third variable by comparing observations across the values of a control variable.

statistical regression: Change in dependent variable due to temporary nature of extreme values.

statistical significance: An indication of whether an observed relationship could have occurred by chance.

stratified sample: A probability sample in which elements sharing one or more characteristics are grouped, and elements are selected from each group in proportion to the group's representation in the total population.

stratum: A subgroup of a population that shares one or more characteristics.

strength of a relationship: An indication of how consistently the values of a dependent variable are associated with the values of an independent variable.

structural-functionalism: An approach that seeks to explain the nature and function of public organizations. It identifies variables common to all organizations such as complexity, centralization, formalization, stratification, adaptiveness, production, efficiency, and job satisfaction.

survey instrument: Schedule of questions to be asked of respondent.

survey research: Research based on interview method of data collection.

symmetrical statistic: A nondirectional measure of association that is used when the direction of a relationship is not being predicted, the lambda statistic, for example.

systematic sample: A probability sample in which elements are selected from a list at predetermined intervals.

tau statistics: Bivariate statistics used with ordinal-level data. They are used as symmetrical (nondirectional) statistics.

tautology: A hypothesis in which the independent and dependent variables are identical, making it impossible to disconfirm.

telephone interview: Questioning of respondent via telephone.

testing: Effect of pretest on a dependent variable.

test-retest method: Calculating reliability by repeating the same measure at two or more points in time.

test stimulus: The independent variable.

theoretical implications: The predicted effect that research findings will have on the theory being used to guide the research effort.

theoretical population: See *population*.

theory: A statement or series of statements that organize, explain, and predict knowledge.

threats to measurement: Possible occurrences that could detract from the reliability and validity of a measure, for example, history or regression artifacts.

Thurstone scale: A multi-item measure in which the goal is to select items that represent the entire range of an attitude at equal intervals.

time-series design: Multiple measurements of dependent variable before or after experimental treatment.

topic evaluation: The process whereby a researcher analyzes a topic for research. According to Richard Cole it involves ensuring (1) the topic is of interest; (2) the topic is manageable, and (3) it does not broach the ethical considerations associated with research.

total variance: The variation in a dependent variable that a researcher is attempting to account for.

transmissible knowledge: Knowledge for which the method of knowing is made explicit.

triangulation: The use of several observers, data collection techniques, or sources of data to enhance the reliability and validity of a research effort.

two-sided question: A question with two substantive alternatives provided for the respondent.

two-way analysis of variance: An extension of the analysis of variance procedure to allow controlling for a third variable.

unexplained variance: That portion of the variation in a dependent variable that is not accounted for by the variation in the independent variable(s).

unit of analysis: The type of actor (individual, group, institution, or nation) specified in a researcher's hypothesis.

univariate data analysis: Analysis of a single variable.

unobtrusive measure: A measure of phenomenon that does not involve reaction to measurement.

validity: The correspondence between a measure and the concept it is supposed to measure.

variability: The heterogeneity of a sample or population. Also used to describe variation in the range of values of a variable.

variance: The measure of dispersion of data points about the mean for interval- and ratio-level data.

war: The use of armed conflict as a way that nation-states play politics to achieve their goals.

weak relationship: A small association between variables. With statistics, a measure of association between variables having a value close to zero, is a weak relationship.

weighting factor: A mathematical factor used to make a disproportionate sample representative.

written record: Documents, reports, statistics, manuscripts, and other written, oral, or visual materials available and useful for empirical research.

Y-intercept: The value of Y (the dependent variable) in a regression equation when the value of X (the independent variable) is 0.

Z score: The number of standard deviations that a score deviates from the mean score.

zero-based budgeting (ZBB): A system of budgeting that requires all spending for a program or an agency to be justified anew each year. It was proposed by analytical budgeting advocates as an alternative to the typical line-item, incremental approach to public budgeting.

BIBLIOGRAPHY

Abramson, Rudy. 1991. "Curbs Sought on 11.6m Acres to Protect Owls." *The Boston Globe*, April 23, p. 1.

Almond, Gabriel, and James Coleman. 1960. *The Politics of Developing Areas.* Princeton, NJ: Princeton University Press.

Almond, Gabriel, and Sidney Verba. 1963. *The Civic Culture.* Princeton, NJ: Princeton University Press.

Almond, Gabriel, and G. Bingham Powell. 1966. *Comparative Politics: A Developmental Approach.* Boston: Little, Brown.

Almond, Gabriel, and Sidney Verba. 1980. *The Civic Culture Revisited.* Boston: Little, Brown.

Arnand, R. P. 1981. *Cultural Factors in International Relations.* Columbia, MO: South Asia Books.

Aristotle. 1962. *The Politics.* Baltimore: Penguin Classics.

Augustine. *City of God.*

Babbie, Earl R. 1983. *The Practice of Social Research,* 3rd ed. Belmont, CA: Wadsworth.

Bacharach, Peter, and Morton S. Baratz. 1962. "The Two Faces of Power," *American Political Science Review* 56 (December): 947–52.

Bacharach, Peter. 1967. *The Theory of Democratic Elitism.* Boston: Little, Brown.

Banfield, Edward C. 1968. *The Unheavenly City Revisted,* 7th ed. Boston: Little, Brown.

Barbour, William, and Carol Wekesser. 1994. *The Breakup of the Soviet Union.* San Diego: Greenhaven Press.

Becker, Howard S. 1967. "Whose Side Are We On?" *Social Problems* vol. 14: 239–47.

Benn, S. I., and R. S. Peters. 1959. *The Principles of Political Thought.* New York: Free Press.

Bernstein, Robert A., and James A. Dyer. 1984. *An Introduction to Political Science Methods,* 2nd ed. Englewood Cliffs, NJ: Prentice-Hall.

Berry, Jeffrey. 1989. *The Interest Group Society,* 2nd ed. Glenview, IL: Scott-Foresman.

Biskup, Michael. 1994. *Europe.* San Diego: Greenhaven Press.

Blaylock, Hubert M., Jr. 1979. *Social Statistics,* 2nd ed. New York: McGraw-Hill.

Bowen, Bruce D., and Herbert F. Weisberg. 1977. *An Introduction to Survey Research and Data Analysis.* San Francisco: Freeman.

Bullock, Alan. 1961. *Hitler: A Study in Tyranny.* New York: Bantam Books.

Butler, Sanera, and Weinrod. 1984. *Mandate For Leadership II.* Washington, D.C.: The Heritage Foundation.

Campbell, Angus, et al. 1960. *The American Voter.* New York: John Wiley.

Campbell, Donald, and Julian Stanley. 1966. *Experimental and Quasi-Experimental Designs of Research.* Chicago: Rand-McNally.

Cantori, Louis, and Andrew Ziegler. 1988. *Comparative Politics in the Post-Behavioralist Period.* Boulder, CO: Lynne Rienner Publishers.

Childe, Gordon. 1982. *Man Makes Himself.* New York: Mentor Books.

Chilcote, Ronald. 1981. *Theories of Comparative Politics.* Boulder, CO: Westview Press.

Clausewitz, Karl von. 1976. *On War.* Princeton: Princeton University Press.

Cobb, Roger W., and Charles D. Elder. 1972. *Participation in American Politics: the Dynamics of Agenda Building.* Boston: Allyn and Bacon.

Cole, Richard L. 1980. *Introduction to Political Inquiry.* New York: Macmillan.

Congressional Research Service. 1987. "Voter Participation Statistics from Recent Elections in Selected Countries." Report to Congressman Biaggi. November 18, 1987.

Cronin, Thomas. 1989. *Direct Democracy.* Cambridge, MA: Harvard University Press.

Crotty, William, ed. 1991. *Political Science: Looking to the Future, Volume Two.* Evanston, IL: Northwestern University Press.

Dahl, Robert. 1956. *A Preface to Democratic Theory.* Chicago: University of Chicago Press.

———. 1958. *Who Governs?* New Haven, CT: Yale University Press.

———. 1976. *Democracy in the United States: Promise and Performance,* 3rd ed. Chicago: Rand McNally.

———. 1982. *Dilemmas of Pluralist Democracy: Autonomy vs. Control.* New Haven, CT: Yale University Press.

———. 1991. *Modern Political Analysis,* 5th ed. Englewood Cliffs, NJ: Prentice-Hall.

Davis, James A. "A Partial Coefficient for Goodman and Kruskal's Gamma," *Journal of the American Statistical Association,* 62 (March, 1967) 189–193.

Deutsch, Karl. 1988. *The Analysis of International Relations,* 3rd ed. Englewood Cliffs, NJ: Prentice-Hall.

Dometrius, Nelson C. 1992. *Social Statistics Using SPSS.* New York: HarperCollins.

Domhoff, William. 1990. *The Power Elite and the State.* New York: D. Gruyter.

Downs, Anthony. 1957. *An Economic Theory of Democracy.* New York: Harper and Row.

Drucker, Peter. 1954. *The Practice of Management.* New York: Harper and Row.

Drucker, Peter F. 1978. "Management by Objectives and Self Control," in *Classics of Organizational Behavior.* ed. by Walter E. Natemeyer. Oak Park IL: Moore Publishing Company.

Dye, Thomas. 1990. *Who's Running America: The Bush Era,* 5th ed. Engelwood Cliffs, NJ: Prentice-Hall.

Easton, David. 1952. *The Political System.* New York: Alfred Knopf.

———. 1965. *A Framework for Political Analysis.* Englewood Cliffs, NJ: Prentice-Hall.

Ebenstein, William, and Allan Ebenstein. 1992. *Introduction to Political Thinkers.* Englewood Cliffs, NJ: Prentice-Hall.

Etzioni, Amatai. 1978. "Two Approaches to Organization Analysis: a Critique and a Suggestion." In Jay M. Shafritz and Philip W. Whitbeck. *Classics of Public Administration,* 2nd ed. Oak Park, IL: Moore Publishing.

Eulau, Heinz. 1963. *The Behavioral Persuasion in Politics.* New York: Random House.

Evans, Peter. 1979. *Dependent Development: The Alliance of Multinational, State and Local Capital in Brazil.* Princeton, NJ: Princeton University Press.

Finer, Sam. 1969/70. "Almond's Concept of 'The Political System': A Textual Critique." *Government and Opposition* V (Winter) 4:3–21.

Fiorina, Morris. *Congress: Keystone of the Washington Establishment,* 2nd ed. New Haven: Yale University Press.

Fox, William. 1993. *Social Statistics Using MicroCase.* Chicago: Nelson-Hall Publishers.

Frank, Andre Gunder. 1970. "The Development of Underdevelopment." In *Imperialism and Underdevelopment.* ed. Robert Rhodes. New York: Monthly Review Press.

Frankfort-Nachmias, Chava, and David Nachmias. 1992. *Research Methods in the Social Sciences,* 4th ed. New York: St. Martin's Press.

Freedman, David, Robert Pisani, and Roger Purves. 1978. *Statistics.* New York: Norton.

Freedman, Lawrence, ed. 1994. *War.* New York: Oxford University Press.

Gardner, John W. 1990. *On Leadership.* New York: Free Press.

———. 1987. *Attributes and Contexts.* Washington, DC: Independent Sector.

Gaus, John M. 1936. "The Responsibility of Public Administration." In *The Frontiers of Public Administration,* pp. 39-40. Chicago: University of Chicago Press. Quoted in Larry B. Hill and F. Ted Hebert, *Essentials of Public Administration.* North Scituate, MA: Duxbury Press, 1979, pp. 422–23.

Gerth, Hans H. 1973. *From Max Weber: Essays in Sociology.* London: Oxford University Press.

Goldenberg, Sheldon. 1992. *Thinking Methodologically.* New York: HarperCollins.

Goldwin, Robert A. 1979. "Of Men and Angels: A Search for Morality in the Constitution." In *The Moral Foundations of the American Republic*, 2nd ed. Ed. Robert H. Horwitz. Charlottesville, VA: University Press of Virginia.

Goodnow, Frank J. 1987. "Politics and Administration." In Jay M. Shafritz and Albert C. Hyde, *Classics of Public Administration*, 2nd ed., pp. 26–29. Chicago: Dorsey Press.

Groth, Alexander. 1970. "Structural Functionalism and Political Development: Three Problems." *WPQ* 23 (September): 485–99.

Hardin, Charles. 1974. *Presidential Power and Accountability*. Chicago: University of Chicago Press.

Heilbroner, Robert. 1977. "The Multi-National Corporation and the Nation-State." In *At Issue: Politics in the World Arena*. ed. Steven Spiegel. New York: St. Martin's Press.

Hess, Stephen, and Michael Nelson. 1985. "Foreign Policy: Dominance and Decisiveness in Presidential Elections." In *Elections of 1984*. Ed. Michael Nelson. Washington, DC: Congressional Quarterly Press.

Hill, Larry B., and F. Ted Hebert. 1979. *Essentials of Public Administration*. North Scituate, MA: Duxbury Press.

Hobbes, Thomas, 1651. *Leviathan*. New York: Macmillan, 1947.

Holsti, K. J. 1965. *International Politics: A Framework for Analysis*. Englewood Cliffs, NJ: Prentice-Hall.

Holt, Robert, and John Turner. 1966. *The Political Basis of Economic Development: An Exploration in Comparative Political Analysis*, pp. 12–13. Princeton, NJ: D. Van Nostrand.

———, eds. 1970. *The Methodology of Comparative Research*. New York: The Free Press.

Horowitz, Donald L. 1977. *The Courts and Social Policy*. Washington, DC: The Brookings Institute.

Huntington, Samuel. 1968. *Poltical Order in Changing Societies*. New Haven, CT: Yale University Press.

Isaak, Alan C. 1981. *Scope and Methods of Political Science: An Introduction to the Methodology of Political Inquiry*, 3rd ed. Hometown, IL: The Dorsey Press.

Ithiel de Sola Pool. 1981. *Symbols of Democracy*. Westport, CT: Greenwood Press (originally published in 1952).

Jones, Bryan D. 1983. *Governing Urban America: A Policy Focus*. Boston: Little, Brown.

Jones, Laurence F., and Delbert A. Taebel. 1993. "Hispanic Representation in Texas County Government." *Texas Journal of Political Studies* 16, no. 1 (Fall).

Johnson, Janet Buttolph, and Richard A. Joslyn. 1986. *Political Science Research Methods*. Washington, DC: Congressional Quarterly Press.

Jowitt, Kenneth. 1971. *Revolutionary Breakthroughs and National Development: The Case of Romania, 1944–1965*. Berkley, CA: The University of California Press.

Kant, Emmanuel. 1914. *Eternal Peace and Other International Essays.* Trans. W. Hastie. Boston: World Peace Foundation.

Kateb, George. 1968. *Political Theory, Its Nature and Uses.* New York: St. Martin' Press.

Kay, Susan Ann. 1991. *Introduction to the Analysis of Political Data.* Englewood Cliffs, NJ: Prentice-Hall.

Key, V. O. 1961. *Public Opinion and American Democracy.* New York: Knopf.

———. 1966. *The Responsible Electorate.* Cambridge, MA: The Belknap Press of Harvard University Press.

Kingdon, John. 1984. *Agendas, Alternatives, and Public Policies.* Boston: Little, Brown.

Kissinger, Henry. 1982. *Years of Upheaval.* Boston: Little, Brown.

Lane, Frederick S. 1994. *Current Issues in Public Administration,* 5th edition. New York: St. Martin's Press.

Lasswell, Harold. 1938. *Politics: Who Gets What, When, How.* New York: McGraw-Hill.

Lasswell, Harold, and Abraham Kaplan. 1950. *Power and Society.* New Haven, CT: Yale University Press.

Leedy, Paul D. 1985. *Practical Research: Planning and Design,* 3rd ed. New York: Macmillan.

Lenin, V. I. 1975. In *The Lenin Anthology.* Ed. Robert, Tucker. New York: Norton.

———. 1961. "Imperialsm: The Highest Stage of Capitalism." Excerpted in Harrison Wright, *The New Imperialism.* Lexington, KY: D.C. Heath.

Levy, Marion. 1966. *Modernization and the Structure of Societies: A Setting for International Affairs.* Princeton, NJ: Princeton University Press.

Lindbloom, Charles E. 1987. "The Science of Muddling Through." In Jay M. Shafritz and Albert C. Hyde, *Classics of Public Administration,* 2nd ed., pp. 299–318. Chicago: Dorsey Press.

Lineberry, Robert, George C. Edwards III, and Martin P. Wattenberg. 1990. *Government in America,* 4th ed. New York: HarperCollins.

Lipset, S. M. 1959. *Political Man.* New York, NY: Doubleday.

———. 1963. *The First New Nation.* New York: Doubleday.

Locke, John. 1689. *Two Treatises on Government.* New York: Mentor Books, 1963.

Long, Norton E. 1954. "Public Policy and Administration: The Goals of Rationality and Responsibility." *Public Administration Review* 14 (Winter): 22. Quoted in Delbert Taebel, *The Bureaucracy and Democratic Theory,* unpublished, p. 18.

Lorch, Robert S. 1980. *Democratic Process and Administrative Law.* Detroit: Wayne State University Press.

Lowi, Theodore. 1979. *The End of Liberalism,* 2nd ed. New York: Norton.

———. 1987. *The Personal President.* Ithaca, NY: Cornell University Press.

Lynn, Laurence E., Jr. 1994. "Policy Analysis." In Frederick S. Lane, *Current Issues in Public Administration,* 5th ed., pp. 336–44. New York: St. Martin's Press.

Mackie, Thomas T. Voting turnout figures published in *The European Journal of Political Research*, 1990.

Macridis, Roy. 1955. *The Study of Comparative Politics. Studies in Political Science*. New York: Random House.

Madison, James. 1961. In Clinton Rossiter *The Federalist Papers*, pp. 77–84. New York: Norton.

Mann, Thomas. 1987. *A Guide to Library Research Methods*. New York: Oxford University Press.

Mansbach, Richard. 1994. *The Global Puzzle*. Boston: Houghton Mifflin.

Marx, Karl, and Friedrich, Engels. 1968. *Selected Works*. Moscow: Progress Publishers.

———. 1969. *The Communist Manifesto*. Baltimore: Penguin Classics.

McClosky, Herbert. 1964. "Consensus and Ideology in American Politics." *American Political Science Review* 58 (June): 361–82. Quoted in Larry B. Hill and F. Ted Hebert, *Essentials of Public Administration*, p. 423. North Scituate, MA: Duxbury Press, 1979.

McConnell, Grant. 1966. *Private Power and American Democracy*. New York: Vintage.

McCoy, Charles A., and John Playford. 1967. *Apolitical Politics: A Critique of Behavioralism*. New York: Thomas Y. Crowell.

Meier, Kenneth J., and Jeffrey L. Brudney. 1981. *Applied Statistics for Public Administration*. Boston: Duxbury Press.

Meier, Kenneth J. 1993. *Politics and the Bureaucracy: Policymaking in the Fourth Branch of Government*, 3rd ed. Belmont, CA: Wadsworth.

Melanson, Philip, and Lauriston King. 1971. "Theory in Comparative. Politics: A Critical Appraisal." *Comparative Political Studies* 4 (July): 205–31.

Meltsner, Arnold. 1976. *Policy Analysts in the Bureaucracy*. Berkeley: University of California Press.

Meulemans, William. 1989. *Making Political Choices*. Englewood Cliffs, NJ: Prentice-Hall.

Mills, C. W. 1965. *The Power Elite*. London: Oxford University Press.

Modelski, George, ed. 1979. *Transnational Corporations and the World Order*. San Francisco: W. H. Freeman.

Moore, Barrington. 1966. *The Social Origins of Dictatorship and Democracy: Lord and Peasant in the Making of the Modern World*. Boston: Beacon Press.

Morganthaur, Hans. 1963. *Politics Among Nations*, 3rd ed. New York: Knopf.

Mosteller, Frederick, and David L. Wallace. 1964. *Inference and Disputed Authorship: The Federalist*. Reading, MA: Addison-Wesley.

Neustadt, Richard. 1960. *Presidential Power*. New York: John Wiley.

Niehbur, Reinold. 1938. *Beyond Tragedy*. New York: Charles Scribner and Sons.

Norusis, Marija J. 1988. *SPSS/PC +*. Chicago: SPSS.

O'Brien, David. 1990. *Storm Center: The Supreme Court in American Politics*, 2nd ed. New York: Norton.

Olson, William Clinton. 1991. *The Theory and Practice of International Relations,* 8th ed. Englewood Cliffs, NJ: Prentice-Hall.

Papp, Daniel. 1988. *Contemporary International Relations,* 2nd ed. New York: Macmillan.

Parenti, Michael. 1978. *Power and the Powerless.* New York: St. Martin's Press.

Phillips, Kevin. 1993. *Boiling Point.* New York: Random House.

Phyrr, Peter A. 1987. "The Zero-Base Approach to Government Budgeting." In Jay M. Shafritz and Albert C. Hyde. *Classics of Public Administration,* 2nd ed., pp. 495–505. Chicago: Dorsey Press.

Plato. 1953. *The Republic.* New York: The Modern Library.

Plato. 1957. *The Republic.* New York: Random House.

Prottas, Jeffrey Manditch. 1979. *People-Processing.* Lexington, MA: Lexington Books.

Redford, Emmette S. 1969. *Democracy in the Administrative State.* New York: Oxford University Press.

Redhead, Brian. 1988. *Political Thought From Plato to NATO.* Chicago: Dorsey Press.

Robson, William A. 1964. *The Governors and the Governed.* Baton Rouge, LA: Louisiana State University Press, p. 18. Quoted in Larry B. Hill and F. Ted Hebert, *Essentials of Public Administration.* North Scituate, MA: Duxbury Press, 1979, p. 426.

Rossiter, Clinton, ed. 1961. *The Federalist Papers.* New York: Mentor Books.

Rostow, Walt. 1960. *Stages of Economic Growth: A Non-Communist Manifesto* New York, NY: Cambridge University Press.

Rourke, Francis E. 1969. *Bureaucracy, Politics, and Public Policy.* Boston: Little, Brown.

Rubin, Irene S. 1994. "Budget Reform and Political Reform: Conclusions from Six Cities." In Frederick S. Lane, *Current Issues in Public Administration,* 5th ed. pp. 306–26. New York: St. Martin's Press.

Rustow, Dankwart, and Kenneth Erickson, eds. 1991. *Concepts and Models in Comparative Politics: Political Development Reconsidered and its Alternatives.* New York: HarperCollins.

Rousseau, J. 1974. "A Discourse on the Origins of Inequality." In *On the Social Contract, Discourse on the Origins of Inequality, and Discourse on Political Economy.* Trans. G. Grubes. Indianapolis: Hackett.

Scarrow, 1969. *Comparative Political Analysis.* New York: Harper & Row.

Schick, Allen. 1987. "The Road to PPB: the Stages of Budget Reform." In Jay M. Shafritz and Albert C. Hyde, *Classics of Public Administration,* 2nd ed., pp. 299–318. Chicago: Dorsey Press.

Schmidt, Diane E. 1993. *Expository Writing in Political Science: A Practical Guide.* New York: HarperCollins.

Schmidt, Steffen W., Mack C. Shelley II, and Barbara A. Bardes. 1993. *An Introduction to Critical Thinking and Writing in American Politics.* Minneapolis/St. Paul: West Publishing.

Schrems, John J. 1986. *Principles of Politics: An Introduction.* Englewood Cliffs, NJ: Prentice-Hall.

Schwarz, John. 1988. *America's Hidden Success,* rev. ed. New York: Norton, 1988.

Segal, Jeffrey A., and Albert D. Cover. 1989. "Ideological Values and the Votes of U.S. Supreme Court Justices." *The American Political Science Review* 83: 557–65.

Shively, W. Phillips. 1990. *The Craft of Political Research,* 3rd ed. Englewood Cliffs, NJ: Prentice-Hall.

Smith, Adam. *The Wealth of Nations.*

Snow, C. P. 1962. *Science and Government.* New York: Mentor Books.

Spanier, John. 1990. *Games Nations Play,* 7th ed. Washington, DC: Congressional Quarterly Press.

Spero, Joan Edelman. 1985. *The Politics of International Economic Relations.* New York: St. Martin's Press.

Spiegel, Steven, and David Pervin. 1994. *At Issue: Politics in the World Arena,* 7th ed. New York: St. Martin's Press.

Sullivan, Michael P. 1990. *Power in Contemporary International Politics.* Columbia, SC: University of South Carolina Press.

Sunkel, Osvaldo. 1973. "Transnational Capitalism and National Disintegration in Latin America." *Social and Economic Studies* 22: 132–76.

Sylva, Ronald D. 1994. *Public Personnel Administration.* Belmont, CA: Wadsworth.

Taylor, A. J. P. 1964. *The Origins of the Second World War.* Middlesex, UK: Penguin Books.

Thompson, T. L. 1963. *Plato: Totalitarian or Democratic?* Englewood Cliffs, NJ: Prentice-Hall.

Tolchin, Martin. 1989. "Tracking a Foreign Presence in U.S. Military Contracting." *New York Times* ("The Week in Review"), January 1, 1989.

Toqueville, Alexis. 1956. *Democracy in America.* Ed. Richard Heffner. New York: John Wiley.

Truman, David. 1951. *The Governmental Process.* New York: Knopf.

University of Michigan. 1991. 1988 National Election Study and 1988 Senate Election Study. In Robert L. Lineberry, George C. Edwards III, and Martin P. Wattenberg. *Government in America: People, Politics, and Policy,* 5th ed. New York: HarperCollins.

Verba, Sidney, and Norman H. Nie. 1972. *Participation in America: Political Democracy and Social Equality.* New York: Harper & Row.

Waldo, Dwight. 1955. *The Study of Public Administration.* New York: Random House.

Waltz, Kenneth. 1959. *Man, The State, and War.* New York: Columbia University Press.

Wang, Chamant. 1992. *Sense and Nonsense of Statistical Inference.* New York: Morrel Dekker.

Wayne, Stephen J., G. Calvin Mackenzie, David M. O'Brien, and Richard L. Cole. 1995. *The Politics of American Government.* New York: St. Martin's Press.

Weber, Max. 1947. *The Theory of Social and Economic Organization.* New York: Oxford University Press.

———— 1958. *The Protestant Ethic and the Spirit of Capitalism.* New York: Scribner's,

Welch, Susan, and John Comer. 1988. *Quantitative Methods for Public Administration,* 2nd ed. Pacific Grove, CA: Brooks/Cole.

Wiarda, Howard. 1987. *Latin America at the Crossroads: Debt, Development, and the Future.* Boulder, CO: Westview Press.

————. 1988. *The Relations Between Democracy, Development, and Security: Implications for Policy.* New York: Global Economic Action Institute.

————. 1991. "Concepts and Models in Comparative Politics: Political Development Reconsidered and its Alternatives," in Dankwart Rustow, and Kenneth Erickson, *Comparative Political Dynamics.* New York: HarperCollins.

Wiarda, Howard, ed. 1985. *New Directions in Comparative Politics.* Boulder, CO: Westview Press.

Wildavski, Aaron. 1984. *The Politics of the Budgetary Process,* 4th ed. Boston: Little, Brown.

Williamson, John B., and Michael Rustad. 1985. *Social Problems: The Contemporary Debates.* Boston: Little, Brown.

Wills, Gary. 1981. *Explaining America: The Federalist.* Garden City, NY: Doubleday.

Wilson, Woodrow. "The Study of Administration." In Jay M. Shafritz and Albert C. Hyde. 1987. *Classics of Public Administration,* 2nd ed. pp. 10–25. Chicago: Dorsey Press.

Woll, Peter. 1977. *American Bureaucracy,* 2nd ed. New York: Norton.

INDEX

Abramson, Rudy, 82
Abstract, 32–33
Administrative ethics, 122–127
Adverse personnel actions, 106
Agenda setting, 112–113
Almanac of American Politics, 239
Almond, Gabriel, 133, 14, 1441
American political process, 61–62,
    67–100
Analytical budgeting, 109–110
  alternatives, 109
  advantages, 109–110
  disadvantages, 110
Antecedent variable, 189
Aristocracy, 58–59
Aristotle, 53,57–58
Arnad, R.P., 172
Association, 294
Authority, 52–53
  dejure, 52
  defacto, 52

Bachrach, Peter, 57, 82, 262
Bar graph, 269
Baratz, Morton, S., 82, 262
Becker, Howard, S., 15
Behavioralism, 14, 136
Benn, S.I., 52
Bernstein, Robert A., 191, 195
Berry, Jeffrey, 79
Beta weights, 347–348
Bibliographic cards, 35
Bivariate statistics, 293–335. *See also*
  measures of association

Bivariate tables, 294–301
  rudiments of association, 294
  format conventions, 296–301
Blank foreign elements, 243
Book reviews, 35
Budget process, 108–110
Bureaucracy, 104
Bureaucratic approach, 118–119
Butler, Sanera, 122

Campbell, Donald, 215
Case studies, 134, 225–226
Causal explanations, 185–197
Causal relationship, 193–195
Census data, 239
Checks and balances, 76
Chi square, 313–320
Chilcote, Ronald, 136
Civil Service Reform Act (CSRA), 1978,
  107–108
Class, 263
Class boundary, 265
Class frequency, 263
Class interval, 265
Class midpoints, 265
Classic experimental design, 216–218
Cluster of elements, 243
Cobb, Roger W., 114
Codebook, 254–255
Codesheet, 254
Coding, 253–255
Coefficient of determination (r-square), 329
Coefficient of multiple determination
  (R-square), 347

Coefficient of variation, 283–284
Cole, Richard L., 3, 23, 204–205, 253, 260, 262, 296
Coleman, James, 133
Comparative politics, 62, 132–155
Comparison, 218
Compensation plans, 106
Composite index, 206–207
Composite political research, 15–16
Concepts, 187–188
    definition, 187
    operationaliztion, 187
Concordant pair, 306
Confidence level 252–253
Congressional Research Service, 88
Consent, 69, 73
Constitutionalism, 75–79
Content analysis, 240–241
Content validity, 202
Control, 219, 336–341
Correlation coefficient (Pearson's r), 327–329
Covariation, 194
Cover, Albert D., 240–241
Cramer's V, 304
Crisis of distribution, 144
Crisis of lititimacy, 143
Crisis of participation, 143
Crisis of penetration, 143
Critique, 37
Crotty, William, 147
Cumulative frequency distributions, 268–269

Dahl, Robert, 46–47, 54, 80, 163
Data archives, 238
Data collection, 236–259
Data input, 236–259
Decision-making institutions, 92–96
Deduction, 8–9
Degrees of freedom, 318320
Democracy, 56–59, 69, 73–75
Dependent variable, 188
Descriptive statistics, 261
Deterrence, 171
De Toqueville, Alexis, 89
Dictatorship, 56–59
Direct observation, 237
Discordant pair, 307

Discriminate validity, 202
Distributive policy, 112
Downs, Anthony, 186187
Durkheim, Emile, 9
Dye, Thomas, 82
Dyer, James A., 191, 195

Easton, David, 11, 47
Economic dimension of power, 169–170
Economic security, 167–168
Edwards, George C., III, 75
Elder, Charles D., 114
Elite theory (elitism), 82–83
Engels, Friedrich, 53
Epistemology, 5
Equality, 68–69, 71–73
Etzioni, Amatai, 121
Eulau, Heinz, 135
Expected frequency, 314–320
Experimental designs, 215–223
Experimental mortality, 230
Explanatory, 7
External validity, 230–231

F ratio, 313, 329–330
Federalism, 76
Field research, 226–227
Finer, Sam, 140
Fox, William, 358
Frankfort-Nachmias, Chava, 5, 205, 210, 215, 227, 232–233, 240
Freedman, David, 246
Freedom, 59
Frequency distribution, 263–267, 321
    definition, 263
    constructing, 265–267
Frequency polygon, 271

Gallup Opinion Index, 240
Gamma, 307–308
Gardner, John W., 124
Gaus, John, M., 123
General, 6–7
Goldwin, Robert A., 125
Government, 53–54
Graphic presentations, 269–271
Groth, Alexander, 140
Guttman scale, 208–211

Hebert, Ted, 123
Heffner, Richard, 89
Heilbroner, Robert, 162
Hill, Larry, 123
Histogram, 269–270
History, 229
Hobbes, Thomas, 58, 70
Holsti, K.J., 163
Holt, Robert, 140
Huntington, Samuel, 133, 148
Hypothesis, 189–192
  definition, 189
  purpose of, 190
  requirements of, 189–191
  common errors, 191–192

Ideology, 168
Incomplete frame, 243
Incremental approach, 121
Independent variable, 189
Indices, 32–33, 206–211
Induction, 7–8
Inferential statistics, 261–262
Influence, 49–50
Input functions, 139
Instrumentation, 230
Internal validity, 227–228
International law, 164165
International organizations, 160–163
International relations, 63, 155–181
International system, 163–165, 175
Interval level of measurement, 201
Intervening variable, 189
Issak, Alan C., 14
Ithiel de Sola Pool, 241

Jacobellis v. Ohio, 1964, 71
Jefferson, Thomas, 12, 57
Jenkins v. Georgia, 1974, 70
Johnson, Janet Buttolph, 6–7, 204
Jones, Bryan D., 12
Jones, Laurence F., 32–33, 264
Journal, 33–35
Joslyn, Richard A., 6–7, 204
Justice, 58

Kant, Emmanuel, 174
Kay, Susan Ann, 261
Key, V.O., 85, 88

Kingship, 58–59
Kissinger, Henry, 173

Lambda, 304–305
Lasswell, Harold, 46–47
Leedy, Paul D., 36, 198
Lenin, V.I., 57
Levels of measurement, 199–202
Lindbloom, Charles, 121
Lowi, Theodore, 78–79
Liberty, 68, 70–71
Likert scale, 207–208
Limited government, 69, 76
Linear regression line, 323–326
Lineberry, Robert, 75
Line positions, 118
Linkage institutions, 8692
Lipset, S.M., 61, 133, 144–145
Literature review, 16–17, 30–40
  purpose of the review, 30–31
  how to begin a search for related
    literature, 31–35
  how to write the literature review,
    36–39
Locke, John, 12, 57
Long, Norton E., 124
Lorch, Robert S., 125–126

Mackie, Thomas T., 13
Macridis, Roy, 62, 134
Madisonian Model, 75–76
Main diagonal, 295
Majoritarian model, 80
Management-By-Objectives (MBO), 109
Manipulation, 218–219
Mansbach, Richard, 166
Marbury v. Madison, 1803, 77
Marx, Karl, 6, 46, 53
Matching, 228
Maturation, 230
McCulloch v. Maryland, 1819, 78
Measurement, 198–212, 244
Measurement validity, 202–203
Measurement reliability, 203–204
Measures of association, 301–310
  tests of association for nominal data,
    302–305
    general, 302
    the Phi coefficient, 302–303

Cramer's V, 304
Pearson's Coefficient of
    Contingency, 304
Lambda, 304–305
tests of association for ordinal data
    general, 305–307
    concordant pair, 306
    discordant pair, 307
    tied pair, 307
    gamma, 307–308
    tau statistics, 308–309
    Sommer's DYX and DXY, 309
tests of association for interval data,
    320–330
    frequency distribution, 321
    scattergram, 321–323
    regression analysis, 323–327
    correlation coefficient, 327–329
    coefficient of determination, 329
Measures of central tendency, 271–278
    mode, 271–273
    median, 273–274
    mean, 274–275
    and grouped data, 275–276
    comparison of, 277–278
Measures of dispersion, 278–284
    variation ratio, 278
    range, 278–279
    mean deviation, 279–280
    variance, 280–281
    standard deviation, 281–282
    coefficient of variation, 283–284
Mean, 274–276
Mean deviation, 279–280
Median, 273–276
Meier, Kenneth, J., 122, 127
Meulemans, William, 54
Methods used to investigate the scope of
    politics, 12–16
    modern methods, 13–15
        the behavioral method, 14
        the postbehavioral methods, 14–15
    traditional methods, 12–13
        the philosophical method, 12–13
        the historical method, 13
        the comparative method, 13
        the juridical method, 13
Military dimension of power, 170–172
Mills, C.W., 82
Mixed-scanning approach, 121–122

Mode, 271–273
Modelski, George, 161
Moore, Barrington, 144
Morganthau, , Hans, 169
Mosteller, Frederick, 241
Multinational corporations, 161–162
Multiple causation, 195
Multiple regression, 345–349
Multivariate analysis, 336–352
Multivariate crosstabulation, 338–342
    description of, 338–341
    disadvantages of, 341–342

Nachmias, David, 5, 205, 210, 215, 227,
    232–233, 240
Nation-state, 157–160
National prestige, 167
National security, 166
Neustadt, Richaard, 95
Nominal definition, 187–188
Nominal level of measurement, 200
Nonexperimental designs, 223–225
Nongovernmental organizations,
    162–163
Nonnormative, 6
Nonrandomized control group design,
    224
Nonspuriousness, 194
Normal curve, 286–288
Null hypothesis, 312

Observed frequency, 314–320
Off diagonal, 295
Oligarchy, 58–59
Operational definition, 188
Order, 70
Ordinal level of measurement, 200–201
Osborne v. Ohio, 1990, 70
Output functions, 139

Papp, Daniel, 157–158, 160
Parameter, 244
Parenti, Michael, 12
Partial correlation, 343–345
Partial slope, 345, 348
Partial tables, 340–341
Participatory democracy, 103
Pearson's Coefficient of Contingency, 304
Pendelton Act of 1883, 103
Percentage distribution, 267–268

Personal interview, 238
Personnel administration, 104–108
Pervin, David, 160
Peters, R.S., 52
Phi coefficient, 302–303
Pisani, Robert, 246
Planning, Programming, and Budgeting System (PPBS), 109
Plato, 6, 57
Pluralist model, 80–82
Policy adoption, 113
Policy agenda, 113
Policy evaluation, 113
Policy formulation, 113
Policy implications, 354
Policy implementation, 113
Policy triggering devices, 114
Political concepts, 48–53
Political decay, 148
Political development, 142
Political power, 50
Political questions, 53–59
    How should people be governed?, 54–56
    Who should govern?, 56–57
    What is the purpose of government?, 57–59
Political research, 4
Political resource, 50–52
Political science, 4, 59–63
    the discipline, 59–60
    subfields, 60–65
Political structures, 139
Political system, 46–48
Political world, 44–66
Politics, 44–46
    and human nature, 46
Polity, 58–59
Population, 192, 242
    finite population, 242
    infinite population, 242
Position classifications, 105–106
Postbehavioralism, 14–15, 136
Posttest, 216
Posttest-only control group design, 222–223
Predictive validity, 203
Pretest, 216

Primary data, 237–238
Problem recognition, 112

Problem statement, 25
    statement and clarity 25–26
    what to avoid when writing your problem statement, 26
Progressive movement, 103–104
Prottas, Jeffrey Manditch, 123
Provisional, 7
Psychological dimension of power, 172–173
Public administration, 62, 101–131
    definition, 102
Public opinion, 84–86
Public policy, 62, 96–97, 101–131
    definition, 110
    types, 112
    the process, 112–114
Purves, Roger, 246

Random assignment, 229
Random error, 345
Range, 278–279
Ratio level of measurement, 201–202
Rational approach, 120–121
Raw data, 263
Redford, Emmette S., 124–125
Redistributive policy, 112
Regression analysis, 323–327
Regression artifact, 230
Regression model and euation, 324–326
Regulatory policy, 112
Republicanism, 75–76
Research
    applied, 4
    basic, 4
Research design, 214–235
    definition, 214
    purpose, 215
    factors affecting the choice of design, 215
Research problem, 22–29
    deciding on a potential topic, 23
    sources of topics, 23
    topic evaluation, 23–25
Robson, William A., 124
Rostow, Walt, 145
Roth v. United States, 1957, 70
Rousseau, J., 57
Rustad, Michael, 11–12

Sample designs, 244–250

probability samples, 244–250
  simple random samples, 246
  systematic samples, 247–248
  stratified samples, 248–249
  cluster samples, 249
nonprobability sample designs,
  245–246
  convenience samples, 245
  puposive samples, 245
  quota sample, 245–246
Sample error, 252–253
Sample size, 250–252
Sampling, 241–255
Sampling frame, 243–244
Sampling unit, 242
Satisficing, 121
Scales, 206–211
Scarrow, T., 62
Scattergram, 321–323
Schrems, John J., 12–15
Schwartz, John, 79
Scientific knowledge, 5
  characteristics, 5–7
  definition, 5
  obstacles, 9–10
Scope of political science, 10
Secondary data, 237–241
Segal, Jeffrey A., 240–241
Selection, 312–313
Separation of powers, 76
Smith, Adam, 6
Shape of the distribution, 284–288
  skewed distribution, 284–285
  symmetrical distributions, 285–286
  the normal curve, 286–288
Shively, W. Phillips, 4–5, 8, 24–25, 186
Slope, 325–326
Solomon Four-Group design, 219–222
Sommer's DYX and DXY, 309
Spanier, John, 168–169, 172
Specification, 312
Spero, Joan Edelman, 162
Spiegel, Steven, 160
Split-half method, 205
Spurious, 194
Staff positions, 118
Standard deviation, 281–282
Standard scores. See Z scores
Stanley, Julian, 215
State of nature, 58

Statistical Abstract of the United States,
  239
Statistical significance and hypothesis
  testing, 310–320, 348
Statistics, 244
Structural-functionalism, 138–141
Survey, 237–238
Systems approach, 119–120
Systematic research process, 16–19
  literature review, 16–17
  identifying the topic of research, 17
  clarifying the research elements, 17
  the research design, 18
  the remaining steps, 18

Taebel, Delbert A., 264
Tau statistics, 308–309
Telephone interview, 238
Testing, 229
Tests of significance
  Chi Square, 313–320
  F test with the correlation coefficient,
    329–330
Test-retest method, 205
Theoretical implications, 353–354
Theoretical justification, 194–195
Theory, 186–187
  investigating the scope of politics,
    10–11
  goals theory, 12
  power theory, 11–12
  systems theory, 14
Tied pair, 307
Time order, 193–194
Time series with control group design, 225
Time series without control group
    design, 224–225
Tolchin, Martin, 167
Topic selection, 27–28
  select the topic early, 27
  limit the range of the topic, 27
  consider duplicating another study,
    27–28
  abandon topics that are impossible to
    complete, 28
Total frequency, 263
Transmissible, 6
Triangulation, 205–206
Tucker, Robert, 57
Turner, John, 140

Tyranny, 58–59

Unidimensionality, 208–211
Units of analysis, 192
Univariate statistics, 260–292

Variation ratio, 278
Variability, 251–252
Variables, 188–189
Verb, Sidney, 14, 144

Waldo, Dwight, 124
Wallace, David L., 241

Waltz, Kenneth, 163, 172–174
Wattenberg, Martin P., 75
Wayne, Stephen J., 112
Weber, Max, 52, 57, 118
Wiarda, Howard, 133, 146, 14149
Williamson, John B., 11–12
Wilson, Woodrow, 101, 103–104
Woll, Peter, 126–127

Y intercept, 324–326, 345–347

Z scores, 287–288
Zero-Based Budgeting (ZBB), 109